THE REDISCOVERY OF AMERICA

THE REDISCOVERY OF AMERICA

*Essays by Harry V. Jaffa on the
New Birth of Politics*

**Edited by Edward J. Erler
and Ken Masugi**

ROWMAN & LITTLEFIELD
Lanham • Boulder • New York • London

Published by Rowman & Littlefield
An imprint of The Rowman & Littlefield Publishing Group, Inc.
4501 Forbes Boulevard, Suite 200, Lanham, Maryland 20706
www.rowman.com

6 Tinworth Street, London SE11 5AL

British Library Cataloguing in Publication Information Available

Library of Congress Cataloging-in-Publication Data

Names: Jaffa, Harry V., author. / Erler, Edward J., editor. / Masugi, Ken, editor.
Title: The rediscovery of America : essays by Harry V. Jaffa on the new birth of politics / edited by Edward J. Erler and Ken Masugi.
Description: Lanham, Maryland : Rowman & Littlefield, [2019] / Includes biographical references and index.
Identifiers: LCCN 2018031641 (print) / LCCN 2018045573 (ebook) / ISBN 9781538122105 (electronic) / ISBN 9781538122099 (cloth : alk. paper)
Subjects: LCSH: Political science--United States--Philosophy. / United States--Politics and government--Philosophy. / Founding Fathers of the United States.
Classification: LCC JA84.U5 (ebook) / LCC JA84.U5 J34 2018 (print) / DDC 320.97301--dc 23
LC record available at https://lccn.loc.gov/2018031641

∞ ™ The paper used in this publication meets the minimum requirements of American National Standard for Information Sciences Permanence of Paper for Printed Library Materials, ANSI/NISO Z39.48-1992.

Printed in the United States of America

To the students of Harry V. Jaffa

CONTENTS

INTRODUCTION

Harry V. Jaffa's profoundest book was *A New Birth of Freedom* (2000). His earlier *Crisis of the House Divided* (1959)[1] is justly regarded as the best book written by a student of Leo Strauss. Yet Jaffa's later book revisits one of the central premises of his earlier book—the radical modernity of the American founding. Jaffa had once argued that Aristotelian elements were introduced into the American regime by Lincoln's refounding. Now he came to believe, with Lincoln, that they were always present in the founding. *New Birth* explains Lincoln's perpetuation of the founding. This "discovery of America" also comes to light in the collection of essays presented in this volume, each of which reflects the development of his thought that came to maturity in *New Birth*.

These essays are organized chronologically, with the exception of the first essay, "Aristotle and Locke in the American Founding" (2001). Written since 1986, they reflect a turn in Jaffa's career, which he discussed in this essay and more thoroughly in *A New Birth of Freedom*. See especially chapter 2, "The Declaration of Independence, the Gettysburg Address, and the Historians." *New Birth* is a chronological midpoint between the publication or composition of the first and last essays of this volume.

In the first essay, "Aristotle and Locke in the American Founding" (2001), Jaffa described his reassessment of both America (and its place in the modern world) and of Leo Strauss.

> My critics, friendly and unfriendly, may ask why it took me so long to see the purloined letter on the mantelpiece. The reason is that I took

for granted that the account of the Hobbesian Locke in Leo Strauss's *Natural Right and History* represented the Locke that informed the American Founding.

The key essay in his new understanding is the 1987 work, "Equality, Liberty, Wisdom, Morality and Consent in the Idea of Political Freedom." Its themes dominate these essays, whether in the previously unpublished critiques of Harvey Mansfield and Irving Kristol or in his final essay on the *Dred Scott* case. In particular, we see a deeper understanding of the theological-political problem that Leo Strauss said was the principal focus of his work. (See, among other works, his autobiographical Preface to the English translation of *Spinoza's Critique of Religion*, especially on his changing views of Spinoza).[2] Jaffa realized that the distinction that Strauss drew between ancients and moderns was a distinction in the history of political philosophy, not a distinction within philosophy itself. In Strauss's work ancients and moderns served a largely rhetorical purpose. What this all portends is a deeper understanding of political philosophy and its relation to politics and political life. Jaffa could now present the American Founding in a way that an unreflective adherence to the ancients and moderns paradigm would have prevented. Due to its philosophic origins in the Declaration of Independence, American political life provides unique instruction in political philosophy.

In judging the activity of political philosophy within Jaffa's mind, a reader must also consider his last book, the whimsically titled *Crisis of the Strauss Divided*, which contains his intellectual autobiography, "Straussian Geography"; his disputes with some political theorists; and a variety of essays and occasional pieces, plus an essay by Leo Strauss.[3] The essays in the second *Crisis* should be read in light of those collected here. And of course both these later books should be kept in mind when rereading his two earlier, major books.

The essays in this volume have been lightly edited for typos and incomplete references.

The editors collaborated on the Introduction; Edward Erler edited the "Decline and Fall of the America Idea" chapter and provided the introductions for it and the "Equality, Liberty, Wisdom, Morality, and Consent in the Idea of Political Freedom" chapter. With the assistance of Erler, Ken Masugi edited and provided introductions for the remaining chapters.

The editors thank Ben Judge of Monument Valley, Inc.; Tom Klingenstein and Ryan Williams of the Claremont Institute; and Larry Arnn and Douglas Jeffrey of Hillsdale College for their support at various stages of this project. Ken Masugi thanks his wife, Althea Nagai, for her invaluable assistance from start to finish.

We hope this work perpetuates the Socratic revolution in political theory that Harry V. Jaffa dedicated his life to fostering.

NOTES

1. Harry V. Jaffa, *A New Birth of Freedom: Abraham Lincoln and the Coming of the Civil War* (Lanham, MD: Rowman & Littlefield, 2000). Harry V. Jaffa, *Crisis of the House Divided: An Interpretation of the Issues in the Lincoln-Douglas Debates* (Garden City, NY: Doubleday & Co., 1959); republished with a new introduction in 1973 by University of Washington Press; republished in 1982 with a new preface by the University of Chicago Press; a Fiftieth Anniversary Edition was published in 2009 by the University of Chicago Press with a new introduction. See the reviews of *New Birth* by Thomas G. West and Edward J. Erler, *Interpretation* 28, no.1, Spring, 2001. http:// interpretationjournal.com/backissues/Vol_28-3.pdf.

2. Leo Strauss, *Spinoza's Critique of Religion*, E. M. Sinclair, trans. (New York: Schocken, 1965).

3. Harry V. Jaffa et al., *Crisis of the Strauss Divided: Essays on Leo Strauss and Straussianism, East and West* (Lanham, MD: Rowman & Littlefield, 2012).

I

ARISTOTLE AND LOCKE IN THE AMERICAN FOUNDING

INTRODUCTION

In this brief 2001 essay, Harry Jaffa replies to Charles Kesler's review of *A New Birth of Freedom* (*Claremont Review of Books*, Fall 2000). Jaffa recapitulates his turn from *Crisis of the House Divided* (1959) to *New Birth* (2000):

> That the Founding, which Lincoln inherited, was dominated by an Aristotelian Locke—or a Lockean Aristotle—has been a conspicuous theme of my writing since 1987. It has gone largely unnoticed because it contradicts the conventional wisdom of certain academic establishments. Like the "Purloined Letter," however, it has been in plain view all along.

As with other essays in this volume, Jaffa notes the importance of social contract theory, the state of nature, and government by consent in the constitution of free governments. "The ancient conception of law would, in the modern world, serve only tyranny, while the very purpose of law, according to Aristotle, is to prevent tyranny." Contrary to the imprudent and unphilosophic arguments of many scholars, these "modern" notions do not require a choice between rights and virtue in order to have a moral and just political order. The necessity of accommodating revealed religion, specifically Christianity, requires we rethink what we thought we knew about the difference between the ancients and the moderns, the best regime and its alternatives. In other words, we need to rethink the meaning of and relationship among "Equality, Liberty, Wisdom, Morality, and Consent" in order to understand the "idea of freedom." The editors thank the *Claremont Review of Books* for permission to reprint from the *Claremont Review of Books* Vol. 1, No. 2 (Winter 2001).

ARISTOTLE AND LOCKE IN THE AMERICAN FOUNDING, *BY HARRY V. JAFFA*

In his review of *A New Birth of Freedom: Abraham Lincoln and the Coming of the Civil War*, in the inaugural issue of the Claremont Review of Books, Charles Kesler writes, "Jaffa doesn't draw attention to his revised view of Lincoln or of the American Founding. In fact, he is strangely silent about the whole subject, leaving it to the readers to figure out the relation between the two remarkably different accounts in Crisis and A New Birth."

I do not think that I have been as silent, or strangely so, as Professor Kesler seems to think. That the Founding, which Lincoln inherited, was dominated by an Aristotelian Locke—or a Lockean Aristotle—has been a conspicuous theme of my writing since 1987. It has gone largely unnoticed because it contradicts the conventional wisdom of certain academic establishments. Like the "Purloined Letter," however, it has been in plain view all along.

After speaking of our unalienable rights, to secure which governments are instituted, the Declaration of Independence goes on to say that "whenever any form of government becomes destructive of these ends, it is the right of the people to alter or abolish it, and to institute new government, laying its foundations on such principles and organizing its powers in such form, as to them shall seem most likely to effect their safety and happiness." Notice that in the second institution, or reinstitution of government, "rights" become "ends." And these ends are now said to be "Safety" and "Happiness," the alpha and omega of political life in Aristotle's *Politics*.

In one form or another, the metamorphosis of Lockean " rights" into Aristotelian "ends" (or vice versa) recurs in many of the documents of the founding. Washington in his first inaugural address as president, says that "there is no truth more thoroughly established than that there exists in the economy and course of nature an indissoluble union between virtue and happiness." The pursuit of happiness is thus understood as the pursuit of virtue. It is difficult to imagine a more forthright Aristotelianism in Hooker or Aquinas. Nor do Washington and the founders generally suppose that either virtue or happiness is something private or idiosyncratic. In *Federalist* 43, Madison speaks of the "transcendent law of nature and of nature's God, which declares that the safety and happiness of society are the objects at which all political institutions aim, and to which all such institutions must be sacrificed." The pursuit of happiness, while that of individuals in the state of nature, is a social or political happiness, within civil society.

Neither Washington nor Madison imagined for a moment that, in speaking of the happiness of society, he was contradicting the idea of all human individuals being equally endowed by their Creator with unalienable rights. In his letter transmitting the Constitution to the Congress of the Confederation (September 17, 1787), Washington speaks of "Individuals entering into society [having to] give up a share of liberty to preserve the rest." But where—except in the state of nature—can individuals be, before "entering society"? How can they enter society, except by a social contract—or compact—in which each recognizes the equal natural rights of all, in a society dedicated to preserving the equal natural rights of each? It is this mutual recognition which is the foundation, at once, of majority rule and minority rights, of the rule of law.

* * *

One might object that the idea of rule of law arising from a social contract is purely Lockean, and has no tincture of Aristotelianism. To think this, however, is to ignore what Aristotle says about all of natural right being changeable. Consider that, according to Aristotle, whatever the law does not command, it forbids. This is perfectly consistent with the idea of law in the Mosaic polity, which is another example of the ancient city. Remember that, according to Aristotle, a city with more than 10,000 citizens would be too large. Law for an ancient city and for a modern state—whether the 4 million inhabitants of the 13 original American states, or the 280 million of the twenty-first-century America—must of necessity be very different. It must be very different as to the ways and means by which it is formed, yet altogether the same for the human ends that it must serve. The ancient conception of law would, in the modern world, serve only tyranny, while the very purpose of law, according to Aristotle, is to prevent tyranny. The common ground of the ancient and the modern conception of law is shown by Aristotle's dictum that law is reason unaffected by desire.

Locke's state of nature is not a merely hypothetical construct. It is rather a dictate of that very prudence which is, according to Aristotle, the hallmark of all political wisdom. It arises from that fundamental transformation in the human condition from the world described in Fustel de Coulanges' Ancient City—from a world in which each city had its own god—to one in which there was but one God for the human race. This God however was not the God of any one city, or the author of its laws. The obligation of a citizen of an ancient city to obey its laws followed from the obligation to the god of that city. Under Christian monotheism each individual has a relationship with God that is prior, both logically and ontologically, to his membership in his political community. Each individual is a citizen, actual or potential, of the City of God, before being a citizen of his own particular country.

The meaning of this distinction I have discussed at some length in chapter 2 of *A New Birth* in the context of Shakespeare's discussion between Bates, Williams, and King Henry V (in disguise) around the campfire, before the battle of Agincourt. Their conclusion is that each man has an unconditional duty to the King who is alone responsible for the justice of his cause. But the king is not responsible for the fate of each man's soul. Every man is responsible to God, but not the king, for this. Shakespeare, while displaying unflinchingly the defects of kingly rule, does not in the English histories have on his horizon any alternative to divine right monarchy. The American Founding's Lockean republican political theory provides an answer to the defects of Christian divine right monarchy, the answer that Lincoln inherited. This supplied as well the theoretical foundation for Lincoln's assault on slavery.

According to St. Peter and St. Paul, all power was held to come from God. Submission to the power of the Emperor was submission to God. This theory underlay the authority of the king, as Bates and Williams saw it in Henry V. In the Declaration of Independence, the origin of political authority is held to reside, not in emperor, king, or church, but in those unalienable rights with which every human individual is equally endowed by his creator. From the fact of this equal endowment, no one has by nature more authority over another than the other has over him.

Hence the state of nature, and hence the social contract that takes men from the state of nature into civil society, a contract which initially is unanimous, and based upon mutual recognition of that equality of right. It is this unanimity which authorizes majority rule, rule which is understood in principle to be in the interests of the indefeasible rights of the minority no less than of the majority. The "just powers of the government" are moreover understood to be only those to which there has been unanimous consent a priori. Excluded thereby from all political control are the rights of conscience which make man a citizen of the City of God. From this follows the separation of state and church, from which is derived the distinction between state and society, from which, in turn, are derived those civil rights which are the outstanding feature of all decent modern constitutions. These limitations upon political power have no standing whatever in the constitutions of the ancient city. From all of the foregoing, I concluded long ago that, had Aristotle been called upon, in the latter half of the 17th century, to write a guide book for constitution makers, he would have written something very closely approximating Locke's *Second Treatise*. For he would have recognized instantly those differences from his *Politics* that prudential wisdom required, in the world of Christian monotheism, with all its peculiar dangers of tyranny, especially from the union of divine right monarchy and established church.

❈ ❈ ❈

My critics, friendly and unfriendly, may ask why it took me so long to see the purloined letter on the mantelpiece. The reason is that I took for granted that the account of the Hobbesian Locke in Leo Strauss's *Natural Right and History* represented the Locke that informed the American Founding. That rights were prior to duties, that duties were derived from rights, that civil society arose from a contract solely for mutual self-preservation, and that the goods of the soul were subordinated in all decisive respects to the goods of the body, were conclusions of Strauss's interpretation. Strauss himself never said this Locke was the founder's Locke, but the spell cast by his book led many of us to apply it to the founders. Many former students of Strauss, to this day, regard it as heresy to think that Strauss's chapters on Hobbes and Locke do not constitute the authoritative account of the philosophic foundations of American constitutionalism. When presented with the evidence of Aristotelianism in the founding, they react like the scholastics who refused to look into Galileo's telescope: "If it confirms Aristotle it is redundant; if it contradicts him it is false." Strauss himself said that Aristotle would have been the first to look through the telescope.

Strauss was clear, in *Natural Right and History*, that his was an account of Locke's esoteric teaching, but that Locke's exoteric doctrine was far more conventional, and far more consistent with both traditional morality and traditional (albeit more tolerant) Christianity. Strauss also taught us that the authors of the past—and this certainly included political men no less than philosophers—were to be understood as they understood themselves, before the attempt was made to understand them differently or better. It was, and is, an anachronism to assume that the founders read Locke through the eyes of Strauss! One is reminded of Shakespeare's *Troilus and Cressida*. Hector, himself a young man, denounces the elders of Troy, who are so bewitched by Helen's beauty that they are unwilling to return her to her husband, and thus save their city from destruction. "You gloz'd [commented]," he said, "[like] young men whom Aristotle thought unfit to hear moral philosophy." It seemed to me that imputing to the Founding Fathers Leo Strauss's esoteric interpretation of Locke would be not unlike finding the *Nicomachean Ethics* in Hector's library.

2

EQUALITY, LIBERTY, WISDOM, MORALITY, AND CONSENT IN THE IDEA OF POLITICAL FREEDOM

INTRODUCTION

Harry Jaffa mentioned several times to me that the essay reprinted above was a "breakthrough" in his thinking. The only time he explicitly expressed such sentiments in any of his subsequent published writing was in his "Aristotle and Locke" essay, reprinted above, although many of the ideas introduced in this essay make their appearance in his seminal works *A New Birth of Freedom: Abraham Lincoln and the Coming of the Civil War* (2000) and *Crisis of the Strauss Divided: Essays on Leo Strauss and Straussianism East and West* (2012). Jaffa explores the possibility that Lockean elements of the Founding might be understood in Aristotelian terms. For example, Locke's concept of the "state of nature," and "social compact," Jaffa argues, should be understood as prudential adaptations of Aristotelian principles which modify but at the same time "preserve the idea of man as by nature a political animal." This interpretation seems to contradict Leo Strauss's discovery of a radically modern Locke buried deep in his esotericism. The esoteric Locke viewed man as apolitical and possessed of rights by nature but having no obligations by nature. Man was, from Locke's point of view, a radical egoist. The American Founders, insofar as they placed any reliance on Locke, therefore incorporated this radical individualism into their notion of natural rights, particularly the right to property—which

Locke emphasized was derived exclusively from "self-ownership"—and provided no ground for obligations or morality of any kind. In other words, the Founders could not escape the inevitable forces of modernity—the American Founding was radically modern.

But, of course, the Founders were not philosophers; they were, in Aristotle's terms *phronemoi*, practically wise statesmen or "enlightened statesmen," in Madison's terms. Strauss's reading of Locke was revolutionary. No one had ever before read Locke with the skill, innovation and penetration of Strauss, including, as far as we know, the most insightful philosophers. It is impossible to believe that the Founders read Locke the way Strauss did. They were philosophic statesmen, open to philosophy and guided by the "elementary books of public right," including "Aristotle, Cicero, Locke, Sydney, etc." (Jefferson). The exoteric Locke, according to Strauss, presented an unbroken line of natural law teaching that led directly to Aristotle. Thus Jefferson's pairing of Aristotle and Locke, unmindful of the philosophic dispute between ancients and moderns, was perfectly sound Lockeanism. As Jaffa points out, for Locke equality is the ground of political liberty, and consent is the ground of just government. Equally important is the fact that in the state of nature every individual possesses equal rights by nature but also has by nature *equal obligations*. Under the law of nature, therefore, rights and obligations are reciprocal. The law of nature—reason—is the ground of morality; reason therefore informs rights and obligations as well as consent. The Founders accepted Locke's view that reason governs morality, rejecting Hobbes's position that reason is the slave of the passions.

These prudential adaptations of Aristotelian natural right, Jaffa maintains, are fully consistent with "Aristotle's principles." Aristotle's principles did not change, but they required adaptation because of "the transformation of the human condition—and of political life." What had changed the "human condition" and "political life" was a radically different theological-political problem," one that could not have been anticipated by Aristotle. The question of obligation—and religious freedom—was never an issue for the classical *polis*, but it became the principal political and theological concern after the advent of Christianity. The American Founders looked to Locke for guidance on the theological-political issues and they found Locke's solution—separation of church and state—the most salutary political resolution available, and the only one consistent with constitutional government and religious liberty. As Jaffa never tired of repeating, the theology of the Declaration was one of reason and revelation. This reconciliation of reason and revelation on the level of politics and morality was made possible by Locke. The question of what provides or informs the highest human good—reason (philosophy) or revelation (faith)—is an unanswerable question, but there can be agreement on the level of politics and morality, and that was achieved for the first time in the American Founding. And it was that agreement—made possible by a providential dispensation whose ground had been prepared by Locke—that was largely responsible for the success of the Founding. What allowed Jaffa to see the Aristotelian elements in Locke and the American Founding was his understanding of the crucial theological-political problem that confronted early modern political philosophers and the American Founders. Jaffa believed that for Strauss the most important distinction for political philosophy—as opposed to the history of political philosophy—was not between ancients and moderns, but between reason and revelation. That truth is crucial for understanding Locke and the American Founding, but it is a truth that has not been understood by some of Jaffa's most prominent critics because they are guided not by philosophy but the history of philosophy.

   This essay was originally prepared for a Conference on the Constitution at the Center for the Study of Democratic Institutions, Santa Barbara, California, February 12, 1986. The editors thank *Interpretation* for permission to reprint from *Interpretation* Vol. 15, No. 1 (January 1987).

EQUALITY, LIBERTY, WISDOM, MORALITY, AND CONSENT IN THE IDEA OF POLITICAL FREEDOM, BY *HARRY V. JAFFA*

I have written many times that the American Revolution—and the American Founding—represent an idea: the idea of political freedom. This revolution and this founding do indeed also represent an event, or a series of events, which are recorded in what we call history. But our interest in these historical events is derivative, derivative from the fact that we discover at work in the events such an idea as that of political freedom. The particular historical circumstances in which the idea of political freedom took root are certainly interesting, but they can be neither as interesting nor as important as the idea itself. Not the time or place in which the idea was blazoned forth to the world, or when (or even how) it was put into practice, but the idea itself, deserves the first rank in our attention and esteem. Gladstone called "the American Constitution the most wonderful work ever struck off at a given time by the brain and purpose of man." But the "brain and purpose" is prior to the "work." For it was the former which made the latter "wonderful." The Creator must always take precedence of his Creation, in our wonder and admiration. The Constitution has become our inheritance, and we ought to honor the intelligence, the devotion, and the sacrifices, of those who bequeathed it to us. Yet such a legacy cannot be transmitted by inheritance, in the sense that money, land, or other external goods can be transmitted. A constitution, a regime, a way of life—no more than courage, temperance, justice, or wisdom—cannot be "willed" to posterity. In its origin our regime was proclaimed to be a matter of reason: "We hold these truths to be self-evident." And truth is a possession of the mind—not of the will—and of the mind only when it is properly employed. Truth is the possession not of one to whom it is willed, but of him only who understands. There are no lawful inheritors or unlawful usurpers in the possession of truth. But we must also bear in mind that the understanding of truth—although in these premises the condition of virtue—is not itself virtue. Just as the individual virtues represent an habituation of the will to principles of reason, so a free society must not only understand the principles of freedom, but must implement them by those institutions of education and of government, by which such principles become the actual ground of the way of life of a people. I am sure that many of you will wonder why it was that a nation dedicated at its birth—as Lincoln said at Gettysburg—to the proposition that all men are created equal, continued for fourscore and seven years the institution of chattel slavery. This is an important question, and deserves the most serious discussion. Yet I would assert a priori that, as an object of wonder and concern, it is far less significant than the question of how it was that a nation of slaveholders declared that all men are created equal. How was it that this nation declared its independence, not by an appeal to any virtues or rights that were distinctively its own, but to rights that it shared with all men everywhere—

with human beings of every caste and class and every race and nation and creed. Is it, however, wonderful that having made this proclamation of the universal right to freedom of all men—the first time in human history that such a proclamation was made—the American Founders were yet puzzled as to how to implement it? The early history of the republic is one of the fiercest controversy. The ratification of the Constitution was fiercely disputed. In the 1790s, the party controversy among republicans and federalists surpassed in ferocity and rancor anything that we have witnessed in our time. And such animosity even divided some—such as Madison and Hamilton (the principal authors of the celebrated *Federalist*)—who had worked shoulder to shoulder in securing the adoption of the Constitution. Yet each now accused the other of an interpretation of the Constitution which would turn it into an engine, not of freedom, but of despotism. To repeat, no one before the American Founding had ever before proclaimed the principles of freedom—the principles of freedom for all mankind—as the principles of a particular people. Yet how to convert these principles into political institutions, even for themselves, was hardly a settled matter. And how to extend them to all those to whom they were rightfully bound to extend them, represented still another challenge. Nor was it a challenge that could be met merely by a recourse to the principles. Even in the lives of individuals, it is no easy matter to discover the connection between, let us say, good health and healthy habits. Yet even when that knowledge has been gained, it is frequently a matter of greater difficulty to implement the practices that the knowledge would dictate.

To repeat, our national existence began with the proclamation of certain propositions held to be true. The sense of these propositions was understood to be entirely independent of any "climate of eighteenth century America" or of any other time or place. I recall being taken to task once at an English university, by an historian, for treating the Declaration of Independence—an eighteenth-century document, as he thought—as if it had been contemporary. I replied that I was confident that the one thing Jefferson never for a moment dreamed of himself as doing as he drafted the Declaration, was composing an eighteenth-century document. No one believed in the idea of progress more firmly than Jefferson, yet he wrote "Nothing is unchangeable but the inherent and inalienable rights of man." "The rights of man" to Jefferson meant, moreover, the fundamental principles of political right and the moral principles that they embodied. Washington, in 1783, wrote that "The foundation of our empire was not laid in the gloomy age of ignorance and superstition but at an epoch when the rights of mankind were better understood and more clearly defined than at any former period." It was axiomatic for both Jefferson and Washington that "the rights of man" (or mankind) were no different in ages of ignorance and superstition than in ages of enlightenment. But, of course, where they are unknown they can hardly form the basis of governments. The Declaration of Independence itself speaks both of "barbarous ages" and of "merciless savages," and by so doing indicates that barbarism and savagery are ever-present threats to civilization. They may have been more widespread at certain times and places than at others, but they may occur at any time and place. They are negations of enlightenment—and of the wisdom and virtue that may be founded upon enlightenment. The opposition between despotism and freedom is at bottom that of "right and wrong, between whose endless jar Justice resides" (*Troilus & Cressida*, I.iii.116). The same thought was expressed by Lincoln, thus:

> Slavery is founded in the selfishness of man's nature—opposition to it in his love of justice. These principles are an eternal antagonism. Repeal the Missouri Compromise—repeal all compromises—repeal the Declaration of Independence—repeal all past history, you still cannot repeal human nature (Speech at Peoria, Illinois, October 16, 1854).

Before proceeding, some preliminary remarks about language are in order. The words "equality" and "liberty" are in reality adjectives that have been turned into nouns. In more pretentious philosophical discourse, they represent hypostatization—the linguistic transformation of attributes into substances. But attributes, except as attributes of substances, can have no real existence. There can be a red barn. And although one can speak of redness, we cannot see it—or even imagine it—except in a red something: a sunset, a dog, or a red-headed woman. Hence there cannot be equality, except between things that are equal. "Things equal to the same thing are equal to each other" is a Euclidean axiom. By it, equality may be said to subsist between the things that are equal to the same thing, but only in the respects in which that equality is said to subsist. A bed and a chair each of which cost $100.00 may be said to be equal in their monetary value. They may also be said to be equally "furniture." But a bed is not equally a chair, nor a chair equally a bed! There cannot be equality except as a relationship of the things said to be equal, and in the respects in which they are said to be equal. It is then perfectly vain to debate whether all men are created equal, without making clear *in what respects* we are asking whether such equality subsists. Chickens and human beings are two-legged animals, and it would be perfectly correct to say that all chickens and human beings are born equal, if one meant by it equally two-legged.

In defining justice and the just, Aristotle declares that the just subsists in equality, but he then distinguishes the equality that may subsist in exchanges from the equality that may subsist in distributions—of honors, emoluments, or other external goods. The one is called commutative justice, and the other distributive justice. One bed that exchanges for $100.00 may be said to be "equal" to another bed (or any other commodity) that also exchanges for $100.00. The two beds may be of different styles, materials, workmanship, but they are both equal to the same thing, namely, $100.00, and *in that sense* equal to each other. This equality, moreover, defines a sense in which two things, otherwise different, are the same. The value of $100.00 which is placed upon either or both of the beds is a single number. The equality is therefore numerical. There is identity, and no difference, in that respect in which the two beds are said to be equal. On the other hand, in the distribution of the dividends of a corporation, the owner of 200 shares will receive twice as much as the owner of 100 shares. We cannot and do not say that the man receiving twice the amount was receiving an unequal share. On the contrary, his share would be unequal if, having invested twice as much, he were to receive the same amount of dividends as the other man. Here the *same* amount is unequal, and the double amount is equal. Here equality subsists as an equality of *ratios* and not of *numbers*. The ratio of 2/1 in dividends corresponds to the ratio of 2/1 in shares. And so it is with honors and awards based upon merit: the gold medal goes to the winner, the silver to second place, and the bronze to the third.

With these preliminaries behind us, let us turn to the great proposition, "That all men are created equal," and to the axiomatic premises which accompany it, and which together constitute the core of the idea of political freedom. The philosophic source *par excellence* is without question, the opening section of the second chapter ("Of the State of

Nature") of Locke's *Second Treatise of Civil Government*. It is as follows.

> To understand political power aright, and derive it from its original,
> we must consider what state all men are naturally in, and that is a
> state of perfect freedom to order their actions and dispose of their
> possessions and persons as they think fit, within the bounds of the
> law of nature, without asking leave, or depending upon the will, of
> any other man.
>
> A state also of equality, wherein all the power and jurisdiction is
> reciprocal, no one having more than another; there being nothing
> more evident than that creatures of the same species and rank, pro-
> miscuously born to all the same advantages of nature, and the use of
> the same faculties, should also be equal one amongst another without
> subordination or subjection, unless the Lord and Master of them all
> should by any manifest declaration of His will set one above another,
> and confer on him by an evident and clear appointment an un-
> doubted right to dominion and sovereignty.

Before considering this text by itself, we turn to the opening sentence of the "Declaration of the Causes and Necessity of Taking Up
Arms," of the Continental Congress, July 6, 1775. The draftsmen were
John Dickinson and Thomas Jefferson, but we do not know which of
them was responsible for this sentence. It anticipates, however, lacking
only two days to the year, the great trumpet call of the Declaration of
Independence. And whether we consider the declaration of July 6, 1775
or July 4, 1776, what we find are distinct reminders of Locke's famous
phrases.

> If it were possible for men, who exercise their reason to believe, that
> the divine Author of our existence intended a part of the human race
> to hold an absolute property in, and an unbounded power over oth-
> ers, marked out by his infinite goodness and wisdom, as the objects
> of a legal domination never rightfully resistible, however severe and
> oppressive, the inhabitants of these colonies might at least require
> from the Parliament of Great Britain some evidence, that this dread-
> ful authority over them has been granted to that body.

The demand of the Congress that Parliament offer evidence that God had invested "that body" with the right of property—or "dominion and sovereignty"—over "the inhabitants of these colonies" is irony of cosmic grandeur. Sidney in his *Discourses on Government* had expressed a similar thought by saying that some men are not born with saddles on their backs, and others booted and spurred to ride them. (Jefferson would repeat Sidney's words in the letter written just before his death in 1826.) The "saddles on their back" figure of speech means that there is no such natural difference among men, as there is between men and horses, to indicate that one is by nature the master and the other by nature the servant. It is fair to point out, however, that neither horses nor men are born with saddles on their backs! Horses are, however, born apt for serving the purposes of man, although it is left to men to train them to serve those purposes. There is a natural difference be- tween men and horses that makes it according to the natural order, or natural right, that men ride horses. Although we say that men should treat horses humanely—that is to say, with the kindness consistent with the purposes for which the horses are properly used—we do not say that the horses' natural rights are violated, by taking them out of their herds and subjecting them to the service of men. For we reason *a posteriori* from the powers and faculties inherent in the species found in nature, to the distinctions in rank among them. And we say that it is just that the lower serve the higher. It is also true that there are many species of plants and many of animals that are good for food for other species. There is a natural aversion among human beings as there is also among other species—to eating their own kind. But that some species should serve as food for others—whether we consider all plants and animals in relationship to man, or plants in relationship to animals, or the herbivorous animals in relationship to the carnivorous—also seems part of the order of nature and hence of natural right. In each such case, we discover "dominion" or the right to appropriate and to use, the right of property, inhering in beings held superior, in relationship to those held inferior, in the order of nature. A *prima facie* objection to this is, of course, that we have merely equated right with power. Within the lower order of Creation this is undoubtedly true. But as we shall see in due course, it is not true with respect to man. Man's sensibility of what is due to his own humanity, will be seen to result in the idea of power being controlled by right, by something called moral obligation. Even in man's dealings with brute creation, the unlimited power of man is not understood to result in permission to use that power indiscriminately. It is no accident that associations to monitor the dealings of human beings with brutes are called "humane" societies!

Turning to the text of John Locke, we are told, to begin with, that in order "to understand political power aright, we must consider what state all men are naturally in." This is "a state of perfect freedom to order their actions and dispose of their possessions and persons as they think fit, within the bounds of nature, without asking leave, or depending upon the will of any other man." But this is "a state also of equality, wherein all the power and jurisdiction is reciprocal, no one having more than another. . . ." This state, of perfect freedom, but also of equality, is the state of nature. It is a state in which there is no political authority. No man is subject to another. Each is his own master. Each is free—equally free—to obey himself alone. Freedom or—liberty—and equality are then two names for two aspects of the same thing. The "balance between equality and liberty" must be sought in another relationship than that of men in the state of nature.

Locke writes that "there [is] nothing more evident than that creatures of the same species and rank, promiscuously born to all the advantages of nature, and the use of the same faculties, should also be equal one amongst another without subordination or subjection. . . ." When Locke says that nothing is more evident, he means what Jefferson meant in saying that it was self-evident, that all men are created equal. For a proposition to be self-evident means that it cannot be made clearer, or better known, by any form of demonstration. If one grasps the terms of the proposition, one understands it as well as it can be understood. "Self-evident truths" may refer either to analytical or to empirical propositions. "Things equal to the same thing are equal to each other" is analytical—or, if you will, tautological. "That all men are created equal" arises from reflection upon our experience of a class of beings called "men." We abstract from the experience of a number of individual human beings the common noun "man." (A common noun differs from a proper noun as the name of a species differs from the name of an individual of that species. In "Fido is a dog," "Fido" is the proper noun, and "dog" is the common noun.) We do so in the same way that we abstract from the experience of a number of individual dogs, the abstract noun "dog." Having performed the act of inductive

reasoning by which these common nouns are understood, we can articulate attributes which reflection shows were implied in the act of grasp-
ing that noun. We discover, for example, that in understanding "man,"
we not only distinguish the characteristics of individual human beings
from "man in general," but we also distinguish man from "nonman." We
distinguish the human from the nonhuman. And we distinguish, moreover, the nonhuman that is subhuman from the nonhuman that is
superhuman. We conclude, for example, that there is no such difference between man and man, as there is between men and dogs, that
makes men by nature the ruler of dogs, and dogs by nature the servants
to men. But that very experience of man and dog also instructs us that
God is as much above man as man is above dog. Nor is it necessary to
"experience" God in the same sense that one experiences man and dog,
in order to arrive at this conclusion. It is evident that it is by the power
of reason by which we draw this conclusion that man is elevated above
the brute creation. But the power of reason by which man discovers his
elevation in the scale of being, instructs him in the idea of a being
higher in that scale, a being also possessed of reason but without the
evident limitations upon the perfection and use of reason that every
man discovers in his own soul, at the same moment that he becomes
aware that he is a rational being. By the power of reason we form the
conception of a perfectly reasonable Being, in whom there are no passions to act as impediments to reason. From this perspective, it might
be said, reason forms an adequate idea of the essence of God, without
necessarily implying His existence. But whether or not faith is necessary
for the mind to make the transition from God's essence to His existence, it is unnecessary to make that transition "to understand political
power aright, and derive it from its original." Natural theology, stopping
at the idea of God's essence, informs us of the meaning of the difference between man and beast, by informing us of the difference between man and God. Thereby we understand anew what Aristotle declares in the *Politics*, that man is the in-between being, the being that is
neither beast nor God. We understand therefore that the rule of man
over man must differ, not only from the rule of man over beast, but
from the rule of God over man. For the difference between the idea of
man and of God is such, that it would be absurd to suppose that God
would need to secure the consent of man in order to exercise His
providential government. It would be as absurd as that of men securing

the consent of their dogs as a condition of exercising authority over them. Hence, it was that the men of Malden, Massachusetts, as independence approached (May 27, 1776), declared "we can never be willingly subject to any other King than he who, being possessed of infinite wisdom, goodness, and rectitude, is alone fit to possess unlimited power." Hence Tom Paine declared that "In America, the law alone is King." For the conception of God informs us of the idea of law—in Aristotle's words, the rule of "reason unaffected by desire." And therefore is it that all the elements of the rule of law—responsibility of the government to the governed, freedom of speech, press, and religion, subordination of military to civilian authority, separation of powers, independence of the judiciary, writ of habeas corpus, trial by jury, etc.—are discoveries of human reason, whereby the rule of men will, under the denomination of rule of law, be as free as possible from the effects of those infirmities by which human nature is understood to differ from that of God.

It is frequently objected to this, that the rule of law is an illusion, that laws must be interpreted and administered by men, and that there is no escaping the rule of men. If this means that the rule of law can never completely achieve its goal of being "reason unaffected by desire," it is of course perfectly true. If however it means that the law can never approximate this goal, it is wrong. The signers of the Declaration of Independence appealed to "the Supreme Judge of the world, for the rectitude of our intentions." No one expected them to ask God for a jury trial! But the very same reasoning led the framers of the Bill of Rights in the first Congress to insist (in Article VI) upon the right of trial by jury. No one would say that trial by jury in criminal cases yields perfect justice; that the guilty never escape, or that the innocent are never convicted. Yet criminal jurisprudence over the centuries has developed many safeguards against arbitrary judgments by juries. The rules of evidence have constantly been refined in the light of experience to enable judges better to concentrate the attention of juries upon the facts that are material, and to remove from their consideration facts that are immaterial. With this we have been quite reasonably able to impute a very high degree of reasonableness to the judgments of juries in criminal cases. We do not say that these judgments are perfectly reasonable, or that criminal jurisprudence has reached a state of absolute perfection. The debate today about such matters as the Miranda rule is

sufficient evidence of this. Yet no one seriously proposes the replacement of the adversary system of our courts with an entirely different
one. No one seriously doubts that the enfranchisement within the
courtroom of equal and opposite interests—before a jury that (to the
best of the knowledge of the court) shares no interest with either side—
is well adapted to making judgments untainted by the interests of either
of the contending parties. Nor could the court be impartial if there
were no separation of powers, if the judge could be threatened or
bribed by anyone who had an interest in the cases that came before
him. We say, of course, that judges should, so far as possible, be incor-
ruptible. But we take great pains to arrange things so that the corruption of judges is difficult, and that the probable losses of those who
would participate in any attempts at bribery far outweigh their probable
gains. At every step of the way, the idea of "reason unaffected by desire," informed by a realistic understanding of human nature, improves
the operation of the legal system, and acts to make the justice of the
regime genuine.

But is it true, as Locke proposes, and as the Founding Fathers assumed, that "all men," all human beings, "promiscuously born to all the
same advantages of nature, and the use of the same faculties, should
also be equal one to another without subordination or subjection[?]" Do
not human beings differ greatly, both as to their natural endowments,
and as to the degree to which those endowments are or may be cultivated? Are not these differences politically relevant? Is not government,
like all the arts by which human life is benefited, itself benefited by
being conducted by "the wise and the good"? Is it not best conducted,
in the words of the 10th *Federalist*, by those "whose wisdom may best
discern the true interests of their country, and whose patriotism and
love of justice will be least likely to sacrifice it to temporary or partial
considerations[?]" Is not the fact that man is the rational animal reason
to place in authority—to use one of Locke's favorite phrases "the rational and industrious"? The answer to all these questions is, of course, an
emphatic affirmative.

In considering the application of reason to human affairs, however,
we are reminded of an argument advanced by Socrates in the first book
of Plato's *Republic*. All the arts involve knowledge of opposites. Medicine is knowledge of health and disease. The function of the doctor, we
say, is to preserve health and prevent disease, or to cure disease and

restore health. To know how to do these things, however, the doctor must know equally well how to cause disease and prevent or injure health. The art of medicine—considered simply as the knowledge of the causes of health and disease—is an art or knowledge of opposites. And we know that medicine can be employed, and is employed—as in the invention of the instruments of nuclear and biological warfare—for killing as well as for curing. We also know that physicians have been known to enter into conspiracies against their patients. (For example, plots in collusion with heirs to collect insurance.) More profoundly, we know that despotic regimes especially those peculiarly malicious forms of despotism which, in our time, are called "totalitarian"—regularly employ the medical art against those they call enemies of the regime. Hitler employed thousands of physicians—not only Dr. Mengele—to murder "undesirables": Jews, gypsies, homosexuals, invalids, the chronically ill. The Soviet Union today has suborned the entire psychiatric profession within its borders to treat political dissidents as "insane," to testify against them in court, and to turn their hospitals and sanatoria into prisons and torture chambers. These "doctors" inject their patients with mind and body-destroying drugs.

The "ethical neutrality" of the arts and the sciences (τέχναι καί ἐπιστῆμαι) was recognized equally by Aristotle, in the *Nicomachean Ethics* when, in Book VI, he makes it clear that the exercise of none of the intellectual virtues requires moral virtue, with the exception only of prudence, or practical wisdom. This moral defect of the arts and sciences was recognized in the ancient world by the Hippocratic oath, taken even today by all physicians before entering into practice. Whatever may be the noble and just intentions that lead most young physicians into the medical profession, there is nothing in the art of medicine, considered merely as a knowledge of the causes of health and disease, that directs it towards healing and away from injuring. It is the addition of the Hippocratic oath to medical knowledge—that is to say, the addition of moral virtue to intellectual virtue—which together constitute what we call the healing art. From this example, which can be multiplied many times over, we conclude that something must be added to each of the arts, considered merely as forms of knowing, or know-how, or knowledge of causes, to assure that it will benefit those who are to be governed by it. Aristotle classified governments into those of the one, the few, and the many. But each kind of government could be either good or bad, depending upon whether the government was directed to the common good, or towards the private advantage of the government. A government, whether of the one, few, or many, may be skillful or unskillful in the art of governing. But whether skillful or unskillful, it could not be good, if it directed its efforts to rewarding the rulers at the expense of the community as a whole. The principle of the "consent of the governed" is the supreme discovery of the political art for directing government towards the benefit of the governed.

When we go to the doctor, we subject ourselves to his regimen. We consent to be governed by him, in one of the most important respects in which, during our lives, we subject ourselves to the rule of others. We do so because we think that it is better to be governed by one with medical knowledge than by ourselves, with respect to our health. But we also think that it is essential, that the full extent of the doctor's skill be devoted to our benefit. We want him to be neither negligent nor lackadaisical, because of any indifference towards us. Nor do we want him to be distracted in any way, by having any reason to ask himself, why he should exert himself fully on our behalf. We want assurance, or even reassurance, on this point. First of all, it is essential, for the "health" of our relationship, that it be voluntary. However much we may, or must, rely upon advice, both lay and professional, in choosing a doctor, it is essential that his government over us is based upon our consent. To the hypothetical objection, that this is a case of the wise depending upon the unwise, for the exercise of wisdom, the reply must be: the unwise have an interest in choosing well that goes a long way towards compensating for the defect of their knowledge. Of course, we are supposing a people who, however "unwise" as laymen, are nonetheless "enlightened," aware of their ignorance, and therefore intelligent and vigilant in their own interests. The very proposition "that all men are created equal" (the ground of "the consent of the governed") as a philosophical truth, implies a civilized understanding of civilization generally shared by the people as a whole. "If a nation expects to be ignorant and free . . . it expects what never was and never will be," wrote Jefferson in 1816 (letter to Charles Yancey, January 6 1816). We are not then considering people who would not know the difference between witch doctors and highly trained graduates of modern medical schools. And, in general, we do not expect that the choice of doctors by private individuals will be guided by nonmedical considerations. If you are in urgent need of medical attention, you do not look for someone whose diagnosis is intended to flatter you, rather than cure you! Or if, in some cases, some people are guided more by the doctor's "bedside manners" than by his professional knowledge, this does not constitute a reason why in general the choice of physicians should not be voluntary. The medical profession as a whole, in a political society constituted by the principle of the consent of the governed, depends very much upon the reputation it enjoys with society at large. The chances are not great, therefore, that someone will choose a very bad doctor because he has chosen him for considerations that are less than strictly professional. Because our patronage of the medical profession is voluntary, the medical profession, through professional organizations, and through the licensing laws (usually administered in cooperation with the professional medical organizations) has a great incentive to police itself. And however we may complain of our medical bills, we really want the doctor to be paid, and paid well, for his services. We want him to have the greatest possible incentive to apply his wisdom as skillfully as possible to our advantage. Paying him, however, is only one aspect of a system of incentives and constraints with which we surround him. It is important also that the payment be as nearly as possible a "market" price. The individual doctor ought to have the incentive to be able to charge higher prices because of the superior reputation for excellence he may gain in the course of his practice. A fixed price for a fixed service does not produce the unqualified incentive for unqualified devotion, each of us likes to think that the doctor is giving him. Further: we surround the doctor with a web of law (including the aforesaid licensing laws), civil law by which he may be sued for any form of negligence or incompetence (malpractice), and criminal law by which he may be prosecuted if he is thought to have deliberately inflicted injury, for whatever motive.

The Hippocratic oath reminds us that the medical art, taken merely as knowledge of causes, is amoral. But we expect our doctors to be moral men, whose moral intention combined with their knowledge makes their art the healing art. Yet we surround the practice of medicine with a myriad of institutional arrangements—with both rewards for good behavior and punishment for bad behavior—designed to assure that physicians will act morally, whether or not they are actually moral. In taking these precautions we do not regard their actual character as a matter of indifference. In fact, we recognize that habitual good behavior—whether of doctors or anyone else—even if begun for nonmoral reasons is a good foundation upon which genuinely good character may develop. All moral education is of this sort.

In health care, as in criminal justice, the aim is behavior reflecting the standard of "reason unaffected by desire." Here "reason" refers to medical knowledge pure and simple, uninfluenced by any nonmedical considerations of economic (or other) advantage. Yet it is well to remember, when we consider the "government" of ourselves by medical doctors, that the good health we seek through their assistance depends only partly on the skill and virtue of the doctors. Our desire for health is indeed a powerful incentive to obey the doctors' government. Patients who flinch at the least pain will undergo drastic surgery when the alternative is sufficiently stark. Those who are ordinarily self-indulgent to the last degree will follow regimens of abstinence and self-denial when the thread of life is slender. But the end intrinsic to medicine—which is to contribute to human health—is not a final end, but a means to human well-being. No doctor, we presume would want to be remembered as the man whose supreme skill in 1935 saved Adolph Hitler's life (even if such a doctor rightly believed he was only doing his duty). If physicians are the moral men we wish them to be (and as moral men— and not merely as physicians—they will have higher ends than health) then they too will recognize a distinction between repairing the ravages of gluttony, greed, or promiscuity and in providing that relief to the human estate which is required by the ills to which all flesh is heir.

There are those, however, who think that the modern project for the relief of man's estate justifies the abolition of what is sometimes alleged to be the greatest of all burdens upon the human condition: the burden of virtue. Modern philosophy conceives of a project in which a much higher degree of felicity is imagined, if the passions do not have to be controlled, and in particular if they are not controlled by reason. (In the comparison between the life of the tyrant, and the life of the just man, sketched in both the *Republic* and the *Gorgias*, they—in opposition to Socrates—choose the life of the tyrant. This is the starting point for Machiavelli, and for all modern political philosophy.) It does not, however, mean that men must become tyrants in the classical sense. The conquest of nature by science will make nature the universal slave, so that men can become tyrants in principle without becoming tyrants in fact. That is to say, science will enable them to live lives unrestrained by moral principle, yet somehow without injuring themselves and without injuring each other. This last is the greatest of the illusions of modern man. It imagines a surpassingly greater happiness, in the unfettered release or indulgence of the passions, and imagines that reason performs a truer function as a slave to the passions than as their ruler. In the light of this enterprise, the essential purpose of medicine is not health, as conceived traditionally (or by common sense). Health in the traditional sense was a good thing because it contributed to the *summum bonum*, happiness. A happy life was one lived well, because lived in accordance with the moral and intellectual virtues. The restraints upon the human passions imposed by the habits of the moral virtues are by this dispensation no longer regarded as goods in themselves. Whatever goodness is seen in restraint is such only as it may be a temporary necessity or exigency which will in due course make way for unrestraint. Thus, in Marxist-Leninist theory, the dictatorship of the proletariat will be followed in due course by the withering away of the state. Under the "pure communism" which follows, there will be no constraints upon human behavior, either political or moral. Pure communism represents the return to the Garden of Eden—but with this difference: there will be no forbidden fruit (and hence no possibility of a Fall, or expulsion from the Garden!). Contemporary ideological liberalism—or at least its libertarian wing—differs from Marxism-Leninism only in this: it sees no reason why anyone should wait for the Revolution, or the withering away of the state! For example, sodomy is not something one ought not to engage in, although it may be wise to abstain from it until a cure for AIDS is found. Meanwhile, unlimited resources may be demanded for finding a cure for AIDS. The reason for this demand is only incidentally to avert the evil of the disease. It is essentially for the sake of the felicity of unrestrained sodomy. Nor can medicine object to the use of drugs that are unhealthy, if they give pleasure through illusions beyond the natural powers of the mind or of the imagination. Doctors might advise patients to abstain from them until an adequate antidote to their deleterious side effects might be found. But it is as much a purpose of medicine to find antidotes to pleasant "vices" as to find cures for painful diseases. The physician, *qua* physician, may not make moral judgments as to how his healing art may be exercised.

But what of the physician *qua* moral man? Is there not a contradiction in wishing doctors to be just, to genuinely care for the good of their

patients, but yet to be neutral or indifferent to all other moral distinctions? Does not the goodness of the doctor depend upon an understanding of goodness rejected by those who would thus commandeer
the art of medicine? Does not the good doctor, *qua* good man, have an
obligation to refuse to serve Hitler or Stalin? Does he not also have an
equal obligation not to serve a regime in which every man is as free to
do as he likes, without regard to moral considerations, as a regime in
which only one man—for example, a Hitler or Stalin—is? Is not government by the consent of the governed (whether we think of medical
government or political government) controlled inexorably by the idea
of "reason unaffected by desire"? And does it not therefore inexorably
commit us to the control of the passions by reason?

The example taken from medicine, may be repeated with law, engi-
neering, architecture, and even strategy. Benedict Arnold was probably
the greatest military talent in the American cause—until he attempted
to betray that cause. It was he, more than Gates, who was responsible
for the victory at Saratoga—the only substantial American victory before Yorktown, and the one that tipped the balance in favor of France's
decision to intervene on the American side. It is not immaterial that one
reason for George Washington's selection to command the American
army before Boston in 1775, was his very considerable wealth, which
represented a fundamental pledge of (or, if you will, hostage to) his
loyalty to the American cause. Benedict Arnold, unlike George Washington, proved to be a talented but unreliable military adventurer. He
lacked both Washington's moral character and Washington's stake in
the community he was appointed to defend.

Two other reasons for Washington's appointment by the Continental
Congress are also noteworthy. They were his unusual—and highly regarded—military record, gained in the Seven Years' War with France;
and the necessity of having a Virginian in command of an American
army outside Boston. For this latter consideration also sought to seal
the loyalty of the commander and his regional interests as a Virginian to
the larger cause of America as a whole. Had the Revolution broken out
in Virginia, and had the American army been situated, let us say, on the
Yorktown peninsula, it is probable that a Massachusetts man would
have been sought for the command. Massachusetts and Virginia were,
so to speak, the Dan and Beersheba of the thirteen colonies. But the
rebellious colonists were Whigs, and had remembered as if it were only

yesterday, the British experience of Oliver Cromwell. It was their intention, in the Revolution, and in both the state and federal constitutions
which ensued upon the Revolution, to avoid the dangers of a profes-
sionally commanded army following a gifted commander—the Caesar-
ean formula represented to them by the army of Cromwell. Because of
that experience, for nearly two hundred years commissions in the British army had to be purchased. It was thus assured that the officer corps
would share an overriding interest with the propertied classes—and
civilian society—which would keep them from ever "crossing the Rubi-
con." Thus the constitutional axioms of the dependence of the sword
upon the purse, and of the military upon the civilian authority. (The
American Constitution makes the President, who must be a civilian,
commander-in-chief of the armed services; but it makes him dependent
upon the Congress for supplies. It also makes the House of Representatives—the more popular branch—the origin of all money bills, while it
requires the consent of the Senate for the appointment of all the higher
military offices.)

It is clear that British experience underlies much of American constitutionalism. Underlying this experience, however, is this relationship—rooted in the nature of things—of the subpolitical, or nonpolitical
arts to the political art or to political science. Different institutional (or
other) devices may be required in different circumstances, but the purpose is the same: to bring the different practical disciplines of human
life (whether, e.g., strategic, medical, or economic) under moral control, and under the control of the master discipline which is the political. The "consent of the governed" is the foundation, not only of the
responsibility of the government to the governed in the political sense,
but in the broader sense in which under such a government "wisdom"
in all the arts and sciences may become beneficial to the whole community.

The natural equality of man, as we have seen, results in government
by the consent of the governed. This consent must be uncoerced, although it becomes, in turn, the foundation of lawful coercion. But a
civil society organized upon the principle of voluntary association alone
can implement the voluntary principle in all those other relationships of
life resulting from the cultivation of knowledge and wisdom. And it is by
the voluntary principle that the means are found by which wisdom—
and not freedom alone—becomes an effective force in the life not only

of individuals, but of the polity. But the wisdom which "rectifies" (so to speak) all other wisdom, is wisdom in a more fundamental sense. And this is that political wisdom—defined originally by Aristotle—which stands in the supervisory or architectonic relationship to all other practical arts and sciences. The foundation of this architectonic discipline, within its Lockeian context, is to be found in that "law of nature" by which "the state of nature" is said to be governed.

But is not the "state of nature" merely imaginary? Does it not refer to a hypothetical rather than a real past? Or if some time in the actual past a group of men came together to form civil society by a social compact, what relevance does that have for us today? Our natural liberty does not consist in being bound by what others have agreed to. These are typical of the objections to Lockeianism heard today, and to any Lockeian interpretation of the Constitution (such as that of Abraham Lincoln).

In reply, we observe that it is necessary, that we, living in civil society, understand what the law of nature is in the state of nature, to understand the foundation of our rights and our duties here and now. Whatever status the idea of the state of nature may possess, as a historical concept, it is a permanent attribute of our consciousness as members of a free society.

Everyone knows that he may, if necessary and at any time, take "the law into his own hands," either to defend himself, or to defend other innocent persons from unlawful violence. No positive law can repeal this natural law. That every normal human being does understand this proves that we are conscious of the law of nature in the state of nature, whether we conceptualize this consciousness or not. Hence we also understand that where there are no police, or impartial courts in which to seek damages, it is not unjust to seek redress for injuries by whatever means are available, including force. Again, international law tries to supply the defect of the state of nature, when individuals—meaning here both individual nations, and individual citizens of different nations—having no common judge (Locke's definition of the state of nature)—attempt to provide juridical means for redress. All of these examples are testimony that, however ineffective the law of nature might be in the state of nature, the understanding that such a law exists, is entirely independent of its enforcement. That is to say, the law of nature, as Locke says, is the law of reason. We thus look to the state of nature a priori to understand what is the law of reason, the law which ought to govern, whether or not it does govern. From this we instruct ourselves of the ground of our rights and duties in civil society, under government. Reason teaches us not to inflict injury upon other human beings, except as just punishment for offenses they may have committed. It instructs us that murder, theft, adultery, perjury, the abandonment or neglect of children, ingratitude towards parents, are injuries, offenses against reason, and therefore against the law of nature. They are offenses against the law of civil society because we understand antecedently that they are wrong, that they ought not be done, and if done, punished. This understanding of right and wrong is in us all, and we become aware of it when we become aware of our own humanity. By it we become aware of what we owe to others, because of the humanity that they share with us. That is to say, we understand that there is a ground of friendship in nature, apart from the more obvious ground in family, clan, nation, or any other form of personal relationship, arising from particular circumstances or shared interests. We understand, of course, that these other forms of friendship are naturally more intense, and nobler and better than those of mere humanity. But we also understand that these friendships are potentialities of our common humanity, and would not be possible without it. We understand ourselves—and our own humanity—in the light of this underlying resemblance we bear to each other. We understand particular manifestations of our humanity—including its negations in barbarism and savagery—in the light of what is consistent with, or inconsistent with, this underlying resemblance. And this resemblance is understood, on the one hand, by the light of both the resemblance and the difference between all human beings and the lower order of Creation, and on the other, by the light of the resemblance and the difference between man and God.

The state of nature is then to be understood primarily in analytical terms: as an inference from man's place in that "great chain of being" that both links and distinguishes the higher and the lower natures. It recurs whenever men meet who have "no common judge." It may at some point become a feature of the history of a people as it progresses from family and clan and tribe to civil polity. Or it may arise in virtue of the revolutionary right of human beings both to dissolve particular societies, and to break up oppressive governments and institute new ones. But its most common utility is to be found, not in extreme situations, but in normal ones: and that is to understand the ground and purpose of our citizenship. It is to enable us to judge the tendencies, whether in ourselves or in others, away from, or towards, government that fulfills the purposes implicit in our human nature. It enables us to reflect upon that fact that, being neither beasts nor gods, we are yet a compound of both, with potentialities in ourselves, both individually and collectively, for descending into bestiality, or ascending towards the divine.

We may illustrate the foregoing from documents of the era of the Revolution and the Founding. In the Lockeian language of the Massachusetts Bill of Rights (1780),

> The body politic is formed by a voluntary association of individuals; it is a social compact by which the whole people covenants with each citizen and each citizen with the whole people that all shall be governed by certain laws for the common good

And the premise of this compact is that

> All men are born free and equal, and have certain natural, essential and unalienable rights; among which may be reckoned the right of enjoying and defending their lives and liberties; that of acquiring, possessing, and protecting property: in fine that of seeking and obtaining their safety and happiness.

"Safety and happiness" constitute the alpha and omega of human beings joined together in a body politic. How safety is to be achieved, and how happiness is understood, are inferences from the understanding of human nature either expressed or implied in the compact by which civil society is formed. The powers granted—as well as the powers denied to—government, are also understood from the same implied reference.

The ubiquity of the social compact theory in the American Founding is nowhere better illustrated than in the thought of the Father of the Constitution, James Madison. In one of his last extended discourses in political theory ("Sovereignty," *The Papers of James Madison*, edited by Gaillard Hunt, Vol. IX. p. 569), Madison wrote that "it is proper to keep in mind that all power in just and free governments is derived from compact. . . ." Throughout his career, Madison repeated over and over again that all free government is founded upon "compact." What he meant he explained as follows.

> To go to the bottom of the subject, let us consult the Theory which contemplates a certain number of individuals as meeting and agreeing to form one political society, in order that the rights, the safety, and the interest of each may be under the safeguard of the whole.
>
> The first supposition is, that each individual being previously independent of the others, the compact which is to make them one society must result from the free consent of *every* individual.
>
> But as the objects in view could not be attained, if every measure conducive to them required the consent of every member of society, the theory further supposes, either that it was part of the original compact, that the will of the majority was to be deemed the will of the whole, or that this was a law of nature, resulting from the nature of political society itself, the offspring of the natural wants of man.
>
> Whatever be the hypothesis of the origin of the *lex majoris partis* it is evident that it operates as a plenary substitute of the will of the majority of the society for the will of the whole society; and that the sovereignty of the society as vested in and exercisable by the majority, may do anything that could be *rightfully* done by the unanimous concurrence of the members; the reserved rights of individuals (of conscience for example) in becoming parties to the original compact being beyond the legitimate reach of sovereignty, wherever vested or however viewed (*Ibid.*, pp. 570, 571).

"To go to the bottom of the subject"—the nature of sovereignty in the Constitution and government of the United States—it was necessary for Madison to consult a "Theory." And this theory requires us—as we have said it must—to contemplate man in the state of nature: "a number of individuals ('each individual being previously independent of the others') meeting and agreeing to form one political society, in order that the rights, the safety, and the interest of each may be under the safeguard of the whole." In order to be competent to make the contract, each must be free of any antecedent human authority, and be the equal of each of the persons with whom he is contracting. Having made the contract, each is under an equal obligation to cooperate in the establishment of the government. The rights that each individual possesses by nature, and the freedom and equality of each in the possession of such rights, defines the nature of the compact, and instructs us both in the nature of the powers of government which result therefrom, and in the limitations upon such power.

No one in the state of nature leaves the state of nature—to become a member of a body politic, properly so-called—except as a consequence of a compact or contract freely entered into. Subsequent generations born into a free society retain the right—upon coming of age—to accept or reject the polity into which they are born. Of course, civil society cannot be torn down and begun anew with each generation. But each individual succeeds to the same political rights as those who preceded him, including the Founders. Everyone is equally born into a world that is not of his making, and everyone has the same natural right to accept or reject, in whole or in part, what he finds. That is to say, each one has the same right to choose among the alternatives he finds. No one can say that he rejects the society into which he is born, simply because it is not what he wants. He is of course at liberty to persuade others to join him in remaking it, but their relative contentment—if it be such—does not entitle him to reject its authority. But he must be permitted to leave, if he wishes. That there is a natural right of emigration is a corollary of the idea of civil society as a voluntary association. One's obligations flow from the fact that one is a voluntary member of a voluntary association. But the obligations that flow from the exercise of one's free will are themselves binding. Paying taxes and serving in the military are not optional, because one disagrees with some (or any) of the purposes of the laws which have resulted from the political process.

As a citizen of a polity constituted by the social contract, one has an equal right to share in the making of the law one is to live under. And those who make the law must live under the identical laws that they make for the rest of their fellow-citizens. There can be no privileged classes. To say "You—but not I—shall pay taxes" is another way of saying "You work, I'll eat." Still, we must recognize that the operation of laws may be unequal without intending to be so, and laws which are surreptitiously intended to be unequal may not appear to be so. A regime of equality cannot be expected to be perfectly so, either in appearance or in reality.

One must also recognize that there is no abstract answer to the question of what constitutes an "equal" share in lawmaking. Although the principle can and must be stated in abstract or universal terms— that all men are created equal—the means of implementing this principle must follow the dictates of prudence, taking into consideration circumstances that are not universal, but particular. The idea that proportional representation, for example, more nearly implements the principle of equal rights than other electoral systems, involves a fundamental misunderstanding. The purpose of voting in a free society is not to assure an equal weight in the voting process but, in Lincoln's words, "an equal voice in the government." How that "equal voice" may be achieved in any particular government—indeed, what sensible meaning may be assigned to it—cannot be discovered by any abstract formula. We cannot here enter more largely into the complexity of different electoral systems. Suffice it that proportional voting (of which there are many forms) generally encourages the fragmentation of the citizenry into splinter groups, who must then be compounded into working majorities. Since such majorities are not bound by party loyalties, they tend to be fragile, the resulting governments weak, and the rights both of majority and minority in jeopardy. A voting system—such as that of district representation, in which "the winner takes all"—that compels the coalescence of smaller minorities into a larger minority, and of minorities into a majority—produces stronger and more stable governments. This is to the advantage of both majority and minorities. The electoral system in a free society ought to be designed to facilitate coalition building in the electoral process. This coalition building should, so far as possible, take place before the elections. The loyalties generated by the discrete minorities, to each other, as they form themselves into ever larger parties, assist the process of compromise, in the service of a common good. This makes possible a two-party system, the only system compatible, in the long run, with popular government. In a two-party system, the broad base of the major parties is such that each is competing for members of the other's coalition. In this way minorities may obtain political influence—and protection for their rights as minorities—far beyond what may be represented by their numbers. Thus the real interest of minorities is much better served than in a system of proportional representation, where their status as minorities is preserved by the voting, but where they are separated, if not isolated, from the political influence of loyal members of a major party.

Majority rule, says Madison, arises from the fact that the most essential purposes of government—not to mention lesser ones—could not be achieved if the action of the government depended upon the unanimity which lies at its foundation. That unanimity, in short, implies necessarily a willingness to be governed by the majority, either as a part of the "original compact" or as "a law of nature." Henceforth "the will of the majority" will be "deemed the will of the whole." The unanimous consent by which civil society is constituted, itself invests the majority with the authority of the whole. But this authority of the majority is not without limitations. The two criteria that limit the authority of the majority, according to Madison here, are unanimity and rightfulness. There is, we say, unanimous consent for majority rule. But that unanimous consent implies that the majority is the trustee of the rights of the minority. The majority does not act in its own name, but in the name of the minority as well. And the minority is supposed to look upon the decisions of the majority as its own decisions. (The man elected President of the United States is the representative of every citizen of the United States, not only of those who voted for him.) But this would not be realistic, if we did not understand the rights under the protection of our common government, to be at bottom the same. If fellow citizens looked upon each other, in the way that Protestants and Catholics looked upon each other, during the wars of the Reformation, or as medieval Christians looked upon medieval Jews, then Protestants, Catholics, and Jews could not be fellow citizens. Majority rule would be chimerical, because what divided majorities and minorities would be more fundamental than what united them. It is in this light that we recall Washington's declaration that the American Founding "was not laid in the gloomy age of ignorance and superstition." And that age survives today in Khomeini's Iran, and in many other parts of the world as well. Nor are superstitions to be associated only with man's prescientific religious consciousness. The demon of persecution in National Socialism and Marxism-Leninism arises from an allegedly "scientific" interpretation of the world. The moral education of the whole community in the common natural rights of humanity, as the ground of the social compact, is a necessary condition of free society, of a polity in which majority rule may be combined with minority rights. And no free society can perfect itself beyond the point that has been made possible by its progress in this education.

The Virginia Bill of Rights of 1776 expresses the common faith of the Revolution, when it declares:

That no free government, or the blessings of liberty, can be preserved to any people but by a firm adherence to justice, moderation,
temperance, frugality and virtue and by frequent recurrence to fundamental principles.

By this it is implied that the citizens of a free community must be
characterized by a morality that generates trust among them. And the
moral virtues, as virtues of the will, are themselves grounded upon
"fundamental principles," which are virtues of the mind or intellect. It
is then not "individuals" of any description whatever, who are united
into a polity by the social contract, but those possessed of a rational will
who give unanimous consent to majority rule. By reason of their understanding of what unites them on the fundamental level, the citizens of a
free society, while becoming partisans (and even "factions") with respect to the interests that divide them, will be able to transcend these
distinctions, when these threaten the genuine interests they share as
fellow citizens. It will teach them, above all, as members of a majority,
not to permit the endangering of those rights of the minority, which
ought to be their common care.

   Madison, we recall, said that the majority, acting for the whole, "may
do anything that could be *rightfully* done by the unanimous concurrence of the members. . . ." (emphasis in the original). He thus adds
rightfulness to unanimity, as a criterion of majority rule, and even gives
it a particular emphasis. Clearly, unanimity acts as a check on majority
rule, by inviting each member of the majority to ask himself, whether
he is doing anything to another, that he would not have another do to
him. In a free society men rule and are ruled in turn. In representative
government, they may "rule" either by holding office, or by forming
part of the victorious electoral majority. No one, in the majority, may
act to deprive others of those civil or political rights, in virtue of which
members of the minority may hope to rule in their turn. But unanimity
by itself, although a necessary criterion, is not sufficient. Men may be
unanimous and wrong. Madison gives us but one example, but it is one
whose importance cannot be exaggerated. The rights of conscience may
not become a matter of governmental action, no matter how unanimous
opinion may be with respect to them. Religious homogeneity is not a
justification for laws expressing that agreement among the citizens. A
community of Christians (or of a particular denomination of Christians)
may ask themselves whether, in compelling non-Christians (or Chris-

tians of another denomination) to join their church, they are violating the golden rule of doing to others what they would not have others do to them. But it is not likely that they will think in Kantian or categorical terms of what it would mean if everyone were at liberty to compel everyone else in matters of religious faith. It is much more likely that, thinking only of their own faith as an unqualified blessing, they would see nothing wrong in itself, or contrary to the golden rule, in using the compulsion for the sake of an end of whose goodness they have no doubt. (Shakespeare was confident that few members of an Elizabethan audience would doubt that the forced conversion of Shylock at the end of *The Merchant of Venice* was as philanthropic as it was just.)

The very idea of a social compact, founded upon the common rights of man in the state of nature excludes from legislation whatever is not intrinsic to those rights that men share, and for which they need common protection, in the state of nature. The Statute of Virginia for Religious Liberty of 1786—the doctrinal basis of the religious clauses of the First Amendment—declares that our civil rights have no more dependence upon our religious opinions, than upon our opinions in physics or geometry. A sequel to this statute might have declared that our civil rights have no more dependence upon the color of our skin, or of our national origin, than upon our religious opinions. In the course of time, as we know, such amendments to the Constitution, and statutes to enforce such amendments, have in fact become the law of the United States. For this reason, we tend to view as illegitimate political parties whose aim—like the Ku Klux Klan, the Nazis, or the Communists—it is to deprive others of their equal rights of citizenship. Are not those, we ask, who do not accept the premises of free society, and of majority rule, themselves justly excluded from participating in the political processes of a free society?

The answer to the foregoing question must be a prudential one. Denying civil or political rights to those who are intolerant of the equal rights of others, however just in itself, may be counterproductive. It may in some circumstances actually serve the interests of those we suppress. Contemplating this question however like contemplating man in the state of nature instructs us in the fundamental rights and duties of the citizens of a free government. It teaches us that education of the citizens in the principles of the regime is the most fundamental task of any free government. For a free society cannot be neutral towards the convictions of its citizens with respect to their mutual rights and duties. It cannot be neutral towards the morality of citizenship, without being neutral towards itself. And this is absurd. Without that frequent recurrence to (that is to say, frequent re-education in) fundamental principles enjoined by the great documents of the American Revolution "no free government . . . can be preserved to any people." These principles as the ground of our patriotism must be defended, whenever the nation itself is defended, if necessary, by the sword. But they cannot be defended politically or by force, if they are not defended first and last, in the souls of the citizens. The greatest threat is in the souls of those who believe that reason as a guide to the ends or purposes of man's moral and political existence is either blind or impotent, and who think that reason is relevant to human life, only as the slave, and never as the master, of our passions.

APPENDIX

Walter Berns has written (*This World*, Fall 1983, pp. 97, 98) that

> the champions of separation [of church and state] in the United States—Madison, Washington, and Jefferson, for example—were not Christians, except perhaps in the most nominal of senses . . . I would go further: the very idea of natural rights is incompatible with Christian doctrine and, by its formulators, was understood to be incompatible. In fact, Thomas Hobbes and John Locke were enemies of all revealed religions.

I have commented elsewhere (*This World*, Spring/Summer 1984, pp. 3–7, but see also *National Review*, November 29, 1985, pp. 34–36) on this thesis of Berns—now very popular—that Christianity and all revealed religion is "incompatible" with "the very idea of natural rights." According to Berns himself the idea of natural rights, as expressed above all in the Declaration of Independence (but not less so in the Virginia Statute of Religious Liberty) is the very foundation of our constitutional and political order. To say that these foundations are "incompatible" with revealed religion, means that the success of the one must end in the withering away, if not the ultimate extinction, of the other.

I believe Berns is mistaken, and that the doctrine of natural rights is not only compatible with Christianity (and a fortiori with revealed religion as such), but is understood to be a requirement of it. The ground of individualism that we find in Locke's state of nature is anticipated by Christianity, in the idea of an individual, personal relationship, between each human soul and God, arising from Creation itself. This relationship is understood to be outside the natural order, and yet one that is reflected in the government of the natural order. It is, as such, independent of the political community. The Virginia Statute of 1786 begins with the assertion that "Almighty God hath created the mind free" and goes on to cite the example set by "the holy author of our religion" who "being Lord of both body and mind, yet chose not to propagate it by coercions on either, as was in His Almighty power to do." The success of Christianity—not its demise, as Berns suggests—depends upon its influence upon the mind, altogether free of "temporal punishments or burthens or civil incapacitations. . . ." Wealth or power in this world, or fear of persecution, may beget "hypocrisy and meanness," but not true faith. Inducements to the profession of faith, apart from the evidences presented to faith itself, are responsible for establishing and maintaining "false religions over the greatest part of the world and through all time." The doctrine of the Virginia Statute, the doctrine of natural rights, understands itself to contribute to true religion, and not to the elimination of religion. By contributing to the purity of religion, it is meant to contribute to the purity of society, and thereby to the moral foundation of civil government.

Prior to the rise of Christianity in the Roman world, every ancient city had its own divine law. The attribution of the laws of the Mosaic polity to Moses' God was typical of the ancient world. Every city either had a god as its lawgiver, or received them from a legislator who had in turn received them from a god. The God of Israel Himself appears for some time as if He were "one among many" gods. First He must persuade the children of Israel that He alone is their god: then he moves on to that most shocking of paradoxes: their God alone is God.

In the ancient world, when cities were defeated in war, they often ceased to exist. If the inhabitants were not all killed, then the survivors—usually the women and children only—were carried off into slavery. Their altars were destroyed, and their gods ceased to exist—even for them. They became "clients" of the religion of their masters—the way in which black slaves in America forgot their native religions, and became in time Christians. The only conspicuous exception was the Jews, who strangely (to the rest of the world) clung to their God, perhaps even more adamantly in defeat.

As Rome conquered the cities of the ancient Mediterranean world, it found it more profitable (only incidentally more humane) to leave them to their own internal self-government. The Romans no longer exterminated their defeated enemies—as they did Carthage—or even enslaved them. Rome imposed tribute, which it found it could collect more efficaciously if it left their civic life as nearly intact as possible. After the Republic was succeeded by the Empire, and after the destruction of the Senate and the patriciate of Rome by Caesar and his successors, Rome itself ceased in any proper sense to be a political community. All power was concentrated within the Imperial palace, and the Praetorian guard. Eventually, the distinction between Rome and the provinces, and the distinction between citizens and noncitizens, became so attenuated, that Roman citizenship was extended to everyone. The Roman empire—in its own self-understanding—became universal—that is, catholic—and to be a citizen of Rome was to be a citizen of the world. Of course, to be a citizen of the world meant equally not to be a citizen at all. Citizenship as such was divorced from ruling and being ruled. It was divorced in fact from all political identity, properly so-called. As citizens of the United States, we are not citizens of Great Britain, or Italy, or Israel, or China, or the U.S.S.R. Citizenship is a matter, not of sameness as such, but of sameness in the light of otherness. (We are, we recall, human beings insofar as we are *not* beasts, and *not* God.) If Rome was the world, then political life as heretofore understood—above all, as understood in Aristotle's *Politics*—ceased to exist. The Roman empire became by anticipation, the secular antecedent of the city of God: in which also there are no political identities recognizable as such, and no ruling and being ruled.

Once Roman citizenship became universal citizenship, the separate gods of the separate cities, whose worship Rome had both permitted and protected, lost their reason for being. If everyone was a Roman, then Roman law was everyone's law. The separate gods of the separate cities had been the lawgivers of their cities. If there was but one law there must be only one God. Some form of monotheism was thus destined to become the Roman religion. The only question was what form.

We observe here only that Christianity was able to combine the monotheism of Judaism with the universality of Roman citizenship.

The idea of universal political empire sustained by universal monotheistic religion certainly gripped the West for nearly a millennium. From the moment of the establishment of Christianity within the Roman Empire, the contest for supremacy began between the civil and the ecclesiastical powers. With varying degrees of success, and in different ways, political nature reasserted itself. That is to say, men were not content to be citizens of the world, without recognition of their greater attachments to their own ancestors, their own families, their own clans, their own soil, and their own ways of life. Men in their political existence seek an identity that they do not share with everyone else. Patriotism reasserted itself, and as it did so, the Holy Roman Empire became ever more feeble and ever more contemptible. The spirit of universal empire gradually faded. But the spiritual dominion of the One God did not. The City of God—in any one of many manifestations—endured. Since loyalty to God takes precedence by definition to any lesser loyalty, loyalty to one's separate polity here and now became problematical. It therefore became a necessity of political theory, that the unity of human nature might be reflected in the diversity of civil polities, without calling into question the unity of the City of God. It also became a necessity of political theory, that men might conceive of themselves as perfectly loyal to the God who, being One, was common to them all, without sharing an equal loyalty to their separate polities. As we have observed, Christianity had established within the souls of men the idea of a direct, personal, trans-political relationship between the individual and his God. But this relationship did not determine what the laws were to be, or the precise character of the obligation owed to those laws. The idea of the state of nature—the idea of a non-political state governed by moral law—corresponded to the relationship which every Christian had with every other Christian as he considered himself prior to and apart from his membership in a particular civil society. Just as every Christian was under the moral law, without being a member of civil society, so every human being was under the moral law of the state of nature, prior to entering a particular civil society by way of the social contract. Hence Madison's assertion that, in entering civil society, in making the social contract, a man does not—indeed cannot—surrender his rights of conscience. He is, both as man and Christian (or Jew), limited by the moral law in what he may, and may not, agree to, in making the social contract.

Christianity we might say, when it was established in the Roman empire, continued the political role of the gods in the ancient cities. In so doing, it performed a function, and filled a role, consistent with its genesis, as the successor to the gods of the ancient city. Yet however intelligible in the light of these originating circumstances—and however necessary it may have continued to be in ages of "barbarism and superstition"—this function and role was essentially at odds with its intrinsic nature. Only by the separation of church and state, under the aegis of the doctrine of natural rights, did it find a role fully consistent with its avowed mission of spiritual salvation. In Aristotle's *Politics* man is seen as, by nature, a member of the political community. No consent is necessary to establish the authority of the city, or of its laws, since those laws are given by gods. Aristotle himself understands the authority of the city in the light of man's perfection, which is the perfection of a being by nature rational and political. But the presence of priests in his polities, is evidence that for the nonphilosopher, that is, for the citizens, divine sanction will support the authority of the laws. Divine sanction will support the authority of the laws, although the intrinsic ground of that authority is its reasonableness. There must then be either immediate divine sanction for the laws, or a natural sanction translated from that form visible only to philosophers, to one that is intelligible to nonphilosophers. Nowhere in the *Politics* does Aristotle confront the question of how the citizens will be persuaded to obey the laws, if there are no gods to whom those laws will be ascribed. Nowhere does he confront the question of how the authority of an unmediated universal nature will replace the authority of the gods. The state of nature and the social contract supply that mediation. Aristotle recognizes that particular polities will require particular institutions—that they will be the work of legislators acting in particular circumstances. But if these legislators can no longer crown their work by appealing to the authority of particular gods as the foundation of their laws, they must appeal directly to nature. They must have some way of translating the authority of a universal nature into the ground of particular laws. This, to repeat, is exactly what the doctrine of the state of nature, as we have described it above, accomplished. Moreover, it did so by defining nature itself in the light of the differences between man, beast, and

God. That is to say, it did so by a natural theology consistent with monotheistic revealed theology. It is then a necessary emendation in Aristotle's own teaching required not by any transformation in Aristotle's principles, but by the transformation of the human condition—and of political life—in which those principles are applied. The idea of the state of nature modifies and yet preserves the idea of man as by nature a political animal. Moreover the idea of the state of nature, by treating civil society as a voluntary association, lays a firmer foundation for the idea of the rule of law than in Aristotle's *Politics*. It is guided, as we have shown, by Aristotle's idea of law as "reason unaffected by desire." It enshrines the doctrine of popular sovereignty—which in itself is un-Aristotelian. Contrary to what is often said, however, it enshrines not the people's will, but only their rational will. The people, in unanimously agreeing to form a civil society, may enjoin in the social contract as the ground and purpose of law only those things that are consistent with the law of nature in the state of nature. They may enjoin only as Madison said what may be willed unanimously and rightfully. Hence the rule of law, resulting from the social contract, contains guarantees against despotism, which are not guaranteed by the rule of law as described by Aristotle. For Aristotle's polity—with less than 10,000 citizens—had natural checks against tyranny or despotism, that would have been absent from any political society formed in the wake of the post-republican Roman Empire. The anarchy and despotism accompanying both theological and ideological politics in the post-classical era has shown the necessity of firmer foundations for the rule of law than Aristotle anticipated. The theory of the state of nature—whose law is reason—as the ground of political obligation, emancipates church and state to pursue their proper goals in a manner both complementary and harmonious. Those goals are as distinct, and yet inseparable, as the concavity and the convexity of a curved line. For they are both grounded in that ultimate unity of human life which is itself grounded in the equality of man and the unity of God.

3

HUMANIZING CERTITUDES AND IMPOVERISHING DOUBTS

A Critique of *The Closing of the American Mind*
by Allan Bloom

INTRODUCTION

Among Harry Jaffa's trenchant book reviews, his response to Allan Bloom's surprise best-selling critique of the contemporary American soul ranks among the most instructive and memorable. It should be read along with Jaffa's exchanges with various political theorists in his last book, *Crisis of the Strauss Divided* (2012). These exchanges present Jaffa's moral-political sense and what he learned from Leo Strauss about the theological-political question.

Jaffa argues that Bloom, his co-author of *Shakespeare's Politics*, misleads both Bloom's students and a greater public about the related questions of the meaning of America and how to study political philosophy. As he does with Irving Kristol in this book's last essay, Jaffa attacks Bloom's scrubbing of principled conflict from American political history. Bloom, however, attempts to understand America in terms of great books that stand behind the Founders and not the Founders' and Lincoln's thoughtful deeds. Because Bloom does not know politics as Americans have practiced it, Jaffa complains, he cannot understand political philosophy. "For Bloom the question is not, What is Justice? It is, Which book about justice do you like best." And Bloom does not even pick the proper books, at least when it comes to America: "Bloom cannot form or accept an opinion about the United States that has not come to him from a European source." This echoes Bloom's distortion of morality: "Bloom does not, repeat not, find 'the immorality of relativism appalling.' What Bloom rejects is only "'easy going' relativism."

As with Jaffa's other post-1987 work, he revives the practical teachings of natural right and revelation to advance a theological-political scholarship of the politics of freedom. He further presents a philosophically grounded liberal arts alternative to Bloom's approach to higher education in chapter 4, "The Reichstag Is Still Burning."

The editors thank *Interpretation* for permission to reprint from *Interpretation* Vol. 16, No. 1 (Fall 1988).

HUMANIZING CERTITUDES AND IMPOVERISHING DOUBTS: A CRITIQUE OF *THE CLOSING OF THE AMERICAN MIND* BY ALLAN BLOOM, BY *HARRY V. JAFFA*

At the end of July 1987, Mark McGwire, of Claremont, California, and the Oakland As, had hit 37 home runs, and led both major leagues. He had equaled the home run record for rookies in the American League, and was only one short of the National League record. Records, however, are for full seasons, and young Mr. McGwire still had nearly half the year's games to play. He is without question what in sports is called a "Feenom."

At about the time McGwire was taking his first turn at bat that spring, a book entitled *The Closing of the American Mind,* by Allan Bloom, was published. Its rise to the top of the nonfiction best seller list has been as explosive as young McGwire's bat. Its staying power at the top of that list—extending over many months is no less astonishing than its swift anabasis. The demand for it is widespread—radiating outwards from Chicago, New York, Boston, and Washington (not to mention Paris, where it is said to be going like "hot crêpes")—to top most regional lists, as well as the national. It is surely as much a "Feenom," as any event in recent sports history.

Whatever the ultimate judgment may be as to the book's merits, there can be no doubt that its tremendous sales are evidence that it has touched an exposed nerve of public concern. Something, no doubt, must be conceded to the fact that its "defense" of traditional morality is accompanied by a great deal of prurient denunciation of immorality—like the famous reformer who, at the turn of the century, made highly publicized invasions of the red light districts of New York City. His church was always jammed on the ensuing Sundays, when his congregation (as well as numerous reporters) assembled to hear of his virtuous forays into these dens of iniquity. With much greater sophistication, Bloom also preaches, and does it very well.

> Meanwhile [that is, in the wake of women's "liberation"] one of the strongest, oldest motives for marriage is no longer operative. Men can now easily enjoy the sex that previously could be had only in marriage. It is strange that the tiredest and stupidest bromide mothers and fathers preached to their daughters—"He won't respect you or marry you if you give him what he wants too easily"—turns out to be the truest and most probing analysis of the current situation (p. 132).

Reading the first part of *The Closing of the American Mind,* with its discussion—along the foregoing lines—of such topics as "Equality," "Race," "Sex," "Divorce," "Love," and "Eros," one is forcibly struck by its resemblance to the moral (as distinct from theological) aspects of the sermons of the Rev. Jerry Falwell and of the homilies of the Rev. Pat Robertson. Bloom is certainly correct about relativism seducing young women—thereby saving their boyfriends that trouble. And he is also right in pointing to the other—and much greater—troubles that young men find themselves in, when in the company of their "liberated" women. If all moral choices are "values" and all are equally unsupported by reason or by revelation, which becomes just another "opinion" or "value"—then all moral choices are equally significant, or insignificant. Thus Bloom quotes young women as saying that sex is "no big deal." Yet the truth is that sex is always a big deal, and those who think and act otherwise, leave an ever-widening trail of disaster, disease, and death in their wake.

There is, however, one surprising omission in Bloom's catalogue of the evils of relativism. He is vigorous in his portrayal of the human cost of sexual promiscuity, as the foregoing quotation indicates. Yet his observations of the aberrations of the counterculture seem frozen in "The Sixties," as the title of his most memorable chapter suggests. (Bloom left Cornell for Toronto at the end of that decade, and remained in self-imposed exile for most of the decade that followed.) His remarks about feminism, and the changing roles of men and women, for example, are dated not because they are mistaken, or irrelevant, but because in the intervening years the so-called "gay rights" movement, which Bloom hardly mentions, has emerged as the most radical and sinister challenge, not merely to sexual morality, but to all morality.

As I have argued in "Sodomy and the Academy: The Assault on the Family and Morality by 'Liberation' Ethics" (*American Conservatism and the American Founding*, Carolina Academic Press, 1984, pp. 263–78), the demand for the recognition of sodomy as both a moral and a legal right represents the most complete repudiation—theoretical as well as practical—of all objective standards of human conduct. The reason why we regard the killing of other human beings—but not the killing of cattle as murder, is because we are members of the same species. That is to say, we share a common nature. The reason we regard the enslavement of human beings—but not of cattle—as wrong, is because we recognize an equality of rights among fellow members of the same species. This is also the reason for regarding racial or religious or even sex discrimination as wrong. Every moral distinction that can be called to mind can, I believe, be shown to have the same origin or ground, including the very idea of human rights—to which the sodomites and lesbians themselves appeal. But the word nature means generation. A species is defined by the presence in it of individuals of opposite sexes who can generate new individuals of the same species. Nature is the ground of all morality, but maleness and femaleness is the ground of nature. The Bible, in describing man as created in the image of God, adds "male and female created he them," implying that God's own existence is grounded in the same distinction as nature's. The so-called "gay rights" movement is then the ultimate repudiation of nature, and therewith the ground of all morality. Of course, sodomy has been around for a long time—as we know from the Bible. What we are faced with here is not a demand that homosexuality be a private matter between consenting adults. We are faced with a public demand for the admission into law and morality of an equal right of homosexuality and heterosexuality. There has never in my experience been anything like the Gay and Lesbian Centers, now on virtually every campus—with a GLAD week (Gay and Lesbian Awareness Days) sanctioned and encouraged by the college administrations, and patronized by local (and even national) politicians. I have been teaching many more years than Bloom, and I have never seen students as morally confused as they are today. It is difficult enough for young people, as Bloom shows so well, to have to work out anew, with no authoritative conventions, the roles to be followed in boy/girl, man/woman relationships. But this difficulty is compounded a thousand times, when the boy/girl, man/woman relationship is itself called into question. This is as much as to say, that whether you want to belong to the human race is now a matter of personal preference. Tens of thousands—perhaps hundreds of thousands—of students across the country, who never had the least homosexual tendencies, have been seduced (and their lives ruined) by the overpowering pressure of the official patronage of the gay rights propaganda. Many young men, who do not know how to deal with "liberated" women, and many "liberated" women, who do not know how to deal with men any more (except as enemies), take refuge in sodomy and lesbianism. This has constituted the great moral crisis of the eighties on American campuses, and Bloom is almost entirely silent about it.

The chronology of the AIDS epidemic corresponds precisely with this public movement to establish sodomy and lesbianism as a recommended lifestyle. In nothing has the power of relativism—and the disgrace of American higher education—manifested itself more than in its endorsement of homosexuality. But whatever the attitude of the educational authorities, God and nature have exacted terrible retribution. This lifestyle has proved to be a deathstyle. For the first time since modern relativism has mounted its assault upon man's humanity, chastity and the monogamous family may be seen to be recovering some of their standing. Unfortunately, the new argument for the old ways is entirely based upon the argument for self-preservation. This argument will not survive the discovery of new scientific cures. Last spring I told a class of freshmen (and women) that there was a race on, between God and science, for their moral allegiance. And, I added, somewhat sententiously, that it would be very unwise for them ever to bet against God. A few years ago, this remark would have provoked gales of laughter. This time I looked out upon the most solemn faces I had ever seen! Thanks to AIDS then, we have a little breathing time to reassert the true arguments—the "enriching certitudes" (as in the *Nicomachean Ethics*), not merely Bloom's "humanizing doubts." Morality must be seen, as Aristotle sees it, as a means to implement the desire for happiness, and not merely as a restraint upon the desire for pleasure. The arguments must be made not only as to how one may avoid a bad death, but how one can pursue a good life. But one will not find those arguments in *The Closing of the American Mind.*

Notwithstanding the foregoing, Bloom speaks eloquently and even wisely of the evils of relativism. And, to the surprise and pleasure of many, it turns out that he is not just another Bible thumper. (I do not mean to suggest that these are to be despised, but only that they have no standing in our "elite" universities.) He is, rather, of all things, a professor of political philosophy, pointing to his fellow university teachers as the source of this poisonous and literally demoralizing doctrine. This surely must go a long way towards accounting for the book's apparently wide appeal to middle America. Yet those who turn to Bloom for solace and guidance are apt to find their optimism short-lived. Having eloquently portrayed the disastrous consequences of relativism he does not advocate a return to those standards of human conduct implied in its rejection and, most notably, in his own invocation and praise of the ancient "bromides" concerning chastity. Thus he writes

> It is not the immorality of relativism that I find appalling. What is astounding and degrading is the dogmatism with which we accept such relativism, and the easy going lack of concern about what that means for our lives (p. 239).

In one issue of *Insight* magazine, as well as in feature stories in *The Washington Times,* Bloom was hailed as "the general in the war against relativism." But those who thus hailed him seemed to assume that his critique of relativism implied a stand in favor of traditional morality. If so, they did not read him with sufficient care—or astuteness. Bloom does not, repeat not, find "the immorality of relativism . . . appalling." What Bloom rejects is only "easy going" relativism.

When Bloom looks at the "low" in the light of the "high," the "high" turns out to be the "extraordinary thought and philosophical greatness" of German nihilism. One might say that American relativism is comic in its blandness and indifference to the genuine significance of human choice, whereas in its German version fundamental human choices take on the agonized dignity of high tragedy. But none of Bloom's philosophical heroes—for example, Nietzsche or Heidegger—wrote tragedies.

Shakespeare did. And Bloom himself once wrote extraordinarily well on *Othello*. (See *Shakespeare's Politics,* by Allan Bloom, with Harry V Jaffa, Basic Books, 1964, Chapter 3. See especially, pp. 53ff.) Desdemona cannot imagine that a woman would betray her husband even "for the whole world." One can only surmise how students for whom sex is "no big deal" read the play. One guesses only that for them it is a black comedy about crazy people. The greatness of *Othello* is inextricably bound up with the fact once so powerfully expounded by Bloom himself—that the covenantal act of choice of partners in marriage reproduces the covenantal act of choice of the Children of Israel by the God of Israel. Bloom wants to turn his students from their "impoverishing certitudes" to "humanizing doubts." But it seems to me that his own argument requires rather that "impoverishing certitudes" be replaced by "enriching certitudes." After all, it was a necessary condition of the tragedy in *Othello* that there be no doubt whatever in the minds of Othello and Desdemona as to the absolute significance of fidelity in marriage. "Humanizing doubt," no less than any other kind, would dissolve the tragedy into a tale of silly mistakes. It seems to me that Nietzsche's and Heidegger's theoretical teaching is far more profoundly subversive of the universe of Shakespearean tragedy, than the sitcoms of Woody Allen, which draw so much of Bloom's attention. And we must ask the same Bloom who recommended the "bromide" about chastity, whether a young woman would be more or less apt to benefit from it, if her cheap generic drugstore relativism had been replaced by the high and tragic nihilism the parent of all relativism—of Nietzsche and Heidegger? Do we really want her to look into the abyss of nothingness and agonize over whether to have sex with her boyfriend? As Bloom must know from the literature (to borrow a familiar phrase of Leo Strauss), the outcome, in at least nine times out of ten, will be the same, whether the girl agonizes first, or just hops into bed. Thus Aristotle, in the *Nicomachean Ethics*

> Nor does goodness or badness with regard to such things [viz., passions such as spite, shamelessness, envy, and actions such as adultery, theft, murder] depend upon committing adultery with the right woman, at the right time, and in the right way, but simply to do any of them is to go wrong (1107a15ff.).

Aristotle directs the argument of his *Ethics* only to those whose characters are already formed by basic moral education. He does not suppose
that liberal education should form the basis of moral choice—on the
contrary, he supposes that moral education should form the basis of
liberal education. Bloom, it seems to me, has got it exactly backwards.

A moving passage in *The Closing of the American Mind,* and the one
that to me conveys Bloom's critique of relativism most effectively, is the
following:

> My grandparents were ignorant people by our standards, and my
> grandfather held only lowly jobs. But their home was spiritually rich
> because all the things in it, not only what was specifically ritual,
> found their origins in the Bible's commandments, and their explana-
> tion in the Bible's stories and the commentaries on them, and had
> their imaginative counterparts in the deeds of the myriad of exem-
> plary heroes. My grandparents found reasons for the existence of
> their family and the fulfillment of their duties in serious writings, and
> they interpreted their special sufferings with respect to a great and
> ennobling past. Their simple faith and practices linked them to great
> scholars and thinkers who dealt with the same material, not from
> outside or from an alien perspective, but believing as they did, while
> simply going deeper and providing guidance. There was real respect
> for real learning, because it had a felt connection with their lives.
> This is what a community and a history mean, a common experience
> inviting high and low into a single body of belief (p. 60).

I do not remember a more eloquent evocation of the idea of authoritative tradition, and of how it dignifies human life. Of course, Bloom is
referring to the Jewish tradition—the most conservative of all traditions, beginning as it does "in the beginning." I am confident that
Bloom's grandparents—like my grandparents—found a home for that
tradition within the American political tradition that for them was represented by Washington, Jefferson, and Lincoln. I am sure that they
felt, as did Moses Seixas, sexton of Newport's Touro Synagogue in 1790,
on the occasion of Washington's visit to Newport. He hailed Washington as another Joshua who had been led by the Lord, as he himself had
led the American people into the Promised Land of this new Zion of
political and religious freedom. For American Jews at the time of the
Revolution—and even for those today who have not become victims of
a university education have always seen this nation as also a chosen

nation. From the beginning, America as the new Israel, as a light to lighten all the nations, concerning the principles of political and religious liberty, has been a theme of public discourse. And for the very reason that America could become a Zion to all the nations, it could become a Zion to the Jews themselves. George Washington's letter to the Touro Synagogue represented the first time in more than 2,000 years that Jews had been recognized as citizens of any nation. It represented the first time in human history that Jews had been recognized, as equal and fellow citizens of a non-Jewish polity. And that recognition was authoritative because it came from the one man who, as President and Head of State, and as Father of his Country, surpassed all others in moral authority. Washington's greeting to the Jews recognized them as possessing not only a technical legal equality, but as equal human participants, under the One God, in the moral and providential order which was the source of all the nation's blessings. Let me just add here, that Lincoln's greatest speeches are characterized by the combination into a peculiarly American synthesis of the moral and providential order of the Bible, and of the no less moral and no less providential order of the Declaration of Independence. In Lincoln's second inaugural address we see in absolute perfection an authoritative tradition encompassing the teachings of the Bible—both Old and New Testaments and the teachings of the Revolution. I am confident that Bloom's grandparents understood this, in their humble—but profound—way. Why then does Bloom look only abroad, to that acid solvent of all traditions, German nihilism, for that which is already his by right of inheritance?

Here is the denouement of Bloom's genuinely poetic—and nostalgic—tribute to his grandparents.

> I do not believe that my generation, my cousins who have been educated in the American way, all of whom are M.D.s or Ph.D.s, have any comparable learning. When they talk about heaven and earth, the relations between men and women, parents and children, the human condition, I hear nothing but cliches, superficialities, the material of satire. I am not saying anything so trite as that life is fuller when people have myths to live by. I mean rather that a life based upon the Book is closer to the truth, that it provides the material for deeper research in and access to the real nature of things. Without the great revelations. epics, and philosophies as part of our natural vision, there is nothing to see out there, and eventually little left

inside. The Bible is not the only means to furnish a mind, but without a book of similar gravity, read with the gravity of the potential believer, it will remain unfurnished (p. 60).

Bloom says that his generation—his cousins—have no "comparable learning" to that of their grandparents. But why does Bloom assume without argument that there is any learning "comparable" to the Torah and the Talmud? Bloom makes no attempt to understand his grandparents as they understood themselves, and he tacitly rejects their way of life, even as he recognizes in it something rich and wonderful that is lacking in his own.

Bloom's evocation of his grandparents is touching, but it is barren. He denies that he is saying "anything so trite as that life is fuller when people have myths to live by." What then is he saying? That "a life based on the Book is closer to the truth [and] provides access to the real nature of things"? But what is the source or ground of knowledge that enables Bloom to judge the Bible's proximity to the truth? According to Leo Strauss, the concept of "nature" is a discovery of philosophy, and is alien to the Old Testament. By asserting that the world is created by God, the Torah denies that there is a self-subsisting reality independent of the will of God. Of course, rabbinic Judaism, like medieval Christianity, assimilated the idea of "the laws of nature and of nature's God" within the framework of Creation. The perfect expression of this assimilation is of course in our own Declaration of Independence. Bloom's easy going judgment of the truth of the Bible is however—from the viewpoint of the Bible itself—a judgment of the high in the light of the low.

"Without the great revelations," Bloom writes, " . . . there is nothing to see out there. . . ." The descent of the Bible is now explicit—to being only one of many "revelations." And such "revelations" are now lower case "books," along with "epics" and "philosophies." We need them says Bloom, "as part of our natural vision." But books are artifacts. If, however, artifacts determine the content of our vision, if without these artifacts there is nothing to see, then visual reality is in truth an artifact. "Natural vision" would then be an illusion, although not an optical illusion (since there is no optical reality)! Conversely, if there is such a thing as natural vision, then there must be natural objects of sense perception, and of knowledge. And the existence and perception of these must be independent of books. Books then would be accounts of reality, or interpretations of reality, but not themselves the ground of the reality of which they speak. To say that without books there is nothing to see, is nihilism. Yet Bloom's nihilism, manifest in these words, is, as we have seen, contradicted by his reference to both "natural vision" and "the real nature of things." This contradiction runs throughout his book from beginning to end.

Although the title of the book speaks of an "American Mind," there is in truth little or nothing American about the mind or minds that are characterized, other than Bloom's reports about his students. Bloom writes in the tradition of the great expatriates: Henry James, T. S. Eliot, Ezra Pound, and (in a somewhat different sense) Henry Adams. He reminds one of the avant-garde Parisian-Bohemians of the 1920s that included Joyce and Hemingway. He can breathe freely only in the presence of the symbols (and ruins) of Europe's aristocratic past. American democracy, as Americans themselves have understood it, is a closed book to him.

Bloom writes often about French and German philosophy and literature. Names drop upon his pages like summer flies. There are the great modern thinkers—Rousseau, Kant, Hegel, Nietzsche, and Heidegger. There are the more literary types, Ibsen, Joyce, Dostoyevsky, Proust, Kafka, Céline, Molière, Flaubert, Schiller, and of course Goethe. There is not a single reference to Cooper or Hawthorne or Emerson or Whitman or Howells. Nor any to Dreiser or Sinclair Lewis or Edith Wharton or Willa Cather. Thoreau is mentioned, but only because he represented a "side of Rousseau's thought . . ." (p. 171). Above all, there is nothing about Melville or Mark Twain! In "Tom Sawyer: Hero of Middle America," (*Interpretation,* Spring 1972, reprinted in *The Conditions of Freedom,* The Johns Hopkins University Press, 1975) I attempted to capture the art by which Mark Twain had transformed Plutarchian into Machiavellian (and Lockean) heroism, how in *Tom Sawyer* we see the regime refounded, how we witness the coming into being of a "new order, of which Tom is a new prince [and where] the boy is father of the man, and the old are ruled by the young." Tom may be a rogue, but he is a charming one. Bloom's Tom Sawyer is Céline's Robinson, the hero of *Journey to the End of the Night,* described as an "utterly selfish liar, cheat, and murderer for pay" (p. 239).

Bloom complains loud and long that Americans do not have national books that form and represent national character, as do Frenchmen or Germans or Italians or the English. There is some justification for this complaint. But that is because the genius of America as a civilization is above all to be found in its political institutions, and its greatest writers have been its greatest political men, Jefferson and Lincoln and Washington. The American book of books is the story of America itself, as the story of the secular redemption of mankind.

> It was not the mere matter of the separation of the colonies from the motherland [said Lincoln on his way to Washington in February of 1861] but that sentiment in the Declaration of Independence which gave liberty, not alone to the people of this country, but, I hope, to the world, for all future time. It was that which gave promise that in due time the weight would be lifted from the shoulders of all men and that all should have an equal chance.[1]

Lincoln's metaphor, of course, was that of Christian, in *Pilgrim's Progress*, with the great pack on his back—representing original sin. In the Gettysburg Address the messianic theme would be consummated in the transformation of the death on the battlefield into the rebirth of the nation. What national poetry has ever surpassed that of Lincoln? When did epic poetry and poetic tragedy ever so coincide in the actual life story of a people—a coincidence in itself no less improbable than that of philosophy and kingship—than in the movement of thought and of events from the Revolution to the Civil War?

Of course it is the themes of the Civil War that supplied the themes of America's greatest literary works. *Huckleberry Finn* confronts convention with nature, and slavery with freedom, in a uniquely American poetic transformation of the teachings of Rousseau. It is one that, I believe, equals, if it does not surpass anything that European literature of the last 200 years can show. The great white whale, like the weight that Lincoln wished to see lifted from the shoulders of men, is also a distinctively American confrontation of the problem of evil, within the framework of Biblical allegory ("Call me Ishmael"). *Moby Dick* too is a "people's book"—as much in the tradition of the *Iliad* and of the *Odyssey*—as any modern book could be. Of either of them, however, Bloom says nothing. There is irony too in the Foreword by Saul Bellow, who seems only to have this in common with Bloom: that "European observers sometimes classify me as a hybrid curiosity, neither fully American nor satisfactorily European, stuffed with references to the philosophers, the historians, and poets I had consumed higgledy-piggledy . . ." (pp. 14, 15).

Bloom writes:

> Reading Thucydides shows us that the decline of Greece was purely political, that what we call intellectual history is of little importance for understanding it. Old regimes had traditional roots, but philosophy and science took over as rulers in modernity, and purely theoretical problems have decisive political effects. One cannot imagine modern political history without a discussion of Locke, Rousseau and Marx (p. 197).

Leaving aside the begged question of what is meant by "purely political" history, can one imagine a discussion of "modern political history" that is *only* "a discussion of Locke, Rousseau, and Marx"? Elsewhere Bloom asserts that

> What was acted out in the American and French Revolutions had been thought out beforehand in the writings of Locke and Rousseau, the scenarists for the drama of modern politics (p. 162).

He adds that Hobbes had "led the way" and, as he proceeds, it becomes clear that he regards Locke as essentially Hobbes with a fig leaf covering the hedonism, atheism, and materialism that is so prominent in the former, but no less essential although concealed in the latter. We will return to this point presently. But think of it, the American and French Revolutions "scenarios" written by Locke and Rousseau! The embattled farmers who "fired the shot heard round the world" and the great protagonists in the world historical events that followed—Samuel Adams, Patrick Henry, Benjamin Franklin, John Adams, George Washington, Thomas Jefferson, Alexander Hamilton, are mere actors, following a script. Do we not have here an historical determinism equal to Hegel's? Only the "cunning of history" is replaced by the cunning of the modern philosophers. But this is the purest nonsense.

Leaving the French Revolution to others, I comment only on the American Revolution and the American Founding. The statesmen of the era, among them those just mentioned, were, if not "a graver bench

than ever frowned in Greece" or Rome, certainly the equal of any
(Coriolanus, III.i. 106). And they possessed a core of conviction
which—if we are to make any attempt to understand them as they
understood themselves—formed the basis of everything they did.
Bloom purports to write about "the American mind." But he is perfectly
oblivious of the presence of this expression in one of the most famous
documents of American history. In a letter to Henry Lee, May 8, 1825,
Thomas Jefferson explained the sources, the purpose, and the manner
of the writing of what Lincoln would call that "immortal emblem of
humanity," and Calvin Coolidge (observing in 1926 the sesquicentenni-
al of the event) called "the most important civil document in the world."

> But with respect to our rights and the acts of the British government
> contravening those rights, there was but one opinion on this side of
> the water. All American whigs thought alike on these subjects. When
> forced therefore to resort to arms for redress, an appeal to the tribu-
> nal of the world was deemed proper for our justification. This was
> the object of the Declaration of Independence. Not to find out new
> principles . . . but to place before mankind the common sense of the
> subject; in terms so plain and firm as to command their assent nei-
> ther aiming at originality of principle nor yet copied from any partic-
> ular and previous writing, it was intended to be an expression of the
> American mind, and to give to that expression the proper tone and
> spirit called for by the occasion. All its authority rests then on the
> harmonizing sentiments of the day, whether expressed in conversa-
> tions, in letters, printed essays or in the elementary books of public
> right, as Aristotle, Cicero, Locke, Sidney, etc. . . .[2]

We must ourselves lay the greatest emphasis upon Jefferson's emphasis
upon the "one opinion" on this side of the water. There really was a
"public philosophy" at the time of the Revolution and the Founding.
The party conflict of the 1790s exceeded in intensity anything that has
come after even that of the decade before the Civil War. Yet Jefferson,
in his inaugural address in 1801, could say "We have called by different
names brethren of the same principle. We are all Federalists, we are all
Republicans." To speak as Jefferson did, in the letter to Lee, of the
"harmonizing sentiments of the day," is to imply a consensus transcending the normal differences of opinion among a free people. Of "the
elementary books of public right" mentioned by Jefferson, two are an-

cient, two are modern. I think it safe to assume that according to Jefferson's understanding of the American mind, that mind found harmonizing sentiments among the books of public right no less than among the conversations, letters, and printed essays. Certainly that would suggest that Americans then read John Locke's *Second Treatise* in *its* "harmonizing" sense, in which Locke quotes Hooker for authority for his doctrine, and through Hooker reaches back to Christian scholasticism, and through it to Aristotle.

Bloom not only believes that the English and American Revolutions were scenarios by Locke—he says that "the new English and American regimes founded themselves according to his [Locke's] instructions" (p. 162). According to Bloom one can save oneself all the trouble of reading political and constitutional history like Bloom—and just read Locke. But how does Bloom read Locke?

"Perhaps the most important discovery" upon which Locke's teaching was based, according to Bloom, was that "there was no Garden of Eden . . . Man was not provided for at the beginning . . . God neither looks after him nor punishes him. Nature's indifference to justice is a terrible bereavement for man. He must [therefore] care for himself" (p. 163). The complete break with Biblical religion, as well as with classical philosophy, as represented by Aristotle and Cicero, is the necessary presupposition of Bloom's Locke.

> Once the world has been purged of ghosts or spirits, [meaning of any belief in God or immortality] it reveals to us that the critical problem is scarcity. . . . What is required is not brotherly love or faith, hope, and charity, but self-interested rational labor (p. 165).

"Americans" says Bloom,

> are Lockeans: recognizing that work is necessary (no longing for a nonexistent Eden), and will produce well-being; following their natural inclinations moderately, not because they possess the virtue of moderation but because their passions are balanced and they recognize the reasonableness of that; respecting the rights of others so that theirs will be respected. . . . From the point of view of God or heroes, all this is not very inspiring. But for the poor, the weak, the oppressed—the overwhelming majority of mankind—it is the promise of salvation. As Leo Strauss put it, the moderns "built on low but solid ground" (p. 167).

We need not dispute Bloom's interpretation of Locke to deny that the American mind has ever been the mind represented by that interpretation. Let us however turn here to Bloom's obiter dicta at the end of the foregoing passage. This is his only mention (or quotation) of Leo Strauss, although Strauss's words and Strauss's thoughts echo and re-echo (without attribution) throughout his book. However, as Kirk Emmert recently reminded me, the words attributed to Strauss are not Strauss's but Churchill's—albeit words Strauss himself frequently quoted. But can a regime to which a Churchill could give such unstinting devotion—a regime in whose finest hour so many would come to owe so much to so few; a regime whose glory would not be of a day, but of a thousand years—be a regime despised by God and heroes?

Bloom is the first person I have ever known to suggest that "the point of view of God" is adverse or indifferent to "the poor, the weak, the oppressed." How can a regime which Bloom himself calls the "promise of salvation" for "the overwhelming majority of mankind" be anything but a theme for the greatest heroism? Why did the Union armies march to battle singing, "As He died to make men holy, let us die to make men free. . . ." Why did Churchill himself leave orders for the singing of the Battle Hymn of the Republic, in Westminster Abbey, at his funeral? Abraham Lincoln is reported as saying that God must have loved the common people—he made so many of them. But who that has ever read either the Prophets of the Old Testament, or the Sermon on the Mount in the New, could have said what Bloom says here? And may not "rational labor" be in service of faith, hope, and charity? I am sure that Bloom's grandparents thought so. Bloom's own account of the success of American Lockeanism is testimony to the proposition that this is precisely the kind of regime that the God of the Bible, who cares for the poor, the weak, and the oppressed, would favor. Bloom to the contrary notwithstanding this is the kind of God most Americans have always believed in. This is what they believe when they sing "God bless America."

Let us again consult Jefferson, at his inaugural, declaring of the American mind that it is one

> enlightened by a benign religion, professed, indeed, and practiced in various forms yet all of them inculcating honesty, truth, temperance, gratitude, and the love of man; acknowledging and adoring an over-ruling Providence, which by all its dispensations proves that it de-

lights in the happiness of man here and his greater happiness here-
after (p. 333).

As far as I can see, everything Bloom says on subject of the American
Founding is derived from his readings of Hobbes, Locke, or Tocqueville. I have found not a word of serious interpretation—apart from his
birdseed scatterings—coming from an American source: not Jefferson,
Washington, Madison, Hamilton, or Lincoln. No one has maintained
more persistently than I have, during the past thirty-five years, the
importance in the American Founding of Locke's teachings—as they
were understood and incorporated into their handiwork by the Founding Fathers. But to say that a radical atheism discovered in Locke's
esoteric teaching was part of what they understood, believed, and incorporated into their regime—when every single document bearing on the
question contradicts it, and there is not a shred of evidence to support
it—is just plain crazy.
  Bloom writes:

> It should be noted that sex is a theme hardly mentioned in the
> thought underlying the American Founding. There it is all preserva-
> tion, not procreation, because fear is more powerful than love, and
> men prefer their lives to their pleasures (p. 187).

Surely no sillier remark has ever been made in a work purporting to be
serious. One can only wonder what Bloom could have in mind: a treatise on the joy of sex by the Father of his country? Something to vindicate the symbolism of the Washington monument? In point of fact,
Benjamin Franklin penned some of the raciest lines of the 18th century. And Jefferson's "Dialogue Between the Head and the Heart," although in no way indecorous, is nonetheless highly charged with the
passions that are its subject. That moreover was written in Paris, and
during Jefferson's romance with Maria Conway. I'm sure Bloom would
have approved, if only he had known about it.
  But Bloom writes about the thought *underlying* the Founding. And
what he says can refer only to the thought of Thomas Hobbes. For it
was only that old bachelor for whom self-preservation meant individual
self-preservation, and who divorced preservation from procreation, the
family, and civil society. What is true of the political thought of Thomas
Hobbes is not however true of the American Founding. It is not even

true of Locke. The centrality of property in Locke's teaching gives place as well to the family, as the object of self-preservation. Nor is it true of nature generally—notwithstanding Bloom's Hobbesian remarks about fear and love. In nature generally self-preservation is directed to the species rather than to the individual. A cock robin will attack a cat that comes too near the nest where the hen is brooding. In the case of humans, the instinct of self-preservation may be transferred from the family to the political community, as the guarantor of the family. But whatever the behavior of particular individuals, the instinct of self-preservation is almost never understood to be directed by nature to the preservation of the individual as such. Consider the following from the 43rd *Federalist*—which happens to be the central number. Madison writes, with respect to the question of the right of the Convention to scrap the Articles, rather than revise them, that it is to be

> answered at once by recurring to the absolute necessity of the case; to the great principle of self-preservation; to the transcendent law of nature and of nature's God, which declares that the safety and happiness of society are the objects at which all political institutions aim, and to which all such institutions must be sacrificed.[3]

There is no question that "the great principle of self-preservation" refers to "the safety and happiness of *society*," and not to individuals. Moreover, in using the very words of the Declaration of Independence, Madison gives us a gloss on that document as well, and on "the common sense of the subject." There is then no contradiction—as some have supposed—between the unalienable right to life, proclaimed in the second paragraph of the Declaration, and the mutual pledge of the Signers, to each other, of "our lives, our fortunes, and our sacred honor." It would have been inconceivable to them that the right to life, with which they had been endowed by their Creator, was a right to act basely, to save their skins at any cost. Moreover, the law of nature, as stated by Madison, is dedicated to the ends of safety and happiness, the alpha and omega of political life. This is in entire agreement with Aristotle's *Politics*. The teaching of the Founding, expressed in the Declaration and the Federalist, takes nature as the ground of political life in the teleological sense, not in the non-moral purposeless sense of modern science. Bloom has completely misread not only the American Founding, but all political life, since he does not read political speeches to discover the form of the consciousness of political men. He assumes that political men are mere epigones of philosophers whether they know it or not. The political nature of man is however understood by the Founders—if one reads what they say, and not only what Hobbes or Locke or Kant say—in the light of the inequality of man and beast, as well as in the light of the inequality of man and God. This understanding corresponds very closely with the first book of the *Politics,* and as it does with the first chapter of *Genesis.* But such inequalities imply that morality and the principles of political right are grounded in a purposeful reality accessible to reason, one that corresponds as well to the teachings of biblical faith. When Madison speaks of the sacrifice of all institutions to the safety and happiness of society, he implies a fortiori that the safety and happiness of individuals may or must he sacrificed too. For the Founders, the safety or happiness of society—that is to say, of a society constructed according to the principles of legitimacy and right set forth in the Declaration of Independence—always takes precedence over the mere interests or subjective judgments of individuals. That is why Lincoln in 1861, while conceding that the citizens of the seceding States possessed the same right of revolution as their Revolutionary ancestors, denied that they ought to exercise that right for any purpose inconsistent with the purposes for which their ancestors had exercised that right. To extend slavery was inconsistent with the purposes of the Revolution. The Founding Fathers, no more than Aristotle, could conceive of a life worth living without friendship. The baseness of self-preservation at any cost—the principle of Hobbesianism—as a *moral* principle, was beyond their imagination. Hence for them there could be no interest in self-preservation separate from or independent of the survival and well-being of everything they loved. In truth, fear is not more powerful than love.

   The Founding Fathers, as one of the most exceptional generations of political men who ever lived, are not to be understood as primarily Hobbesians, Lockeans, or Aristotelians. They were rather *phronimoi,* morally and politically wise men, the kind of characters from whom Aristotle himself drew his portraits of the moral and political virtues. And Aristotle understood what these virtues were, not from speculative thought as such, but from contemplating such actual examples of the virtues as came under his observation. The source of his ability to recognize these virtues, was not philosophy, but nature, the reality which was the ground of philosophy. Bloom looks to philosophy only as the source of "humanizing doubts." For him, political philosophy is nothing more nor less than the cleverly disguised question, "What have you done for me lately?" But men who lead revolutions, who found and preserve states, cannot be guided only by their doubts. They require convictions. And they do not look upon themselves as responsible only to those who raise doubts about those convictions. Looking only to books, politics for Bloom is a closed book. And no one can comment instructively on the relationship between political life and the philosophic life who does not know what political life is.

The vitality of classical political philosophy—why it is so close to the spirit of the statesmanship of the American Founding—is that it is grounded in the reality of political life itself. In the light of that reality one does not speak of rights divorced from right. There can be no such thing as a right to do wrong—as Lincoln said when he denied that the consent of the governed could justify the extension of slavery. And we must never forget, as Lincoln never forgot, that the rights Americans valued so highly were the rights with which they had been endowed by their Creator. Their duty to respect the rights of others did not ensue—as Bloom, following Hobbes, thinks—solely because it was to their advantage, however enlightened the self-interest which dictated that advantage. Their duty to respect the rights of others was part of their duty to God—a duty which was entirely unconditional. Hence Jefferson, in the *Notes on Virginia,*

> And can the liberties of a people be thought secure, when we have removed their only firm basis, a conviction in the minds of the people that these liberties are of the gift of God? That they are not to be violated but with his wrath?

Concerning the central event in American history—in which Abraham Lincoln found entirely plausible Jefferson's prophetic judgment concerning the wrath of God for the sin of slavery—Bloom has this to say:

> The only quarrel in our history that really involved fundamental differences was over slavery. But even the proponents of slavery hardly dared assert that some human beings are made by nature to serve other human beings, as did Aristotle; they had to deny the humanity

of the blacks. Besides, that question was really already settled with
the Declaration of Independence. Black slavery was an aberration
that had to be extinguished, not a permanent feature of our national
life. Not only slavery, but aristocracy, monarchy and theocracy were
laid to rest by the Declaration and the Constitution (p. 248).

Except for Russell Kirk's allocution excommunicating the Declaration
of Independence ("not conspicuously American . . . not even characteristically Jeffersonian . . . not a work of political philosophy or an instrument of government") I cannot recall another place in which so few
words encompassed such great errors.[4]

We note first of all Bloom's thesis: that our "differences of principles
are very small compared to those over which men used to fight" (p.
248). This opinion was certified by Tocqueville (who visited here in the
early 1830s and who died before the Civil War). It is therefore canonical for Bloom. It is nonetheless mistaken. I remember in 1940 trying to
tutor in English a refugee Polish university professor. I finally abandoned the effort. My pupil had a German English textbook that he had
brought with him from Europe, and he simply would not accept anything I told him about the English language that did not agree with his
German authority!

Bloom cannot form or accept an opinion about the United States
that has not come to him from a European source. Tocqueville was a
great and wise writer but, as Aristotle says of the discourses of Socrates,
however brilliant, original, and searching they may have been, "it is
difficult to be right about everything" (*Politics*, 1265a14). It hardly
seems to detract from Tocqueville's greatness to say that he is not the
greatest interpreter of a war he did not live to see. Bloom writes about
the "fundamental differences" in the Civil War, yet there is no attempt
to characterize those differences. He ignores the pronouncements of
Lincoln, which represent the peak of what is American, pronouncements that belong in the company of Demosthenes, Cicero, and Burke.
Leo Strauss believed the Gettysburg Address to be a greater funeral
oration than that of Pericles, just as Lincoln was clearly a greater war
leader. In the Preface to the University of Chicago Press reprint of
Crisis of the House Divided I noted that I had first encountered the
Lincoln-Douglas debates in 1946 when I was reading Plato's *Republic*
with Leo Strauss. I was astonished to discover that the issue between
Lincoln and Douglas was identical in principle with that between Soc-

rates and Thrasymachus. For Douglas's doctrine of popular sovereignty was simply the democratic form of the proposition that justice was the interest of the stronger.

> We in Illinois . . . tried slavery [said Douglas], kept it up for twelve years, and finding that it was not profitable, we abolished it for that reason (Joint Debate, Alton, Illinois, October 15, 1858. *Collected Works of Abraham Lincoln,* Vol. III, p. 297.)

Whatever the people think is in their interest, said Douglas, they may vote in, and whatever they think is not in their interest, they may vote out. This is exactly what Thrasymachus thought democratic justice to be. This implies, of course, that when the tyrant does what is in his interest, he is being neither more nor less just than the people. Tyrannical justice is no less justice than democratic justice. In Douglas's version of popular sovereignty—as in the Southern version—the distinction between tyrannical and democratic justice disappears. But Lincoln thought differently. Like Socrates (and Plato and Aristotle) he thought that the principles of natural justice limited—as they ought to guide human choice. There is a distant echo of *Crisis of the House Divided* when Bloom writes (p. 29) that "for Lincoln . . . there could be no compromise with the *principle* of equality, that it did not depend on the people's choice or election but is the condition of their having elections in the first place. . . ." But Bloom sees Lincoln's argument as a demand for consistency, a demand that the people defer to the logic of the principle of their regime. But he does not inquire into the status of that principle or of the regime embodying it: is it theirs because it is right, or is it merely right for them because it is theirs? Bloom never asks. He never entertains the possibility that the foundation of this allegedly "low" regime is, as Lincoln believed it to be, "an abstract truth applicable to all men and all times" *(Ibid.,* III, p. 376).

To the best of my knowledge, the election of 1800 in the United States was the first time in human history that a national government was replaced by its bitter political enemies on the basis of a free election. Those who lost their offices gave them up without any physical struggle. Those who gained the offices did nothing to proscribe—to execute, imprison, expropriate, or exile—those who lost. And those who lost looked forward confidently to a future in which they or others like themselves might again hold those offices. We are so accustomed to such blessings in what we are pleased to call the free world, that we fail to appreciate the uniqueness of this event, and to realize how much everything we hold dear depended upon the successful test of the principles of the Declaration of Independence in the election of 1800.

It is well to bear in mind that in the Glorious Revolution in England in 1689 the King was driven into exile just because there was no constitutional way of changing the chief executive on the basis of the elections to Parliament. Although that Revolution established the principle of Parliamentary supremacy, the King (or Queen) remained the executive head of the government until after the Reform Act of 1832. The ministers of the crown remained responsible to the unelected Crown, and not to the elected House of Commons. The Crown could not, of course, govern effectively without majorities in the Parliament, but these majorities were assembled as much by manipulation of the patronage (that is to say, by buying the votes it needed in the Commons) as by deference to the electorate. And the electors of the unreformed Parliament—with its "rotten" boroughs as well as equally "rotten" rural seats—were very far from the American standard of democratic representation in 1800. All this is, I believe, what Alexander Hamilton had in mind when he said that the British Constitution, purged of corruption, would become unworkable. The idea of a King or Queen who reigned but did not rule, and of a Prime Minister—and cabinet—that was responsible to a democratically elected legislature, had not yet been born. And so the idea of changing the executive whenever the vote of the people changed the majorities in the House of Commons, was yet unknown. The idea of a government resting upon the continuing and changing consent of the governed, registered in free elections, was a discovery of the American Founding, and was its precious gift to the world.

But the trail blazed in 1800 proved to be inconclusive. In 1860, the losing party in a national election refused to accept the results of the voting, and "seceded" to form another government. Here indeed was a supreme test of whether

> societies of men are really capable or not of establishing good government from reflection and choice, or whether they are forever destined to depend for their political constitutions on accident and force (Alexander Hamilton, *Federalist* No. 1, Modern Library edition, p. 3).

In his inaugural address, Lincoln declared that

> A majority, held in restraint by constitutional checks and limitations, and always changing easily with deliberate changes of popular opinions and sentiments is the only true sovereign of a free people (*Collected Works,* IV, p. 268).

And so it remained for the American people to demonstrate to the world

> that ballots are the rightful and peaceful successors of bullets; and that when ballots have fairly and constitutionally decided, there can be no successful appeal back to bullets . . . (*Ibid.*, p. 439).

Bloom to the contrary notwithstanding, this question of bullets versus ballots represented as fundamental a difference as any over which men have ever fought.

We noted Bloom's pronouncement above that the antebellum "proponents of slavery hardly dared assert that some human beings are made by nature to serve other human beings, as did Aristotle. . . ." He has got the matter exactly backwards. The American defenders of Negro slavery did assert that that slavery was by nature just. They did so by asserting—long before Nazi theory—the biological inequality of the races. Aristotle says that someone of human birth would be servile by nature, if he differed from the generality of mankind "as widely as the soul does from the body and the human being from the lower animal" (*Politics*, 1254a16). The usefulness of such persons, by reason of the imperfection of their rational faculties, "diverges little from that of animals: bodily service for the necessities of life is forthcoming from both . . ." (*Ibid.*, 1254b25). Aristotle only calls those slaves natural who are so defective mentally as to be functionally akin to the lower animals. In the modern world, such persons are called retarded, and are usually confined to what are somewhat euphemistically called "mental" institutions. (This is supposed to distinguish them from universities.) One might however ask, how could Aristotle expect such persons to form such a social class as slaves actually formed in the ancient world? The answer is that he did not. In Book VII of the *Politics* he says that "it is advantageous that all slaves should have their freedom set before them as a reward. . . . " (1330a32). But a natural slave, properly so called, *cannot* be rewarded by freedom, any more than a horse or a dog or an ox. Aristotle's discussion of natural slavery leads to the conclusion that the actual institution of slavery rested, not on nature, but on convention or law. Its sanction was force, or justice understood as the interest of the stronger (cf. 1255a19 with 1255b15). Aristotle's proposal in Book VII of the *Politics,* applied to antebellum America, would have led to the policy that Lincoln commended: that of gradual, compensated emancipation. The fact that no such policy was politically conceivable— that is to say, that no legislation to this end could be adopted by consti- tutional means—made the Civil War inevitable. Slavery was in fact destroyed by the only means that could have destroyed it: military ne- cessity.

The antebellum Southern defense of Negro slavery was much harsh- er than Bloom recognizes. Aristotle's argument has nothing to do with "race" (as in "racism," a term of modern politics). Nothing in Aristotle's argument would justify the enslavement of an intelligent Negro by a stupid white. Bloom thinks that American slavery was an "aberration" whose place was "settled" by the Declaration of Independence. Noth- ing could be further from the truth. This is shown by the following excerpts from the famous "cornerstone" speech of April 1861 (before the fall of Fort Sumter) by Alexander Stephens, Vice President of the Confederacy.

> The prevailing ideas entertained by [Jefferson] and most of the lead- ing statesmen at the time of the formation of the old Constitution, were that the enslavement of the African was in violation of the laws of nature: that it was wrong in principle, socially, morally, and politi- cally.

Now, however, we know that

> those ideas were fundamentally wrong. They rested upon the as- sumption of the equality of the races. Our new government [the Confederate States of America] is founded upon exactly the opposite idea; its foundations are laid, its cornerstone rests upon the great truth that the negro is not the equal of the white man. That slavery— the subordination to the superior race, is his natural and normal condition.[5]

Stephens further asserted that the natural inferiority of the Negro—his allegedly natural aptitude for slavery—was a discovery of modern science, and he compared it to Harvey's discovery of the circulation of the blood. He identifies the idea of the social, moral, and political progress of mankind with the progress of science. The Confederacy—based upon just such an advance of science—is therefore superior to the "old" Constitution of 1787. The notorious claims made later in behalf both of National Socialism and Marxism-Leninism—that they represented political regimes grounded in the progress of scientific truth—were anticipated in principle by this most articulate spokesman for the Confederate South. Bloom's assertion that slavery "was an aberration that had to be extinguished" is itself merely the counterpart of Stephens' conviction in 1861 that opposition to Negro slavery was an aberration to be extinguished. Like all new truths, he said, it would take time for its diffusion and general recognition. With this recognition, however, would come acceptance of the justice and propriety of Negro slavery. Bloom simply dismisses—if he has not altogether forgotten—Lincoln's House Divided speech, which warned that the nation was at a crossroads, and that a decision had to be reached and taken, whether the nation was to become all free or all slave. Bloom writes as if "all slave" was never a possibility, and Lincoln an irresponsible inflammatory politician. He writes precisely as most "revisionist" American historians wrote before the publication of *Crisis of the House Divided* in 1959. In truth, however, the idea of progress can be used to vindicate either freedom or slavery. In 1861, however, no one could tell which would prevail.

The question of slavery extension went to the root of the meaning of free government, but it was the obverse of the question of whether free elections would continue to decide who would govern in a republic. By 1860 the doctrines of John C. Calhoun—which had taken the deepest root throughout the South—had completely divorced the idea of natural rights and human equality from the idea of political sovereignty, and hence from the idea of State sovereignty. It was this divorce which gave legitimacy to the idea of a constitutional right of secession. Popular sovereignty, seen in the light of the Declaration of Independence, is the collective expression of the equal right of each human person to be governed with his own consent under the rule of law. And the rule of law was itself understood to be the implementation, in accordance with the dictates of prudence, of "the laws of nature and of nature's God."

These laws of nature were understood to be both moral and rational. They were understood to secure the equal rights to life, liberty, property, and the pursuit of happiness of each human person. In severing the connection between natural rights and constitutional rights, Calhoun severed the connection between law and morality altogether. This fact was disguised to some extent because of Calhoun's typical mid-century commitment to the idea of progress—to the belief that those who were scientifically and technologically advanced were morally superior.

> The discovery of gunpowder and the use of steam as an impelling force. and their application to military purposes have *forever* settled the question of the ascendancy between civilized and barbarous communities, in favor of the former. (A *Disquisition on Government*, Cralle ed., p. 62. Emphasis added.)

Calhoun assumed—as did his contemporary Karl Marx, whose *Manifesto* was written about the same time as the *Disquisition*—that the outcome of physical conflict, whether that of proletariat and bourgeoisie, or that of white and colored races—would indicate moral no less than material superiority.

State sovereignty, in Calhoun's thought, refers then ultimately to nothing more than the force (*assumed* to be moral) at the command of the government. In his *Disquisition* there is no abstract or rational way to distinguish—as in the Declaration of Independence—between the just and the unjust powers of government. Those who are slaves are assumed to be rightfully slaves, and those who are masters, to be rightfully masters. And if the slaves suddenly arise and enslave the masters, then each will still be rightfully what he is! This latter was not something Calhoun contemplated, but it follows the logic of his argument. It is not for nothing that Calhoun has been rightly called (by Richard Hofstadter, in *The American Political Tradition*) "the Marx of the Master Class." This is to imply—correctly, I believe—that Calhoun anticipated, in certain fundamentals, the thought underlying the two great tyrannies of the twentieth century. If it was true, as Bloom says, that "slavery, aristocracy, monarchy, and theocracy" had been "laid to rest by the Declaration and the Constitution," then why had the thought of John C. Calhoun become so powerful? Why indeed was there ever a Civil War? (See "Defenders of the Constitution: Calhoun versus Madison," by the present writer. A Bicentennial Essay published by the Bicentennial Project of the University of Dallas.)

Next, I come to Bloom's account of the "The Sixties." Bloom was forced to live through a revolutionary political event which he never really understood. It was an event in American history, the serious study of which Bloom has always regarded as superfluous. He looked upon the student radicals as Americanized versions of the Nazi youth of the 1930s, and there is some validity in this analogy. The deeper resemblance, however, is to the historicism and nihilism already present in the intellectual defense of the Confederacy—notably in the thought of both John C. Calhoun and Alexander Stephens. And there are important parallels to Calhoun in Thoreau, contemporaries who, ostensibly on opposite sides of the slavery question, were yet nearly perfect mirror images of each other. For the fact is that abolitionism and slavery, although theoretical antagonists, nonetheless collaborated in a way that, had it succeeded, would have crushed the Constitution. Their radical hostility and practical cooperation closely resembles the way in which in our century Nazis and Communists worked together to destroy the Weimar regime, which both hated worse than they hated each other. But Weimar lacked the strength of the American Founding, and Germany had no Lincoln.

The Black Power movement which brought Cornell University to its knees in 1969 (and drove Bloom into exile) was a transformation of the Civil Rights movement, in the aftermath of the victory of that movement by the enactment of the great civil rights laws of 1964 and 1965. In this transformation there was the same severance of the connection between civil and constitutional rights, on the one hand, and natural rights on the other, as had been earlier accomplished in the thought of Calhoun. Black Power became its own justification for whatever demands it could exact, just as the ownership of slaves once justified whatever the owners of slaves could exact. That the ideas animating the Black Power movement were at bottom the same as those of the leading defenders of slavery, however ironical, is nonetheless true. Bloom, however, is unconscious of this, because he is unconscious of the power and magnitude of the ideas in conflict that made the American Civil War perhaps the least avoidable great war ever.

Bloom's alienation from the American political tradition is illuminated by his pride in the fact that some of his students went among the rioters distributing a pamphlet which reprinted the passage from Plato's *Republic* (491e–492b) in which Socrates characterizes the *demos* itself as the greatest of sophists, the greatest of the corrupters of the young. Most radical students—and many who were not radical—would think that what it revealed most of all was Plato's antidemocratic prejudices. But the passage also lends itself easily to a Marxist interpretation—however spurious—because, according to the *Republic,* among the causes of the corruption is private property, and the leading cure for it is communism. It is difficult to imagine what effect—other than inflammatory—Bloom thought this Platonic passage might have had on the rioters.

One might reflect, however, as Bloom does not, that Socrates' characterization of democracy in the *Republic* is peculiarly inapplicable to the popular government envisaged by the American Founding Fathers. Theirs was a regime of law in principle and aspiration, one of reason unaffected by desire. To the extent that human ingenuity could make it so, it was intended as a regime in which equal recognition was given to the requirements of wisdom and of consent. Consent was necessary however because, as Plato himself insisted, the designs of tyrants are always masked as the claims of wisdom.

Leo Strauss, in "On Classical Political Philosophy," remarks that

> "aristocracy" (rule of the best) presented itself as the natural answer of all good *men* to the natural question of the best political order. As Thomas Jefferson put it, "That form of government is the best, which provides the most effectually for a pure selection of [the] natural *aristoi* into the offices of government."[6]

Professor Colleen Sheehan of Villanova University has been kind enough to point out to me that in this celebrated essay, Strauss illustrates the central thesis of *classical* political philosophy—the nature of the best regime—with a quotation from a renowned letter of Jefferson to Adams. She has also pointed out that it appears to be the central passage in Strauss's essay. However one finally judges the wisdom of the Founding, there is little doubt that Strauss, like Jefferson, regarded this assimilation of aristocracy into democracy as its guiding thought. Elsewhere Strauss has written that

> Liberal education is the ladder by which we try to ascend from mass
> democracy to democracy as originally meant. [7]

The American Founding, insofar as it is "democracy as originally
meant" is thus inadequately characterized—to say the least—as something "low." After all, why would anyone need a ladder to ascend to it?

Yet Bloom is not altogether oblivious of the higher ground. He
writes,

> The students were unaware that the teachings of equality, the prom-
> ise of the Declaration of Independence, the study of the Constitu-
> tion, the knowledge of our history and many more things were the
> painstakingly earned and stored-up capital that supported them (p.
> 334).

Someone who can write of the American and French Revolutions as
scenarios thought out beforehand by Locke and Rousseau, and who can
say that "the English and American regimes [had been] founded according to [Locke's] instructions," is hardly in a position to reproach
others for the lack of "the study of . . . history." But were the students
simply unaware of this history as Bloom says here—or were they not in
agreement with Bloom's own view of the Founding as "not very inspir-
ing," and as spiritually impoverishing? Was the revolt of the sixties not
at bottom a middle class revolt against the successful materialism of
American life? Did not the students themselves however misguided—
believe that they were rejecting the low in favor of the high? Had not
Bloom himself nurtured this revolt, even if it took forms that he did not
expect or wish?

On February 21, 1861, President-elect Abraham Lincoln addressed
the Senate of the State of New Jersey. He spoke of his recollection,
from the earliest days of his childhood, of a small book, Weems's *Life of
Washington*.

> I remember all the accounts there given of the battle fields and
> struggles for the liberties of the country, and none fixed themselves
> upon my imagination so deeply as the struggle here at Trenton . . .
> the crossing of the river; the contest with the Hessians; the great
> hardships endured at that time, all fixed themselves on my memory
> more than any single Revolutionary event; and you know, for you
> have all been boys, how these early impressions last longer than any

others. I recollect thinking, then, boy even though I was, that there must have been something more than common that those men struggled for. I am exceedingly anxious that that thing which they struggled for; that something even more than National Independence; that something that held out a great promise to all the people of the world to all time to come; I am exceedingly anxious that this Union, the Constitution, and the liberties of the people shall be perpetuated in accordance with the original idea for which that struggle was made, and I shall be most happy indeed if I shall be an humble instrument in the hands of the Almighty, and of this, his almost chosen people, for perpetuating the object of that struggle (*Collected Works.* IV, pp. 235, 236).

Leo Strauss's—and Jefferson's—"democracy as originally meant," and Lincoln's "original idea" of what the Almighty had promised "to all the people of all the world" by this "his almost chosen people," is the noble legacy—the moral no less than the intellectual foundation—that was lacking in the education of the disaffected students. Lincoln's speech at Trenton, not Socrates' denunciation of democracy, is what was needed to illuminate the folly of the rioters who, in rejecting their inheritance,

> Like the base Indian, threw a pearl away, Richer than all his tribe
> (*Othello*, v.ii.407).

Lincoln, who had opposed Douglas's idea of popular sovereignty on the same ground that Socrates had opposed Thrasymachus' cynical definition of justice as nothing but the interest of the stronger, could have provided a better introduction to the *Republic* than Bloom's. He could have shown the students the inner connection between the principles of classical political philosophy and those of the Declaration of Independence. Bloom could not do this because everything in his account of the American mind proves that he does not believe it to be true.

The argument of Bloom's book founders on the fact that he cannot decide between the classical rationalism that may be traced to Socrates and Socratic skepticism, and the rejection of all rationalism—and all skepticism—by Nietzsche and Heidegger. He is only certain that his "humanized" doubt is superior to any alternative, or to any decision for example, in favor of the principles of the Declaration of Independence. Yet he concedes that the issue may yet be resolved.

Are Nietzsche and Heidegger right about Plato and Aristotle? They rightly saw that *the* question is here, and both returned obsessively to Socrates. Our rationalism is his rationalism. Perhaps they did not take seriously enough the changes wrought by modern rationalists and hence the possibility that the Socratic way might have avoided the modern impasse. But certainly all the philosophers, the proponents of reason, have something in common, and more or less directly reach back to Aristotle, Socrates' spiritual grandchild. A serious argument about what is most profoundly modern leads inevitably to the conclusion that study of the problem of Socrates is the one thing needful. It was Socrates who made Nietzsche and Heidegger look to the pre-Socratics. For the first time in four hundred years, it seems possible to begin all over again, to try to figure out what Plato was talking about, because it might be the best thing available (p. 310).

The study of the problem of Socrates was a life-long preoccupation of Leo Strauss, who was Bloom's teacher and mine. Indeed, much of the foregoing passage might have been transcribed from Strauss's familiar conversation. In addition to his many writings on virtually all aspects of classical and modern political philosophy, Strauss wrote three books on Xenophon's Socratic writings, all of them with forewords by Bloom. In addition, he wrote *Socrates and Aristophanes.* Together, these constituted an exhaustive articulation of "the problem of Socrates," as it might be uncovered in non-Platonic (and pre-Socratic) sources. These writings of Strauss were in addition to his lengthy commentaries on the Platonic Socrates as he is presented in the *Republic,* the *Laws,* the *Statesman,* the *Apology,* the *Crito,* and yet other dialogues. Of all this Bloom makes no mention. In his overview of the history of political philosophy, "From Socrates' *Apology* to Heidegger's *Rektoratsrede*" (pp. 243–312) there is no mention of Strauss.

In our time, Bloom writes, "it was Heidegger, practically alone, for whom the study of Greek philosophy became truly central . . . " (pp. 309, 310). How anyone who had studied with Strauss or had read "What Is Political Philosophy?" or "On Classical Political Philosophy"—could have written this is almost beyond comprehension. To speak thus of Heidegger, without mentioning Strauss, is like speaking of Hitler, without mentioning Churchill. For, if the truth were known, Strauss was as surely Heidegger's nemesis as Churchill was Hitler's. One can only conclude that if Bloom says that the one thing needful is the study of the problem of Socrates, and yet makes no mention of Strauss's study of the problem of Socrates (or of Greek philosophy), then he cannot think that Strauss's study is the needful one.

Strauss moreover never reached such a lame conclusion as Bloom's, that we might now—after four hundred years—"try to figure out what Plato was talking about, because it might be the best thing available." This makes the quest for the right way of life sound like the quest for prewar whiskey during the era of prohibition! In fact, Bloom's "to figure out" is an echo of a passage from Strauss's *Preface to Spinoza's Critique of Religion:*

> For Spinoza there are no natural ends. . . . He is therefore compelled to give a novel account of man's end (the life devoted to contempla-tion): man's end is not natural but rational, *the result of figuring it out.* . . . He thus decisively prepares the modern notion of the "ideal" as a work of the human mind . . . as distinguished from an end imposed on man by nature. *(Liberalism Ancient and Modern,* p. 241. Emphasis added.)

What Bloom is looking for is a "figuring out" of Plato which is in fact not Plato at all, but a modern "ideal," ostensibly grounded in Plato, but designed like all modern ideals, to gratify a passion, rather than to subordinate passion to reason. Bloom has no intention of facing square-ly the issue of philosophical realism (Socrates, Plato, and Aristotle) ver-sus nihilism (Nietzsche and Heidegger). He has no such intention be-cause he knows that Strauss has presented the case for the former in terms he cannot refute but will not accept. Consider the following from the end of Strauss's chapter on "The Crisis of Modern Natural Right" in *Natural Right and History.* Rousseau, according to Strauss, had a reser-vation against society in the name of the state of nature.

> To have a reservation against society in the name of the state of nature means to have a reservation against society without being either compelled or able to indicate the way of life or the cause or pursuit for the sake of which the reservation is made. The notion of a return to the state of nature on the level of humanity was the ideal basis for claiming a freedom from society which is not freedom for something (p. 294).

Rousseau, as interpreted here by Strauss, is the core of Bloom's soul. It is Rousseau who informs Bloom's reading of Plato's *Republic,* and who has tipped the balance within him irrevocably towards Nietzsche and Heidegger. Bloom's ideal of the university is just such a place where one can "return to the state of nature on the level of humanity." The attractiveness of this supposed return, says Strauss, is that

> It was an ideal basis for an appeal from society to something indefinite and undefinable, to an ultimate sanctity of the individual as individual, unredeemed and unjustified. This was precisely what freedom came to mean for a considerable number of men.

In the "ultimate sanctity of the individual as individual"—meaning thereby a sanctity unfettered either by God or nature—Strauss has defined the core of modern liberalism. And Bloom, a quintessential liberal, is one of that "considerable number of men." Concluding, Strauss writes that

> Every freedom which is freedom for something, every freedom which is justified by reference to something higher than the individual or than man as mere man, *necessarily* restricts freedom or, which is the same thing, establishes a tenable distinction between freedom and license. It makes freedom conditional on the purpose for which it is claimed.

Of course Bloom does not claim unconditional freedom for man in society—any more than did Rousseau. Nor does he attack those necessary conventions of academic life that make it comfortable and agreeable to persons like himself. But he does not admit within his own soul—nor does he teach any idea of freedom that is conditional upon anything higher than man as man. That excludes both Athens and Jerusalem and Leo Strauss.

Bloom to the contrary notwithstanding, we have known all along what Plato was talking about. He was talking about Justice (for example, in the *Republic*), and in the other dialogues about moderation, courage, law, and, in general, what was good and bad for man. The question about Plato is not what he was talking about, or even whether what he said appears wise or just, but whether the good and bad for man was grounded in any ultimate reality, whether it existed by nature, by convention (or law), or by some unknowable divine dispensation. For Bloom the question is not, What is Justice? It is, Which book about justice do you like best? At the end of *Thoughts on Machiavelli* Strauss, rejecting Machiavelli's teaching, says "that the notion of the beneficence of nature or of the primacy of the Good must be restored by being rethought through a return to the fundamental experiences from which it is derived" (p. 299). In Strauss's rejection of progress in favor of return, the books of the classical philosophers would be indispensable to us as modern men, needing emancipation from our peculiarly modern cave. But Strauss, unlike Bloom, never failed to distinguish books from the "fundamental experiences" the books were meant to articulate. The "primacy of the Good"—the upper case emphasis is Strauss's—is a primacy with respect to all books and all art, even that of Plato.

Plato's dialogues always reveal to us far more of our ignorance of each subject discussed, than knowledge of that subject. In revealing our ignorance, however, they always reveal something of our knowledge of that ignorance. And that knowledge of ignorance always reveals something—never enough to satisfy us, but something—of what it is that we wish to know. It is enough to whet our appetites, to make us wish to go on, and know more of what it is that we do not know. The life lived in accordance with the knowledge of ignorance—the truly skeptical life, the examined and examining life—is, by the light of unassisted human reason, the best life. The regime that is best adapted to the living of this life is the best regime. All other lives and regimes are to be judged in relationship to this life and this regime. The goodness of the best life and the best regime is not arbitrary. It is not to be characterized—as Bloom suggests—as merely the "best thing available." On the contrary, that goodness is "according to nature." And hence the moral and intellectual virtues which are in harmony with this goodness are not arbitrary, but also are good "according to nature."

We return to Bloom's assertion that Nietzsche and Heidegger "returned obsessively to Socrates." They did so, he says because "Our rationalism is [Socrates'] rationalism." He adds, however, "perhaps they did not take seriously enough the changes wrought by the modern rationalists and hence the possibility that the Socratic way might have avoided the modern impasse." One might encapsulate the life work of Leo Strauss in Bloom's "perhaps." For Strauss proved, I believe, that "the changes wrought by modern rationalists" had mistakenly discredit-ed the possibility that reason might discover the right way of life and the best regime. According to Strauss, it was not true that "Our [viz., mod-ern man's] rationalism is his [viz., Socrates'] rationalism." Modern ra-tionalism is "scientific" rationalism, which means that it explains the world and everything in it including whatever is regarded as good or bad for man—in terms of what Aristotle called efficient and material causes, while denying the reality of what he called formal and final causes. All formal and final causes are understood in modern science and modern philosophy as epiphenomena or by-products of efficient and material causes. They are attempts to explain the high by the low.

This is as if one would try to understand Michelangelo's David as the result of the physical force applied by the artist to the chisel on the marble, omitting from one's explanation any reference to the sculptor's brain, purpose, and skill. Socratic rationalism assumes that Michelange-lo's brain had a purpose, even before his hand attempted to give it effect, or even before Michelangelo himself had discovered what it was. Indeed, it assumes that Michelangelo could not have discovered his purpose if it had not pre-existed—through all eternity as a potentiality of his human nature. For modern philosophy, Michelangelo's art is simply an accidental outcome of the causes that generated Michelange-lo, causes utterly indifferent to his art, as they were blind to anything intelligent or intelligible. The premises of modern philosophy are the result of a doubt so radical as to eliminate all further need to doubt: hence its dogmatism. The ambition of modern rationalism was to elimi-nate the skepticism that had accompanied Socratic rationalism, as its shadow. By replacing skepticism with dogmatism in philosophy, it would at the same time obviate any need for faith in God. Strauss, by showing that the self-destruction of reason in modern philosophy was the self-destruction of modern rationalism alone, prepared a return to premodern rationalism. By restoring Socratic skepticism, he restored not only Socratic rationalism, but the place that that skepticism left for biblical faith.

Nietzsche and Heidegger represented the final disillusionment with—and rejection of—modern rationalism, although they seem at the same time to have rejected all rationalism. Not seeing—as did Strauss—any alternative to modern rationalism, however, they discovered: noth-ing. Since there is no purpose, good or evil, in any reality outside of man, all purpose in life must be willed by man. But the will has no source of guidance outside itself. What one wills as good is good. What one wills as evil, is evil. The will is its own justification, because there can be no other. Hitler's famous propaganda film "Triumph of the Will," whatever its defects as art, is an authentic manifestation of Heidegger's teaching. Here then is the core cause of modern nihilism, and of the belief that there is no ground for the existence of God, or of the noble and good things, except as useful fictions or pleasing illusions. These must be willed by man, although they are believable by *hoi polloi* only if their origin is concealed. For the true Thinker—who replaces the Philosopher—there is neither myth nor reality. The Thinker having triumphed over the terror of the abyss—alone lives without illusions, without either hope or fear, but in an unprecedented freedom. Bloom lives with considerable discomfort in this freedom, but he has not yet figured out anything for which he would give it up.

NOTES

1. Lincoln, Address in Independence Hall, Feb. 22, 1861. Collected Works, IV, p. 240.

2. *Basic Writings of Thomas Jefferson*, edited by Philip S. Foner (New York: Halcyon House), p. 802.

3. Modern Library Edition, p. 287.

4. On Kirk's atrocities, see "What Were the 'Original Intentions' of the Framers of the Constitution of the United States?" in *The University of Puget Sound Law Review*, Spring 1987, esp. at 380–83. [Editors' note: Reprinted in Harry V. Jaffa, with Bruce Ledewitz, Robert L. Stone, and George Anastaplo, *Original Intent and the Framers of the Constitution: A Disputed Question,* Foreword by Lewis E. Lehrman (Washington, DC: Regnery Gateway, 1994).]

5. *The Political History of the Great Rebellion,* Edward McPherson ed., Washington, D.C., 1865, p. 103.

6. In *What Is Political Philosophy,"* Glencoe: Free Press, 1959, pp, 85, 86.

7. *Liberalism Ancient and Modern,* New York: Basic Books, 1968, p. 5.

4

THE REICHSTAG IS STILL BURNING

The Failure of Higher Education
and the Decline of the West: A Valedictory Lecture

INTRODUCTION

Harry Jaffa's 1989 farewell to full-time faculty status at Claremont McKenna College exemplifies the moral and intellectual objectives of his entire career. He begins his lecture with an expression of duty, to a faithful patron, and concludes with a quotation from Abraham Lincoln's Cooper Institute speech, to "do our duty as we understand it," thus rising from an expression of gratitude to a justification of a way of life. He recounts the 1968–1969 surrender of a reputed conservative college administration to terrorists and other thugs, a pattern repeated ever since at the college. His story of the collapse of a putatively "conservative" institution under threats of violence remains unremarked.

Jaffa's observations continue his confrontation of Allan Bloom's *Closing of the American Mind*, in chapter 3. He confronts the violent enemies of civilization and their cowardly academic facilitators and then concludes by describing "that metaphysical freedom of the mind that, as Jefferson rightly declared, is the ground of all moral freedom, and hence of civil and religious liberty." Americans who are truly concerned with education will promote the life of the mind by living as free Americans, both knowing and acting upon their fundamental principles. Jaffa's treatise is a guide not only to survival but of living well, in exercising one's rights but even more fulfilling the duties one has to the academy, to America, and to western civilization.

The editors thank The Claremont Institute for permission to reprint the text of this 1989 lecture.

THE REICHSTAG IS STILL BURNING: THE FAILURE OF HIGHER EDUCATION AND THE DECLINE OF THE WEST:

A Valedictory Lecture,[1] by *Harry V. Jaffa*

> *While abandoning the idea of natural right and through abandoning it. . . . German thought . . . was led . . . to unqualified relativism. What was a tolerably accurate description of German thought twenty-seven years ago would now appear to be true of Western thought in general. It would not be the first time that a nation, defeated on the battlefield and, as it were, annihilated as a political being, has deprived its conquerors of the most sublime fruit of victory by imposing on them the yoke of its own thought.* —Leo Strauss, *Natural Right and History*, 1953

> *Professor Strauss has singlehandedly revived the serious study of ancient political thought and shown that it is not merely an object of historical curiosity but is relevant to our most vital present interests.* —Allan Bloom, Foreword to Agora Edition of *On Tyranny*, 1965

> *[I]t was Heidegger, pracitcally [sic] alone, for whom the study of Greek Philosophy became truly central. . . .* [pp. 309–310] —Allan Bloom, *The Closing of the American Mind*, 1987

I dedicate this lecture to the memory of Jerene Appleby Harnish. I met Mrs. Harnish some time during my first year in Claremont, when I was paraded before her—as I was before a number of conservative donors to the college—as a Goldwater speech writer. With her, as with Henry Salvatori, I formed a lasting friendship. Appleby Hall at Claremont McKenna College [CMC] is a reminder of her generosity, as is the Appleby Fund which for a number of years brought Thai students to CMC. Many of our Thai graduates have attained distinction, as well as influence and prestige, within their native land. All of them have remained friends, and some of them very great friends, of the United States, and of the principles upon which the United States was founded. In recent years, the Appleby Fund has augmented the research support I have enjoyed as Salvatori Professor, and I hope this lecture will be some small acknowledgment of that assistance.

Beyond my gratitude and affectionate regard, I intend to record here some of the events over which Jerene and I agonized together, and the convictions we shared during the time of troubles that befell higher education two decades ago.

Allan Bloom began his now famous chapter on "The Sixties" in *The Closing of the American Mind* as follows.

> "You don't have to intimidate us," said the famous professor of philosophy in April 1969, to ten thousand triumphant students supporting a group of black students who had persuaded "us," the faculty of Cornell University, to do their will by threatening the use of firearms as well as threatening the lives of individual professors. A member of the ample press corps newly specialized in reporting the hottest item of the day, the university, muttered, "You said it, brother." The reporter had learned a proper contempt for the moral and intellectual qualities of professors. Servility, vanity, and lack of conviction are not difficult to discern. (*Closing*, p. 313)

The servility, vanity, lack of conviction—and plain cowardice—of the Claremont faculties and their administrations, was certainly not less than that displayed at Cornell. What was different in Claremont was that there was no "ample press corps" to display our shame to the outside world and, incidentally, to offer at least the protection of publicity to those whose lives were threatened. That protection was not inconsiderable if the reporters were—as at Cornell—from a newspaper of the stature of the *New York Times*. Such reporters were less likely to be intimidated by radical students or by local authorities than those from the local press.

In mid-afternoon of a February day in 1969 two pipe bombs exploded in Claremont—some 40 seconds apart. The first went off in a basement restroom of Balch Hall on the Scripps campus. Fortunately no one was there at the time, and no one was injured. The second, in an unaddressed parcel, had been placed in the mailbox of Lee Macdonald, Chairman of the Political Science Department at Pomona College. It detonated when the 19-year-old secretary of the department—the wife of a Claremont Men's College senior—picked it up. Her injuries were terrible, and included disfigurement, the loss of all sight in one eye, and damage to her hands that has required at least twenty-five reconstructive surgeries. According to information received from her attorney, Pomona College has—apart from her medical expenses—paid her no more than what was due to her, as an employee of the college, under the Workmen's Compensation Law. (I was tempted to say "when the accident occurred," except that what occurred was not an accident.) I mention this not merely to suggest that her treatment by the College was cold and mean-spirited, which it was. It is to point out that if she had been a black activist, or a white activist in the cause of black power—she would instantly have been celebrated as a victim of racism. A benefit fund for her relief—and a scholarship fund for her children— would have been established. She would have been the subject of countless articles and speeches, and perhaps even a movie, "Claremont Burning." The one thing that would never have happened, is what did happen: she was forgotten. I recall one AP wire service story that crossed the nation the day the bomb went off, and then, after a short flurry in the local media, silence. In the twenty years that have intervened I have told this story hundreds of times. I have never met anyone outside of Claremont who knew about it. I have never met anyone in Claremont who was not here at the time—and that includes students who came in the fall of 1969, and in all the years that have followed— who knew about it. To the best of my knowledge, the bombs that exploded in Claremont in February of 1969 were the first bombs to explode on any American campus in that time of turbulence across the nation. This dubious distinction is one that has been as thoroughly suppressed as any of the innumerable non-events that have occurred within the Soviet Union, at any time in the last 70 years, or until the arrival of *Glasnost*. The shabby treatment of this innocent victim reflects less the miserliness or parsimony of this extremely wealthy college, than a collective desire of all the colleges to suppress the memory of what happened. She was the "wrong" kind of victim, and therefore didn't count.

But the shame does not stop here. No arrest in the case was ever made, although shortly after the Claremont episode a young Black Panther in San Francisco engaged in putting together a pipe bomb blew himself up. It was common knowledge at the time that there was a Panther unit in the nearby City of Pomona, supplying "technical assistance" to the radical students on campus. Had Pomona or Scripps or any of the other colleges had any real interest in finding the criminals who planted the bombs, they would have offered a substantial reward for information leading to arrests and convictions. They never did. They were perfectly terrified at the prospect of what might happen if there were arrests. (I remember that about this time the President of Yale—Kingman Brewster—took out an insurance policy by declaring that a Black Panther could not get a fair trial in the courts of the United States.) So there was a stream of official statements declaring that they did not know who planted the bombs, but that they were sure nevertheless that it was not any one of our students.

Nor—to the best of my knowledge—was any arrest ever made in connection with the 25 fires that followed the bombings, over the next 10 weeks. Most of the fires were relatively small affairs, usually caused by dousing the draperies in the lounges of the dormitories with kerosene—or lighter fluid—and then igniting them. The damage was limited because the students in the dormitories, not wishing to be incinerated in their sleep, ran night patrol, and most of the fires were extinguished promptly. One of them was in an equipment storage area under the stadium seats of Parents' Field, CMC. One at Mead Hall, Pitzer College, caused—I believe—over $100,000 in damage. The largest of the fires completely destroyed Story House on the Claremont Men's College campus. Of that, more later. It was the iron-clad policy of all six colleges, never to have police on campus, and—to repeat—never to have anyone arrested. If no one was arrested, the question of amnesty—the question that tore the Cornell faculty apart—could not arise. The underlying—or overarching—policy of the colleges, as it became manifest, was one of pre-emptive surrender to the demands of the radicals. And how can you arrest someone to whom you are surrendering?

I may illustrate this policy further by a personal experience. I had written a letter to the Board of Trustees of Claremont Men's College, outlining the sequence of recent events, including therein explicit public threats of arson and other forms of violence. The official view, as I have said, was that no one knew who was responsible for the bombings or the fires and that therefore no one could say that there was any connection between the bombings, the fires, and the threats. In my letter, I was careful not to contradict this official view. I only narrated what was a matter of public record. (It was however like narrating the statistics on smoking and lung cancer, without contradicting the tobacco companies' denial of any causal relationship between them.) I asked the trustees to adopt a policy of making no decision upon any of the demands of the radicals, until the threats had ceased, so that whatever was decided would be the result of deliberation and not intimidation. A copy of my letter got into the hands of the radicals, who promptly published it in the *Collegian*, together with an editorial—and numerous columns and letters—denouncing me for having made false accusations. Since I had made no accusations, it is clear that my adversaries believed that the mere narration of the facts had constituted accusations.

About this time, one of the leaders of the Black Students Union, in Collins Dining Hall on the Claremont Men's College campus, conspicuously and publicly urged that someone should take a gun and shoot me. The threat—if understood to be meant seriously—was a felony. In the wake of the bombings, how could it have been regarded as other than serious? Be that as it may, no criminal complaint was filed—that was altogether out of the question—the young man was subjected to no disciplinary proceedings whatever, and he was not even admonished or reprimanded by anyone in (or, so far as I could tell, out of) authority. The following year found him at Yale Law School, whither he had gone with the enthusiastic recommendation of the College. Had anyone on the faculty—or in the student body—who opposed the Black Studies Center—made such a threat against him, a criminal complaint would certainly have been filed. The offender would have been denounced as a racist, and if the charges were proved he would—whether a student or a tenured faculty member—have been expelled. Let me only add that I believe such punishment would have been just. But such penalties should not be for one side only. When some of my students asked the authorities for protection for me, they were told that I had brought the problem on myself, and it was not their concern. In short, I was at fault for expressing opinions which the advocates of Black Power had found offensive. Civil liberties, not to mention academic freedom, were at a discount.

The climax of the demand for a Black Studies Center came in a meeting of the Black and (Brown) Students' Unions, with the faculty of Claremont Men's College. The meeting was climactic, because all the other five Claremont colleges had endorsed the principle of establishing Black (and Brown) Studies Centers, centers which would be at once autonomous and racially or ethnically pure. CMC was known to be something of a bastion of resistance, and there was at least a question as to whether the other colleges would scale back—if not abandon—the project if CMC did not undertake its share of the cost. In short, we were the nut that had to be cracked.

The meeting, as I recall, began around 4 p.m. President Benson was in the chair, and he announced at the outset that we would adjourn at 6 p.m. When that hour arrived, our guests said that they would decide when we might leave. The assembly then continued for another half hour, when Dr. Benson declared it over. Amid a good deal of tumult he was escorted from the hall by two members of the faculty who happened to have unusually large and powerful physiques.

The demands of the Black Students Union showed it to be—in its own mind—a continuation of the Civil Rights movement. The theme of its pronouncements however was Black Power—the very opposite of the color blind principles espoused by Dr. King on the steps of the Lincoln Memorial in 1963. The Black Power movement demanded recognition, not of "the content of character" but of the color of skin. It wanted a Black Studies Center, not to enrich the curriculum, but to bring Black Power to bear upon it. There was no wish to eliminate racial bias from the courses of study in the Claremont Colleges. Rather did it wish to encounter white bias with black bias. The assumption was that an unbiased education was a delusion. Education was understood to be, not a function of the freedom of the human mind, but of its determination by race and ethnicity. What stands out finally in my memory of this meeting, was the declaration of a Brown leader, that he had been in Vietnam, and had seen there what bullets could do, and that he knew therefore what they could do in Claremont. This was followed by a rhetorical question asked by a Black leader—a young woman who the next year was an assistant dean at Pomona College. The question was, "Do you want this campus burned down this summer or next summer?"

The meeting with the radical students occurred on a Wednesday afternoon. The faculty meeting to consider their demands was scheduled for the following Monday. On the Sunday night before this Monday meeting Story House was gutted by fire. It was about this time that I drafted the letter to the Trustees. Before sending it I called the Fire Chief of Claremont, to ask his opinion of the cause of the conflagration. He answered, without hesitation, that it had been caused by "spontaneous combustion." It was the old steam pipes in the basement, he said. This was the tale told in the local press as well. Sometime later, a group of students from Pomona College's *Student Life*, with the aid of an arson expert, studied the ruins of Story House, and found incontrovertible evidence that the point of origin of the fire was the library, where kerosene had been poured on the books. I trust that this further symbolic identification with the Third Reich will not be missed! What this showed however was not so much the fact of arson—which no one had ever really doubted—as the extent to which (again, as in the Third Reich) the conspiracy to protect those engaged in criminal activity had involved public officials charged with the public safety. Let me anticipate the rest of the story by mentioning here that, from the moment of the capitulation of the Colleges, there were no more campus fires—by spontaneous combustion or by any other cause.

This account indicates the environment within which the CMC faculty met to consider and to vote upon the demands being made upon it. As the event transpired, there were two proposals before the faculty. When the vote was taken, each member could vote for one or the other. One was called the Diamond/Fisk/Jaffa proposal. It called for a program of Black (and Brown) studies, the courses therein to be developed within the framework of the existing academic structure. Courses in Black (or Mexican-American) literature would be developed and taught in literature departments, which would be responsible for hiring competent instructors. The same would be true of courses in, for example, history, economics, political science, or philosophy. This proposal denied that education in itself was a function of race. It implied as well that the colleges, however imperfect, were not inherently racist and corrupt. It implied therefore that a non-discriminatory policy was possible and that non-racial academic standards ought to prevail.

The alternative to the Diamond/Fisk/Jaffa plan represented at once a repudiation of the legitimacy of the existing academic structure and an outright endorsement of the principle of racially exclusive "centers." It contained—altogether incidentally—a financial arrangement designed to minimize the cost of implementing such an endorsement. But everyone—with one possible exception—knew that this was irrelevant to our deliberations. Once the proposal was approved, its implementation by the restructuring of the Claremont Colleges would be accomplished by deliberations *de novo*. The only purpose of our vote was to decide whether we would—or would not—endorse the concept of race as a ground or basis of education. And this endorsement was accomplished fully and unequivocally by a preamble in which it was said that Claremont Men's College had been—and was at that moment—"a white college that gave a white education."

In the course of the ensuing debate I asked repeatedly whether it was true that CMC, providing a "white education" taught white mathematics, or white economics, or white biology, or white physics, or for that matter, white political science. Was there anything in Plato's *Republic*, I asked, that indicated that it was "white justice" that Socrates was seeking to define or discover. Was there anything in the *Nicomachean Ethics*, I asked, to indicate that it was "white happiness" that Aristotle sought as the *summum bonum*? Was there anything in Locke's *Second Treatise of Civil Government* (or in the Declaration of Independence) to indicate that taxation without representation was unjust only for whites? Was their anything in Locke's *Letters on Toleration* (or in the Virginia Statute for Religious Freedom) I asked, to indicate that it was only in the case of white human beings, that "our civil rights have no dependence on our religious opinions, any more than our opinions in physics or geometry"? Although I hammered away at these questions, the opposition was uninterested in debating them. "The philosophers have hitherto interpreted the world," Karl Marx had written. "The point is however to change it." Debate, like religion, had become in their minds only an opiate. You defeated your opponent's arguments by trampling on your opponents, and by treating them with contempt.

The other side, although it did not have a reasoned argument, did have what might be called a position. This consisted in two elements. The one was a confession of white guilt. Of course, the very idea of white guilt contradicted the idea that we were engaged in dispensing only a white education. How could a white mind recognize a black mind as equally a mind, unless mind as such transcends the distinction of color? The response to this question was to be found in something entirely different, in a commitment to relativism. Relativism began with the assertion that the dispositions of our minds or souls, all the grounds upon which we hold anything to be true or good or precious, are rooted in our cultures. But there is no trans-cultural (or trans-historical) point of view from which different cultures can be measured or judged. In fact, there was no objective foundation for the dignity—or indignity—of any culture. All cultures being equally without such a foundation, were objectively equal in dignity. Because our curricula had failed to assimilate the truth of relativism, we had wrongly imputed a superior dignity and importance to American (and Western) culture. The Black and Brown Centers were only the beginning of a new openness—a new commitment to tolerance and diversity—based upon the equality of all human cultures.

The allegedly rational foundation of this openness was the realization of the non-rational foundations, not only of all cultures, but of all moral preferences and all "lifestyles." All were grounded in "value judgments" which were rooted in our subconscious selves, which sometimes produced illusions of reason (called "ideologies"), but which were never rational in themselves. We were off-shoots of white Western culture, in all our habits of thought and feeling and expression, whether we knew it or not. We were guilty—the argument ran—because as members of our culture we shared a collective unconscious ethnocentrism which constituted something very much akin—or so it seemed—to Original Sin. In any event, as an institution of higher learning, we could be saved by the gospel of relativism. We had a duty to lead the way out of the dark night of ego-and ethno-centricity, to the heavenly uplands of diversity and tolerance.

Of course for anyone not completely in the grip of unreason, it should have been apparent that the claims of relativism—which were made with respect to all human cultures, past, present and future— were themselves inherently and necessarily trans-cultural and trans-historical. The argument for relativism was in fact an argument for a totally new culture. There was no existing or previous culture—certainly no African or Mexican culture—among all those to be admitted to equality with western culture, that recognized the alleged truth of relativism. The only civilization that had ever recognized the equal humanity (not the equal dignity) of all cultures was Western civilization. Indeed, the first nation ever to have declared its right to independence, not upon the ground of any peculiar virtues of its own, but upon the ground of rights which it shared with all men everywhere, was the United States of America. And the doctrine of relativism itself, however self-contradictory, was nonetheless an authentic offspring of modern Western culture and philosophy.

Looking back from the perspective of 1989, we may say that the argument in the Claremont Men's College faculty in 1969 followed, as if it had been scripted, the argument sketched in 1949 by Leo Strauss, in the lectures that became *Natural Right and History*. At the bottom of the passionate rejection of all "absolutes" we discern the recognition of a natural right or, more precisely, of that particular interpretation of natural right according to which the one thing needful is respect for diversity or individuality. But there is a tension between the respect for diversity or individuality and the recognition of natural right. When liberals became impatient of the absolute limits to diversity or individuality that are imposed even by the most liberal version of natural right, they had to make a choice between natural right and the uninhibited cultivation of individuality. They chose the latter. Once this step was taken, tolerance appeared as one value or ideal among many, and not intrinsically superior to its opposite. In other words, intolerance appeared as a value equal in dignity to tolerance. But it is practically impossible to leave it at the equality of all preferences or choices. If the unequal rank of choices cannot be traced to the unequal rank of their objectives, it must be traced to the unequal rank of the acts of choosing; and this means eventually that genuine choice, as distinguished from spurious or despicable choice, is nothing but resolute or deadly serious decision. Such a decision, however, is akin to intolerance rather than to tolerance. Liberal relativism has its roots in the natural right tradition or in the notion that everyone has a natural right to the pursuit happiness as he understands happiness; but in itself it is a seminary of intolerance.

The faculty debate, while the embers of Story House still smoldered, was an exercise in the elimination of diversity in a seminary of intolerance. I once asked a teen-aged student who was among the leaders of the Black Students Union, why he was so sure of himself. He replied, "Because of my sincerity." I then asked him if he thought that Hitler had been any less sincere than he was. He merely stared blankly at me. However, by then he knew that he—not I—represented majority sentiment in the faculties. Representing the most resolute and daring part of the community, he had come to be recognized as the embodiment of majority sentiment.

While I do not recall the exact numbers, I remember that the Diamond/Fisk/Jaffa proposal lost by a margin of five votes. Had three of our colleagues voted differently, the result might have been reversed. I do not believe that, in any of the other Claremont Colleges, the cause of human decency came anywhere near as close to success. Nevertheless, there was a large minority scattered among the other colleges who were prepared to unite in resistance to the intimidation to which we are all being subjected, and there was a number of campus wide meetings. The roll of honor was a long one, and I omit attempting any enumeration at this distance in time because it would do injustice to so many. I would not want anyone to think, however, that in articulating such arguments as these, I was fighting alone.

My greatest disappointment however was in the Claremont Men's College trustees. Besides sending the letter I have described, I called several of them. Their attitude was invariably friendly, and invariably patronizing. They all reassured me that I was unnecessarily anxious and apprehensive. They were unanimous in telling me that they would never vote to approve any demand so ludicrous as a Black Studies Center. When the time came, however, they voted unanimously—or so I was told—but not in the sense they had told me. One of those with whom I spoke would one day become an Attorney General of the United States. A year or two later I had a conversation with a trustee of one of the other Claremont colleges, a man notable for his hard-edged Conservative political convictions. I lamented the cowardliness, the utter lack of conviction of the Colleges—including the trustees—in doing their duty in the face of intimidation. He said, "You don't understand, Harry. Rome wasn't built in a day." I replied, "You don't understand. Rome is not being built. Rome is burning." He was as blank and uncomprehending as that teen-age black. All of these trustees were as tough as nails over their brandy and cigars, at the end of comfortable banquets. Apparently however it was not Churchill's brandy that they drank, or Churchill's cigars that they smoked. Since they themselves were far from the bombs and the fires and the threats, it is hard to comprehend their detachment and pusillanimity. They could have made a difference, but they would not do so.

All those who voted for the proposal that we were a "white college" providing a "white education" had been told, over and over again, before they voted, that the idea that education (or the human mind) could have a color or a race—other than that of the human race—was the essential and underlying principle of the Third Reich. They had been told that our nation had been founded, in the words of Abraham Lincoln, upon "an abstract truth applicable to all men and all times." Like jesting Pilate, they asked "What is truth?" and would not stay for an answer. None of them took seriously the idea of such trans-cultural or trans-historical truth, as is represented by either the Declaration of Independence or the Bible. The only truth, in their minds, that was trans-cultural or trans-historical, was the truth that there is no trans-cultural, trans-historical truth. The most radical form of relativism is radical historicism. Leo Strauss has written that it was the contempt for permanent standards for human life and human action that

> permitted the most radical historicist in 1933 to submit to, or rather to welcome, as a dispensation of fate, the verdict of the least wise and least moderate part of his nation while it was in its least wise and least moderate mood, and at the same time to speak of wisdom and moderation. (*What Is Political Philosophy?* p. 27.)

In deferring to the "wisdom and moderation" of teenage gangsters in the re-structuring of higher education, the faculties, administrations and—ultimately, the trustees—of the Claremont Colleges showed a contempt for the idea of civilization—no less than of education—that was not essentially different from that of the German university professors—led by Heidegger—who had welcomed Hitler in 1933. We were saved—at least for the moment—from the full consequences of our folly by the fact that, although the cause of Hitler flourished on our campuses, it did not control the action of the government, as it had done in Germany. That Richard Nixon was President of the United States, and that Ronald Reagan was Governor of California—and that both expressed their sympathy with our beleaguered cause—did much to keep our morale high, even as we lost the battle on the campus itself. Our thanks was due to the genius of our Founding, and the strength of our political institutions. How long that strength could withstand this moral cancer, remained—and still remains—to be seen.

I add here this footnote. Immediately after the vote endorsing the ethnic centers, the faculty turned to the election of representatives to serve on the committee that would draw up the plans for the new centers. One-half the membership of this committee would be students, who would have the same voting rights as the faculty members. At this point I declared my refusal to take part in the discussion or the voting, on the ground that I believed this action to be *ultra vires*. Under our corporate charters, I held, such a delegation of authority to persons without any academic credentials was unlawful. In taking this position I was alone.

Except for the activism centered around Vietnam in the years immediately following 1969, the following decades have been relatively free of violent confrontations. The Vietnam protests were directed at government rather than academic policy. Yet they too assumed the illegitimacy of the principles of Western civilization as embodied in our Declaration of Independence and our Constitution. Presently, Watergate, followed by the fall of Saigon, represented a victory for student— and faculty—radicalism in the political sphere, which paralleled what had earlier been achieved in the academic sphere.

Meanwhile, the attrition of the principles under assault two decades ago has continued unabated. Most of those who resisted the radicalism of the 1960s and 1970s have faded from the scene, and they have been replaced by and large from the ranks of the radicals themselves. If these seem less revolutionary today, it is because they themselves control the levers of power on our campuses.

Let me illustrate the course of events by three incidents. In the early 1970s Claremont Men's College produced a house organ entitled *Res Publica*. Its first issue included an article entitled "Amoral America" by President-emeritus George C. S. Benson, and one by Joseph Hough, the Chairman of the Religion Department at Claremont Graduate School (who was then also Acting Dean—later Dean—of the School of Theology). Hough's article was entitled "Dilemma: The Liberal and the Church." I wrote a critique of both articles, entitled "Amoral America and the Liberal Dilemma."

My criticism of the former was that "Like Socrates . . . Dr. Benson seems better at exhorting us to education in virtue, than in instructing us in what it is." This followed the critique of Socrates in the *Kleitophon*, and the line of criticism that Aristotle takes, in reproaching Plato, in the *Nicomachean Ethics*. In due time I received a response which was not unlike what Plato—or a follower of Plato—might have given to Aristotle.

Dean Hough's article, however, was altogether a different matter. It was essentially an adaptation to the exigencies of liberation theology of Herbert Marcuse's *Repressive Tolerance*. Its thesis was that liberals should not be afraid of being considered illiberal, when it was necessary to adopt the rough methods sometimes required to bring about social change. When Hough published these sentiments, the utility of the bombings and the burnings in bringing about "liberation" in Claremont was fresh in everyone's minds. The true role of the churches was not defined, said Hough, by "the personal salvation style of conservatism." It was rather that of a "social action ministry" which required "group decision and mobilization" of "cadres" of the committed. A "non-political vision of meaning" was rejected by Dean Hough because he found it to be inconsistent with "the neo-Marxist criticism of the separation of meaning from action. . . ." I pointed out that there was no difference, known to me, between a neo-Marxist and a Marxist "criticism of the separation of meaning from action." It was Marx's thesis on Feuerbach—which I have already quoted—which underlay both Marcuse's and Hough's protest against "bourgeois" tolerance. Meaning—and liberation—was to be found in the unity of theory and practice preached by Karl Marx. Hence true liberalism—according to Hough—was not to be found in any overnice attachment to civil liberties. It was to be found in resolute action, otherwise known as revolution.

I have taken pains to summarize my critique of Hough's article—which critique is reprinted both in my book, *The Conditions of Freedom*,[2] and in *A Symposium*, published by the Claremont Committee for Academic Freedom—because *Res Publica* refused to publish it. What Hough wrote was a justification of the policy of the Claremont Colleges in refusing to defend either academic freedom or civil liberty, while submitting to gangsterism. I no doubt offended the editors, in part because I was much clearer in presenting Hough's argument than he was himself; but I was also candid in explicating the implications of his appeal to Marxist principles—although the fact of his appeal to those principles was itself explicit and overt. There was a lengthy correspondence with the editorial authorities—reprinted in *A Symposium*—which even today is instructive reading. I was admonished not to yield to "the temptation of putting down a colleague" and told to learn to write "in a different style." These reproofs were remarkably similar to those once directed to Solzhenitsyn by Soviet authorities. Of course, I was not prevented from publishing what I had written. But I was prevented from addressing the same audience that Hough had addressed in circumstances that might have compelled him to engage in genuine debate. *Res Publica* had declared itself to be a "platform for provocative articles which deal with public affairs. . . ." But the provocation it countenanced was severely limited and certainly one-sided. Thomas Jefferson had written that

> truth is great and will prevail if left to herself, that she is the proper and sufficient antagonist to error, and has nothing to fear from the conflict unless by human interposition disarmed of her natural weapons, free argument and debate, errors ceasing to be dangerous when it is permitted freely to contradict them.

Reasoned argument is the ground of truth. And such truth is the only safe ground either for academic or political freedom. "Provocative articles" are worthless unless they can be tested. Neither Jefferson himself, nor Lincoln, nor Churchill, were nor wished to be accepted on authority. The swords of argument that they wielded were keen because they had been tempered in the fires of controversy.

Today's private and elite colleges and universities are administered in very much the same spirit as other corporate enterprises. They depend very much upon the support of the public—beginning with the competition for bright and talented freshmen who have parents willing to make the considerable sacrifices required to pay the high costs. They must continue to persuade these same students, after they become alumni, to go on paying the old school. Then they must find wealthy donors, corporate and individual, to underwrite buildings, research institutes, scholarship funds, and even professorships. For all these reasons they must maintain a continuous public relations campaign. I am myself flooded with college PR, and know the genre well, since I am on the mailing list of six institutions: besides CMC and CGS, there are the two from which I have earned degrees, and the two from which I have honorary degrees. By far the most sophisticated, and the most intensive, is Yale's. Yet all share one common characteristic: there is not the slightest hint in them of what the real life of the colleges is. Western civilization as a whole—and American civilization in particular—is going through a profound period of inner turmoil and change. No doubt some of it is change for the better. Certainly much of it is change for the worse. But the cockpit of these changes, their dynamic source, is the university. And the one certain and central fact about the universities is not the bitter division of opinion concerning which changes are for the better, and which for the worse, but whether there are any standards by which better and worse can in any way be distinguished. As far as the PR departments are concerned, however, we are all supposed to be so many Mr. (and Ms.) Chips, with our quaint and lovable idiosyncrasies and esoteric—but highly praiseworthy—scholarship. No one, reading official college publications, would have any inkling of the rancid passions, the dislike, animosity, antipathy, and sheer loathing, with which college faculties—and their student followers—look upon each other. The conflicts within the political arena—even such as Watergate, or Irangate, or those that centered around Judge Bork and Senator John Tower—are tepid and polite compared to those within the academy.

There is one thesis that is dominant in the liberal arts curricula today—one that runs through all the social science and humanities departments, e.g., political science, economics, literature, religion, philosophy, history, psychology, sociology, anthropology. That thesis is that there is no objective knowledge of, or rational ground for distinguishing good and bad, right and wrong, just and unjust. All such judgments are said to be value judgments, concerning which reason has nothing to say. The essence of a liberal education consists—at least at first—in becoming a dilettante of the aesthetic ideals expressed in art, architecture, sculpture, music, and literature, and learning to savor the variety of lifestyles expressed in books, religions, philosophies, and cultures. What education displays for us is the variety of forms that human imagination and human taste—including moral taste—takes, but it never tells us that one is truer, more beautiful, or more just than another. It never tells us that human choice can be guided—as the Signers of the Declaration of Independence believed it could be—by the truth about man, God, and the universe.

That the only truth is that there is no truth is however a two-edged sword. As Leo Strauss pointed out, it may at first suggest indifference. But human beings by nature love, and they also hate. By nature, they begin by loving their own. But when they are told that there is no ground for distinguishing their own—or what they love—from the good, they are told that there is no ground for imposing any limits or restraints upon either their loves or their hates. Then the indifference of the dilettante turns quickly into either the adventurism of the scoundrel, or the passionate commitment of the fanatic.

In 1979 Claremont Men's College replaced *Res Publica* with a new publication, *Current*. Its first number featured on its cover a cartoon, of a "Mr. Goodlyfe" who represented, the editors said, what they liked to think of as "the guiding principle" of a CMC education. Anyone who looked closely at the cartoon—which evidently the editors did not do— would have seen that the artist, who was very skillful, had conceived of Mr. Goodlyfe as a thoroughly egocentric and repulsive character. The theme of the good life was chosen however because of the feature article by Professor Steven Smith of CMC's Philosophy Department. It was a celebration of Smith's extremely popular course, "Theories of the Good Life." Cartoon and article together were designed to advertise our commitment to cultural uplift, and to counter the impression among the other Claremont colleges, that CMC was a haven for political reactionaries and cultural barbarians. The fact that students were encouraged by Smith to seek, not merely life, or the means of life, but the good life, was supposed to prove a devotion to the higher things. I say it was "supposed" to do this, although the critique I wrote of Smith's account of his course—entitled "Looking at Mr. Goodlyfe" and reprinted in *American Conservatism and the American Founding* proved I think that it did the exact opposite. The heart of the course was Smith's conviction that he himself knew nothing about what the good life was, and that he had abandoned any idea that he might discover something about it by such an anachronistic method as reading the Bible, Plato, Aristotle, Cicero, Aquinas, Locke, Kant, Hegel Marx, Mill, Dewey, or anyone else. He had abandoned the quest, because he did not think that the good life was or could be an object of knowing. His course was designed to help his students decide—each for himself— what the good life was—not in itself—but *for him*. Since it was assumed *a priori* that there was no *reason* for choosing one life—or lifestyle— over another, the choice was one that could only be made by some nonrational process. And since there was no way to rank the passions— only reason could do that—the course was an exercise in helping one to discover whatever it was that was most agreeable to one's passions.

Some four years later, *Current* again published an article by Professor Smith, entitled "Reflections on Human Liberation." Now what had earlier been implied but not expressed, or not expressed unreservedly, became altogether manifest. The substance, of my critique of this second article—which is also reprinted in *American Conservatism*—is perhaps sufficiently indicated in the title I gave it, "Sodomy and the Academy: The Assault on the Family and Morality by 'Liberation' Ethics." The heart of Professor Smith's thesis, as he now expressed it, is in these two passages:

> The root notion of freedom is, I believe, the spontaneous, uninhibited expression of the integrated self.

And again:

> The absence of freedom means therefore the presence of blocks or limitations that prevent unfettered expressions of the self.

In the immediate context, Smith's argument was directed mainly against the obstacles to liberation that he discovered in what he regarded as sexual stereotypes. His contention was that being born a male or a female was a mere accidental circumstance that ought not in any way to determine the kind of sex role—or sex life—that one might choose. From his perspective, the most inhibiting or limiting of all stereotypes was the traditional family, with its arbitrarily assigned roles, such as masculine fathers and feminine mothers. But Smith's underlying thesis was that all moral ideas were stereotypes that might limit human freedom. Liberation thus conceived is an end in itself in which no distinction can be drawn between moral probity and moral improbity. No *moral* distinction can be drawn between criminal and non-criminal conduct. That is to say, there is nothing in the idea of liberation that decides criminal conduct may not be more liberating than non-criminal conduct. The only question that liberation ethics asks, is whether a proposed course of life or action accords with the spontaneous, uninhibited, unfettered self. The only categorical imperative is, "If it feels good, do it." The only counsel of prudence is, "Can you get away with it?" From Smith's premises, it was clear, the best life, whether in public or in private, was the life of the successful tyrant.

Of course, it goes without saying that *Current* would not publish my critiques of Smith. The editors only saw that I was, once again, "putting down a colleague." Their response was, in effect, "Does General Motors let Oldsmobile attack Chevrolet?" (In fact, General Motors does!) But I am minded of the fact that Smith is a Harvard trained philosophy professor, and that Derek Bok, President of Harvard, recently extracted 20 million dollars from a former Chairman of the Securities and Exchange Commission, under the incredible pretext of establishing an ethics program at Harvard. I am reminded of the occasion, a few years back, when President Bart Giamatti made the central theme of his annual address to the incoming class of freshmen at Yale, to beware of evils of the Moral Majority. Bill Buckley commented that this was like warning someone about to enter a whorehouse of the dangers of the bedbugs. And the rites of spring at Yale these days suggest that the whorehouse analogy has itself become depressingly anachronistic. A recent visitor to New Haven has described to me the booths set up in front of Sterling Library. They represent "closets" from which initiates ritualistically emerge. This seems to symbolize the baptism of the spirit by the new religion of relativism. This is how the sinner's "consciousness" is raised, and the devils of racism, sexism, and homophobia are expelled from his soul, no doubt into the Gadarene swine of reactionary moralists. This is the heart of the new—and vigorously intolerant—Puritanism on our campuses. It is more dominant on some campuses than others but—with a very few very honorable exceptions—it is dominant everywhere. Today's university presidents, selling ethics to gullible donors, seem to me to have all the comic qualities, of Chaucer's Pardoner.

I have said that Abraham Lincoln referred to the proposition of human equality in the Declaration of Independence as "an abstract truth, applicable to all men and all time." I recently had occasion to point out that Jesus' admonition, in the Sermon on the Mount, to do unto others as we would have others do unto us, presupposes that very truth. To whom is the Golden Rule addressed? It is not to Jews only. It is not to any nation or race, other than the human race. Nor is it addressed to any part of the human race more than any other. The rule is addressed equally to all human beings everywhere, because and only because, it is assumed that in the decisive and relevant respect all men are created equal. Human beings are equal with respect to certain rights. As we would have others recognize and respect those rights in us, so must we recognize and respect the same rights in others. The Bible—Old and New Testaments—and the Declaration imply not only moral equality among men, but moral responsibility. But the very notion of responsibility implies human freedom as a metaphysical reality.

I remind you of what Thomas Jefferson caused to be inscribed upon his tombstone, as the three things by which he wished most to be remembered. The first was as the author of the Declaration of Independence; next, as the author of the Statute of Virginia for Religious Freedom; and third as the Father of the University of Virginia. The Virginia Statute, although not first, is nonetheless central. Even as the Golden Rule presupposes human equality, so does human equality presuppose the solemn affirmation that "Almighty God hath created the mind free. . . ."

To hold it as a *truth* that all men are created equal, it is necessary to hold that the mind of man is free to grasp truth. If what the mind thinks—or thinks that it thinks—is the involuntary effect of a cause outside the mind, a mere reaction to that cause, then truth is merely an illusion. To say that the mind can hold something as true implies that there is a conformity of the mind with its object. That the object outside the mind determines thought—not by forcing the mind to respond, but by presenting itself as an object of thought, to which the mind responds by its unforced will to know, is what is meant by objectivity. Relativism in modern philosophy is a by-product of the denial of objectivity in the life of the mind. It goes back to the beginnings of modern philosophy and modern science. Here is the beginning of Hobbes's *Leviathan*, Part I, Chapter I, "Of Sense."

> The cause of sense, is the external body, or object, which presseth the organ proper to each sense . . . which pressure, by the mediation of nerves, and other strings, and membranes of the body, continued inwards to the brain, and heart, causeth there a resistance, or counter-pressure, or endeavour of the heart to deliver itself: which endeavour because *outward*, seemeth to be some matter without. And this *seeming* or *fancy*, is that which men call *sense*, and consisteth, as to the eye, in a *light*, or *colour figured*, to the ear, in a *sound*. . . . All which qualities called *sensible*, are in the object that causeth them, but so many motions of the matter by which it presseth our organs diversely.

According to Hobbes sense perception is not an apprehension of anything outside ourselves. Sense perception—and all thought is generated from sense perception—is purely subjective. Human consciousness is a black box receiving signals from the outside, but it must interpret those signals altogether within itself. For Hobbes, the only metaphysical reality is bodies in motion. Psychological reality is a form of physical reality. Our sense organs record reactions to the bodies that impinge upon them, the way billiard balls communicate their motions to each other when they strike each other. The laws of the mind are then aspects of the laws of the motions of matter. Let me remark only in passing that deconstructionism, the current craze in literary scholarship—and the leading edge in liberal arts education—is merely a remote by-product of Hobbesian psychology. The deconstructionists assume *a priori* that the work they are studying has no objective existence—or if it did we would have no access to it—and that literary scholarship consists only in interpreting our reactions to the work—never the work itself.

> How fundamental for all the modern centuries has been this view of the mind may be shown by the following, quoted from *The Primary World of Senses* by Erwin Straus, and published in 1963.[3] At the Hixon Symposium of 1948, a conference of a small number of physiologists, and psychiatrists . . . (a speaker for the group) formulated an "article of common faith". . . . This "article" states that all phenomena of behavior and mind will ultimately become describable in terms of the mathematical and physical sciences. (p. 106)

This is called by Straus "the credo of objective psychology." For the phenomena of the mind to be described mathematically means, as in the Newtonian universe, that there is no indeterminacy in the record of cause and effect: every action generates an equal and opposite reaction. Any freedom or indeterminacy in the phenomena of the mind would render them not susceptible to scientific description. But without freedom or indeterminacy, there is nothing recognizably human in the human phenomena. The problem that immediately attends this view of the mind, is that it cannot account for the consciousness of the scientific observer. The scientist cannot at once insist upon the superior truthfulness of his account of the mind, while admitting that what he says is itself subject to the determinism which is his axiomatic premise. The mind of the scientist—and therewith human consciousness properly so called—is no part of the universe [of] science studies. Straus lists as corollaries of this article of faith, that

1. There is no consciousness.
2. There might be consciousness, but there is no proof of its existence or its mode of operation.
3. The question of whether there is consciousness or not is irrelevant, for it cannot be explored by scientific, that is, objective, methods.

For twentieth century psychology, no less than for that of the seventeenth century, the great antagonist is Aristotle. Here is Hobbes again:

> But the philosophy-schools, through all the universities of Christendom, grounded upon certain texts of *Aristotle* teach another doctrine, and say, for the cause of *vision*, that the thing seen, sendeth forth . . . a *visible species*. . . . Nay for the cause of *understanding* also, they say the thing understood sendeth forth an *intelligible species* . . . which coming into the understanding, makes us understand..

Descartes' polemic against Aristotle is no less vehement than Hobbes's.

From the point of view of objective psychology, we are all both blind and deaf. I remind you of the allegory of the three blind men and the elephant. One touches the leg and says it is a tree trunk. Another touches the trunk and says it is a huge reptile. Another touches the inside of the ear, and says it is a silk purse. Of course, when the three compare notes, they realize that each had only partial information. If they keep collecting data they will frame hypotheses to cover more and more data. And with each new hypothesis they will come closer to the truth. Now this is precisely how scientists proceed in discovering, let us say, atomic and subatomic particles, which they see no more than the blind men see the elephant. Of course, they are dealing with phenomena which are outside the scope of sense perception. But when they communicate their findings to each other, they do not blindfold themselves, they do not try to discover each other as if they were subatomic particles or the blind men's elephant. As I have written elsewhere, "[s]cientific rationality is a subspecies of human rationality, but it has no life, or being, apart from that pre-scientific rationality which is the condition of its existence."[4] The philosopher of pre-scientific rationality is Aristotle. He alone has given a fundamental account of sense perception, memory, imagination, and reason, as it is experienced in the prescientific consciousness, which remains the fundamental dimension of human experience. Only Aristotle has accounted for that consciousness that the Hixon conferees could not think about because it presented insuperable difficulties. Only Aristotle has given an account of that metaphysical freedom of the mind that, as Jefferson rightly declared, is the ground of all moral freedom, and hence of civil and religious liberty.

I can do no more here than indicate the kernel of that account. For Aristotle the eye really sees, because it apprehends the form of the thing seen, without its matter. The signet ring leaves its form in the wax, after it has been removed. The form in the wax is no less the form of the ring, because the ring is no longer there. Also, a mirror records the form of the thing or person who stands before it. Hobbes says that the form in the mirror is an illusion and he ridicules the very idea of a disembodied "species." He does not grant that anything, separated from its matter, can be real. But we in the world of common sense—the world of pre-scientific rationality, the world of Aristotle—know that what we see in the mirror (however distorted it may sometimes be)—is genuine. The fact that the form of a thing can be separated from its matter is the very heart of human understanding, and of human intelligence. Without this possibility, modern science itself would not be possible, because all science presupposes the detachment of the mind from its object as a condition of human speech about the object. Human speech about an object presupposes that we employ common nouns. To say, for example, that this is a chair, implies that there is an infinite number of possible chairs, each different from this one, and yet all equally chairs. The mind has abstracted the idea of the chairs from the visible forms of particular chairs, just as the eye abstracted the visible forms from their matter. The mind frees itself from all sense perception every time it employs a universal, that is, a common noun. The common noun—the ground and basis of what we call common sense—is at once the principal ingredient of the most ordinary experience, and the greatest of all miracles. It exhibits the mind detached from matter, understanding material things just because it is detached from them. In understanding that this is a chair, to repeat, we understand that there is an infinite number of possible chairs, each different from this. We understand that there is no particular color that makes a chair a chair. If any element in the idea of the chair had color—or any other sensible quality—then to that extent the mind could not comprehend chairs. For the idea of a chair to be the intelligible basis for perceiving any possible chairs, it must be abstracted from all sensible qualities. Only then will it be seen that all chairs are equally chairs. Only when we see that there is an infinite variety of possible human beings, each equally human, do we begin to understand the difference between the human and the non-human. Only then can we see that men are not dogs or hogs or horses—or gods. Only then can the moral function of human intelligence begin to function. A philosophy or a psychology that denies the metaphysical freedom of the mind that was axiomatic for Jefferson can form no part of liberal education, for liberal education means education in freedom and for freedom. It means education in the metaphysical reality of such a universe as the Declaration of Independence proclaims. This is a universe whose purposes are real, because—if we think about it—we participate in those purposes every time we think. Because we know we can think, we know we can think well or ill. Because we know we can think, we know we can think about right and wrong, good and evil. Understanding that we can understand, we can understand what are our rights, and what are our duties. Understanding this, we understand that the fate of our civilization is yet in our hands, because it is in our minds. We can "do our duty as we understand it."[5]

NOTES

1. Valedictory Lecture, delivered at Bauer Auditorium, Claremont McKenna College, Claremont, California, April 14, 1989. It was met with booing and a walkout in protest and cheers in support. All footnotes are by the editors.

2. Harry V. Jaffa, "Amoral America and the Liberal Dilemma" in *The Conditions of Freedom: Essays in Political Philosophy* (Baltimore, MD: Johns Hopkins University Press, 1975), 273–280.

3. Erwin W. Straus, *The Primary World of Senses* (Glencoe, IL: The Free Press of Glencoe, 1963).

4. Harry V. Jaffa, "Judicial Conscience and Natural Rights: A Reply to Professor Ledewitz" 1998 *Seattle Law Review* [formerly *University of Puget*

Sound Law Review] 11:219, 227. Reprinted in Harry V. Jaffa, with Bruce Ledewitz, Robert L. Stone, George Anastaplo, Foreword by Lewis E. Lehrman, *Original Intent and the Framers of the Constitution: A Disputed Question* (Washington, D.C.: Regnery Gateway, 1994), 243.

   5. Abraham Lincoln, "Cooper Institute Address," February 27, 1860.

5

THE END OF HISTORY MEANS THE END OF FREEDOM

Harry Jaffa contrasts Francis Fukuyama's "End of History" argument with that of Leo Strauss in his debate with Alexandre Kojève in *On Tyranny*. Jaffa characterizes this "debate with Kojève on natural right and history" as "a debate that may very well be the greatest intellectual confrontation of the last century, at least." Drawing from Strauss, Jaffa argues that the case for Socratic wisdom is coeval with the case for politics; in the modern world the freedom of the mind and political freedom require one another. "We see accordingly that the case for liberal democracy (and political moderation generally) rests decisively upon the Socratic understanding of human nature—of the humbling but invigorating awareness of the limits of human wisdom and virtue. It rests, in short upon the idea of natural right as Leo Strauss expounded it." Fukuyama, Jaffa contends, dismissed natural right as a serious alternative to historicism of the "end of history" philosophers such as Hegel.

But there is yet another dimension to human life to be considered in a world that promises final solutions to all the great questions.

> The disappearance of any reason for elections will be followed by the disappearance of constitutional government, since such government has no purposes apart from the purpose of elections. It goes without saying, of course, that all revealed religion must also come to an end. What possible role is there for faith or God if History has revealed all?

With the universal administrative state we lack all need for political freedom, philosophy, or a transcendent God.

Jaffa's essay was posted on the Claremont Institute website, www.claremont.org January 17, 1990. The editors thank the *Claremont Review of Books* for permission to reprint from *CRB Digital* (January 2015).

THE END OF HISTORY MEANS THE END OF FREEDOM BY *HARRY V. JAFFA*

In "A Reply to My Critics," (*The National Interest*—Winter 1989/90) Francis Fukuyama writes:

> We owe to Hegel our modern understanding of history as an evolu-
> tion from primitive to modern, through a succession of stages of
> "false consciousness" during which men believed in the legitimacy of
> such things as chattel slavery and the divine right of kings. There is
> hardly an educated person alive who does not have a slightly patron-
> izing view of those great thinkers of the past who were "advanced for
> their times," but whose views have subsequently been superseded by
> more modern, less parochial ones. Among "sophisticated" people,
> there is hardly anyone willing to assert that the views of Aristotle, or
> of Aquinas, or of Locke, are true absolutely and forever.[1]

This assertion is far more fundamental than any of Fukuyama's more highly publicized assertions about the relationship either of liberal de-mocracy or of communism to "the end of history." In the foregoing passage Fukuyama put the word "sophisticated" in quotation marks. However he did not do so in the case of "educated," although referring to the same phenomenon. It is clear that he himself is as patronizing as anyone concerning the great pre-Hegelian thinkers of the past. What "we owe to Hegel . . ." is something that Fukuyama thinks *is* "true, absolutely and forever."

The "modern understanding of history," according to Fukuyama is of an "evolution" from the lower to the higher. To understand the past in the light of the present is—for him—to understand the low in the light of the high. Aristotle belongs to the low—and Hegel (and Marx) be-longs to the high—*ex hypothesi.*

Fukuyama recognizes that this understanding of history might be thought merely to represent a short-sighted relativism in disguise.

> Anyone who accepts the historicist premise—that is, that truth is historically relative—faces the question of the end of history even if he is not aware of it. . . . Anyone who believes that earlier thinkers were simply "products of their time" must, if he is honest and consistent, ask whether he and his own historicism are not also products of their times. . . .
>
> For historicists, there are two ways out of this conundrum.* The first is the path chosen by Hegel, to declare that history had come to an end. Hegel accepted the historical relativity of thought, but argued that in his system opinion finally reached the status of truth and ideology turned into philosophy. Hegel's system also represented the end of philosophy, because it would henceforth be impossible to state a philosophical proposition that was both true and new. Hegel understood with full philosophical clarity that the end of history was a necessary support for the modern state, for otherwise its underlying concepts of right would have no basis in truth. The other path was the one chosen by Nietzsche and his twentieth-century followers like Heidegger, who accepted fully the radical consequences of historicism and realized that it makes impossible any sort of conventional ethics or morality.

The asterisk* above [footnote 2 in Fukuyama's article] is accompanied by this footnote: "Of course, one need not be a historicist; one can simply believe in a doctrine of natural right." In this most remarkable of asides, Fukuyama simply dismisses the alternative to historicism as if it were unworthy of further consideration. In endorsing the thesis "that the end of history was a necessary support for the modern state," he rejects *inter alia* the natural right teaching embodied in the American Declaration of Independence, the Virginia Statute of Religious Liberty, and other documents of the American Founding. And at least one post-Hegelian modern statesman, Abraham Lincoln, found the necessary support for a modern state—a government of the people, by the people for the people—in "an abstract truth, applicable to all men and all times." Commenting on the great crisis of his time—in his Peoria speech of October 16, 1854—Lincoln declared that Slavery is founded in the selfishness of man's nature—opposition to it in his love of justice. These principles are an *eternal* antagonism; and when brought into collision so fiercely, as slavery extension brings them, shocks, and throes, and convulsions must ceaselessly follow. "Repeal the Missouri Compromise—repeal all compromises—repeal the Declaration of Independence—repeal all past *history*, you still cannot repeal human nature." (Emphasis added.) Lincoln clearly thought that the principles of political freedom were grounded in nature and eternity, not in history. And it is to the words of Lincoln and Jefferson—not of Hegel—to whom the peoples of eastern Europe are turning to vindicate their struggles today.

Mr. Fukuyama is a disciple of the late Alexandre Kojève, who re-interpreted Hegel's version of the "end of history" to justify his support of the regime of Josef Stalin. Now Mr. Fukuyama re-interprets Kojève's reinterpretation to justify the principles of liberal democracy. If, however, "the end of history" can—depending upon the way things happen to be going—be used to justify the regimes hailed by Hegel (first that of Napoleon, then the Prussian monarchy), by Kojève, and by Fukuyama, it is difficult to imagine anything that it could not justify. Thus I fail to see the difference that Fukuyama thinks he sees between the paths marked out by Hegel (and Marx and Kojève), and those of Nietzsche and Heidegger.

Leo Strauss—whose best known work is *Natural Right and History* (1953)—is the philosophic representative in our time of natural right. The revised and enlarged edition of Strauss's *On Tyranny* (Free Press, 1991, first published 1963) includes his debate with Kojève on natural right and history, a debate that may very well be the greatest intellectual confrontation of the last century, at least. From the evidence of his footnote, this debate seems to have left no residue whatever in the mind of Fukuyama. At the end of the French edition of the Strauss/Kojève debate, however, Strauss made these observations concerning their differences.

> Philosophy in the strict and classical sense is quest for the eternal order or for the eternal cause or causes of all things. It presupposes then that there is an eternal and unchangeable order within which History takes place and which is not in any way affected by History. It presupposes in other words that any "realm of freedom" is not more than a dependent province within the "the realm of necessity." It presupposes, in the words of Kojève, that "Being is essentially immutable in itself and eternally identical with itself." This presup-

position is not self-evident. Kojève rejects it in favor of view that "Being creates itself in the course of History," or that the highest being is Society and History, or that eternity is nothing but the totality of historical, i.e. finite time.[2]

Here is a profound articulation of what is at stake. Philosophy "in the strict and classical sense" stands or falls, with the idea of "an eternal and unchangeable order." If there is no unchanging ground of changing experience, the philosophical quest for meaning in experience is itself meaningless. Strauss quotes with approval Kojève's characterization of the philosophical presupposition, that "Being is essentially immutable in itself and eternally identical with itself." I think it worth noticing that this definition of Being would apply equally, for example, to Plato's Idea of the Good, *and* to the God of the Bible.

The eternity of the God of the Bible is not in time: He existed before the creation of the world, and will exist after it ceases to be. The world exists in time, but the God of the Bible does not. Hegel's "God" is nothing but History, Being creating itself in time, but having no existence beyond time. Kojève's rejection of the idea of philosophy ("in the strict and classical sense") is equally a rejection of the idea of revealed religion. To say, as Kojève does, that Being creates itself, is to say that man and God are created by the same process. This is as much as to say that what is imperfect—whether man or God—creates what is more perfect. But how can this be possible? How can the unreal and the irrational be the cause of the real and the rational? In truth, there is no intelligible perfection in the Hegelian universe accepted by Kojève (and Fukuyama), and hence no rational understanding of human perfection and imperfection may be found in the difference between man and God, as revealed in the Bible, or in "the laws of nature and of nature's God."

In the tradition of American constitutionalism, all men are equally endowed by their Creator with certain rights. The equality of man is understood in the light of man's inequality with God: because men are not and never can become God or gods—because unqualified wisdom is never available to human beings—only government by the consent of the governed, and under the rule of law, is intrinsically in accordance with the eternal order.

Strauss says that the presupposition upon which classical philosophy—and natural right—depend "is not self-evident" and that Kojève rejects it. Is this rejection reasonable? What we can observe, at this point, is that Fukuyama accepts the proposition that all pre-Hegelian "philosophy" is ideology or false consciousness, that philosophy only comes to be with the end of history, but that philosophy also ceases to be with the end of history! In short philosophy exists neither in the past nor in the future, but only in the moment that separates them! But clearly, such a "moment" can have no duration. Philosophy has no real existence, and neither does the end of history! Does Fukuyama realize that he is courting the fate of John Buridan's ass?

Strauss we see conceded—nay, insisted—that philosophy rested upon a premise, or presupposition, that was neither self-evident nor (as he argues elsewhere) susceptive of proof. For that reason, philosophy is eternally skeptical of itself and can therefore never expect to transform itself from love of wisdom, or quest for wisdom, into wisdom proper—which Hegel (followed by Kojève and Fukuyama) claimed to have done. Socrates, we know, conceded that he might be the wisest of men precisely because, knowing that he knew nothing, he did not think he knew what he did not know. This was Socrates' human wisdom. It is this very wisdom which decides the case for the rule of law in preference to the arbitrary rule of any man or men, however wise they or others may deem them to be. Socratic wisdom is however perfectly compatible with the idea of human equality enshrined in the Declaration of Independence. For this idea of equality in no way disparages the genuine differences among men: in intelligence, virtue, talents, or strength of character. It rather marks off man as man from beasts and from God or gods. It denounces *a priori* as fraudulent any claim to superhuman virtue or wisdom that might be thought to justify any right to rule human beings without their consent. We see accordingly that the case for liberal democracy (and political moderation generally) rests decisively upon the Socratic understanding of human nature—of the humbling but invigorating awareness of the limits of human wisdom and virtue. It rests, in short upon the idea of natural right as Leo Strauss expounded it.

According to Strauss,

> On the basis of the classical presupposition, a radical distinction must be made between the conditions of understanding and the sources of understanding, and the sources of understanding, between the conditions of the existence and perpetuation of philosophy (societies of a

certain kind, and so on) and the sources of philosophic insight. On the basis of Kojève's presupposition, that distinction loses its crucial significance: social change or fate affects being, if it is not identical with Being, and hence affects truth.[3]

According to the classical or Socratic perspective, the conditions for thinking clearly and well—e.g., intelligence, health, a certain amount of wealth, freedom, leisure—do not guarantee that one will think clearly and well. Nothing can *guarantee* understanding. Indeed, from this perspective nothing can guarantee a successful outcome to any human enterprise, practical or theoretical. In Churchill's phrase, one cannot guarantee success, one can only deserve it. To say that the conditions of success—in thinking or anything else—necessarily produce success, would be to reduce man to a cipher of his environment. This is what in effect, the idea of the end of history does. The existence—or comprehension—of truth, is held to be the result of a fate over which the thinker himself has no control. Human consciousness—whether wise or foolish—is no more the result of the individual's intelligence and will respond to the conditions of the individual's existence, that is the consciousness of a dog or of any other species of animal. "Truth" is something that happens to the individual as the result of an historical fate that owes nothing to his individual efforts at thinking. Accordingly, says Strauss,

> On the basis of Kojève's presuppositions, unqualified attachment to human concerns becomes the source of philosophic understanding: man must be absolutely at home on earth, he must be absolutely a citizen of the earth, if not a citizen of a part of the inhabitable earth. On the basis of the classical presupposition, philosophy requires a radical detachment from human concerns: man must be absolutely at home on earth, he must be a citizen of the whole.[4]

According to Fukuyama, Kojève had erred in thinking that a universal homogeneous state presided over by Stalin, or one of Stalin's successors, was what History had fated for its end. In truth, however, the distinction between Stalinism and liberal democracy loses its significance after history has come to an end. If, as Fukuyama (following Hegel and Kojève) contends, philosophy ends with the ending of history, then politics also ends. Politics can subsist only so long as it is thought reasonable for men to differ as to what they ought to pursue. Liberal democracy is merely a civilized and civilizing method for pursuing such differences, substituting ballots for bullets. Once the final truth is proclaimed—as Fukuyama says it must be—then there is no more reason to have elections than there is to have wars. (Wars will be replaced by police actions against philosophers and other dissenters, who by definition will be held to be invincibly ignorant.) As Marx said— quite correctly, on his Hegelian premises—the government of men is transformed into the administration of things. Indeed, it was precisely in anticipation of this end of history that Kojève, disdaining the fame and prominence that might easily have been his as a professor of philosophy, chose instead the career of a technician in the French bureaucracy. In this he was, of course, enacting in his own way the same kind of role as Lenin in Zürich, only at the later (and last) phase of history.

Of this however we may be sure. The bureaucracy that replaces political government at the end of history will, from the point of view of an unwise and invincibly philosophic human nature, be just as tyrannical, whether it has been preceded by a Stalinist or liberal democratic regime. If, as Fukuyama insists, the end of history means that philosophy has been transformed into wisdom, then—as we have noted—politics no less than philosophy must come to end. The disappearance of any reason for elections will be followed by the disappearance of constitutional government, since such government has no purposes apart from the purpose of elections. It goes without saying, of course, that all revealed religion must also come to an end. What possible role is there for faith or God if History has revealed all? The arch-criminal—the Dr. Moriarty of the future that has no future—will be anyone who, like Socrates, continues to question the wisdom of the rulers.

There are those who continue to believe, with Leo Strauss, in the unexhausted meaningfulness of the quest for "an eternal and unchangeable order within which History takes place and which is not in any way affected by History." For them, both faith in God and skepticism towards all human claims to know must remain permanent—and indeed desirable—features of human life on earth. For them, the ultimate dwelling place of the soul is not in time, which is why "man must not be absolutely at home on earth." They recognize that democratic politics, philosophy, and religion all stand or fall together. For them, not Marxism-Leninism, or its Stalinist form, is the greatest of delusions. Rather it is the belief in an end of history itself, which is ineluctably Stalinist. Mr. Fukuyama should realize that because Kojève understood this, he was wiser than his disciple.

NOTES

1. These words were written before the final disintegration of the U.S.S.R. [All other footnotes are from the editors.] Francis Fukuyama, "A Reply to My Critics," *The National Interest*, No.16, Winter 1989–90, 21–28. Fukuyama's original essay, "The End of History?" was published in *The National Interest*, No. 16, Summer 1989, 3–18.

2. Jaffa quotes from the original Strauss "Reply," later reprinted in the "Corrected and Expanded" edition of *On Tyranny*, eds. Victor Gourevitch and Michael S. Roth (Chicago: University of Chicago Press, 2013), 212–213 and before that in Leo Strauss, *Jewish Philosophy and the Crisis of Modernity: Essays and Lectures in Modern Jewish Thought*, edited with an Introduction by Kenneth Hart Green (Albany: State University of New York Press, 1997), 471.

3. Strauss, "Reply" (from Green), 471.

4. Ibid.

6

THE AMERICAN FOUNDING AS THE BEST REGIME

The Bonding of Civil and Religious Liberty

INTRODUCTION

Anticipations of the themes of this essay long preceded its appearance in March 1990 as a monograph published by the Claremont Institute. In fact the list of his books, past and promised, in the prefatory material to *Original Intent and the Framers of the Constitution*[1] contains *"The American Founding as the Best Regime, and Other Essays in Socratic Rationalism* (Forthcoming)." An earlier essay, "The American Regime and the Only Greater Institution," appeared as chapter 17 of *American Conservatism and the American Founding.*[2] The differences between it and the essay that follows make clear Jaffa's new focus. The essays on "Socratic Rationalism" appeared in his last book, *Crisis of the Strauss Divided.* Those essays echo the themes of this "Best Regime" essay, thus showing the philosophic connection between Plato and America. One sees in the 1990 monograph the heart of the argument of chapter 2 of *A New Birth of Freedom*, "The Declaration of Independence, the Gettysburg Address, and the Historians."

The argument of "The American Founding as the Best Regime: The Bonding of Civil and Religious Liberty" is aptly summarized in a single sentence: "The constitutionalism of our Founding is inseparable from its moral realism and its natural theology." The act of founding transcended the tensions between reason and revelation, ancients and moderns, theory and practice. Such a regime or political way of life required a doctrine of disestablishment and religious freedom. Subsequently, "the idea of religious freedom encompasses and promotes moral law independently of any particular dogmas of revealed religion. . . . Equally important, it lays the foundation for the idea of limited government in its full extent, and not only with reference to the question of religion."

From this perspective, the pivotal distinction between ancient duties and modern rights, virtue and freedom, must not be misunderstood as relegating America to a battlefield of individualistic self-interest devised by Thomas Hobbes. "The American Founding limited the ends of government. It did not limit the ends of man." Jaffa presents the truly revolutionary America and the new conception of politics it embodies, along with its abiding ancient human purposes: "The new order of the ages is radically novel in its solution of the political problem within the framework of a cosmopolitan, monotheistic universe. It is radically traditional in its conception of the ends, whether of reason or of revelation, to be served by that order."

The editors thank the *Claremont Review of Books* for permission to reprint from *CRB Digital* (July 2007).

THE AMERICAN FOUNDING AS THE BEST REGIME: THE BONDING OF CIVIL AND RELIGIOUS LIBERTY BY *HARRY V. JAFFA*

> *In the great journal of things happening under the sun, we, the American people, find our account running, under date of the nineteenth century of the Christian era. We find ourselves in the peaceful possession, of the fairest portion of the earth, as regards extent of territory, fertility of soil, and salubrity of climate. We find ourselves under the government of a system of political institutions, conducing more essentially to the ends of civil and religious liberty, than any of which the history of former times tell us.* —Abraham Lincoln January 27, 1838

The Preamble of the Constitution crowns its enumeration of the ends of the Constitution by declaring its purpose to "secure the blessings of liberty to ourselves and our posterity." No words of the Constitution reveal the intention of the Constitution more profoundly than these. The Preamble is the statement of the Constitution's purposes, and this culminating purpose embraces and transcends those that have gone before. Alone among the ends of the Constitution, to secure liberty is called a securing of "blessings." What is a blessing is what is good in the eyes of God. It is a good whose possession—by the common understanding of mankind—belongs properly only to those who deserve it. We remember that the final paragraph of the Declaration of Independence appeals to "the Supreme Judge of the World for the rectitude of our intentions." It is by the authority of the good people of these colonies, that independence is declared. It is because of this assurance of their rectitude that this good people, and their representatives, placed "a firm reliance on the protection of Divine Providence." We commonly call blessed those who enjoy in great measure wealth and health and freedom. And so it is that men pray for these things. Yet the sufferings of the innocent and the flourishing of the wicked—especially the great tyrants—teach us that to be blessed is not the same thing as to be in the enjoyment of worldly goods, of what Aristotle calls external goods. It is an element of the natural theology of mankind—that is partly implicit and partly explicit in the Declaration of Independence—that the compensations, both of evil and of good, are not altogether those visible in the natural order. Hence Aristotle says that what men should pray for is that these external goods be good for them. When men are poor, they seem to wish only for wealth. When they are ill, for health. When they are enslaved, they long only for freedom. This is altogether understandable. Nevertheless, reflection teaches us that the possession of health, wealth, and freedom are not the ultimate measure of human well-being. We know that there have been human beings who, being in the full possession of health, wealth, and freedom, have yet committed suicide. Health, wealth, and freedom must be combined with something else before they become ingredients of the human good, before they become blessings, properly so called. Aristotle says that no man, even with all the other goods for which men pray, would wish to live without friends. And—although they are usually surrounded by flatterers—tyrants do not have friends, certainly not the kind of friends who make life worth living. The Virginia Bill of Rights of June 12, 1776, affirmed a fundamental principle of the Revolution and of the Founding—providing by anticipation a gloss upon the words of the Preamble—when it declared that:

> *no free government, or the blessings of liberty, can be preserved to any people, but by a firm adherence to justice, moderation, temperance, frugality, and virtue, and by a frequent recurrence to fundamental principles.*

The idea of liberty—or the liberty which is a blessing—being an emancipation of the passions from moral restraint had no place in the constitutional doctrine of the *novus ordo seclorum*. The liberty which is a blessing must be good for the one who possesses it. It must therefore be a good in the sight of God, who is the source of blessings. Such a good must point to felicity, whether in this world or the next, as its consummation. By calling the advantages of liberty "blessings," the Constitution, which in certain respects makes perhaps the most radical break in all human history with all that has gone before it, nonetheless, in its understanding of the connection between happiness and virtue, aligns itself decisively with traditional moral philosophy and moral theology.

✿ ✿ ✿

The Constitution of the United States meant to do what, in fact, it has done. By grounding the regime in the doctrine of human equality, proclaimed in the Declaration of Independence, it has, as Lincoln said, cleared paths for all, given hope to all, and, by consequence, enterprise and industry to all. To a degree hitherto unimagined as possible, it has lifted the burden of unjust inequality—"the oppressor's wrong, the proud man's contumely"—from the backs of the common people. As the Virginia Bill of Rights shows, the Framers never conceived the blessings of liberty in nonmoral terms. They never imagined it to encompass the exhibitionism of lesbians, sodomites, abortionists, drug addicts, and pornographers. The people are the source of the authority of the Constitution—of all lawful authority. In Jefferson's words, the people "are inherently independent of all but moral law" (letter to Spencer Roane, September 6, 1819). Let us not, however, forget that "but." Absent the moral law, a people becomes a mob. And mobs give rise not to free government, but to despotism. That is the theme of Lincoln's Lyceum speech in 1838.

✿ ✿ ✿

In the beginning of the Lyceum speech, Lincoln speaks of our political institutions "conducing more essentially to the ends of civil and religious liberty, than any of which the history of former times tells us." Speaking thus has become so idiomatic that it is difficult to recapture the novelty it once possessed. The first amendment, in a single sentence—divided, however, by a semicolon—joins together its civil and religious guarantees. Although it is customary to speak of "civil" before "religious," the first amendment actually reverses this order. This is not accidental. Without the establishment of religious Liberty—without the removal from the political process of sectarian religious questions—a regime combining majority rule with minority rights is not a feasible enterprise. The problem of democratic constitutionalism was expressed succinctly by Jefferson in his inaugural address.

> *All too will bear in mind this sacred principle, that though the will of the majority is in all cases to prevail, that will to be rightful must be reasonable; that the minority possess their equal rights, which equal law must protect, and to violate would be oppression.*

It is clear from the foregoing that "rightfulness" and "reasonableness," being restraints upon the will of the majority, are not themselves mere expressions of will. Here Jefferson is not only saying what the Constitution is, but why it is what it is. In truth, the "what" of the Constitution is inseparable from its "why," and the attempt to understand the former without the latter is—all but the simplest cases—vain. Yet this is precisely what Chief Justice of the Supreme Court William Rehnquist attempts when he writes, for example, that constitutional "safeguards for individual liberty" are grounded neither in "intrinsic worth" nor in "someone's idea of natural justice," but simply in the fact that "they have been incorporated in a constitution by the people." The Framers' ideas of natural justice were the very ground and origin of their intent. To appeal to the conception of "original intent" in interpreting the Constitution—as do Justices Rehnquist and Antonin Scalia and Judge Robert Bork—while denying the ideas of natural justice which formed the "why" of the Constitution, is to go to the uttermost limit of self-contradiction.

James Madison, in his essay on "Sovereignty," written near the end of his life, restated the theoretical arguments that had guided both him and Jefferson in their long political careers. The occasion, of course, was his bitter struggle against Nullification—the South Carolina doctrine whose principal author and exponent was John C. Calhoun. And the necessary condition for Calhoun's entire teaching was the rejection (like Justice Rehnquist) of the idea of natural equality—and natural justice—that had animated the Founding. Legitimate political authority, according to Madison, always arises from an agreement ("compact is the basis of all free government") made between men who are by nature—or originally—equal, none having more authority over another than the other has over him. It is the primordial fact "that all men are created equal" which is the ground both of majority rule and of minority rights. Hence it is that Lincoln would call this proposition "an abstract truth, applicable to all men and all times," and why he would, at Gettysburg, rededicate the nation to it.

Sovereignty, then, has its ground in the natural right to rule oneself that every human being possesses. Sovereignty in the political sense—what we ordinarily call sovereignty—arises when men transfer their right to rule themselves to a civil society, which can do for them what they cannot do for themselves. Civil society, according to Madison, is constituted by the unanimous consent of its constituent members. But civil society is ruled by the majority. The majority is the surrogate for that unanimity which brought the polity into being, but which cannot be the continuing basis for the decisions required by governments if they are to answer the purposes for which they are instituted. That the will of the majority should prevail is a "sacred principle" because the authority of the majority is derived from those natural rights with which all men have been equally "endowed by their Creator." A civil society is perfectly formed, to the extent that each and all of the contracting parties recognize in each other that equality of rights—and of right—which makes the will of the majority "sacred." For the majority, being the substitute or surrogate for the whole, must represent the minority as well as itself. The majority must understand that it is acting on behalf of the people as a whole, and hence the minority no less than the majority. And the minority must look upon the majority as governing in the interests of all, however much it may disagree with the particular measures adopted by the majority. We all recognize this when we speak, for example, of the representative from our congressional district as "our" representative whether we voted for him or against him. And we all recognize that the President of the United States is equally the

President of every citizen of the United States. Majority and minority are then essentially divided only by the questions of what means ought to be adopted, for the sake of the ends which are common to all. Hence the Declaration of Independence proclaims "that whenever any form of government becomes destructive of these ends, it is the right of the people to alter or to abolish it. . . ." The Declaration is speaking here of the people as a whole, but this whole is constituted by its contracting individuals. The right to "alter or abolish" belongs to any majority faced with a will external to itself—as in the case of the King and Parliament of Great Britain. But it also belongs to any minority faced with a majority that ceases, as Jefferson says, to be "reasonable," and which passes laws which violate the "equal rights" of their fellow citizens. Madison, in his essay on "Sovereignty," defines the limits of the authority of the majority by reference to whatever might be done rightfully and by unanimity. The qualification of unanimity refers back to the original constitutive principle of the polity. Unanimous consent is, however, the necessary but not the sufficient condition of government that is nondespotic. The community of Jonestown apparently committed suicide by unanimous consent. Unanimity did not make that action reasonable, or even nondespotic—surely not for the hundreds of children who were put to death by their consenting but deluded parents. Rightfulness implies moral understanding, that "rectitude" upon which the "good people" of the colonies relied in submitting their consciences to "the Supreme Judge of the world." It implies, to repeat, that "moral law" mentioned by Jefferson, without which the authority of the people itself fails. For the rights set forth in the second paragraph of the Declaration of Independence, the rights to "life, liberty, and the pursuit of happiness," are not unconditional justifications for idiosyncratic behavior. They are rights under the "laws of nature and of nature's God." They are not rights authorizing actions which, by those laws, are wrongs. Slavery was, from the outset, no mere paradox in a land of freedom. It was a contradiction of every right to which the American people had themselves appealed when asserting their own right to nondespotic government.

The constitutionalism of our Founding is inseparable from its moral realism and its natural theology. Tocqueville praised the effect of disestablishment in America and called religion the first of our political institutions precisely because of it. By removing theological differences

from the political arena, men could worship God freely according to the
dictates of their consciences. But however differently they might conceive of the divine attributes, or however different the forms of worship
which in their eyes were pleasing to God, there was a common understanding of morality underlying—or transcending—religious differences. This common understanding was strengthened by all the
churches, just by the fact that it was not called into question by their
theological differences. By strengthening this moral consensus, disestablishment promoted confidence and even friendship among the citizens. By doing so, it promoted a regime in which the rule of the majority might be consistent with the rights of the minority. But the practical
achievement of such a regime was a hard one nonetheless. Without the
doctrine of disestablishment and religious freedom it would have been
impossible.

The obstacle to Union that arose over slavery could never have been
surmounted had not the bonds of Union been sowed in the idea of
religious freedom, for the idea of religious freedom encompasses and
promotes moral law independently of any particular dogmas of revealed
religion. Equally important, it lays the foundation for the idea of limited
government in its full extent, and not only with reference to the question of religion. Why this is so, we shall presently say. First, in attempting to define the nature of its limits, let us take note of the crucial tests
in the early years of the Constitution—tests it could never have survived
had not the doctrine of religious liberty placed the religious question
outside its boundaries.

* * *

In the election of 1800, the control of the government of the United
States passed substantially from the hands of the Federalists to that of
the Republicans. To the best of my knowledge, this was the first time in
human history that any such change in the offices of government had
ever occurred on the basis of a free popular election. No such election
happened in England until well into the nineteenth century. It was not
until long after the American Revolution that the King—who could not
be constitutionally replaced by any electoral process—ceased to be the
executive head of government. Ministers were responsible to the
Crown, not to the Parliament. The King secured his majorities in Parliament, not by calling elections, but by manipulating the patronage. That
is what Alexander Hamilton had in mind when he said that without

corruption the British Constitution was unworkable. And, of course, not until after 1832 could there be said to be anything like a popular election even for the House of Commons.

During the 1790s in France, in the course of the French Revolution, something like ministerial responsibility to the elected Assembly did occur, anticipating the future course of parliamentary democracy. Unfortunately, the special ceremony for outgoing ministers made it impossible for them to form a loyal opposition or to contest future elections. The election of 1800 in the United States was the first time that the losers gave up their offices peacefully and the winners did not proscribe their defeated opponents by death, imprisonment, loss of property, exile, or even the loss of civil or political rights.

Exactly what contested elections were to mean under the new Constitution was an unresolved question until 1800. The presidency of George Washington happily postponed many such questions, while the new government gained stability and strength under the shelter of Washington's towering prestige. The election of 1796, while hotly contested, returned the party in power to office. The fact that the Constitution of 1787 called for each elector to cast two ballots for President—with the vice-presidency going to the runner-up—showed that the Framers did not anticipate the kind of partisan contests that actually developed. When Jefferson and Burr received the same electoral vote in 1800, the Constitution had to be amended so that electors henceforth distinguished their votes for President and Vice President. The Alien and Sedition Acts of 1798 revealed profound uncertainties as to what a regime of liberty meant in the face of fierce party contests for control of the government.

It cannot be emphasized too strongly, however, that America was forging the principles of modern democracy for all humanity, and doing so with no precedents to guide her. The party contests of the 1790s were the bitterest in American history—more so, even, than those that preceded the Civil War. In part, this was because the very idea of settling such deeply felt differences by free elections was an idea struggling to be born. And we must never forget that that idea required a rebirth—a new birth of freedom—before it was in any sense finally accepted, for the achievement of the election of 1800 did not survive 1860. That year, the party that lost the decision of the vote withdrew from the government rather than accept that decision.

It was Lincoln's genius to explain more lucidly and compellingly than ever before the inner connection between the great proposition of human equality and the necessity and propriety of free elections. It was Lincoln's fate to explain—in the presence of a gigantic rebellion against the decision of the polls—why the decision of the ballots might not be reversed by bullets. And it was Lincoln's fate to explain why, in the end, the war to defend the sanctity of the ballot box and the war to end slavery had to become one and the same.

But Jefferson was Lincoln's teacher. And Jefferson, who in the electoral contest of 1800 had not been lax in the invidiousness of his description of his political opponents, nonetheless declared, in his inaugural address, that:

> every difference of opinion is not a difference of principle. We have called by different names brethren of the same principle. We are all Republicans, we are all Federalists.

Jefferson did not mean by this that the electoral process was indifferent to differences of principle.

> If there be any among us who would wish to dissolve this Union or to change its republican form, let them stand undisturbed as monuments of the safety with which error of opinion may be tolerated where reason is left free to combat it.

To tolerate error is not to be indifferent to error. Jefferson did not suppose that free government could survive in the absence of sufficient and authoritative opinion in its favor. To worship God according to the dictates of one's own conscience, and not to suffer any civil disability for doing so, is not a matter of tolerance. It is a matter of right. Nor does Jefferson think that there is a right either to dissolve the Union or to change its republican form. Those who would do so merit toleration, but only because of the "safety" with which such toleration may be extended. Yet the day came when it was no longer safe to repeat Jefferson's own condemnation of slavery in many states of the Union. The day came when those states, rather than tolerate anti-slavery speech or contemplate its political consequences, attempted to dissolve the Union. Then it was that Jefferson's confidence in the power of the truth to prevail was put to a supreme test.

✿ ✿ ✿

As we have noted, in the single sentence that is the first amendment, the religious guarantees come first. The guarantees after the semicolon—speech, press, assembly, petition—are all active elements in the political process and are intended to provide for its integrity. Freedom of religion is understood to be necessary for the integrity of the political process in the negative sense that such questions as what religion should be established would be an intolerable burden upon that process. Civil and religious liberty are distinct, yet it is good that we regard them as inseparable. Their "bonding" (to use a currently fashionable phrase) is, in a peculiar sense, the achievement of the United States of America.

Consider the status of religious liberty in England—deemed by all the Founding Fathers as the freest government to precede our own, and the model for many of its features. Let us recall Lord Macaulay's celebrated passage on the Toleration Act of 1689, a constitutional pillar of the Glorious Revolution:

> The sound principle undoubtedly is, that mere theological error ought not to be punished by the civil magistrate. This principle the Toleration Act not only does not recognize, but positively disclaims. . . . Persecution continues to be the general rule. Toleration is the exception. . . . That the provisions . . . are cumbrous, puerile, inconsistent with each other, inconsistent with the true theory of religious liberty, must be acknowledged. All that can be said in their defense is this: that they removed a vast mass of evil without shocking a vast mass of prejudice.

It was wonderful that such a vast mass of evil was removed by this great law. It was wise of the Parliament not to attempt to assert "the true theory of religious liberty" in the face of such "a vast mass of prejudice." We are reminded that a nation can proceed upon the ground of a "true theory" in the face of such prejudice only by imposing upon the nation a will external to the nation itself. This alternative was known to our Founding Fathers as "enlightened despotism," but they rejected it on the ground that the enlightened consent of the governed was the only durable foundation for free or good government. But the necessity for enlightenment in the consent of the governed was never far from their thoughts. Free government was never possible apart from it. The foundations of American government, wrote Washington in 1783,

> were not laid in the gloomy ages of ignorance and superstition, but at an epoch when the rights of mankind were better understood and more clearly defined than at any other period.

And wrote Jefferson in 1816:

> If a nation expects to be ignorant and free in a state of civilization, it expects what never was and never will be.

The American Revolution and the American Constitution became possible only because the rights of man as man—the rights of an enlightened humanity under the moral order of the laws of nature and of nature's God—defined the ground of civic friendship, subordinating the ancient distinctions, not only of religion but of ethnicity and race. Among the most remarkable but least-remarked features of the Declaration of Independence is the passage in which, after assigning a measure of responsibility to "our British brethren" for the tyrannical acts of their government, the Americans "hold them, as we hold the rest of mankind, enemies in war, in peace friends." The ancient distinctions of Greek and barbarian, of Jew and Gentile, of Christian and infidel, here disappear as the ground of human friendship and therewith of civic association.

It is true that the distinction is made, within the Declaration, between civilization on the one hand, and barbarism and savagery on the other. The distinction between the first and the latter two is the distinction between those who do and those who do not respect the rights of others, under the laws of nature. Of course, the necessary ground for such respect is enlightenment: One cannot act on principles of which one is ignorant. As I have often written, the United States is the first nation in the world to declare its independence, not because of any particular qualities or merits of its own, but because of rights which it shared with all men everywhere. In so doing, it declared the ground of "government of the people, by the people, for the people" in a sense absolutely unprecedented. In so doing, it laid an equally unprecedented claim to the character of the best regime of Western civilization.

This latter claim cannot be understood in the light of the doctrine of the best regime as it is found, for example, in Plato and Aristotle. For them, the best regime was that of "the examined life" as defined by Socratic skepticism. Moral virtue, although necessary for human happiness, did not represent in itself the highest of all possible ends: that was to be found in purely contemplative activity. Biblical religion, however, found not the examined life, but the life of obedient love of the living God, to be the highest of all possible ends of human existence. Like classical philosophy, biblical religion finds that man's highest end transcends morality. For man's highest end, his relationship with God, is a transmoral end. Biblical religion presupposes a living God whose existence is primarily and essentially a matter of faith. Whatever demonstrations unassisted reason might make of God's existence and attributes may complement or supplement the teachings of faith. But they can never supplant faith as the ground of belief.

Philosophy, the way of life grounded upon the powers of unassisted human reason, can never refute the existence of the biblical God or the possibility that the best way of life is not that of the examined life. The skepticism that is the core of philosophy, the honest skepticism that must always be distinguished from dogmatic skepticism, always leaves philosophy open to the challenge of revelation. It always leaves philosophers open to the undeniable fact that the claims of autonomous human reason cannot be fully vindicated by that reason. It always leaves philosophers open to the possibility that the fully consistent life—the life that the philosopher himself longs for above all others—is possible only on the basis of revelation.

What we call Western civilization is to be found primarily and essentially in the confluence of the autonomous rationalism of classical philosophy and the faith of biblical religion. As Leo Strauss has said, the vitality—and the glory—of Western civilization is to be found above all in the "mutual influence" of these two irrefutable, irreducible principles of human life. The dynamic of Western civilization is the dynamic of their interaction. The triumph of Western civilization is to be found in the evidence, supplied by both philosophy and revelation, that the human soul, no less by the questions it asks than by the answers it believes it has discovered, participates in a reality that transcends all time and change. The tragedy of Western civilization has been the unfettered attempt, by political means, to vindicate claims whose very nature excludes the possibility that they can be vindicated by political means. To attempt to overcome the skepticism that is the ground of philosophy is like trying to jump over one's own shadow. To attempt to remove the necessity of the free and unconstrained faith that is the ground of the Bible and of biblical religion is like denying the existence of the shadow by jumping only in the dark—or with one's eyes shut!

The unprecedented character of the American Founding is that it provided for the coexistence of the claims of reason and of revelation in all their forms, without requiring or permitting any political decisions concerning them. It refused to make unassisted human reason the arbiter of the claims of revelation, and it refused to make revelation the judge of the claims of reason. It is the first regime in Western civilization to do this, and for that reason it is, in its principles or speech (leaving aside the question of its practice or deeds), the best regime.

But the virtue of the American Founding rests not only upon its defusing of the tension between reason and revelation, but upon their fundamental agreement on a moral code which can guide human life both privately and publicly. This moral code is the work both of "Nature's God"—reason—and the "Creator"—revelation. Religious freedom properly understood is a principle which emancipates political life not only from sectarian religious conflict, but from the far profounder conflict between reason and revelation. Indeed, it makes reason and revelation—for the first time—open friends and allies on the political level. For they are, to repeat, agreed upon the nature and role of morality in the good society.

But radical modernity is the enemy equally of autonomous human reason and of biblical revelation. The core of radical modernity is radical skepticism, a dogmatic skepticism that denies that we do have, or can have, any genuine knowledge of the external world. This dogmatic skepticism denies that either philosophy or revelation in the traditional understanding are possible. It denies that either Socrates or the prophets could ever have distinguished, as Thomas Hobbes put it, whether God had spoken to them in dreams or they had dreamed that God had spoken to them. Hobbes was the precursor of modern scientific positivism, which regards all knowledge as essentially hypothetical and experimental. Its core conviction is that we know only what we make. In constructing a world from hypotheses, we ourselves are the source of all creativity: there is neither need nor room for God. In constructing a world from hypotheses, we have a priori perfect knowledge of that world: there is neither need nor room for philosophy.

Since there is no *a priori* knowledge in nature or of nature (no "self-evident" truths) to guide the human will, the human will must itself be the a priori source of all knowledge. Unfettered will is the ground, then, of all morality. That is why National Socialism—which understood itself as "The Triumph of the Will"—is the prototypical modern regime. Long before Hitler, though, it was Marx who wrote: "The philosophers have hitherto only interpreted the world. The point, however, is to change it." Marx meant by this that traditional philosophy—an attempt to interpret or understand the world—was illusory. He believed that genuine knowledge of the world was possible only by changes in the world that originated in one's will. Hence the highest form of intellectual activity—of philosophy—was to be found not in speculation or theory, but in practice or revolution. The supreme revolutionary is the supreme philosopher. The outcome of the most radical revolution is therefore the highest form of wisdom. Hence "the inner truth and greatness" of Hitler's revolution and of Stalin's is one and the same. As such it is beyond skepticism. To doubt becomes treason and is punishable as such, for the aim or purpose of radical modernity—of modern philosophy in its final form—is the elimination of skepticism from human life, the transcendence of the opposition between reason and revelation by the abolition of both.

Dogmatic skepticism leads, then, to a scientism, of which totalitarian regimes are the natural and culminating manifestations. But the scientism of dogmatic skepticism is today endemic to the universities of the free world. This dogmatic skepticism is typically expressed as "value relativism," and is found in the writings of the Chief Justice of the United States as well as those of nearly all the so-called philosophers and social scientists of our universities. "Value relativism" is commonly but mistakenly associated with toleration of different opinions. In fact, it denies the rational or divine foundation of any virtue, including that of tolerance. But if there is no human or divine reason to prefer one opinion to another, neither is there any such reason to prefer one regime to another. If knowledge is power, the most powerful opinion is the best opinion. And there is no reason why the most powerful opinion—from which any skepticism concerning its own truth has been eliminated—should give place to any less powerful opinion. Relativism thus undermines the confidence that free government once had in its own truth, the kind of confidence with which the United States in 1776 proclaimed its right to an equal station among the powers of the earth. Relativism thus leads ultimately but inevitably toward the worst forms of tyranny.

It is sometimes said that the American Founding, as an expression of modern (notably Lockean) political philosophy, lowers the ends of human life in order to make them more easily attainable. For Americans, comfortable self-preservation, implemented by free-market economics and the scientific enhancement of man's productive powers, replaces eternal salvation or contemplation as the end of man. Whatever may be true of the thought of John Locke, this is not the way in which the American Founding understood itself. The American Founding limited the ends of government. It did not limit the ends of man. The ends of the regime, considered as ends of government, were lowered. But the ends both of reason and revelation served by the regime, in and through the limitations on government, were understood to enhance, not to diminish, the intrinsic possibility of human excellence. As long as the idea of human excellence itself survived, as understood by the great tradition of Western civilization—the civilization of the Bible and of classical philosophy—the dignity of the American Founding remained that of man's highest ends. It is the outright denial—within the very citadels of learning, the universities—of the dignity of reason and of revelation that threatens the eclipse of the American Founding, and therewith of Western civilization itself.

✿ ✿ ✿

We have noted Macaulay's reference to "the true theory of religious liberty." This theory has its classic affirmation in the Virginia Statute of Religious Liberty of 1786, whose author was Thomas Jefferson. It is often said, and correctly, that Jefferson wrote with Locke's *Letters on Toleration* before him. But Jefferson, in writing that "our civil rights have no dependence on our religious opinions any more than our opinions in physics or geometry," was more absolute and categorical than Locke. Jefferson allowed no exceptions for Jews, Catholics, or atheists. (This, incidentally, did not mean that he was an atheist any more than it meant that he was a Jew or a Catholic!) If "the true theory of religious liberty" was not recognized by the laws of England in the seventeenth or eighteenth centuries, neither was it recognized in the public laws of any other government before the American Founding. Indeed, it could not be so recognized as long as the ground of political authority was understood to originate in divine law. In the American Founding, the social contract theory of the Declaration of Independence and the doctrine of religious liberty in the Virginia Statute—both authored by Jefferson—are two sides of one coin. The rights with which all men are by nature equally endowed qualify any man to enter into an agreement with any other man (who is willing to agree with him) to form a civil society.

Political obligations are obligations flowing from such an agreement, and obeying the law is simply keeping one's promise. The authority of government is collective promise-keeping of all the parties to the social contract. Such a contract, by its nature, excludes religious stipulations, since any such stipulations or reservations would be inconsistent with the equality which is the foundation or condition of the contract. Moreover, the sovereignty of the individual who is the party to the social contract means that the government arising from this contract is limited government. This follows from the intrinsic nature of contract itself. A contract can only be made between equals, and can obligate no further than the intentions of the contracting parties.

Here we reflect upon the radical novelty, two hundred years ago, of the idea of limited government based upon the social contract of men created equal. The ancient city understood itself altogether as a creation of divine law. We are familiar, from the Old Testament, with the ancient Mosaic polity. We read it for the story of God's covenant with Israel and the origins of the Messianic promise which Christians believe was fulfilled in Jesus. However unique the Bible is in these respects, in others it is typical. The conception of political obligation—as set forth in the Declaration of Independence—simply did not exist for ancient man.

Plato's *Laws* begins with the Athenian Stranger asking the Cretan and the Spartan, "A god, is it, or some human being, who is credited with laying down your laws?" The Cretan answers for both himself and the Spartan, "A god, Stranger, a god." Ancient man obeyed the laws because they were of divine, not human origin. If a city was defeated in war, that meant its gods were defeated by stronger gods, and men might, without any sense of disloyalty, transfer their allegiance to the gods of their masters. Here the Jews were different in that by holding that their God alone was God, they would not admit that their God could be defeated—nor that they could have any just reason to be faithless to him.

The conception of religion, as we understand it, was as unknown to Socrates as it was unknown to Moses or to Jesus, for we distinguish religious from nonreligious spheres of life, just as we distinguish church from state, state from society, and society from government. In denying the charge of impiety, it seems never to have occurred to Socrates to deny that impiety was a crime. In defending his philosophical mission, he did so by discovering its origin in a command of the oracle of Delphi—a god recognized by the city of Athens. He insisted that it would be impious for him to disobey that command. The worship of the golden calf was a revolt against the authority of Moses—and of God. There was no ground for distinguishing the infidelity of the rebelling Israelites from their lawlessness, since there was no other source of law than God. In this, however, we see the principle of every ancient city, and not of Israel alone.

The laws of Moses regulated all aspects of human life, mental as well as physical, private as well as public. If we think of orthodox Judaism today, we think of freely chosen personal obligations. But in ancient Israel, these laws were inescapable. We have recently had something of a glimpse of the ancient city in the Islamic republicanism of the Ayatollah Khomeini and in the exhortations of Meir Kahane. How typical of the ancient city were the laws of Moses, however, we may glean from Aristotle's dictum: "Whatever the laws do not permit, they forbid." It took one of the greatest revolutions in human consciousness to change that to "Whatever the laws do not forbid, they permit."

In the New Testament, we see ancient Israel not as an independent polity, but as a conquered province of the Roman empire. When Jesus said to render to Caesar the things that were Caesar's and to God what was God's, he was making an eminently prudent statement. Contrary to a common opinion, he was not distinguishing between church and state, private and public, or religion and government. Jews had to pay tribute because the Roman legions were there to enforce payment—and to crucify anyone who resisted the authority of Rome. But the Romans were interested only in collecting tribute, and were content to let the peoples they had conquered live under their own laws and gods—these being indistinguishable. Had Jesus lived at the time of Moses or Joshua or David or Solomon, he would never have distinguished, as he did, between God and Caesar. Hence Jesus never meant to characterize all political authority as that of Caesar. When he spoke of "Caesar" he was not speaking symbolically; he meant the conqueror of his people, whose regime rested upon force alone. Government deriving its just powers from the consent of the governed is no more properly characterized as "Caesar" than is the government of ancient Israel under the laws of Moses. Nevertheless, it was the transformation of the Rome of the Caesars into the Holy Roman Empire that ended the ancient world and created the distinction—and opposition—of church and state.

The ancient world—the world of the ancient city—may be said to have come to an end when, in the third century of the Christian era, the Roman emperors extended Roman citizenship to the provinces. This, we observe, represented less of an elevation of the provinces than it did a leveling of Rome. Rome had become an imperial military despotism. The emperor's horse—or perhaps merely the latter half of his horse— could become a Senator. The self-governing institutions of republican Rome were dead. Rome was the administrative center of a regime that had no political center, because "the government of men had been replaced by the administration of things." The heart of the process whereby politics is replaced by administration is presented to us unforgettably in Shakespeare's *Antony and Cleopatra*.

Rome's conquest of the ancient world ended the civic life of the independent polis. The gods of the conquered cities continued a shadowy existence for some time. When, however, everyone might become a Roman citizen, there was in principle but one authority for law. The gods who had been the many authors of the many laws of the many cities flickered out and died. There was only one city, which was no longer an ancient city, but the empire of the world. But by the logic of the ancient city—which to this point dominated the consciousness of civilized mankind—a single source of law implied a single God. It took little more than a century after the extension of Roman citizenship to the provinces before Constantine's conversion to Christianity began the process of transforming Rome (and the world understood as Rome) from polytheism to monotheism. Whether there was a providential necessity in this—as Aquinas and Dante and Shakespeare seem to have thought—there was certainly an inherent compulsion of reason in saying: one city, one law, one world, one God. That this God should be the

God of Israel partakes of the same logic, for the God of Israel was not only understood to be the only God, but one who transcended the universe of which He was held to be Creator. Such a God could not be defeated by the legions of Rome or of any other power, whether in the world or out of the world.

The establishment of Christianity in the Roman empire obeyed the logic of the ancient city, in that membership in the political association carried the implied requirement of acknowledgment of, and obedience to, the God of that empire. The concept of heresy was virtually unknown to the ancient city. What Socrates was accused of is better understood as resembling what we might call being "un-American," that is, of disloyalty. Ancient cities lived on narrow margins of survival, and defeat in war could mean extinction or slavery. All the civic gods tended to be jealous gods for that reason. Belief as such was not central to fidelity. Obedience was central. But the Christian empire made belief central to fidelity, and heresy assumed an unprecedented gravity as an offense against the good order not merely of civil society, but of the world. While belief was elevated to an unprecedented level, obedience sank correspondingly. The decline and fall of the ancient empire replaced centralized Roman administration with the most decentralized, and most lawless, of regimes: feudalism. The Christian God of the Holy Roman Empire was not the author of the laws of France, Germany, England, Spain, or any other part of the Holy Roman Empire, in the sense in which He had been the author of the laws of Moses. He was the sanction for obedience to all the rulers—or laws—that were to be obeyed. But these laws were regarded as laws for a variety of reasons, ancient custom or tradition being foremost. And the divine law—the characteristic form of all law in the ancient world—was no longer the law of the earthly but of the heavenly city.

The extension of Roman citizenship to the provinces, followed by the establishment of Christianity, created a problem that went unsolved in the Christian West for a millennium and a half. That problem was how to discover a source of law for particular political communities within the larger framework of the cosmopolis of the city of God. A single political structure for all of Christendom, much less all of mankind, proved to be impossible. As Thomas Aquinas taught, human law must embody the prudence of the ruler. But who ought to be the ruler? And how are the governed to recognize their obligation to obey him?

Aristotle addressed himself to the question of who should rule, and did so in terms of the moral and intellectual excellences that might comprise regimes. His answers were designed to gain acquiescence by philosophers and gentlemen. But he expected the generality of mankind to accept the judgments of the wise because they would be attributed to the gods. Thomas followed Aristotle, but Aristotle offered no solution to the problem of Christian empire. Dante, in one of the most remarkable works ever composed, developed an argument for universal empire based upon Aristotle's *Metaphysics*, while ignoring his *Politics*. This fact itself illuminates wonderfully the dilemma of the Christian West—and the causes of the wars of the Reformation—before the American Revolution.

In Protestant countries, the Reformation removed the anointing (and the excommunicating) of secular rulers from the jurisdiction of Rome. The doctrine of the divine right of kings was invented to enable kings to be anointed by bishops they had themselves appointed, rather than by appointees of the Pope. The interests of national kings and their peoples were certainly closer than those of popes or emperors. But however much the interest of kings and their peoples might seem close at a time of national peril—as at the time of the Spanish Armada—at other times they might be in the harshest conflict, with ensuing revolutions and civil wars. The national Church of England, established by Henry VIII's break with Rome, had as its most fundamental doctrine that of passive obedience to the king, under all circumstances and at any cost. But such a doctrine could not survive the contingency of the King himself becoming Catholic. In the Glorious Revolution of 1689, the Church of England itself was converted from the divine right of kings to popular sovereignty, exercised in and through the Parliament.

Long before the writings of Hobbes and Locke, Christianity sowed the seed of what we have come to call individualism by establishing a direct personal relationship between God and every human being. Nothing dramatizes this better than the opening scene in Bunyan's Pilgrim's Progress, in which Christian is fleeing from his family, crying out "What shall I do to be saved?" Salvation—citizenship in the City of God—is individual. Individuals are held to be saved by Christ's merit, but not by that of father or mother or brother. I do not mean to say that Christianity in any way devalued the family, only that family, clan, tribe, nation, the community of blood descendants, ceased to have the integral moral, political, and religious unity they possessed in the ancient city. A citizen of ancient Israel, living under the laws that God had given to Moses, believed himself to be already living in the city of God. In the ancient city—and the Old Testament here is typical—the individual sees himself primarily as a link in the chain of ancestors and descendants. Individuality—including personal immortality—plays virtually no role as a paramount concern. In the Christian Roman Empire, the Church was the visible representative of the City of God, but the City itself was not of this world. As personal immortality in the City of God came to be the paramount concern of Western man, political life was displaced from the central place in human life it had occupied in the ancient city.

The social contract theory embodied in the American Declaration of Independence solved a problem that had plagued Western civilization for more than a millennium and a half. Political authority was to be rooted in each particular political society as the result of the voluntary action of naturally free and equal individuals, whose natural freedom and equality was seen to be as much a dispensation of God as membership in the City of God. These free and equal individuals are enfranchised in the rights that they bring with them into civil society by the fact that they are a priori under the universal "laws of nature and of nature's God." There is then no tension between one's membership in that larger community, which in principle embraces all mankind, and one's particular obligations to one's own community, here and now. The Declaration of Independence recognizes, as did the medieval church, the divine government of the universe. But this government, while providing a pattern for human government, does not cause any divided allegiance in one's political obligation here on earth. The role played by the power of the Church to excommunicate rulers, and to dissolve the allegiance of their subjects, becomes in the Declaration the right of revolution.

But the power of the church—that is to say, of all the churches, or of whatever means a man may choose to direct his own way to his highest end—remains free of civil authority. This bonding of civil and religious liberty is the core of the idea of limited government, and hence of freedom in our world, for we are compelled both to rely upon and to enjoy a degree of personal autonomy that was inconceivable in the ancient city. But the principles by which this autonomy is to be guided—what Jefferson called the moral law—remain the same. And the ground of that autonomy is still the revelation and the reason that are our inheritance from the ancient cities of Athens and Jerusalem. The new order of the ages is radically novel in its solution of the political problem within the framework of a cosmopolitan, monotheistic universe. It is radically traditional in its conception of the ends, whether of reason or of revelation, to be served by that order.

Today we are faced with an unprecedented threat to the survival of biblical religion, of autonomous human reason, and to the form and substance of political freedom. It is important to understand why the threat to one of these is also the threat to all. It is above all important to understand why this threat is, above all, an internal one, mining and sapping our ancient faith, both in God and in ourselves. The decline of the West is the paramount reality facing us today. Perhaps our most immediate danger comes from the historical pessimism of those who counsel us that this is inevitable and that nothing can be done by taking thought. But this danger is itself a danger only if we believe it. It is precisely by taking thought that this superstition can be dispelled and, with it, the unreasoning fears that it breeds. As we enter this third century of the Constitution, let us renew our ancient faith, the faith of Abraham Lincoln,

> that right make might, and in that faith let us, to the end, dare to do our duty *as we* understand it.

NOTES

1. Harry V. Jaffa, with Bruce Ledewitz, Robert L. Stone, George Anastaplo, Foreword by Lewis E. Lehrman, *Original Intent and the Framers of the Constitution: A Disputed Question* (Washington, D.C.: Regnery Gateway, 1994).

2. Harry V. Jaffa, *American Conservatism and the American Founding* (Durham, NC: Carolina Academic Press, 1984).

7

THE DECLINE AND FALL OF THE AMERICAN IDEA

Reflections on the Failure of American Conservatism

INTRODUCTION

"The Decline and Fall of the American Idea: Reflections on the Failure of American Conservatism" is published here for the first time, along with the transcript of Harvey C. Mansfield's response (prepared for the 25th Anniversary Symposium of the Henry Salvatori Center for the Study of Individual Freedom, Claremont McKenna College, Claremont, California, April 18–20, 1996). The transcript is followed by three unanswered letters from Jaffa to Mansfield, also published for the first time. In the first unanswered letter, Jaffa proposed a continuation of the debate begun at the conference sponsored by the Henry Salvatori Center at Claremont McKenna College. Mansfield, like many of Jaffa's critics, refused the invitation for reasons that remain unknown, although his reluctance may have stemmed from a personal distaste for the kind of no-holds-barred polemical disputes that Jaffa preferred, or perhaps his reluctance stemmed from a recognition of Jaffa's superior dialectical skills. We do, nevertheless, have something of a dialogue in Jaffa's letters to Mansfield since Jaffa answers, almost line by line, Mansfield's conference responses. Had Mansfield accepted Jaffa's challenge, however, we would surely have benefited from a debate between two intellectual giants discussing at the highest level the most serious issues facing the American polity.

In the transcript Mansfield accuses of Jaffa of lurking behind the battle lines in the war with ideological liberalism and shooting fellow conservatives in the back. This charge stems from the fact that Jaffa asserts the "self-evident truth" that "all men are created equal" is the central principle of the American Founding. Mansfield believes this puts Jaffa at odds with conservatives and on the side of the liberals since any reference to equality as a regime principle will inevitably degenerate into permissive egalitarianism.

In the conference paper, Jaffa examines the opinions of prominent conservatives of all stripes and subjects their arguments to severe scrutiny, demonstrating how each rejects the principles of the Founding—even those who profess fealty to those principles! Liberals and conservatives equally reject the principles of the Founding because they reject the Declaration of Independence. Mansfield and other conservatives have, in the most fundamental respects, joined the liberals who likewise reject the principles of the Founding. Jaffa argues, however, that conservatism has no future if it is not grounded in the *conservative* principles of the Declaration. Thus in defecting to the side of the ideological liberals, Mansfield and conservatives have joined the liberal skirmish line firing against Jaffa.

Mansfield provides the most thoughtful and radical criticism of the Founding. Principles—natural law or natural right—are not relevant for understanding the American Founding or any political founding. Mansfield supposedly takes Aristotle as his authority, who he says contends that there is nothing behind the political. All politics are therefore partisan, and all claims of justice are partisan claims. The fact that the Founders appealed to "the Laws of Nature and Nature's God" was either a way to disguise their partisanship or it was a self-deception.

Jaffa defends natural law and natural right; his opponents, both liberal and conservative, defend positive rights or partisanship. He sees the issues of what Leo Strauss called the "theological-political" dilemma being played out in the drama of the American Founding where, for the first time in human history, reason and revelation conspired to create a regime based on "the Laws of Nature and of Nature's God." Jaffa challenged Mansfield to show that the Founders believed their work was merely a matter of partisanship, that principles of natural law and natural right were not the principles they relied upon to inform their work. The same challenge could be made in the case for Aristotle, who famously advanced the idea that natural right was an essential part of political right. If it is true, as Aristotle claims, that man is by nature a political being, then natural right is more or less part of every political community. The degree to which natural right can manifest itself depends on particular circumstances and whether or not practically wise statesmen ("enlightened statesmen") are present to measure what is best under the circumstances against what is best simply. Jaffa argues that the fundamental (and antecedent) political-theological question is always an essential part of any consideration of natural right as a part of political right.

Mansfield seems to believe that Machiavelli killed the possibility of natural right; he thus rejects Aristotle in favor of Machiavelli and effective truth, as Jaffa argues in a few terse paragraphs in the third unanswered letter. Mansfield has rendered a great disservice to the scholarly and political world by his refusal to engage Jaffa. The republic of letters that Mansfield has created among some followers of Leo Strauss looks with disdain at the criticism of non-initiates.

This chapter consists of Jaffa's lecture, "The Decline and Fall of the American Idea"; an exchange between Jaffa and Mansfield; an Afterword by Jaffa and three open letters from Jaffa to Mansfield. The editors thank Hillsdale College for permission to print these previously unpublished materials.

THE DECLINE AND FALL OF THE AMERICAN IDEA: REFLECTIONS ON THE FAILURE OF AMERICAN CONSERVATISM, BY *HARRY V. JAFFA*

the ideas of economists and political philosophers, both when they are right and when they are wrong, are more powerful than is commonly understood. Indeed, the world is ruled by little else. Practical men, who believe themselves to be quite exempt from any intellectual influences, are usually the slaves of some defunct economist. Madmen in authority, who hear voices in the air, are distilling their frenzy from some academic scribbler of a few years back. I am sure that the power of vested interests is vastly exaggerated compared with the gradual encroachment of ideas. Not, indeed immediately, but after a certain interval; for in the field of economic and political philosophy there are not many who are influenced by new theories after they are twenty-five or thirty years of age, so that the ideas which civil servants and politicians and even agitators apply to current events are not likely to be the newest. But, soon or late, it is ideas, not vested interests, which are dangerous for good or evil. —John Maynard Keynes, from the last paragraph of the *General Theory of Employment, Interest, and Money*, 1935.

I

In contemplating the quarter century of the Salvatori Center, we can take heart in the great triumph of freedom represented by the fall of the Evil Empire. That triumph has now been celebrated often enough that we need not dwell on it at length. Over the forty year period of the Cold War, American policy amid many turns and twists and even some remarkable failures, showed nonetheless remarkable consistency: from Churchill's Iron Curtain speech ("The Sinews of Peace") in 1946, followed by the enunciation of the policy of containment by Harry Truman a year later, until Ronald Reagan sounded the trumpets that brought down the walls of the Evil Empire.

In the collapse into the "dustbin of history" of the regimes presided over by Hitler and Stalin we have much reason to rejoice. But we should remember Scipio, weeping amid the ruins of Carthage, who saw foreshadowed therein the fate of Rome itself. Like Rome then, we are at a peak of power and influence unprecedented—even by Rome—in the history of the world. We have every reason to rejoice in the power of our free institutions. We ought not to be disheartened by the apparent mindlessness, as it seems sometimes, of the political process. The Constitution was designed to bring about results better than any envisioned in the day to day activities of politicians and parties. Hegel's "cunning of history" may have been an illusion. The cunning of our constitutional regime is not. In *Federalist* #10, Madison recognized the role of factions in a free society, and the difficulty of bringing just laws out of the welter of mean spirited conflict.

It is vain to say that enlightened statesmen will be able to adjust these clashing interests, and render them subservient to the public good. Enlightened statesmen will not always be at the helm.

Madison believed that the Constitution could make the clashing interests subservient to the public good, even in the absence of enlightened statesmen. More precisely, he believed that the statesmanship of the wise and the good that went into the architecture of the Constitution would compensate for the lack of wisdom and virtue in those who would thereafter dwell within its precincts. But neither Madison nor anyone else ever imagined that it would compensate entirely, or over too great periods of time, or in the presence of great crises, for the absence of wisdom and virtue. Above all, it would not compensate for too great ignorance of the Constitution itself, or of the reasons why the Constitution—if not the politicians and parties—deserved to be respected and revered.

Every four years, before entering upon the duties of his office, a president takes an oath to preserve, protect, and defend the Constitution. That oath, however, represents more than a commitment by the person taking it. It represents a covenant between him and the citizens, whose president he has become. He cannot support his oath, unless his lawful actions are supported by the people. In Lincoln's words, it is public opinion that makes it possible, or impossible, for laws to be executed. The obligations of the president, in fulfilling his oath, are the mirror images of the obligations of the citizens to that same Constitution and the laws made in pursuance thereof.

In 1838, in his Lyceum address on "The Perpetuation of Our Political Institutions," Lincoln surveyed the danger upon his horizon.

Shall we expect some transatlantic military giant to step the Ocean, and crush us at a blow? Never!—All the armies of Europe, Asia and Africa combined, with all the treasure of the earth (our own excepted) in their military chest; with a Buonaparte for a commander, could not by force, take a drink from the Ohio, or make track on the Blue Ridge, in a trial of a thousand years.

At what point then is the approach of danger to be expected? I answer, if ever it reach us, it must spring up amongst us. It cannot come from abroad. If destruction be our lot, we must ourselves be its author and finisher. As a nation of freemen, we must live through all time, or die by suicide.

The view Lincoln expresses here of our international security is not intended to be a sober assessment of our strategic place in the world, although it had at least a superficial plausibility in 1838. It is meant to lend greater emphasis to the reality of the internal danger, which was far more than merely plausible. It was just a quarter century that separated the Lyceum speech from the firing on Fort Sumter. Had the Union failed to survive—as very nearly happened—the United States may well have had "death by suicide" upon its epitaph.

We are told by the Gettysburg Address that the nation was conceived in liberty and dedicated at its birth to the proposition that all men are created equal. The Civil War was a test, whether that nation, or any nation, so conceived and so dedicated, might endure. In the years intervening between the Revolution and the Civil War a large part of the nation had fallen away from the principles of its Founding. It had done so, driven in part by the exigencies of slavery, but still more by the abandonment of the belief in the natural law and natural rights expressed in the Declaration of Independence. Lincoln viewed this falling away much as the prophets of Israel had looked upon the sins of their people. Lincoln, the prophet-statesman, recalled the American people to the "ancient faith" that had given them life as a nation.

Our situation has some remarkable similarities, as well as obvious differences, from Lincoln's. The division within the nation does not correspond with any geographical line. Nor are the consequences of the division focused upon a single issue, although the differences over abortion, by itself, bear a striking resemblance to the differences over slavery. The nation is suffering, more than anything else, from the multiple effects of what Alan Keyes has called the dissolution of the marriage based family, which means the dissolution of the moral substance at the core of Western civilization as a whole. There are neighborhoods in our central cities encompassing many millions nationwide, in which there are virtually no marriage based families at all. Even outside the central cities, there are many millions of single parent households, some of whose female heads have never been married, some of whom have been married but abandoned, some divorced, nearly all in badly straitened circumstances. Nor is this confined to the welfare culture, or to blacks. Some time ago, Larry King had a caller who was a high school senior in a well-to-do white Atlanta suburb. She complained that she was something of an outsider to her peer group, since she was the only one in her class whose parents had not been divorced. Clearly, the dissolution of the marriage based family has affected all classes and all income levels. From this single fact has come a plethora of the social pathologies that preoccupy us in the political arena: abortion, crime, drugs, unemployment, low educational achievement, low productivity. At the core of the problem of the dissolving family is the dissolving morality that supported the family. When was the last time any one of us heard an illegitimate child called a "bastard"? When was the last time an errant daughter was driven into the snow by an enraged father? Certainly ours is a "kinder, gentler" society. Illegitimacy, and divorce and abortion—and sexual promiscuity generally—have lost their stigma, and have become not merely commonplace, but acceptable as normal and moral. The distinctions between right and wrong, good and bad, just and unjust, as they apply to wide areas of human behavior, have been attenuated to the point of irrelevance. Nowhere is that more evident than in the acceptance of homosexuality. Although more than twenty states still have antisodomy laws, the word "sodomy" is rarely pronounced. The euphemism "gay" has replaced it entirely, in conversation, in newspapers, magazines, and in political discourse. Yet the word itself, in this sense, is not even to be found in dictionaries except the most recent. "Don we now our gay apparel," in the traditional Christmas carol would, in present parlance, refer to transvestitism, not to the happy celebration of the birth of a child. Along with the aforementioned euphemism is a matching pejorative, "homophobia."[1] It implies that refusal to accept homosexuality as normal and moral, must represent an irrational passion. By this one word, anyone who even questions the morality of homosexuality is condemned in advance and without argument. We find words assimilated into our vocabulary that subvert our moral understanding, sometimes without our even being aware of the fact.

Dinesh D'Souza's monumental work, *The End of Racism*, has as its main thesis that moral relativism, not race prejudice, is the cause of most of the phenomena that are characterized as racist today. The title of the book is justified by the hypothesis that when we stop calling racist things that are not properly called racist, there will, for all practical purposes, be an end of racism. Like the "poverty industry" and its huge bureaucracy that thrives on poverty, there is a "civil rights industry." It too has its own bureaucracy, both governmental and non-governmental, with thousands of well-paying jobs, and with enormous patronage and profits. It lives and prospers by continuing to discover "racism," a concept which has become as pervasive, elusive, and multifaceted as original sin. The civil rights bureaucracy is particularly adept at discovering racism where it also discovers deep pockets. The fear of being called racist leads to widespread blackmail and extortion, not only of money, but of a wide variety of undeserved favors and preferments. D'Souza's book is an honorable and memorable addition to the venerable journalistic tradition of muckraking, in which scholarship of a high order is brought to bear in exposing fraud and deceit.

A review in the *Wall Street Journal* of Mary Lefkowitz's *Not Out of Africa* tells of a Martin Luther King Memorial Lecture at Wellesley. The lecturer—with a fashionably exotic name—declared that Aristotle had stolen all his philosophy from the books of African authors in the library in Alexandria. When Professor Lefkowitz pointed out that Aristotle died before the library was built, she was given short shrift. When she complained to her Dean, she was told that "everyone had a different but 'equally valid' view of history." What constitutes equally valid Afrocentric history is illuminated by that great scholar and savant, the Reverend Al Sharpton, who is quoted as saying that "white folks was in the caves while we was building empires. . . . We taught philosophy and astrology and mathematics before Socrates and them Greek homos ever got around to it." Perhaps the Reverend Sharpton should have added grammar to astrology!

Surely the foregoing provides the kind of amusement that made the Kingfish in "Amos and Andy" so popular in the 1930s. In those days, the intellectual pretensions of *any* black-person were regarded as entertainment, like a dog walking on its hind legs, as Dr. Johnson might have said. Such condescension sixty years ago was certainly deplorable, but it was largely unselfconscious and even innocent. When however a dean at Wellesley (or Harvard) commends the academic validity of a minstrel show performance, he is far more demeaning of human dignity than any re-run of Amos and Andy. If moreover history—the account of events in time—could ignore chronology, then it would quite literally cease to exist.

We know however that Nazi "history," "proving" the inferiority of Negroes and Jews, and no more fallacious than the aforesaid King memorial lecture, would not be granted equal standing at Wellesley or at any recognized academic institution in this country. The Wellesley dean's assertion of the equal validity of different conceptions of history would not apply to Hitler's. What the dean meant was the equal validity of politically correct conceptions of history. And who decides what is politically correct? Obviously, those who are politically correct! The Afrocentrists—or the patrons of Afrocentrism—might reply that it is unacceptable to employ rationalism (or "logism") to challenge the proposition that Aristotle—after his death—stole from African authors in the library at Alexandria. Rationalism, they say, is Eurocentric, and as much a culture-bound mode of thinking as any other, and cannot therefore be used to contradict a mode of thinking enshrined in a different culture. The difficulty with this reply, however, is that the Afrocentric culture they celebrate is grounded in European, not African culture. Cultural relativism and its derivatives are not to be found in non-European cultures. The charge of Eurocentrism is itself Eurocentric!

Dinesh D'Souza's analysis is sound in tracing the obsession with racism to cultural relativism. Here is a case of the frenzy of academic scribblers dominating the minds of the most powerful elites in a whole society. That different conceptions of history—or of any systems of morals or politics—are equally valid certainly underlies the multicultural condemnation of the alleged hegemony of Western civilization. D'Souza is certainly right in pointing out that cultural relativism is itself a unique feature of Western civilization. It is not true, however, that there is any necessary or rational connection between cultural (or moral) relativism, and the doctrine that all cultures are equally valid. If one believes, as the cultural relativists do, that there are no trans-cultural norms by which different cultures may be judged, then there is no rational basis for saying one is better or worse than another. All that this means however is that one's preference cannot be governed by reason. Reason tells us that it can make no objection to one's preferences. Reason cannot tell us that white European culture is superior to black African culture. But neither can it tell us it is *not* superior. If reason cannot decide, that does not mean there will be no decision: only that the decision will not be by reason. Hitler's "Triumph of the Will" is as good an example of the application of the principles of cultural relativism as Afrocentric history. The widespread assumption among multi-culturalists that a "value free" social science is inherently tolerant and sympathetic towards differences, is a perfect non-sequitur. Those who—like the Wellesley dean—may not themselves subscribe to the lunatic claims either of Afrocentrism or Nazism are disabled by their own belief in relativism from resisting those claims. And this is the prototypical situation of American Conservatism today. It can only pit its preferred "value judgments" against those it opposes, but it cannot justify them in any other court than that established in the first place by the enemies of tradition and of reason.

II.

Of all the words that have poisoned public discourse, none has done so as profoundly as the word "value," used as a synonym for moral or political choice. Today it is commonplace for those who think themselves social conservatives to speak of "family values," or even "traditional family values." They are not conscious of the fact that, by using the word "value" to characterize a moral choice, they are subscribing to the validity of the fact-value distinction, and thereby to the essential principle of moral relativism. Referring to moral principles as "values" would have provoked blank unrecognition until a time that is very recent. In his inaugural address, President Washington spoke as follows:

> the foundations of our national policy will be laid in the pure and immutable principles of private morality . . . since there is no truth more thoroughly established than that there exists in the economy and course of nature an indissoluble union between virtue and happiness [and moreover] we ought to be no less persuaded that the propitious smiles of Heaven can never be expected on a nation that disregards the eternal rules of order and right which Heaven itself has ordained.

The "pure and immutable principles of private morality" are not the same as "family values" whether traditional or nontraditional. The "truth . . . thoroughly established" of the "indissoluble union of virtue and happiness" is as good a short description of the central thesis of the *Nicomachean Ethics* as Aristotle himself could have written. It depends upon the conviction that the meaning of virtue and happiness is to be found in an immutable human nature, not in human choosing. It is up to man to discover what the good of nature is, and how to acquire it; but man is not free to determine the human good on the basis of his subjective preferences. The pursuit of happiness is not idiosyncratic. Virtue, happiness, and the "eternal rules of order and right" are objective conditions of human well-being. In no sense can they be regarded as "values" to be distinguished from "facts." The essence of well-being, whether for a man or a nation, is conforming human will to a standard of reason set by God and nature. Principles of human choice are in no sense "values," they are "facts." Here is the antithesis of moral relativism and all its progeny.

How far what is called Conservatism today has distanced itself from genuine tradition is manifested with great clarity by Mr. Justice Rehnquist's argument against liberal judicial activism. This judicial activism is the propensity of judges to discover rights in the Constitution, not because they are there, but because the judges want them to be there. Inventing judicial remedies for violations of these alleged rights is judicial legislation. This not only violates separation of powers, but—more profoundly—the principle that government should be by the consent of the governed. Judges are appointed to interpret the law that the people or their representative have made, not to make the law for them. Here is how Mr. Justice Rehnquist defends the Constitution from this perverse notion of the function of judges and courts. It is wrong, he says, because

> it seems to ignore totally the nature of political value judgments in a democratic society. If such a society adopts a constitution and incorporates in that constitution safeguards for individual liberty, these safeguards do indeed take on generalized moral rightness or goodness. They assume a general social acceptance neither because of any intrinsic worth nor because of any unique origins in someone's idea of natural justice but instead simply because they have been incorporated in a constitution by a people.

Mr. Justice Rehnquist takes his bearing by what he thinks is popular sovereignty. But the idea that is in his mind has nothing in common with the idea that was in the minds of those who framed and those who ratified the Constitution of 1787, and the bill of rights appended to it shortly thereafter. For them the sovereignty of governments is derived from the natural rights with which all human persons have been "endowed by their Creator." It is these rights, incorporated by a social contract that constitutes the sovereignty of a people.

Safeguards for individual liberty, Rehnquist says, in flat opposition to the Founders, do not have *any* intrinsic worth. That is to say, they do not have any compelling reason or reasons to justify their incorporation into the constitution. The "generalized moral rightness or goodness" that they "take on" is not intrinsic. In fact, it is an illusion, as is shown by Rehnquist's commitment to the same moral relativism that justifies Afrocentrism.

> There is no conceivable way in which I can logically demonstrate to you that the judgments of my conscience are superior to the judgments of your conscience, and vice versa.

The foregoing sentence is not addressed to any particular individual, and the "my" and "your" can refer to any two persons whose moral opinions differ. Now the difference of opinion in regard to the morality of slavery is the greatest of all such differences in American history. The Constitution of 1787 contained many great safeguards for individual liberty. But it also contained notable safeguards for slavery. According to Rehnquist's premises, the safeguards for slavery and the safeguards for liberty, being incorporated by the same people into the same constitution, took on the same "moral rightness and goodness." This was the argument of John C. Calhoun in demanding equal rights for the slave states, with the free states, in the federal territories. It was the contest between the free states and the slave states for control of the territories that was the direct cause of the Civil War. Calhoun however was not a moral relativist: he believed slavery to be a "positive good." He did so because he believed in the inequality of the races, on a principle closely resembling that of Adolph Hitler. But he did say that the Constitution was neutral on the question of the morality of slavery, and that it forbade any preference for the rights of the free states over those of the slave states in the territories. Whether knowingly or not, Rehnquist has clearly endorsed Calhoun's position.

It follows from the assertion that there is no logical way of demonstrating the superiority of any conscience to any other conscience, that there is no logical way of demonstrating the superiority of an antislavery conscience to a proslavery conscience. Here is moral relativism stark naked. It is presented by the Chief Justice of the United States as the *reason* informing the authority of the people to ordain and establish the Constitution of the United States. The *a priori* equality of all moral judgments as value judgments, all being equally indemonstrable, is merely asserted and assumed. By what course of reasoning does Rehnquist believe this is true? He does not say. By whose arguments has he been persuaded to believe this? He does not say. Here most certainly is a case of a practical man in authority distilling the frenzy of an academic scribbler of a few years back. But this frenzy had become the received wisdom in his college classes, and in his law school classes, and like most of the others in those same classes, he has had neither the time nor the inclination to question it. Yet this received wisdom is the very antithesis of what was believed by those who framed and ratified the Constitution. Therefore to call it a jurisprudence of original intent is no less anachronistic or absurd than saying that Aristotle had plagiarized his work from the library at Alexandria!

Those who signed the Declaration of Independence appealed to the Supreme Judge of the world for the rectitude of their intentions. They did not think that the moral judgment enshrined in the document to which they affixed their signatures represented "value judgments" which were merely personal or individual. Although belief in the righteousness of their cause gave them strength, they did not believe that that righteousness was dependent upon its success, whether on the field of battle or in an election. In the *Summary View of the Rights of British America*, in 1774, Jefferson told the King that

> The God who gave us life, gave us liberty at the same time: the hand
> of force may destroy, but it cannot disjoin them.

The American people in that time and place believed in the timeless truth of the propositions they held to be self-evident, and in the reasoning which followed from those propositions.[2] The dignity of their cause depended upon the thoughtfulness of their actions.

Rehnquist says that safeguards for individual liberty—that is to say, a free constitution—are not chosen for any intrinsic worth or "any unique origins in someone's idea of natural justice." The Americans who fought the Revolution and who framed and ratified the Constitution thought otherwise. They believed in the intrinsic rightness of their cause, and that they were acting in accordance with the laws of reason, of nature, and of God, which they held to be one and the same. It is important to see that Rehnquist's position, in rejecting out of hand the beliefs of the framers and ratifiers, also rejects any support, in God, nature, or reason, for the goodness of the Constitution. Indeed, it reduces all moral choices, all morality, to mere preferences that have no support beyond themselves. In the words of Leo Strauss, this is nihilism. It is this opinion, diffusing itself from our elites, downward and outward through our society that will destroy it, that is destroying it. One may ask how complex theories like nihilism and relativism can control the minds of the juvenile delinquents of the ghettos of our central cities. That question leads to another: how did they come to control the mind of the Chief Justice of the United States, and his brethren of the conservative legal establishment? How can we generate respect for law and morality in the lower ranks of society when there is no argument in their favor at the top?

Rehnquist's position is that morality rests upon value judgments for which there is no cognitive support. Accordingly, the proslavery and the antislavery elements of the Constitution of 1787 represented different value judgments, which by their presence represented the political strength mustered by their advocates. But we are forbidden to say that either can "demonstrate" its superiority to the other!

According to Rehnquist,

> Representative government is predicated upon the idea that one who feels deeply upon a matter of conscience will seek out others of like view or will attempt to persuade others who do not initially share that view. When adherents to the belief become sufficiently numerous, he will have the necessary armaments required in a democratic society to press his views upon the elected representatives of the people, and to have them embodied into positive law.

Taken by itself, the foregoing is perfectly commonplace. What is remarkable is not what it says, but what it omits. Consider this passage from Jefferson's first inaugural address.

> All too will bear in mind this sacred principle, that though the will of the majority is in all cases to prevail, that will to be rightful must be

reasonable, that the minority possess their equal rights, which equal
law must protect, and to violate would be oppression.

Rehnquist sees the political process as one of rallying support for one's
own "value judgments." But what are the rights of the losers? On his
theory, losers have no rights except what the winners allow them. If
Protestants are in the majority they can trample on Catholics, and
Christians can trample on Jews. And, of course, whites can trample on
blacks. And, given the opportunity, blacks can trample on whites. Rehnquist, in his eagerness to oppose the tyranny of liberal judicial activism,
has in principle endorsed the tyranny of the majority. Nothing concerned the "original intent" of the Founders more than preventing the
tyranny of the majority by elected legislatures. That tyranny was happening in the states under the Articles of Confederation. The "value
judgments" of the more numerous debtors were voting to cancel their
obligations to the "value judgments" of the less numerous creditors.
The many were voting to confiscate the property of the few, the ultimate reproach of democracy, in Aristotle's *Politics*. It was to prevent
this reproach of popular government that the Constitution of 1787 forbade states to impair the obligation of contract, or to tamper with the
money supply. In introducing on the floor of the House the amendments that would become the Bill of Rights, Madison said that their
enactment would make the judiciary an "impenetrable bulwark" against
any invasion of these "great rights of mankind," by either of the elected
branches of the government. Government by majority rule is unthink-
able without freedom of speech, press, assembly, the right of petition,
or the free exercise of religion. These are natural rights, not "value
judgments." They represent an objective reality, without which government by majority rule is not a viable option.

In the Kentucky Resolutions Jefferson denounced the Alien and
Sedition Acts as violations of the Constitution and of natural rights.
These violations were no more acceptable because they were enacted
by a representative government than if they had been enacted by the
King and Parliament of Great Britain. In fact, the resemblance between
the Declaration of Independence and the Kentucky Resolutions is remarkable. In the latter, as in the former, the ultimate remedy is the
right of revolution. There is the same right to resist the usurpations of
elected governments as of absolute monarchies.

How far the "originalism" of present-day legal positivism is from the generation that framed and ratified the Constitution may be illustrated by a bizarre effusion by Judge Robert Bork.[3] In the May 1995 *Commentary*, in reply to a critic of an article of his on the first amendment, he wrote:

> It is particularly nonsensical to quote the Declaration of Independence's enunciation of a right to alter or abolish government. That right was asserted against an English government in which Americans had no say and which they regarded as tyrannical. Having established a representative government here, the Founders proceeded to enact laws that denied any right of revolution on these shores.

The Founders never enacted laws denying the right of revolution, on these or any other shores! They could never have imagined anything so foolish. The right of revolution is identical in principle with the right of self-preservation, which has the authority of the law of nature. In the 43rd *Federalist* James Madison asked,

> On what principle the Confederation, which stands in the solemn form of a compact among the States, can be superseded without the unanimous consent of the parties to it?

This question, he said,

> is answered at once by recurring to the absolute necessity of the case; to the great principle of self-preservation; to the transcendent law of nature and of nature's God, which declares that the safety and happiness of society are the objects at which all political institutions aim, and to which all political institutions must be sacrificed.

The right to alter or abolish governments—the right of revolution—as set forth in the Declaration of Independence is thus invoked to justify abolishing the authority of the Articles of Confederation, as it had been invoked to justify abolishing the authority of the King and Parliament of Great Britain. The action of the American people, in "overthrowing" the Articles of Confederation, although entirely peaceful, was no less revolutionary in principle than their action in overthrowing the government of Great Britain by war. According to James Madison, therefore, the right of revolution, under the transcendent law of nature and of nature's God, is the justification of the institution of the Constitution, no less than of the separation from Great Britain. To deny or disparage this right is to deny or disparage the authority of the Constitution itself.

Abraham Lincoln has—as usual—rendered the thought of the Founding Fathers with finality as with beauty.

> This country with its institutions, belongs to the people who inhabit it. Whenever they shall grow weary of the existing government, they can exercise their constitutional right of amending it, or their revolutionary right to dismember or overthrow it.

If Judge Bork thinks the Founding Fathers repealed the laws of nature he might join the Rev. Al Sharpton's history faculty.

III

The late Russell Kirk's *The Conservative Mind: From Burke to Santayana* was first published in 1953, and re-issued as *The Conservative Mind: From Burke to Eliot* in 1986. "Movement" Conservatives, thrilled to be told—what they had not hitherto known—namely, that they had a "mind," have regarded Russell Kirk as their prophetic voice ever since. In recent years, with the rise of Neo-Conservatism, Kirk has been increasingly identified with Paleo-Conservatism. The core of Paleo-Conservatism has always been its identification with the so-called State Rights tradition, originating with John C. Calhoun. This version of State Rights has been the doctrinal core of the defense of slavery, secession, and the Confederacy. Since the Civil War and the end of Reconstruction it has been the doctrinal core of the defense of Jim Crow and segregation. State rights in the Calhounian sense have nothing in common, however, with the State Rights as understood by those who framed and those who ratified the Constitution. For them, all the rights of all legitimate governments, whether state or federal, are derived from the equal natural rights of individuals proclaimed in the Declaration of Independence. It is "to secure these rights" that all constitutions of government are instituted. In the State rights of Calhoun and his paleocon descendants, individual rights are assimilated into the collective rights of the States. Calhoun's doctrine closely parallels that of his contemporary (and fellow neo-Hegelian) Karl Marx. In the former, all individual rights are derived from the collective rights of the state, as in the latter they are all derived from the collective rights of the proletariat. It is not without reason that Calhoun has been called "the Marx of the master class."[4] In both Calhoun and Marx the necessary condition of the collectivization of rights is the abandonment of the doctrine of individual natural rights in the Declaration of Independence.

Kirk has never directly espoused the cause of the old South, or of Jim Crow. But he has often and loudly praised Calhoun. He has written articles on Calhoun for *The Southern Partisan*, a journal fanatically devoted to the Confederacy and openly espousing the cause of slavery to this day. Without the open espousal of these causes, Kirk has been rabid in his denigration and disparagement of the Declaration of Independence and of the principle of human equality. Of course, Kirk's dismissal of the Declaration applies *a fortiori* to the Gettysburg Address, and I cannot recall his ever saying anything good about Abraham Lincoln.

A word here is in order about the origins of Kirk's Burkean conservatism. It is descended, not from Burke himself, but from the highly selective use made of Burke by the victorious enemies of the French Revolution after the defeat of Napoleon. It was the political creed of those who would restore hereditary monarchy, hereditary aristocracy, established religion, and the union of altar and throne that constituted the *ancien regime*. The history of the nineteenth century is largely that of the struggle of the Holy Alliance and its heirs to stem the rising tide of popular government, of government by the consent of the governed. The bitter reactionaries who wanted to turn back the clock to the *status quo ante* the French Revolution—those who could learn nothing and forget nothing—saw the seeds of the tyranny in any attempt by the people to govern themselves. Any movement towards recognizing the equality of man was believed to have as its necessary fulfillment the Reign of Terror and Napoleon. In America, this was the view of European history taken by John C. Calhoun. He denounced the proposition "that all men are born free and equal" (or, alternatively, "that all men are created equal") as "the most false and dangerous of all political errors." He held that the French Revolution and Napoleon were its inevitable consequences, and he saw in the antislavery movement of his day all the evils that his European counterparts had seen in the French

Revolution. Here is the doctrinal source of Kirk's understanding of the American political tradition.

The antislavery movement in Great Britain, whose efforts culminated in the abolition of slavery in the British West Indies in 1833, energized the antislavery movement in America. It did so notably with the inauguration of William Lloyd Garrison's *Liberator* in 1831, and the founding of the American Antislavery Society in 1833. When European Conservatism crossed the Atlantic, its American version substituted the defense of the *ancien regime* with the defense of slavery. The romanticizing of slavery paralleled the romanticizing of Europe's pre-revolutionary monarchies and aristocracies. In the celebration of sentiment over reason, the conservative movement, both in Europe and America—and most notably in the person of Russell Kirk—has been completely enthralled by Rousseau's romanticism. Denunciations of Rousseau as the philosopher-king of Jacobinism by Conservatives are nothing to the purpose: Rousseau stands at the headwaters equally of the most radically democratic and the most radically antidemocratic streams of nineteenth and twentieth century political thought. And the concept of "tradition" espoused by Kirk and others of the Southern school, is a radically modern invention. It has nothing in common with tradition as understood by Aristotle, Cicero, Thomas Aquinas, Hooker, or even Burke himself.

The generation of the Founding Fathers had almost without exception regarded Negro slavery as an evil, even if an evil so deeply rooted that it had to be endured for some time. It was evil because it violated the moral law in degrading human beings below the level of human nature, making them chattels, subject to being bought and sold like beasts of the field. And it violated the axiomatic premise of the Revolution, what Lincoln would call "the father of all moral principle among us," "that all men are created equal." Not until the 1830s did there arise a new school of thought on slavery, in opposition to the doctrine of the Founding Fathers. With Calhoun as its most powerful and influential voice, it proclaimed slavery to be no evil at all, but a positive good, beneficial alike to masters and slaves.

The doctrine of human equality implied that the "just powers of government" were derived from the rights all men had by nature, and with which they had been "endowed by their Creator." These rights had no reference either to the color of their skin, or to the manner or mode

by which they worshiped their God. As we have seen, government by
majority rule is impossible without minority rights. No one could consent knowingly to the rule of a majority that could enslave him, or that
could decide what his religious opinions ought to be. In the wars of the
Reformation, millions of Christians had been slaughtered by other
Christians, either because they did believe, or did not believe in transubstantiation. Before government by majority rule could be contemplated, there had to be a decision to recognize that, in Jefferson's words,
"our civil rights have no dependence on our religious opinions, any
more than our opinions in physics or geometry." The Constitution of
1787 was the first in the world that provided that there should never be
a religious test for office. How far Russell Kirk—who celebrated tradition as the source of political principles—was alienated from the
American political tradition is demonstrated by his call in 1989 for an
establishment of Christianity. His reliance upon T. S. Eliot as an authority is a further illustration of how profound that alienation was.
What follows is my reply to his article in *This World*, which reply was
rejected by the editors, and has not hitherto been published.

❋ ❋ ❋

ELIOT, AMERICA, AND THE JEWS: A REPLY TO RUSSELL KIRK

In "Eliot and a Christian Culture" (*This World*, Winter 1989) Russell
Kirk invites us to accept T. S. Eliot as a champion of that common
culture of the West which (according to Kirk on Eliot) has Christianity
as its core. The following is I believe a succinct summary of what we are
asked to believe.

> Christianity prescribes no especial form of government. Yet the
> source of any political order is a religious creed—or else the inverted
> religion of ideology. A principal function of the state is the mainte-
> nance of justice; and justice can be defined only upon ethical as-
> sumptions, ultimately derived from religious insights. If the state
> stands in opposition to the religious dogmas of a society, or is indif-
> ferent to those teachings, then either the state or the society is not
> long for this world. For our civilization, Christianity has provided
> both the principles of personal order and the principles of social

order. If we repudiate or ignore those principles, our only alternative is the Pagan State, obeying the commandments of the Savage God. So it is that we must labor to restore the Christian State.

That the "principal function of the state is the maintenance of justice" and that "justice can be defined only upon ethical assumptions, ultimately derived from religious insights" are premises upon which Russell Kirk and I can agree. That the principles of both personal and social order in our civilization are derived exclusively from Christianity is I believe not only untrue but inconsistent with Christianity itself. St. Paul, in the "Letter to the Romans" (2:10 ff.) writes:

> There will be tribulation and distress for every human being who does evil, the Jew first and also the Greek, but glory and honor and peace for everyone who shows no partiality. . . . For it is not the hearers of the law who are righteous before God, but the doers of the law who are justified. When the Gentiles who have not the law do *by nature* what the law requires, they are a law unto themselves. . . . They show that what the law requires is written on their hearts.

Consistent with Paul's pronouncement is the teaching of Thomas Aquinas, that the natural law is the rational creature's participation in the eternal law, which is God's law. Human beings are rational animals by nature, not by faith. For Thomas, moreover, the highest authority for the moral and intellectual virtues (including justice) was Aristotle, who represented the perfection of unassisted human reason. Dante, in the foreword to *De Monarchia*, asks, Who would write on happiness after Aristotle? Or on old age after Cicero? He implies that Christian wisdom is itself formed upon the wisdom of these classical (pagan) authors.

It is then against the best traditions of the Christian West that Russell Kirk—the disciple of Eliot—believes that

> it is necessary that the state should recognize the moral order which Christianity outlines, and should conform the public order—so far as possible in this imperfectible world—to that ethical understanding.

The United States of America declared its independence by invoking the authority of "the laws of nature and of nature's God." The Congress, in making its declaration, did so after appealing to the Supreme Judge of the world for the rectitude of our intentions.

The Congress did so

in the name and by the authority of the good people of these colonies.

It was because this people was a "good people"—because it acted in accordance with the laws of nature, which were also God's laws and because they were confident of what a Judge who could search men's hearts would see, when he looked into theirs—that the Signers of the Declaration were able to place such

a firm reliance on the protection of Divine Providence [for] our lives, our fortunes, and our sacred honor.

President Calvin Coolidge, in a speech celebrating its 150th anniversary, said that

In its main features the Declaration of Independence is a great spiritual document. It is a declaration not of material but of spiritual conceptions. Equality, liberty, popular sovereignty, the rights of man—these are not elements we can see and touch. . . . They have their source and roots in the religious convictions. Unless the faith of the American people in these religious convictions is to endure, the principles of our Declaration will perish. We can not continue to enjoy the result if we neglect and abandon the cause.

It precisely because Russell Kirk has been a determined enemy of the Declaration of Independence and because he has never recognized the truth of its principles, or their moral and religious significance, that he—and his hero Eliot—are alienated from the political tradition of their native land. Here is what Kirk has written about the Declaration in the introduction to a reprinting (in 1983) of Albert Jay Nock's *Mr. Jefferson*.

Nock's book has very little to say about the Declaration of Independence. That is as it should be, for the Declaration really is not conspicuously American in it ideas or its phrases, and not even characteristically Jeffersonian. As Carl Becker sufficiently explains, the

Declaration was meant to persuade the court of France, and the *philosophes* of Paris, that the Americans were sufficiently un-English to deserve military assistance. Jefferson's Declaration is a successful instrument of diplomacy; it is not a work of political philosophy or an instrument of government, and Jefferson himself said little about it after 1776.

I do not think that the history of the world records an example of greater errors being compressed into fewer words. Think of it, the Declaration of Independence "not conspicuously American!" In fact, what Carl Becker wrote was exactly the opposite of what this Christian moralist represents him as having written. Here are Becker's actual words.

> In France, we are told, the Declaration was officially "well received." Everything considered, to be received at all was to be well received. Democratic impudence could not well go farther than to ask the descendant of Louis XIV to approve a rebellion based upon the theory that "governments derive their just powers from the consent of the governed." If the French government received the Declaration, it did so in spite of its political philosophy because it could not forego the opportunity to take a hand in disrupting the British empire. (*The Declaration of Independence* 1922, 1942, pp. 229 ff.)

Carl Becker did not for a moment doubt that the Declaration of Independence was a work of "political philosophy." Nor, to my knowledge has anyone else before Russell Kirk doubted it—with the exception only of another Kirk hero—John C. Calhoun. That the Declaration was also an "instrument of government" is the testimony of Madison and Jefferson. In 1825, in recommending to the Overseers of the University of Virginia that certain works be regarded as *norma docendi* for the teaching of law, they commended as the "first" of the "best guides" to the "distinctive principles" of the governments of both Virginia and the United States,

> The Declaration of Independence, as the fundamental act of Union of these States.

As the legal instrument of the "Union of these States" the Declaration is, at this day, according to the United States Code, the first of the organic laws in the United States.

* * *

In a famous passage of *Democracy in America* Tocqueville pronounced religion to be the first of political institutions here. It was the morality common to all the churches, whatever their dogmatic theological differences, which made majority rule possible. A shared morality contributed to the confidence that enabled minorities to accept the will of the majority as the ground of the rule of law. This confidence—Tocqueville recognized—was possible only because of the separation of church and state. George Washington, in 1791, in a message to the Barbary States—which were Muslim—declared that the government of the United States was not in any sense founded upon the Christian religion. Precisely because the United States was not a Christian state, because Christian doctrine could not become a subject of political difference, the churches could pursue their pastoral missions undisturbed by the political differences that had plagued Christianity in the Old World. For this reason, Tocqueville believed, the moral influence of Christianity was far greater in America than in Europe. I believe that—notwithstanding the ravages wrought by science and ideology upon faith on both sides of the Atlantic—this observation holds true today.

Eliot and Kirk to the contrary notwithstanding, America was founded upon the wise conviction that to make a state officially Christian would defeat the ends of Christianity. This conviction was fortified by the devastation wrought upon Christian civilization by the internecine wars and persecutions of Christian states in the centuries preceding the American Revolution. These wars and persecutions, waged in the name of Christian truth, were in their own way every bit as cruel as those waged in the name of atheistic ideologies in the 20th century. The memory of the wars of religion was still fresh in the minds of both Madison and Jefferson, who led the movement—supported by George Washington—for disestablishment in Virginia. The great "Act for establishing Religious Freedom" in Virginia—the second of the three things by which Jefferson wished most to be remembered—begins as follows:

> Whereas Almighty God hath created the mind free . . . all attempts
> to influence it by temporal punishments or burthens, or by civil

incapacitations, tend only to beget habits of hypocrisy and meanness, and are a departure from the plan of the Holy author of our religion, who being Lord both of body and mind, yet chose not to propagate it by coercions on either.

We see that all the authority of Christianity itself—notably that of the "Holy author of our religion"—is against

the impious presumption of legislators and rulers, civil as well as ecclesiastical, who being fallible and uninspired men have assumed dominion over the faith of others

It is this impious presumption that has

established and maintained false religions over the greatest part of the world, and through all time

Separation of church and state is the enemy only of "false religion."

truth is great and will prevail if left to herself . . . she is the proper and sufficient antagonist to error, and has nothing to fear from the conflict, unless by human interposition disarmed of her natural weapons, free argument and debate, errors ceasing to be dangerous when it is permitted freely to contradict them.

T. S. Eliot, born in St. Louis, and educated at Harvard, spent most of his life in England, a refugee from the "wasteland" of American liberal democracy. Kirk, unlike Eliot, has remained in the United States, but in his imagination living as a high Tory who has invented his own version of American history that omits the Declaration of Independence—and the Gettysburg Address. He speaks constantly about transcendence, but ignores the natural law tradition that has informed both Christianity and the American political tradition at its Founding.

❈ ❈ ❈

Throughout his article, Kirk moves warily and grudgingly around the subject of Eliot and the Jews. He writes

I am inclined to think that some of the folk who growl about Eliot's alleged anti-Semitism are not really worried about "Bleistein with a Cigar" or passing references to "free-thinking Jews" in *After Strange Gods*. . . . What really alarms such adversaries of Eliot is not his

fancied attitude towards Jews, but his indubitable attachment to
Christian culture.

Kirk does not consider that many today—for example Pope John Paul
II—would think that Eliot's attitude towards Jews was inconsistent with
Christianity. In the passage in *After Strange Gods* to which Kirk refers,
Eliot is clear that his idea of a Christian society excluded "free thinking
Jews." For Eliot the emancipation of the Jews—their full and equal
citizenship in a democratic polity—symbolized everything wrong with
modern secular society. By implication he would return them to where
he thinks they belong: to the Ghetto, where Jewish Orthodoxy would be
left to deal with the "free-thinking" element among them—as it did
with Spinoza.

Eliot belonged to the European Right who loathed both the French
and American revolutions. In France, it was the Right of the Dreyfus
Affair, and of those who, a generation later, said "Better Hitler than
Blum." In England, it was the Right of the Cliveden set, the very heart
and soul of British appeasement. Whatever objection to Hitler these
British Conservatives might have had, it was certainly not his anti-Jew-
ish policy.

In 1919, long before Hitler appeared on the scene, Eliot wrote "Burbank with a Baedeker: Bleistein with a Cigar." There are eight stanzas
of four lines each. Its theme, briefly stated, is the "decline of the West"
or, if one pleases, the decline of Christian civilization. The first three
verses are a nostalgic evocation—obscure in Eliot's familiar way—of a
beautiful but archaic past. Burbank is a weak and sybaritic representative of a failing culture. The next three verses are however anything but
obscure.

> But this or such was Bleistein's way:
> A saggy bending of the knees
> And elbows, with the palms turned out,
> Chicago Semite Viennese
>
> A lustreless protrusive eye
> Stares from the protozoic slime
> At a perspective of Canaletto.
> The smoky candle end of time
>
> Declines. On the Rialto once.

> The rats are underneath the piles.
> The jew is underneath the lot.
> Money in furs. . . .

Hitler had no propagandists with Eliot's poetic gift, who could invest "the wardrobe of our moral imaginations" with a caricature as effectively loathsome as Eliot's lower case "jew." Bleistein, like Hitler, was a native of Vienna. One may surmise that it was just about the time that Eliot was writing this poem that Hitler—observing the Bleisteins around him—was forming his sick fantasy that the Jews' treachery was responsible for Germany's defeat in the first World War. But Bleistein had emigrated to Chicago. He is now symbolic of the cultural atavism of Eliot's native middle west. The "lustreless protrusive eye" which "stares from the protozoic slime" is that of a reptile—the first and lowest form of animal life in the evolutionary process. This sub-human—nay, sub-bestial—eye looks upon a work of high culture, dooming it by its uncomprehending gaze. Here is the very quintessence of Nazi race theory: the characterization of the Jews as so profoundly dysgenic a force as to justify their extermination.

"On the Rialto once" refers to Shylock's encounter with Antonio in *Merchant of Venice*, to money-lending, and to the exacting of the famous pound of flesh. "Canaletto" is a Venetian painter of the eighteenth century, and his name reminds us of the canals, celebrated also in his paintings. It reminds us of the precarious supports upon which Venice—and civilization—rests, and how fragile are the props that stand between it and the aboriginal slime.

Decline and fall seem probable to Eliot, not because of the rats beneath the piles but because of the "jew" beneath everything. Nothing in the "Protocols of the Elders of Zion" more succinctly or powerfully expresses the idea of Jewish malignancy: "money in furs." This also, be it noted, is the view that Karl Marx took of the connection between capitalism and Jews—"the cash nexus"—and high culture.

There was a Nazi propaganda film in the 1930s called "The Eternal Jew." It featured scenes of millions and millions of swarming rats—followed by scenes of Jews, probably Hasidic Jews from eastern Europe, shown first in beards and then shaven, so that their alien features could be clearly identified. Scenes of the Jews are cut to scenes of the rats, and of the rats to the Jews, and of the Jews to the rats, again and again. The mounting disgust for rats becomes disgust for Jews. I do not know whether the Nazi film makers were inspired by Eliot's poem, but they very well could have been. In a letter dated February 15, 1920, Eliot wrote of "Bleistein" that it was a work "intensely serious . . . and . . . among the best I have ever done." I know of no evidence that this opinion ever changed. It was reprinted in every edition of his *Collected Poems* until the end of his life. This, without any apology or explanation, in the aftermath of the Holocaust, can be compared with Heidegger's unapologetic reference in 1953 to the "inner truth and greatness" of National Socialism.

❊ ❊ ❊

Not many readers of *This World*, scanning Russell Kirk's light dismissal of Eliot's "fancied attitude towards Jews" will have had the occasion, or will have taken the time, to look at these passages of "Burbank with a Baedeker: Bleistein with a Cigar." This I thought it necessary for them to do. This paradox of evil intermixed in poetic greatness should not astonish any student of Plato. The banishment of the beloved Homer from the *Republic* was testimony long ago, that great poetry divorced from moral wisdom could become dangerous—the greater the poetry the greater the possible danger. That Eliot and Kirk should identify the moral law not with the law of nature, not with morality itself—as do St. Paul and St. Thomas—but with a Christianity divorced from reason, is to confound utterly the relationship of nature, reason, and faith, even in Christianity itself. It is to be blind to the moral and intellectual greatness of the American Founding, to the noble and just regime of Jefferson, Madison, Washington, and Lincoln. We must not so defer to pretensions of civility as to acquiesce in so tragic an error.[5]

IV.

The hostility to Jews and blacks, rooted in the attachment to the *ancien regime* of the European right has, as we have noted, long tainted American paleo-conservatism. The flagship journal of American Conservatism since 1955 has been *National Review*. For 25 years or more Russell Kirk was a major presence within it. But Willmoore Kendall, Frank Meyer, Jeffrey Hart, M. E. Bradford were among others who operated within the same basic framework in which loyalty to the *ancien regime* was transformed into loyalty to the Old South.[6] This did not of itself necessarily imply hostility to Jews, since Jewish communities, North and South, had flourished in America since the Revolution, and a Jew—Judah Benjamin—had been Jefferson Davis's Secretary of State and closest adviser.[7] For many years however I was the only writer in the pages of *National Review* who had a good word to say about Jefferson or Lincoln, the Declaration of Independence, or the idea of equality. That came to an end in the Independence Day issue of *National Review* in 1979, with the cover article "The Special Meaning of the Declaration of Independence" by Charles Kesler. That was an essay— perhaps the longest until then to appear in *National Review*—rediscovering Lincoln's assertion that this nation had at its birth been dedicated to the proposition that all men are created equal. Kesler viewed Lincoln, as did I, as the savior, not only of the Union, but of that "father of all moral principle among us" that had condemned slavery, and had thereby laid down the fundamental conditions for combining majority rule and minority rights. Buckley had commissioned the essay, and had found a grant to enable the young scholar (he was still an undergraduate at Harvard) to write it. Buckley knew, of course, that Kesler's thesis ran against the grain of the persuasion that had dominated *National Review* almost from its beginning. Like my articles which had preceded it, however, nothing in *NR* that came after Kesler's seemed influenced by it even in the slightest degree.[8] Where Kesler's influence was brought to bear however was in his joint editorship, with Buckley, of *Keeping the Tablets*, the second and greatly revised edition of the Buckley's 1970 *American Conservative Thought*.° A prominent place in *Tablets*[9] was given to "Equality as a Conservative Principle," the first chapter of *How to Think About the American Revolution*, a book equally divided in its critique of paleocons (Kendall, Bradford) and Neocons (Kristol, Diamond.) Anyone reading that book would have seen that, whatever their other differences, paleocons and neocons were united in their rejection of any authority to the Declaration of Independence, or to the rationalism enshrined in the laws of nature and of nature's God.[10]

The hatred of the French Revolution by European Conservatism was in its origins linked to the emancipation of the Jews by Napoleon. Long before the "Protocols of the Elders of Zion," the overthrow of the *ancien regime* was seen as a Jewish conspiracy, an opinion brilliantly captured by Eliot's "Bleistein." While Buckley had, from the beginning of *National Review*, renounced any fellowship with the traditional Jew-haters[11] within the ranks of American nativists, opinions hostile to Israel were not uncommon in its pages. For *NR*'s first twenty-five years there was little appreciation of why many Jews, with no *a priori* Zionist leanings, had become ardent supporters of Israel: they had come to believe that if there had been a state of Israel before World War II, the Holocaust would not have happened.[12] Nor was there appreciation of the fact that American Jews had come to believe that, had Hitler won the war, as he came very near to doing, their American citizenship would not have saved them, or their children, from the gas chambers.[13] The swing of *National Review* away from its connection with this engrained prejudice began with a gradual reassessment of its attitude towards Israel. The story of this movement[14] may be condensed by noting that Buckley in 1984 wrote a column endorsing King Hussein of Jordan's claim to the West Bank; and that about ten years later, he wrote a column calling for Israeli annexation of the West Bank! The consummation of this change came, however, with the publication in 1992, first as an article in *NR* and then, with many additions, as a book, *In Search of Anti-Semitism*. One of the evident purposes of this book was to detach, once and for all, *NR*'s conservatism from any suspicion of a connection with the hostility to Jews transmitted originally from the hatred of the Enlightenment and the French Revolution by European conservatism.

It is ironic that Buckley's book reminds one of nothing so much as a medieval heresy hunt. The opinions of Joe Sobran and Pat Buchanan are condemned as "anti-Semitic" although their persons are spared Buckley's ultimate anathemas. Although Buckley did not "turn his back" on Sobran[15] he did formally denounce his remarks on Jews and Israel. Sobran was demoted within the editorial ranks of *NR* and later quietly disappeared from the magazine altogether. In the dialogue between Norman Podhoretz and Buckley, some differences had remained: the former held out for a fuller measure of inquisitorial condemnation. But clearly there was at the end little reason for the powers centered upon *National Review* and *Commentary* to stand apart from each other.

Buckley's policy of detente bore its fruit in the March 1996 *Commentary* in Podhoretz's lead article "Neoconservatism: A Eulogy." The summary on the contents page is: "A once distinctive political tendency now contributes its ideas, its energies, and its style to the larger movement it invigorated." Podhoretz did not so much celebrate the death of neoconservatism as its resurrection, not as a sectarian movement within conservatism, but as its all-embracing form. This became possible when, thanks largely to Bill Buckley, Pat Buchanan's "amen corner" had become—as far as conservatism was concerned—the whole congregation. The *entente cordiale* between *Commentary* and *National Review* was symbolized by Buckley's review in the *Weekly Standard* of Irving Kristol's latest collection of essays, *Neoconservatism: the Autobiography of an Idea*. The *Standard* is the spirited new flagship of the reborn neopaleoconservatism, presided over most appropriately by Bill Kristol, Irving's son, in close association with John Podhoretz, Norman's son.[16] At about the same time as Buckley's review in the *Standard*, a review by Harvey Mansfield appeared in *National Review*. The two reviews— equally lavish in their praise, and unblemished by any perception of blemishes in their hero—were virtually indistinguishable. No clearer indication can be imagined of the merging of the gene pools. Kristol had indeed gone, as Norman Podhoretz says—in more senses than one—from being the godfather to being the grandfather.

✦ ✦ ✦

It is not a grateful task to intervene, like a wasp or a gadfly, at this picnic of mutual admiration. No one destined for obscurity has ever in his lifetime had more acclaim by his peers than Kristol. I should hasten to add that there is virtually nothing praised by either Buckley or Mansfield that I too do not praise. No one has been more energetic than I in hailing Kristol for his role, in the very midst of the anti-McCarthyite frenzy in the early 1950's, in leading old New Deal liberals out of the fever swamps of anti-anti-communism. The same applies to his discovery of the virtues of capitalism, and the defense of "bourgeois values" against the "counter culture" of the '60s, and against the insanities of "political correctness" that has followed. As far as I know we have always held identical views on Israel, and on the wisdom of a political alliance of Jewish conservatives with the Christian coalition, as with its predecessor, the Moral Majority.[17] It would be otiose and redundant to repeat all the praise that is his due, and that has been given to him so generously.

Irving Kristol is the very incarnation, if not the apotheosis, of the sensible man, always saying sensible things about the political issues of the day. He reminds us of Disraeli's character who said "Sensible men are all of the same religion," and when asked what that was answered,

"Sensible men never tell." But Kristol, like Russell Kirk, says he finds in tradition and religion the principles that make him so overwhelmingly sensible. While Kirk looked to England's feudal class structure and religious establishment, Kristol looks to the American political tradition and American Protestantism. The difficulty with Kristol's principled appeal to tradition and religion is that it bears no relationship to the tradition and religion that is enshrined in the historical documentary record. Kristol's version of American history denigrates all of its heroes. It has only one hero. All this is amply proven in *How to Think About the American Revolution* (1978), supplemented by "Human Rights and the Crisis of the West" in *American Conservatism and the American Founding* (1984). Both Buckley and Mansfield have for many years been familiar with my critiques of Kristol, and both chose for their own reasons—like Kristol himself—to ignore them.

Kristol is an outstanding example of what Leo Strauss called "retail sanity and wholesale madness." Here is what Kristol wrote about the American Founding in his 1973 lecture on "The American Revolution as a Successful Revolution," a lecture that inaugurated the American Enterprise Institute's highly publicized series celebrating the 200th anniversary of our independence.[18]

> To begin at the beginning: the American Revolution was successful in that those who led were able, in later years, to look back in tranquility at what they had wrought and to say that it was good. This was a revolution which, unlike all subsequent revolutions, did not devour its children: the men who made the revolution were the men who went on to create the new political order, who then held the highest elected positions in this order, and who all died in bed. Not very romantic, perhaps. Indeed positively prosaic. But it is this very prosaic quality of the American Revolution that testifies to its success. It is the pathos and poignancy of unsuccessful revolutions which excite the poetic temperament: statesmanship which successfully accomplishes its business is a subject more fit for prose. Alone among the revolutions of modernity, the American Revolution did not give rise to the pathetic and poignant myth of "the revolution betrayed." It spawned no literature of disillusionment; it left behind no grand hopes frustrated, no grand expectations unsatisfied, no grand illusions shattered. Indeed, in one important respect the American Revolution was so successful as to be almost self-defeating: it turned the attention of thinking men away from politics, which now seemed

utterly unproblematic, so that political theory lost its vigor, and even the political thought of the Founding Fathers was not seriously studied. This intellectual sloth, engendered by success, rendered us incompetent to explain this successful revolution to the world, and even to ourselves. The American political tradition became an inarticulate tradition: it worked so well we did not bother to inquire why it worked, and we are therefore intellectually disarmed before those moments when it suddenly seems not to be working so well after all.

Like Protagoras, Kristol casts such a spell with his myths that they disarm the critical faculties. However, they cannot withstand the slightest exercise of those faculties, if they awaken from the spell. If Irving Kristol ever took a course on American history from the Revolution to the Civil War, he must certainly have slept through it, as surely as Rip van Winkle slept through the Revolution itself. The intensity of the party conflict in the 1790s exceeded even that of the decade before the Civil War. The Founding Fathers fell into the most vigorous controversy over assumption, the bank, tariffs, the Jay Treaty, and above all over the French Revolution. The Alien and Sedition Acts provoked the Virginia and Kentucky Resolutions, in the latter of which Jefferson warned that the States might be driven into "blood and revolution." Jefferson's election in 1801 put an end to that danger. If however we push our fast forward button, we come to the Missouri crisis of 1820, the Nullification crisis of 1833 (in which civil war was barely averted), the crisis of 1850 (in which civil war was barely averted), and the ensuing crises over Kansas, Dred Scott, and John Brown, after which civil war was not averted at all.

If there is intellectual sloth anywhere in this picture it is not to be found in the historical record. Webster, Hayne, Calhoun, and Clay, were not men who found politics unproblematic. Madison's service to his country in confronting Calhoun in 1830 rivaled in importance his other great achievements. John Quincy Adams' confrontation with Calhoun over the right of petition is one of the greatest episodes in the history of free government. Of the Lincoln-Douglas debates I need say nothing further here. Jackson's proclamation against the nullifiers may have been written by Edward Livingston, but it is a great state document. Together with Webster's reply to Hayne, it provided Lincoln with indispensable precedents and arguments for his inaugural address. Not in the Athens of Pericles, nor the Rome of Cicero, nor in the

England of Burke and Pitt, or of Gladstone and Disraeli, did rhetorical power or dialectical precision reach greater heights. How anyone with the slightest acquaintance with the American political tradition could say that it had become inarticulate is beyond comprehension.

The moving force of the American Revolution, as the Gettysburg address tells us, was the doctrine of human equality. When, in 1774, the Continental Congress issued its "Declaration of the Causes and Necessity of Taking Up Arms," it denied that it was possible for men possessed of the use of reason to believe that any part of the human race could hold an absolute right of property in any other part of the human race. Then and thereafter, the Americans asserted rights which were not uniquely their own, but which—under the laws of nature and of nature's God—they shared equally with all mankind. The test of which Lincoln would speak at Gettysburg was therefore from the outset a test for all mankind. The principles of the Founding constituted in themselves an unqualified condemnation of human slavery, anywhere in the world. When the thirteen colonies rejected the claim of the British Parliament to bind them "in all cases whatsoever" they did so therefore on behalf of all mankind. However, the American Revolution, by denouncing slavery as against the laws of God and nature, raised a moral standard for America itself, which it was unable to satisfy until fourscore and seven years had passed, and many great battles had been fought. The American Revolution was therefore not the comedy (or fairy tale) of Kristol's imagination. It was rather the first act of a tragedy, a tragedy that ended—if it did end—not at Yorktown but at Appomattox.

Here is an example of the drowsy complacency engendered by the Revolution. This is Thomas Jefferson writing about the Missouri crisis in 1820.

> this momentous question, like a fire bell in the night, awakened and filled me with terror. I considered it at once as the knell of the Union. It is hushed, indeed, for the moment; but this is a reprieve only, not the final sentence. A geographical line, coinciding with a marked principle, moral and political, once conceived and held up to the angry passions of men, will never be obliterated; and every new irritation will mark it deeper and deeper. . . . I regret that I am now to die in the belief that the useless sacrifice of themselves by the generation of 1776, to acquire self-government and happiness to their country, is to be thrown away.

So much for Kristol's self-defeating success story!

The success of Kristol's successful American Revolution is said to lie in its practice, not in its theory.

> To perceive the true purposes of the American Revolution, it is wise to ignore some of the more grandiloquent declamations of the moment—Tom Paine, an English radical who never really understood America, is especially worth ignoring—and to look at the kinds of political activity the Revolution unleashed.

Here is what a leading historian[19] of the American Revolution says about Paine:

> Chiefly influential in leading patriots towards formal separation was Thomas Paine, whose *Common Sense* came anonymously from the press in January, 1776. A gifted writer and propagandist, he now burst like a meteor into the arena of public affairs. In phrases at once eloquent and passionate, Paine denounced the masters of his native country and pleaded for an American proclamation of independence . . . *Common Sense* had an enormous circulation, 120,000 copies being printed within three months . . . and it has been described not infrequently as the determining factor in the debate over independence.

According to Samuel Eliot Morrison, George Washington had been toasting the King nightly in his officers' mess until—as he related in a letter to Joseph Reed, January 31, 1776—he encountered the "sound doctrine and unanswerable reasoning contained in the pamphlet Common Sense." We see accordingly that the man who persuaded George Washington to make the most important decision of his life—and possibly the most important decision for our lives—is someone the "wise" Irving Kristol tells us to ignore![20]

When American fortunes were at their lowest ebb of the war, Paine's flaming eloquence in *The Crisis* was to Americans what Churchill's would be to the British after the fall of France in 1940. Here is Paine's counterpart to Churchill's "we will fight on the beaches" speech.

> These are the times that try men's souls. The summer soldier and the sunshine patriot will, in this crisis, shrink from the service of his country; but he that stands it NOW deserves the love and thanks of

man and woman. Tyranny like hell, is not easily conquered; yet we have this consolation with us, that the harder the conflict the more glorious the triumph.

Kristol invites us to ignore "the more grandiloquent declamations" of the Revolution. It is one of the notable features of Kristol's writing on historical topics, that he rarely if ever quotes or even cites any documentary sources. Here, however, he is certainly inviting us first and foremost to ignore the principles set forth in the Declaration of Independence. He invites us to look away from the Declaration to the constitution-making of the States. What do we find there? Consider the beginning of Virginia's constitution, which preceded independence (June 12, 1776).

> That all men are by nature equally free and independent, and have certain inherent rights, of which, when they enter into state of society, they cannot by any compact deprive or divest their posterity; namely, the enjoyment of life and liberty, with the means of acquiring and possessing property, and pursuing and obtaining happiness and safety.

And consider the beginning of Massachusetts' constitution of 1780.

> All men are born free and equal, and have certain natural, essential, and unalienable rights; among which may be reckoned the right of enjoying and defending their lives and liberties; that of acquiring, possessing, and protecting property, in fine, that of seeking and obtaining their safety and happiness.

It was a moral impossibility for American patriots of the Revolution to embark upon the framing of any government, without the reasoned "declamations" of natural rights that Kristol treats with such patronizing contempt. These defined the purposes, and marked the limits, for governments based upon the consent of the governed. Since Irving Kristol—like William Rehnquist, Robert Bork, or Russell Kirk—does not believe in natural rights, he tell us to ignore them. Yet this is to ignore what the Founders said were the reasons for what they did.

* * *

A notable feature of Buckley's "search for antisemitism" is that in it neither he nor Podhoretz nor Kristol ever says why it is bad or why its opposite is good. Like Potter Stewart in search of pornography, they only know it when they see it! Buckley observed that in his childhood expressions of what today would be called "anti-Semitism" by his father and other family members were vigorous and commonplace. Now he would condemn anyone for using the language his father used, but he does not revere the memory of his father any the less for that, nor should he. Many other fashions have changed over these years.[21] Today, racial or ethnic or religious slurs even in private conversation can lead to drastic consequences (like loss of employment) and ostracism from polite (and even from impolite) society. On the other hand, speech about sex in mixed company which would have banished anyone from respectable society then, is bandied about with the greatest freedom now, by women as well as men, and in public no less than in private. In the arena of yesteryear, it was Jews yes, sex no. Today it is sex yes, Jews no. Are there then any permanent standards in these matters or is it all merely a matter of social conventions and changing customs? Is "anti-Semitism" just out of fashion today, like Amos and Andy, or knee breeches and powdered wigs?

In a *Wall Street Journal* article in 1981, "The Common Sense of 'Human Rights'" Kristol declared that "we really must integrate a conception of human rights into our foreign policy. . . . " The reason, he said, is that "Our polity after all is founded on the idea of an individual's rights. . . . " But why should not the Founders' idea of individual rights be out of fashion, like their knee breeches and powdered wigs? And what *was* their idea of individual rights? Was the fact that so many of them were slaveholders consistent, or inconsistent, with their idea of individual rights?

Later, Kristol says that "Religious toleration is an idea so fundamental to the American way of life, so rooted in American tradition, that we simply cannot be indifferent to violations of that idea." But American history is filled with examples of religious intolerance. Willmoore Kendall liked to point out that tarring and feathering was as rooted in American tradition as freedom of speech. He was perfectly right. Only one was a good tradition and the other a bad tradition. The appeal to tradition is meaningless unless we can distinguish the one from the other.

But the meaning of religious toleration was radically transformed by the American Revolution. The Toleration Act of 1689 in England did not recognize a right to the free exercise of religion. The Church of England continued to be the established church. The Act continued to require religious tests for office, and for many of the ordinary privileges of citizenship. It merely relaxed the severity of the tests. Compare this with the following from President Washington's letter to the Hebrew Congregation of Newport, Rhode Island, in 1790. Washington wrote that

> All possess alike liberty of conscience and immunities of citizenship. It is now no more that toleration is spoken of as if it was by the indulgence of one class of people that another enjoyed the exercise of their inherent natural rights.

According to Washington, toleration here would owe nothing to the condescension of those in power. The free exercise of religion was an inherent natural right. It was not granted to Jews any more than to Christians. But neither was it a right granted *less* to Jews than to Christians. It was a right possessed equally by all, because it was a right with which all were equally endowed by their Creator. And in the exercise of this right, no one might have his "immunities of citizenship" disparaged or diminished. Here now is the answer to the question that Buckley and his interlocutors never asked. "Anti-Semitism" is wrong because it is against the natural rights of mankind. But this reason for the wrongness of "anti-Semitism" is the chief among the "grandiloquent declamations" that Kristol wants us to ignore.

Kristol also says that "The rights of racial minorities were not always thought to represent a fundamental human right, but they have unquestionably acquired that status in recent decades." But how can a polity be founded on the idea of individual rights, but not of the rights of racial minorities? What is any minority but a number of individuals? And how could rights of racial minorities "acquire" a status they did not hitherto possess? I do not recall any mention, much less discussion, of slavery in Kristol's celebration of the mind-numbing success or the American Revolution. In the *Notes on Virginia* however Thomas Jefferson, contemplating the institution of black slavery, wrote:

> Indeed I tremble for my country when I reflect that God is just; that his justice cannot sleep forever; that considering numbers, nature and natural means only, a revolution of the wheel of fortune, an

exchange of situation is among possible events; that it may become probable by supernatural interference! The Almighty has no attribute which can take side with us in such a contest.

Jefferson in the very midst of the Revolution—and long before the Missouri crisis—had predicted that unless the rights of Negroes were recognized, and emancipation begun, God would exact a terrible price for the violation of the rights with which he had endowed *all* his creatures. Here in 1782 is a draft of Lincoln's Second Inaugural.

❊ ❊ ❊

Washington's letter to the Newport synagogue represents an epochal event in world history. Leo Strauss has written that "the Jewish problem is the most manifest symbol of the human problem insofar as it is a social or political problem." Washington's recognition of Jews as equal citizens because equal human beings was absolutely unprecedented. But it was absolutely necessary if the doctrine of religious liberty forged in the struggle for disestablishment in Virginia (led by Madison and Jefferson and supported by Washington) was to prevail. In Jefferson's statute of religious liberty of 1786 we have the complement of the Declaration of Independence: together they condense the meaning of the American political tradition into the most lucid and eloquent compass. They join together civil and religious liberty, in an unbreakable bond wherein neither is possible without the other. In the letter to the Jews, Washington illuminates as nothing else could, how and in what respect the American Founding was addressed to the human problem—as a social or political problem—in its most comprehensive form. It defines that in respect to which the principles of the American Founding are the principles of the best regime of Western civilization.

Yet Irving Kristol has delivered this astonishing oracle on religion and the Founding. The authors of the Constitution, he says,

> were for the most part not particularly interested in religion. I am not aware that any of them wrote anything worth reading on religion, especially Jefferson, who wrote nothing worth reading on religion or almost anything else. [22]

This comprehensive disparagement of the great men who made this nation has all the virtuosity of pigeons flying over statues. But statues endure, and pigeons remain. When Kristol sneered at Tom Paine in his

1973 lecture, it was evident that he really meant Jefferson. By 1990 he had lost all restraint. It cannot be repeated too often however that the civil liberty of the American Founding would have been impossible, had there not been widespread acceptance of the principle

> that our civil rights have no dependence on our religious opinions, any more than our opinions in physics or geometry.

This assertion in the Virginia statute did not of course bind any other state, and religious establishments continued well into the 19th century. But in time it came to dominate public opinion everywhere in the United States, and is enshrined today in all the state constitutions. But it was clear to all the Founding Fathers—as we asserted in our critique of Rehnquist's unqualified majoritarianism—that majority rule and minority rights could not be combined in any government in which voting might decide how a man ought to worship his God. Jefferson had said— to repeat—that the attempts to influence a man's religious beliefs "by temporal punishments . . . or civil incapacitations tend only to beget habits of hypocrisy and meanness." The attempt to do so, he had continued, had "established and maintained false religions over the greatest part of the world, and through all time. . . . It is more than noteworthy therefore that in 1965, at the Second Vatican Council, the Catholic bishops of the world (by a vote of 1,954 to 249) approved a Declaration of Religious Freedom. This declaration renounced the old ideal of a confessional state, in which Catholicism would be the official religion. Jefferson, in the *Notes on Virginia* (Query XVII) had said that

> The error seems not sufficiently eradicated, that the operations of the mind, as well as the acts of the body, are subject to the coercion of the laws. But our rulers can have no authority over such natural rights, only as we have submitted to them. The rights of conscience we never submitted, we could not submit.

In Vatican II, the Catholic Church came officially to agree. What many fail to understand is that the separation of state and church is the origin of the separation of state and society, which is the foundation for the entire concept limited government. Here is George Weigel,[23] a prominent Catholic layman, writing on the 30th anniversary of Vatican II.

It turns out that religious freedom is not an inert doctrine; it has dramatic consequences. For if there is a sanctuary of conscience inside every human person where no earthly power can legitimately tread, then the state is, by definition, a limited state. In that sanctuary of conscience, we are wrestling with matters of ultimate importance. To say that the state has no business interfering in that conversation means that the fundamentally important matters in life are the business of other communities. And that implies social pluralism.

Tocqueville's celebration of the role of voluntary associations in American democracy has its foundation in the idea of limited government. But limited government has its origin in the doctrine of religious liberty. Weigel notes that the drive to change this age old position of the church was led by John Courtney Murray, an American Jesuit. Murray's thoughts on this topic were expressed in his book *We Hold These Truths: Reflections on the American Proposition* (1960). It is needless to say whence the inspiration came for a book with that title. Murray's crusade at Vatican II was powerfully aided by the then archbishop of Krakow, now Pope John Paul II. Although Jefferson's doctrine of religious freedom, integral to the heart of American constitutionalism, became the official church doctrine only in 1965, it had long been canonical in the minds and hearts of American Catholics. Bourke Cockran (1854–1923), the greatest lay spokesman of the Catholic Church[24] in his lifetime, in a speech in 1910, declared that

> If every man, woman and child in the United States were Catholic— if full power to change our political system was in the hands of Catholic representatives—not one word of the Constitution could be changed with advantage to the Catholic Church.

When Jefferson said that the union of church and state had been the cause of false religions over most of the world in all human history, he was saying what he himself believed to be a necessary inference from the example of "the Holy author of our religion." He might also have cited the saying of Jesus, of rendering to Caesar what was Caesar's, and to God what was God's as the ultimate doctrinal source for separation of church and state. The doctrines enshrined in Jefferson's two greatest compositions are then the philosophical foundation equally of free government, and pure religion. The final and greatest act of reformation in the Christian West, both of government and religion, are therein enshrined.

❈ ❈ ❈

Irving Kristol has of late come to be regarded as a sage on religion in a free society. He and I agree on the desirability of non-sectarian prayer in public schools. We agree on the importance of the Christian Coalition—and the "social issues" they support—within the conservative movement and within the Republican Party. But I believe that the possibility of a constructive and healthy non-sectarian religious influence in American politics depends upon the rationalism of the natural law tradition that presided over the Founding. Kristol thinks that such rationalism is the enemy of religion, not (as I do) as an integral component of it. The only occasion in the last twenty-five years that Kristol has replied to anything I have written is the following.[25]

> A society of people interested only in their self-interest in the marketplace is a society that is too base to be tolerated [hence only *two* cheers for capitalism]. . . . The religious tradition functions to correct this natural propensity of a commercial civilization to debase itself.
>
> It also provides something else that is critically necessary, namely, some absolute foundation for our moral values. I know that there are some people who think that such values can be rationally created, perhaps by study, by philosophical analysis, or by computer. But, of course, values are not created; values are inherited. There is no such thing as a rationalist religion which gives you an authoritative moral code. . . . There are no rationalist ten commandments. Morality is derived from certain fundamental dogmatic truths, and I emphasize that word dogmatic. It is the function of a religion, in a society such as ours, to provide the dogmatic basis for those truths.
>
> As this pertains to the American political tradition, we enter into some controversy, which will be better understood if I compare my views to those of Harry Jaffa. . . . Mr. Jaffa, quite correctly, feels that in discussing the issue of human rights one must raise the question of what human rights are based upon. One cannot just be arbitrary and say, "I prefer this conception of human rights to yours and that's all there is to it." You have got to have a fundamental, unshakable basis for your conviction in a given set of human rights, and Harry Jaffa's is that the rights expressed in the Declaration of Independence, in the end, rely on the natural law and natural rights tradition which goes back through St. Thomas Aquinas to Aristotle.

> I think he is wrong. As I see it, our dogma in regard to such matters as human rights comes from the Protestantized version of the Judeo-Christian tradition. On what do we base our valuation of human rights? Why do we cherish human rights? Because of something called "the dignity of man," a key phrase. That is something that emerges out of Jewish doctrine, out of Christian doctrine, and in its modern form, out of Protestantism, which insists on the dignity of the individual soul and the relation of this individual soul to the Deity.

I pass over the fact that, in speaking of "moral values," Kristol, like Rehnquist, is using the language of moral relativism, even as he is denying—or thinks he is denying—the relativism of morality. He says "that there are some people who think that such values can be rationally created." Rehnquist, we have seen, thinks that morality—or what passes for morality—is "created" by a number of people having their "value judgments" enacted into law. According to Rehnquist, moral goodness—or what passes for moral goodness—in a law is acquired by being enacted. Accordingly, there was no basis in reason for distinguishing the morality of the laws protecting slavery from those protecting freedom in the original Constitution.

Except for legal positivists and their relativistic cohorts, I do not know anyone who thinks morality is "created" by human agency. If morality is created at all, my ancient faith teaches me that it is by the Creator. I certainly believe it to be my inheritance—from God and nature.

Kristol says there is no such thing as a rationalist religion, which provides "an authoritative moral code." There may not be a rationalist religion, but there is certainly a rational component of any religion comprehended by the protections of the first amendment. The free exercise of religion does not include the right to human sacrifice, to suttee, to temple prostitution, to the use of hallucinatory drugs, or to any other of the thousand and one barbarous and savage religious practices that have been features of barbarous and savage religions. Nor does it tolerate the mutilations, or the handling of poisonous snakes in worship services, that some Protestant sects have practiced, on the basis of literal readings of passages in the New Testament. The first platform of the Republican Party, in 1856, condemned as "twin relics of barbarism" both slavery and polygamy. The war against polygamy was short and relatively bloodless. The war against slavery was long and bloody. Clearly, both slavery and polygamy were ultimately incompatible with the law of reason and of nature, and could not be justified by any appeal to the free exercise of religion. It is a tacit premise of the right to religious freedom that it be circumscribed by the laws of reason and of nature, which laws define the republican form government guaranteed by the Constitution to every state of the Union. Kristol is at his most pontifical—or rabbinical—when he says "our dogma in regard to such matters as human rights comes from the Protestantized version of the Judeo-Christian tradition." But American Protestantism split right across the Mason and Dixon line in 1861. Nothing about the "dignity of man" as it had been interpreted in the Protestant churches of the South prevented them from being as resolute in the support of slavery as their opposite numbers of the North were in opposing it. Protestants North and South "read the same Bible, and prayed to the same God." Protestantism as such did not decide whether slavery was or was not consistent with the "dignity of man." The dignity of man rested only with that Protestantism in which the rational principles of the Declaration of Independence were a vital element.

Kristol uses all the emphasis he can summon, to insist that the foundation of a moral code must be "dogmatic." It has been said, and not without reason, that "If you laid all the philosophers in the world end to end, they still would not reach a conclusion."[26] But the Founding Fathers were not philosophers, they were statesmen. They did not eschew the use of reason, but they put it to work as God's work, to form the character of a nation, just as Moses had done. Kristol says there are no rationalist ten commandments. But the moral components of the ten commandments have always been recognized as according to reason. Mankind has always known that murder, theft, adultery, and perjury were wrong. God certainly lent authority to these prohibitions, especially if it is believed that God will punish their violations, even if they escape human punishment. But the natural law has been recognized within Christianity no less than within philosophy, as we proved from St. Paul, in our critique of Russell Kirk. And Leo Strauss has written that "Jewish orthodoxy based its claim to superiority to other religions from the beginning on its superior rationality. (Deut. 4:6)."[27]

But if Kristol is looking for a dogmatic assertion of moral authority, where will he find one greater than that beginning "We hold these truths to be self-evident. . . ." The Ten Commandments were not issued with more assurance, nor did they express a firmer reliance upon divine providence. Our doctrine of human rights, Kristol says, comes from a "Protestantized version of the Judeo-Christian tradition." Granted. And no purer example of that version is the Declaration of Independence. That is one reason President Coolidge called it a great spiritual document.

Let us then see an actual example in a Protestant sermon of the Protestantized version of the Judeo-Christian tradition that presided at the Founding. Here is an excerpt from the sermon preached before the Governor—John Hancock—and the Senate and House of Representatives of Massachusetts, by the Reverend Samuel Cooper. The occasion was the inauguration—in the midst of the Revolution—of the government of the commonwealth under the new constitution (of 1780).

> We want not indeed, a special revelation from heaven to teach us that men are born equal and free; that no man has a natural claim of dominion over his neighbors, nor one nation any such claim upon another; and that as government is only the administration of the affairs of a number of men combined for their own security and happiness, such a society have a right freely to determine by whom and in what manner their own affairs shall be administered. These are the plain dictates of that reason and common sense with which the common parent of men has informed the human bosom. It is, however, a satisfaction to observe such everlasting maxims of equity confirmed, and impressed upon the consciences of men, by the instructions, precepts, and examples given us in the sacred oracles; one internal mark of their divine original, and that they come from him "who hath made of one blood all nations to dwell upon the face of the earth," whose authority sanctifies only those governments that instead of oppressing any part of his family, vindicate the oppressed, and restrain and punish the oppressor.[28]

We see that natural theology and revealed theology form a seamless web. Kristol to the contrary notwithstanding, in the aforesaid Protestantism, God speaks to us by right reason no less than by revelation. The doctrine of Cooper's sermon in no way differs from that of the Declaration of Independence. But Cooper did not need to have the Declaration in mind since the identical doctrine informed the constitution whose inauguration he was celebrating. That all men are born free and equal, or that they are all created equal, is not only a dictate of reason, but of the sacred oracle which declares that God hath made of one blood all nations. We see that both reason and revelation condemn slavery, and that no scriptural argument can justify it. Whether the natural law embodied in this Protestantism may be traced back through Locke to Hooker to Aquinas to Aristotle is another question. What is important here is not the ancestry of the doctrine but its truth.

✿ ✿ ✿

We have already noted Kristol's Rip van Winkle version of American history from the Revolution to the Civil War. It should not surprise us then that he continues it to include the Civil War.

> our history has been by most reasonable, let us say historical, stan-
> dards, not particularly tumultuous; and the American people seem
> never to have been torn by conflicting interpretations of the
> American political tradition, though scholars may be. Even our very
> bloody Civil War had surprisingly little effect on the course of
> American history. If one were to write an American history textbook
> with the chapter on the Civil War dropped out, to be replaced by a
> single sentence to the effect that slavery was abolished by constitu-
> tional amendment in 1865, very little in subsequent chapters as now
> written, would need revision. The Civil War had even less effect on
> the American political tradition since there never really was a distinc-
> tively Southern political tradition, nor did the war give rise to one. A
> textbook on American intellectual history could safely ignore the
> Civil War, were it not for the fact that one feels it to be almost
> sacrilegious that so much suffering should be so barren of conse-
> quence. The Civil War was and is a most memorable event—but not
> any kind of turning point in American history.

We have cited the passage in Jefferson's *Notes*—written in the midst of the Revolution—in which he anticipates civil and servile war, unless emancipation is begun. From this we know that all intelligent patriots were aware that the Revolution had planted a time bomb, and the ticking of that bomb grew louder and louder as the nation moved to-wards the war that Jefferson had predicted. We have seen that Kristol thinks that the key to our morality is to be found in the Judeo-Christian concept of "the dignity of man." But what greater challenge to that concept can there be than chattel slavery—than a system of society in which men and women and children can be bought and sold like animals of another species? Yet Kristol has not a word to say about it. Kristol's Judaism fails to remind him that Moses was, before he was anything else, an antislavery leader. It does not occur to him that the two greatest antislavery leaders of all time are Moses and Lincoln.

If one added up all the things in American history Kristol invites us to ignore, how much would be left? Imagine an American history with a single sentence on the thirteenth amendment, but none on the Emancipation Proclamation, or on the events that preceded and followed it! Can there be any greater absurdity?

But Kristol has said that hardly anything Jefferson wrote is worth reading. Lincoln had said that "the principles of Jefferson are the definitions and axioms of free society," and that he had "never had a feeling politically that did not spring from the sentiments embodied in the Declaration of Independence." And, of course, Lincoln said that this nation had been "dedicated to the proposition that all men are created equal." So it follows that hardly anything Lincoln said or wrote is worth reading!

Mr. Kristol thinks that scholars, but not the American people, have been torn by differences concerning slavery and race. One wonders why the Civil War was fought by the American people and not by scholars! But Mr. Kristol is such a man that many men and many women and many children believe anything when once they learn that Mr. Kristol believes it. It is painful to speculate what effect such pronouncements have on national standards of historical literacy! But the Civil War not a turning point?

In 1858 Abraham Lincoln declared that a house divided against itself could not stand. Either the nation would become all free, or all slave. Mr. Kristol notwithstanding, Lincoln said that a point had been reached in which either the advocates of slavery would push forward until it became lawful in all the states, North as well as South, old as well as new, or the opponents of slavery would place it "in course of ultimate extinction." A little more than two years after the House Divided speech Lincoln was elected president. Before his inauguration, seven slave states had seceded from the Union, six had already formed the Confederacy, and Jefferson Davis had been sworn in as its president with Alexander Hamilton Stephens as its vice-president.

Lincoln's inauguration was March 4, 1861. Fort Sumter was fired upon on April 13th. Almost exactly midway between these two points in time, on March 21st, Stephens at Savannah, Georgia, delivered what has come down to us as the "cornerstone" speech. Stephens had once been a Whig colleague and friend of Lincoln in the House during the Mexican War, and had powerfully opposed Georgia's secession in both the Georgia legislature and in its secession convention. Yet he was a follower of Calhoun's doctrines of slavery and state rights, and thus went with his state and joined the rebellion. He was, in Burke's phrase, one of the South's most eminent men of light and learning.

The cornerstone speech is certainly one of the important speeches of American history, although it is hard to find today in documentary collections. It was little cited or noted until I quoted from it in *How to Think About the American Revolution*. It is given its name because its theme is taken from Psalms, 118:22.

> The stone which the builders rejected has become the head of the corner.

This verse is repeated at least three times in the New Testament, once by Jesus himself. In every case it is Jesus who is referred to as the "cornerstone."

The importance of this speech is mainly because of what it says, but partly also because of when it was said. After the war Stephens produced his massive *Constitutional View of the War Between the States* in which he defends the defeated Confederate cause as an attempt to defend minority rights against majority tyranny. Here that same cause—undefeated and apparently peacefully triumphant—is vindicated entirely in terms of the rightness and goodness of slavery. His vindication takes the form of a comparison of the obsolete and reactionary thought of the Founding Fathers with the scientific and progressive thought which informs the new Constitution of the Confederacy. Here are some leading excerpts.

> The new [Confederate] Constitution has put to rest forever all agitating questions relating to our peculiar institution—African slavery as it exists among us—the proper status of the negro in our form of civilization. *This was the immediate cause of the late rupture and present revolution* [italics in the original]. . . . The prevailing ideas entertained by [Jefferson] and most of the leading statesmen at the time of the formation of the old Constitution, were that the enslave-

ment of the African was in violation of the laws of nature; that it was wrong in principle, socially, morally, and politically. It was an evil they knew not well how to deal with, but the general opinion of the men of that day was, that somehow or other, in the order of Providence, the institution would be evanescent and pass away. This idea, though not incorporated in the Constitution, was the prevailing idea at the time.

The Constitution, it is true, secured every essential guarantee to the institution while it should last, and hence no argument can be justly used against the constitutional guarantees thus secured, because of the common sentiment of the day. Those ideas however were fundamentally wrong. They rested upon the assumption of the equality of the races. This was an error. It was a sandy foundation, and the idea of a government built upon it; when the storm came and the wind blew, it fell. (Matthew 7:28)

Our new government is founded upon exactly the opposite idea; its foundations are laid, its cornerstone rests upon the great truth that the negro is not the equal of the white man. That slavery— subordination to the superior race, is his natural and normal condition. This, our new government is the first in the history of the world based upon this great physical and moral truth. This truth has been slow in the process of its development, like all other truths in the various departments of science. . . . It was so with the principles of Galileo—it was so with Adam Smith . . . it was so with Harvey and his theory of the circulation of the blood. It is stated that not a single one of the medical profession, living at the time of the announcement of the truths made by him, admitted them. Now they are universally acknowledged. May we not therefore look with confidence to the ultimate universal acknowledgment of the truths upon which our system rests. It is the first government ever instituted upon principles of strict conformity to nature, and the ordination of Providence, in furnishing the materials of human society. . . . The negro, by nature, or by the curse of Canaan, is fitted for that condition which he occupies in our system.

We see the beginnings of that "scientific racism" that came to its full flower in the regime of Adolf Hitler. The Confederate States of America may have been a genteel anticipation of the Third Reich, but it was an anticipation nonetheless.[29] Was it not a turning point that the United States, by the election of Lincoln, and by the preservation of the Union, turned its back upon the neo-Nazi future implied in such doctrine? Was it not a turning point in world history, that the United States did not enter the twentieth century half slave and half free? Was it not a turning point in world history that the United States did not enter the twentieth century divided into hostile federations? Had it done so, what role would it—or they—have played in the great contests of freedom and domination in the twentieth century? The twentieth century has been the bloodiest in human history, but the conflict was ultimately tilted toward freedom only by the weight of the Union that Lincoln had preserved. In that sense the Civil War represents a turning point, not in American history, but in world history.[30]

Lincoln denied the right of any state to secede from the Union without the permission of the Union or of any other state. He did so because, he held, in ratifying the Constitution the states had committed themselves to accepting the results of elections held according to the rules of the Constitution. Lincoln had been elected in strict accordance with those rules. No rights of minorities had been violated in the election, nor had there been any threats of such violations, then or in the future. The election of Lincoln had, however, signaled a decision of the American people against the extension of slavery. That decision the South could not accept. The South wished to extend slavery, not only to the existing territories, but to Cuba and throughout Central America.[31]

If, said Lincoln, the government could be broken up whenever someone did not like the results of an election, this would mean an end to the very idea of free government. Said Lincoln:

> Plainly, the central idea of secession is the essence of anarchy. A majority, held in restraint by constitutional checks and limitations, and always changing easily with deliberate changes of popular opinion and sentiments is the only true sovereign of a free people. Whoever rejects it, does, of necessity, fly to anarchy or to despotism. Unanimity is impossible; the rule of a minority, as permanent arrangement, is wholly inadmissible; so that, rejecting the majority principle, anarchy or despotism in some form is all that is left.

Here is a lesson in Aristotelian political science, delivered with Euclidean clarity, in Shakespearian prose. This is a precious inheritance of every American child—and indeed of every child born to inherit freedom anywhere. What kind of "conservatism" would ignore it?

V.

For many reasons, it is not a grateful task to identify Professor Harvey Mansfield as another defector from the "ancient faith" of Abraham Lincoln, and from that "central idea" from which all the minor thoughts of the American Founding radiate. But Mansfield has joined the ranks of other so called conservatives, in writing of "the self-evident half-truth that all men are created equal. . . ." This is more than a demeaning of both the Declaration and the Gettysburg Address. A half-truth is not merely a falsehood, but a deceitful falsehood. Mansfield knows as well as anyone, that in the course of American history, no one has depreciated the proposition of human equality in this way who was not a defender of slavery. Calhoun did not mince words when he said it was "the most false and dangerous of all political errors." If Mansfield does not mean to be a defender of slavery, why then has he joined the followers of Calhoun in denouncing the proposition that all men are created equal?

The words we have quoted are from an article entitled "Returning to the Founders: the Debate on the Constitution" in the September 1993 issue of *The New Criterion*. It is ostensibly a review of *The Debate on the Constitution: Federalist and Antifederalist Speeches, Articles, and Letters During the Struggle over Ratification* (Library of America, 2 vols. 1993), edited by Bernard Bailyn. The two volumes total nearly 2,400 pages. The Founders, Mansfield writes, "may not be demigods [but] they are far above us. . . . To read anywhere in these volumes is to be overcome with a shameful sense of inferiority."

According to Mansfield, the "original debate [on the Constitution] makes a very ambitious claim for America's greatness that we still need to appreciate and assess." However, in investigating this claim Mansfield turns away almost entirely from the debate recorded in these two volumes. He proceeds instead

> to a beginning long before the Constitution in modern political philosophy. That beginning is none other than the "state of nature" described by Thomas Hobbes and John Locke, a concept that has lost most of its force today but that still had currency among the Founders.

Certainly the state of nature in Locke had great currency in the Founding, but that was not true of Hobbes's version. Hobbes constructed an argument for absolute monarchy from his version of the state of nature, and this was anathema to Americans. For them there was a world of difference between Hobbes and Locke, but not for Mansfield.[32] For Locke, and the American Founders, man in the state of nature was bound by the moral reason of the law of nature. Here is Alexander Hamilton attacking an adversary for holding Hobbesian views.

> [Hobbes's] opinion was exactly coincident with yours, relative to man in the state of nature. He held, as you do, that he was then perfectly free from all restraint of law and government. Moral obligation, according to him, is derived from the introduction of civil society; and there is no virtue but what is purely artificial, the mere contrivance of politicians for the maintenance of social intercourse. But the reason he ran into this absurd and impious doctrine was, that he disbelieved the existence of an intelligent, superintending principle, who is the governor, and will be the final judge, of the universe.[33]

The repudiation of Hobbes's atheism and moral relativism could not be more forceful. Nothing could be more alien to the thought of the American Founding than to identify it with Hobbesianism.

When Mansfield says the concept of the state of nature has lost most of its force today, he is mistaking form for substance. Our fellow citizens may not know the "state of nature" in an academic sense, but they know instinctively and politically that their fundamental rights are antecedent to government and do not come from government, but that government exists to protect those rights. And they have lost little of their ancestors' conviction that taxation without representation is tyranny. These convictions carry with them a logical implication of a state of nature, whether it is recognized or not. In this sense the state of nature has lost none of its original vitality.

Mansfield writes that

> The state of nature was a pre-political condition, to which it was necessary to recur in order to find the basis of politics; politics must be based on what comes before politics. Why? To see the reason for this fateful conception, we need to compare it to the thought it opposed and replaced, which is conveniently found in Aristotle. For Aristotle, there is no beginning behind or before politics that pro-

vides a guide or basis for politics; every beginning of politics is political. That is one thing intended by his statement that man is by nature a political animal. Every kind of politics, every regime, is guided by the principle which rules it from the beginning; a beginning is in accordance with a principle and a rule in accordance with the principle of the beginning. . . . From Aristotle's standpoint, then, to understand America one would first look for its principle of rule in the speeches of its rulers, in the Constitution, and also in the Declaration of Independence.

One wonders why Mansfield does not adopt Aristotle's "standpoint" for his "first look" for the principle of rule in America, but instead turns back the clock more than a century to Hobbes and Locke in England.

Mansfield says we need to compare the state of nature theorists to the thought they opposed and replaced, which he says is "conveniently" found in Aristotle. I think he is mistaken as to the opposition between the Locke of the American Founders and Aristotle. He confuses the history of political philosophy with the history of political thought. Hobbes and Locke may or may not have opposed and replaced Aristotle in their own minds, but there is no evidence of such opposition in the minds of the American Founders. When Jefferson listed the sources of the Declaration of Independence, he mentioned among the books of "public right" Aristotle, Cicero, Locke and Sidney. Certainly there was a belief that there had been improvements in the science of politics, as in other sciences. But improvement is not the same as opposition and replacement. How Locke (or Leo Strauss) understood Locke is an entirely different question from how Jefferson or Adams, or Hamilton or Madison or Washington understood Locke.

What does Mansfield mean by saying that in Aristotle there is no beginning behind or before politics? It is John C. Calhoun, not Aristotle, who says not only that the political state is man's natural state, but that he is "impelled irresistibly" into it. According to Aristotle, on the contrary, the political community is preceded by the family and the village. At some point, the number of families and villages reaches an aggregate sufficient to form a political community. Although, says Aristotle, the impulse to form a political community is in all men by nature, the one who first united them in such a community was the greatest of benefactors. Now the impulse to form an oak tree is in every acorn by nature. But no external intervention—apart from soil, sun, and water—

is required for the transformation to seedling, sapling, and oak. All the energy—all the transformation of matter into form—comes from within. But the political community does not come to be by natural means in this sense. It requires an external artisan to transform the material into the form intended by nature. Neither in Aristotle nor in Locke are human beings, like acorns, "impelled irresistibly" to form governments. Nature does not of itself unite men into political communities, or decide the political forms those political communities will take.

Contrary to Mansfield, the founding of a political community out of a pre-political society of families and villages must have a beginning behind or before politics. Typically, there must be a founding lawgiver, a powerful political leader who forges a political community, usually in circumstances of the greatest difficulty and against great opposition and resistance. As much as Praxiteles or Michelangelo faced with a block of marble, he must have a vision or conception which initiates politics but is not derived from politics.

To compare and contrast Aristotle and Locke one must first compare and contrast the polities, ancient and modern, for which and about which they wrote. We must come to grips with what Leo Strauss meant when he wrote that "a simple continuation of the tradition of classical political philosophy . . . is no longer possible." That this is so is shown by reflecting on Aristotle's dictum "that what the law does not command, it forbids." Certainly today Aristotle would be the first to see that this would be a formula for the worst kind of tyranny. He would be the first to see that in the modern world a decent constitution must assume that "what the law does not forbid it permits." These apparently opposite pronouncements would in fact serve identical ends. Their difference reflects the difference between the ancient world and the modern, illuminating the fact that all of natural right, being subject to the dictates of prudence, is changeable.

However, what Aristotle says about law agrees entirely with what we find in the books of Moses. The Old Testament presents us with a vivid account of the founding of an ancient city. The unique role of the Bible in the history of Western civilization should not obscure the fact that in many respects its story is typical. Plato's *Laws* begins with the Athenian Stranger prompting the Cretan and the Spartan to declare that each of their lawgivers received his laws from a god. In this respect they did not differ from Moses. All the great ancient cities—or polities—understood

their laws to be of divine origin. Hence the question of political obligation—which is central for Lockeians and the Signers of the Declaration
of Independence—did not exist. In the ancient city, the inequality of
God or gods and mortal men decides the answer to the question, "Why
should I obey?" If, however, laws are of human origin, why should the
authority of one or a few decide the obligations of the many, or of all? If
there is no evident reason why one or a few should decide for all, then
political obligation must be derived from human equality, which is the
same as to say from the state of nature.

When Moses led a ragged band of runaway slaves into the desert, he
started with most unpromising material. Or perhaps we should say that
he began with God's promises to Abraham in his knapsack but little
else! It has been well said that it was easier for Moses to get the Jews
out of Egypt, than to get Egypt out of the Jews. In forty years in the
desert, the discipline of the Law transformed those former slaves into
the hardened band of desert warriors that Joshua led to the conquest of
the land that the Lord had promised. This Law did not admit of any
free exercise of religion, or of any other of the private choices enshrined
in modern constitutionalism.

The religion of the ancient city reflected its origin in the religion of
the family which (according to Fustel de Coulanges) was one of ances-
tor worship. We see this in the Bible, in the role of the patriarchs,
Abraham, Isaac, and Jacob. They are not gods themselves, but their
relationship to God establishes the existence and sanctity of a polity to
be descended from them. Those who will constitute that polity will
enjoy their status and their privileges because of the fulfillment of
God's promises to Abraham. Their dignity will be as descendants of
Abraham and as inheritors of his covenant with God. They must themselves continue that covenant by obedience to God's Law, which Law is
itself the most important form of the blessing that descends to them.
There is however no conception of individual rights apart from this
inheritance.

The New Testament begins, in the first chapter of Matthew, with
"the genealogy of Jesus Christ, the son of David, the son of Abraham."
There are three times fourteen generations from Abraham to Jesus, and
this line of direct descent is necessary to connect the promises of God
to Abraham with the fulfillment of those promises by Jesus. This is a
sharp reminder that the ancient city was a community of blood, of

common descent. You were an Athenian—or a Spartan, or a Cretan, or an Israelite—only because of your father and mother. Citizenship was not a voluntary act. The attachment of each city to its gods, and of its gods to its city, which we see so clearly in the relationship to God and Israel, defines the fundamental dimension of human political consciousness in ancient cities.

The ancient world came to an end when the conquests of Rome made all the cities of the ancient world and their gods, dependencies of Rome. When Roman citizenship was finally extended to the provinces, Rome was no longer a particular city—one among many—but the universal city. But the plurality of gods itself depended in the end upon the plurality of cities. By the very necessity of the self-understanding of the ancient city, when there was but one city there would, sooner or later, have to be only one God. The establishment of Christianity formally concluded a process of some centuries in which the monotheism of a universal empire replaced the polytheism of a pluralistic political world. This change represented the greatest of all historic changes in that human consciousness of the human condition within which the political problem presents itself. No comparison of Aristotle and Locke is possible without taking into account the implications of this change for statesmanship and political philosophy. The state of nature is not an opposition to Aristotle but a response to a condition that did not exist for Aristotle.

With the ascendancy of Christian monotheism that particular relationship between God or gods and particular peoples that had hitherto dominated the ancient city came to an end.[34] It brought to an end that connection between God and law which we see so vividly in the Books of Moses, and which had characterized the ancient city. God was now the God of all peoples, but the legislator for none. Why one should obey the law, or what law (or what authority) one should obey, became a question of paramount importance. Jesus with calculated ambiguity distinguished the obligations to Caesar from the obligations to God. In so doing, he said what would have been unintelligible to any Israelite during the reigns of David or Solomon, as it would have been to any Athenian or Spartan or Roman of an earlier age. When Jesus spoke, Caesar and Rome were all powerful, and any challenge to Roman authority was suicidal. But the day would come when Popes, in the name of Jesus—whose kingdom was not of this world—deposed kings and

Caesars in this world. The conflict of civil and religious authority which began with the persecution of Christians and continued with persecution by Christians went on almost without intermission until the American Revolution. It persisted until a theory of religious liberty, grounded in the state of nature, was set forth as law by Thomas Jefferson.

When Jesus was told that his mother and his brothers were waiting to see him, he stretched out his hand towards his disciples and said "Here are my mother and my brothers." (Matthew 12:49). By this act the community of blood and common descent was replaced by a community of faith. The promise to Abraham was transmuted into a promise to every individual human being who accepted Jesus' doctrine. The portion of the sermon of Dr. Cooper quoted above took its text in part from Acts 17:26, that God had made of one blood all the nations of mankind. Henceforth the patriarchs of Israel became the patriarchs of the entire family of man. Dr. Cooper took it for granted—as did Jefferson and Lincoln—that there was perfect agreement between the Gospel and the principle of human equality in the Declaration.[35]

When Lincoln at Gettysburg invoked "our fathers who brought forth this nation . . ." there resonated the identification of the patriarchs of the American Founding with the patriarchs of the Bible. But the parallel runs deeper than that. Here is Lincoln in Chicago, July 10, 1858. He is speaking of the recent celebrations of the 4th of July, and what they mean.

> We hold this annual celebration to remind ourselves of all the good done in this process of time [since 1776], of how it was done and who did it, and how we are historically connected with it; and we go from these meetings in better humor with ourselves—we feel more attached the one to the other, and more firmly bound to the country we inhabit. In every way we are better men in the age, and race, and country in which we live, for these celebrations. But after we have done all this we have not yet reached the whole. There is something else connected with it. We have besides these men—descended by blood from our ancestors—among us perhaps half our people who are no descendants at all of these men, they are men who have come from Europe—Germans, Irish, French, and Scandinavians—men that have come from Europe themselves, or whose ancestors have come hither and settled here, finding themselves our equals in all

things. If they look back through this history to trace their connection with those days by blood, they find they have none, they cannot
carry themselves back into that glorious epoch and make themselves
feel that they are part of us, but when they look through that old
Declaration of Independence, they find that those old men say that
"We hold these truths to be self-evident, that all men are created
equal," and then they feel that that moral sentiment taught at that
day evidences their relation to those men, that it is the father of all
moral principle in them, and that they have a right to claim it as
though they were blood of the blood, and flesh of the flesh, of the
men who wrote that Declaration, and so they are.

Jesus taught that his disciples were his family, and as such shared his
descent from Abraham, Isaac, and Jacob. Lincoln taught that the disciples of the Declaration of Independence were a family, who shared
equally in their descent from the patriarchs of the American Revolution. Lincoln says that they have a right to claim this patrimony "as
though" they were of the same flesh and blood, but adds, "and so they
are." The words of the apostle, that God has made of one blood all
nations, resonates once again.

What does Lincoln mean by calling the equality maxim "the father of
all moral principle?" A little later in the same speech, he remarks

> My friend has said to me that I am a poor hand to quote Scripture. I
> will try it again however. It is said in one of the admonitions of the
> Lord, "As your Father in heaven is perfect, be ye also perfect." The
> Saviour, I suppose, did not expect that any human creature could be
> as perfect as the Father in Heaven; but He said, "As your Father in
> Heaven is perfect, be ye also perfect." He set that up as a standard,
> and he who did most towards reaching that standard, attained the
> highest degree of moral perfection. So I say in relation to the princi-
> ple that all men are created equal, let it be as nearly reached as we
> can. If we cannot give freedom to every creature, let us do nothing
> that will impose slavery upon any other creature. Let us then turn
> this government back into the channel in which the framers of the
> Constitution originally placed it.

Let us consider further the relation of the foregoing to Scripture. Elsewhere Lincoln said, "As I would not be a slave, so I would not be a
master." Clearly this is an application of the injunction that "Whatever

you wish that men do to you, do so to them; for this is the law and the prophets." This is one of two places that Jesus concentrates the ethical core of the entire Bible into the fewest possible words. Let us ask, "to whom is Jesus' admonition addressed?" Certainly not to the disciples only, or to the Jews or the Greeks or the Romans. It can mean nothing unless it is addressed *without exception* to every human being, then in the world or whoever after might be. It concerns the relationship of every actual or possible human being to every other. In this relationship there is neither "Greek nor Jew." With respect to our moral obligations—our rights and duties—arising from the very nature of our humanity, all men are created equal. If there were classes of human beings with respect to whom the reciprocity of rights and duties did not apply, it would be because some were as far below us as beasts, or as far above us as gods. If we are all of one blood, this is not possible. The ethics of the Gospel and of the Declaration are one and the same.

❊ ❊ ❊

Professor Mansfield noted that Aristotle had said that man is by nature a political animal. Aristotle also says that someone who is not by nature part of a political community is either a beast or a god. The "great chain of being," in which man, beast, and God, are both joined and distinguished, is as fundamental to Aristotle as to Jefferson and the Declaration. With respect to sharing in a political nature—as in a human nature—it is as evident to Aristotle as to Jefferson, that all men are created equal. In what then is Mansfield's reservation against the self-evident truth that all men are created equal?

> To this political view [by which every kind of politics, every regime is guided by the principle that rules it from the beginning], which looks at politics in its own terms, there is indeed a nonpolitical background out of which every regime comes, to which it returns. This is the cycle of regimes, in which regimes rise and fall. Regimes arise because previous regimes have fallen. Why do they fall? In every case they fall for accidental causes but also, and especially, for one essential cause: they are all imperfect. They are imperfect because they are partial and partisan. Although they claim to advance the common good, in fact they represent the good of a party, typically the party of the few or of the many. All regimes are typically oligarchies or democracies. Aristotle mentions the possibility of a mixed regime that would have advantages of both parties, and he urges it on the parti-

sans; but he does not have much confidence that it will be adopted. Although every regime is debatable, the debate will be judged by the very partisans who carry it on; and they will surely judge in their own partisan interest.

No actual regime is likely to represent an impartial common good. And yet it is very important to judge regimes by the standard of the truth of their partisan claims. For their partialities will eventually catch up with them and bring them down. For example, a regime based upon the selfevident half-truth that all men are created equal will eventually founder because of its disregard of the many ways in which men are created unequal. Even if such a regime seems powerful at the moment, it will be subject to revolution by the partisans, in this case those of the few whom it ignores. Sooner or later they will gather their forces, pick on a convenient pretext, overthrow the regime and set up their own—only to make a compensating error, leaving their regime also open to revolution or destruction. In the long run therefore human beings make the same mistakes and learn nothing from political experience.

At this point Mansfield notes that the American Founders believed they could break out of this melancholy cycle by building a regime based not on partisanship but upon truth. According to Mansfield, they believed that

> By following Hobbes and turning to the passions that allegedly precede opinions, above all the passion of *fear* [Mansfield's italics] we can discover a universal, non-partisan foundation for politics.

It is astonishing that with more than two thousand pages of documents of the Founding before him, Mansfield does not find a single page or passage to support his Hobbesian thesis. Since Hobbes is unequivocal that courage is not a virtue, and honor not a good, it is hard to imagine Hobbesians pledging to each other their lives, their fortunes, and the sacred honor. The argument that Mansfield builds upon his Hobbesian premise is not without merit: that "the people" was no longer to be a part but the whole, and that the American regime was to be non-partisan in a sense that no ancient regime was non-partisan. The difficulty with Mansfield's presentation is that the actual Founding Fathers built it upon the very proposition of human equality that Mansfield rejects, and not upon any Hobbesian simulacrum. The arrangements in which

Mansfield finds excellence represent the prudence of great statesmen, relying on premises drawn from classical philosophy and biblical religion, and not the fear of violent death, upon which the Machiavellian Hobbes relied.

Let us return to Mansfield's contention that regimes always fail because they are all always imperfect. This contention is however reduced to the alleged fact that "all regime are typically oligarchies or democracies." No mention is made here of tyrannies, which in fact have ruled most of the world most of the time. Throughout these paragraphs Mansfield clearly has in mind the debate between democracy and oligarchy in the third book of the *Politics*. It is not true however that Aristotle has no confidence in the possibility of a mixed regime. In Book V there are a number of examples of how regimes can be mixed in such a way that the partisans can be persuaded to believe that their partisan claims are being satisfied. It is true, however, that Aristotle does not have any utopian expectation of any final solution to the political problem. But he thinks that regimes can be improved, especially by becoming more just, and that they can become more durable by compensating for their characteristic weaknesses. He would have understood without difficulty the intention of the Constitution of 1787 to form only a more perfect Union.

It is in the context of the comparison and contrast of the defective claims of ancient oligarchies and ancient democracies that Mansfield set forth, as a claim of a democracy, the allegedly self-evident half-truth that all men are created equal. This is astonishing, because never—to the best of my knowledge—did any ancient democracy set forth such a claim. Here is a simple test: when did an ancient partisan of democracy denounce slavery? Philosophers may have done so, but only indirectly and never as political partisans. Athenian democracy in the Periclean age subsisted largely upon the work of slaves, without which the partisans of the democracy could not have afforded to attend to the public business. Yet the most obvious fact about the self-evident truth of Jefferson and Lincoln is its condemnation of slavery.

Mansfield says that a regime based upon the proposition in which Jefferson and Lincoln believed without reservation "will eventually founder because of [the Founders'] disregard of the many ways in which men are created unequal." But in what respect are men unequal, that the Founders regarded them as equal? Mansfield does not say. He knows perfectly well that any exception to the "all" in "all men are created equal" has been and can be a justification of slavery. He knows that equality refers only to rights, and not to brains, beauty, or virtue. Consider this exchange on the floor of the Senate, between Henry Wilson of Massachusetts and Jefferson Davis. It took place on April 12, 1860, one year and a day before the firing on Fort Sumter.

> Mr. Wilson. I believe that every human being has the right to his life and his liberty and to act in this world so as to secure his own happiness. I believe, in a word, in the Declaration of Independence; but I do not, as I have said, believe in the mental or moral or physical equality of some of the races, as against this white race of ours.

> Mr. Davis. Then the Senator believes and he does not believe, and he changes his position so rapidly in giving answers that it is impossible to tell what he does believe. He believes in the Declaration of Independence, and intimates that he means by that all men are equal; but he immediately announces that there is a difference between the two races.

> Mr. Wilson. Well, Mr. President, I believe there are a great many men in the world of the white race inferior to the Senator from Mississippi, and I suppose there are quite a number superior to him; but I believe that he and the inferior man and the superior have equal natural rights.

> Mr. Davis. I suppose the Senator knows what he means. I take it for granted that he does; but it is impossible for anybody to get it from his language.

Mansfield seems to have the same difficulty as Jefferson Davis in reconciling equality of rights with inequality of abilities.

Mansfield thinks that a regime based upon equal rights will "founder" because of "the few whom it ignores." But exactly what is it to which the few are entitled which Mansfield thinks is denied to them by the proposition of universal equality? In the controversy concerning democracy in the *Politics* we find the following:

if the poor take advantage of their greater numbers to divide up the property of the rich, is this not unjust? By Zeus [say the people] it is done justly because it is done by the highest authority [viz., the people!] Then what must be pronounced to be the extreme of injustice? (1281 a 15 ff.)

The idea of the rule of numbers riding roughshod over the rights of property was utterly anathema to the Framers and Ratifiers of the Constitution. By the state of nature, the laws of nature, the laws of reason, the rule of the majority was to be carefully circumscribed to protect the rights of persons and property, something completely lacking from ancient democracy. The very idea of individual rights is derived from the fact that in a post classical monotheistic universe, man's relationship to God is personal. Hence the political relationship must be constructed upon the basis of individual rights. Here is James Madison carefully explaining the origin of political sovereignty and the limits of majority rule.

To go to the bottom of the subject, let us consult the theory which contemplates a certain number of individuals as meeting and agreeing to form one political society, in order that the rights, the safety, and the interest of each may be under the safeguard of the whole.
The first supposition is, that each individual, being previously independent of the others, the compact which is to make them one society must result from the free consent of *every* individual. [emphasis by Madison]
But as the objects in view could not be attained, if every measure conducive to them required the consent of every member of society, the theory further supposes, either that it was part of the original compact, that the will of the majority was to be deemed the will of the whole, or that this was a law of nature, resulting from the nature of political society itself, the offspring of the natural wants of man.
Whatever the hypothesis of the origin of the *lex majoris partis*, it is evident that it operates as a plenary substitute of the will of the majority of the society for the will of the whole society; and that the sovereignty of the society as vested in and exercisable by the majority, may do anything that could be *rightfully* done by the unanimous concurrence of the members; the reserved rights of individuals (of conscience for example) in becoming parties to the original compact

being beyond the legitimate reach of sovereignty, wherever vested or however viewed. [emphasis by Madison]

We see that, according to Madison, not even unanimous consent may authorize whatever cannot be done *rightfully*. We may hear Lincoln's reply to Douglas, that a popular majority in the territories had no right to vote for slavery, because slavery was a wrong, and it had no right to vote for a wrong. Consent operates within a moral order, it is itself a creation of that order, and there is no sovereign authority outside that order. In the tenth *Federalist* Madison declared that the first object of government was to protect the "different and unequal faculties of acquiring property." The *equal* protection of *unequal* faculties was inherent from the outset in the doctrine of human equality of the American Founding. I can see no basis whatever for any emendation of that doctrine into a half truth.

The theory that Madison "contemplates" is that of the state of nature. Madison returns in thought to a pre-political state in order to discover the foundation of rightful authority here and now. We observe that in the *Politics* Aristotle said that the *polis* or political community is prior to the family, while in the *Nicomachean Ethics* he said the family is prior to the political community. There is no contradiction, because in the *Politics* he spoke ontologically, and in the *Ethics* chronologically. The same distinction between priority in *being* and priority *in coming into being* applies as well to the state of nature. At some point in the past of any community (as obviously in the case of communities formed on the American frontier) there were states of nature such as that contemplated by Madison. But the enduring significance of the concept of the state of nature lies in its ontological priority, in its forming a ground for reasoning about political right accessible at any time or place. That is what the Founders understood Locke to mean when he said the "state of nature has a law of nature to govern it . . . and reason . . . is that law." And again,

> the law of nature . . . [is] as intelligible and plain to a rational creature and a studier of that law as the positive laws of commonwealths . . . which are only so far right as they are founded on the law of nature, by which they are to be regulated and interpreted.

We are reminded that Jefferson, in his address to the King in *The Summary View of the Rights of British America* in 1774, told him that

> The great principles of right and wrong are legible to every reader; to pursue them requires not the aid of many counselors. The whole art of government consists in the art of being honest.

We may think it hyperbole to say what Jefferson here says is the *whole* art of government. Yet the moral rationality of the distinction between freedom and despotism articulated with transcendent lucidity in the Declaration of Independence was the ground of the righteous cause not only in the Revolution and the Civil War, but in all the great wars (hot and cold) of the twentieth century. When Ronald Reagan pronounced the Soviet Union an "evil empire" he needed not many counselors to say so. Nor did it require a Harvard education to understand what he meant. In point of fact, a Harvard education might have been the only thing that could have prevented someone from understanding it. But the Declaration of Independence stands squarely against tyranny, whether of the one, the few, or the many. Every single human being is entitled by the moral law, whether of reason or of revelation, to be considered an end in himself, to be governed, under the laws of God and of nature, by his own consent. Any exception to this can only be a harbinger of reappearing tyranny.

AN EXCHANGE BETWEEN HARRY V. JAFFA AND HARVEY C. MANSFIELD, JR., APRIL 19, 1996 [36]

Harvey Mansfield (HM): I want to defend myself against Professor Jaffa. I read his paper with interest. [laughter] Let's begin with his first sentence: "For many reasons it is not a grateful task to identify Professor Harvey Mansfield as another defector from the 'ancient faith' of Abraham Lincoln." It may not be grateful, but to me it seems inevitable; since you have been attacking your friends one after the other for years, and I am only the latest—the last—for you to have reached.

You call yourself an academic scribbler. I wish! You are not even a loose cannon because a loose cannon does some of its harm, or maybe all of its harm, by accident. What you do is stand behind the front lines, and point your weapon at the backs of your friends and shoot! And you're not looking. There is a battle going on in this country between those, as you say, who want to continue America on the basis of its fundamental and original principles and those who do not. There is a front line to that battle. You're not in the front line. The front line is receiving fire from the enemy. They don't shoot at you anymore, because you're not shooting at them. You should come up to the front line, and if you have criticisms to make of those on your side who are shooting at the enemy, tell it to them! Mention that they are shooting at the wrong target or they have the wrong aim or something like that.

Now I'd like to make remarks on three of your points, all of which are made with exaggeration. And what's worse, you not only exaggerate your own statements, you impute exaggeration to others. First, I did not say, I did not propound the thesis that the philosophical progenitor of the American Constitution is Thomas Hobbes. I mention Thomas Hobbes and John Locke. I think both are necessary connections. Locke is much, much closer to the American Constitution than is Hobbes; but there is still an important connection between Locke and Hobbes which you recognize in a backhanded way on your note on page 55, when you say, "'Eastern' Straussians have almost without exception assumed that the Founding Fathers read Locke as Leo Strauss read him in *Natural Right and History*." As you know very well, it's true that Strauss is identified with a view that Locke is much closer to Hobbes than has been thought to be the case by the great majority of commentators, at least those before Leo Strauss—except for the Canadian Maple Leaf Marxist, C.B. Macpherson. So I think that it makes a difficulty for your position which seems to depend on a real, deep division between Hobbes and Locke. We could argue this at some length, but I think that that's a good—

Harry Jaffa (HJ): But let's be clear, though, that I referred to the view of the Founding Fathers, and to impute to the Founding Fathers the interpretation of Locke by Leo Strauss is, it seems to me, somewhat anachronistic.

HM: The second point has to do with the state of nature in Locke and in Aristotle. You say that Aristotle's argument about the political nature of man is essentially the same as Locke's argument about the state of nature, or at least, that if Aristotle did come back today (HJ: Yes.) he would have endorsed what Locke had to say about that.

HJ: Because of the difference between monotheism and politics.

HM: Yes. Well, I'm not sure I agree with that suggestion of yours.

HJ: I didn't expect you would.

HM: That's because I think that when Aristotle said the nature of man is a political animal, he meant the nature of man, he didn't mean man just in certain circumstances, such as circumstances of polytheism instead of monotheism.

HJ: Look, let me be clear . . . now wait, let me interrupt.

HM: No, I don't want to have you interrupt. I want to finish and then you can say what you want. It has been, you say, it has been well said that "it was easier for Moses to get the Jews out of Egypt than to get Egypt out of the Jews." I think that's a beautiful example of the point that I was going to make. That, for Aristotle, there isn't anything behind the political. That if the Jews weren't Jews, they were Egyptians. They were one thing or the other. You say, "Typically, there must be a founding lawgiver, a powerful political leader who forges a political community." It's a *political* leader; that again is my point, that politics is already present in the leadership of the man who puts a political community together. I did not say anything about Calhoun or Calhoun's interpretation of Aristotle. You have a fixation on Calhoun which I advise you against. Drop that! Try to forget his name. My third point is—

HJ: You can understand why you're so sympathetic to Irving Kristol, because he wants to forget it, too, and say the Civil War was about nothing at all except a quarrel between scholars.

HM: The third point is about equality in the sense of my statement that the Declaration is a self-evident half-truth. Now, you say on pages 205 to 206 "Mansfield knows perfectly well that any exception to the 'all' in 'all men are created equal' has been and can be a justification of slavery. He knows that equality refers only to rights, and not to brains, beauty, or virtue." There are other things one might mention: talents, athletic ability, sexual prowess, things like that. All those are inequalities. You go on to say, on page 208, you, Jaffa: "I can see no basis whatever for any emendation of that doctrine into a half-truth." I didn't say that the doctrine was a half-truth, I said that the statement was a half-truth. You're the one who said the equal protection of unequal faculties was inherent from the outset in the doctrine of human equality in the American Founding. (HJ: Yes.) So there is a basis for saying that the equality of man is— that "all men are created equal" is—a half-truth, if all men are also created unequal.

What happens, what tends to happen in the American regime is that the state of nature which . . . was a prepolitical basis or foundation for politics, has become a principle of politics in the Aristotelian sense, the ruling principle, a kind of *arche*. So that the state of nature is not understood simply as a basis from which we would prepare to rule, but a basis upon which we would continue to rule.

And this is the argument of Tocqueville's *Democracy in America*, a book which you do not sufficiently appreciate. That book says that we live in the midst of a democratic revolution, that is, we live in a certain kind of democracy, a democracy that democratizes. It has a continuing tendency to make itself more and more democratic as it proceeds. So, it's, I think, not enough, then, to stick simply to the principle that "All men are created equal" if one wants to combat this democratizing tendency which is, I believe, a fundamental danger, perhaps *the* fundamental danger of our democracy as so identified by Tocqueville.

One must begin to take account of and to justify the inequalities which are in our country: that diversity . . . only exists when people are thought to be unequal and not just equal: and I've, in my writings, tried to emphasize that point time and again, that you cannot have diversity without inequality. So the problem today is not so much to put down slavery, but it's to hold down this democratic revolution. To do that, one has to promote, one has to show that America is full of the promotion and encouragement of inequality as well as equality. So, I think that these two principles must be understood together. It's perfectly true that you can understand equality as equal treatment before the law, but it has to be emphasized, and emphasized time and time again, that equality before the law means toleration, or even promotion, of inequality. And so, I really differ with you on the tactics or the strategy for defending our original principles today.

It's true I have a Harvard education, which leads to a burden; despite this handicap I do my best. [laughter].

HJ: I'm very glad we're having this exchange, because I sent you this critique, or most of it, three years ago, and wrote to you and I haven't had an answer. I suppose you thought it wasn't worthy of an answer, but I'm glad that you've given me an answer, whether you think it worthy or unworthy of yourself to do so.

In the first place, let me simply deny categorically that I have been in the back lines and that I have been firing from the rear at the backs of my friends. I don't see how anybody could place that interpretation upon my numerous publications. I haven't tried to hide them and I've been very straightforward about whether I agreed or disagreed. I don't think that in that respect your publications or mine differ at all. But I certainly haven't hidden myself on the west coast. If I didn't get any east coast invitations, I think I know why, but it wasn't because I was trying to shoot at people from behind their backs. I don't think that anybody has been more straightforward; and you've all had a good example of that this afternoon.

You keep using, speaking of, equality and inequality in this generalized sense which I think Tocqueville does. I may not have studied Tocqueville as carefully as you, but I have studied him, and I've always thought that it was a defect of Tocqueville that he didn't distinguish the different senses of equality, and that he never had any thematic discussion of the meaning of equality in the Declaration of Independence. And he said very little about the thought of the founding, although he said a great deal about the origins of self-government in New England and things like that. But you persistently repeat the error that I accused you of, namely, of saying we need, we have to recognize inequality as well as equality. Now, I've always said, and Lincoln was perfectly clear, that equality in the Declaration of Independence does not refer to equality of abilities, or talents, or what have you, but an equality of rights.

Now, what is the foundation of that equality of rights? The recognition of human beings as constituting a species in nature; and that constitution of the species in nature is the basis of all moral imperatives. What is the reason for condemning either genocide or slavery? You don't want me to go on talking about slavery, but I'm sorry I can't accommodate you there because it is a fundamental distinction which underlies all moral distinctions within the American regime. Slavery is wrong because to treat a human being as if he were an animal of a lower species violates that fundamental perception which is necessary to morality: that human beings cannot be bought or sold like animals or dogs, because they are not animals, they are not dogs or hogs. When Lincoln said, replying to his friends of the South, "Equal justice to the South, we are told, requires that if I can take my hog to Nebraska, you can take your Negro." He said, "That's perfectly reasonable, if there were no difference between a Negro and a hog." Now, it's important to recognize that that distinction is based upon a metaphysical distinction, that is to say, one uses the universal, Man, and recognizes that Negroes and white people are equally human, just as two different chairs are equally chairs. I remember once . . . there was a young professor from Yale here who was denouncing metaphysics, and saying that . . . there was no reliable metaphysical truth, that we could only try to cultivate practical reason. So I asked him, "How uncertain are you that a Negro is a human being?" What degree of uncertainty did you ask, metaphysically speaking . . . [break in recording to change the tape] [a] Negro woman," he [Lincoln] said. That she may not be my equal in some respects. Perhaps. He used the word perhaps. "But in her equal right to put into her mouth the bread that her own hand has earned, she is my equal, the equal of Judge Douglas, and of every living human being." Now, that primordial meaning of equality takes into account inequality. But the right to put into her mouth the bread that her own hand has earned: there is no exception to her equal right to that.

Charles Kesler: Well, I think the issues that are being explored, personalities aside, go very deep, and are extremely important for the defense and the understanding of American politics. But since I began [this session] with poetry, I shall end with poetry. The same poem, written by Ralph Waldo Emerson, praising the completion of the Concord Monument. Let me just recite these closing lines as our benediction:

> The foe long since in silence slept;
> Alike the conqueror silent sleeps;
> And Time the ruined bridge has swept
> Down the dark stream which seaward creeps.
>
> On this green bank, by this soft stream,
> We set today a votive stone;
> That memory may their deed redeem,
> When, like our sires, our sons are gone.
>
> Spirit, that made those heroes dare
> To die, and leave their children free,
> Bid Time and Nature gently spare
> The shaft we raise to them and thee.

AFTERWORD AND FIRST OPEN LETTER, BY HARRY V. JAFFA

Afterword to The Decline and Fall of the American Idea
with An Open Letter to Harvey Mansfield

Following a twenty-minute oral summary of the foregoing essay,[37] Professor Mansfield gave an impromptu rebuttal.[38] He began by denouncing me for skulking in the rear, while others carried on the battle. Even worse, he said, I took shots at those on my side while they were occupied by the enemy.[39] All of this presupposed that the difference between friends and enemies was what he supposed it to be. At the end of World War II there was a tremendous struggle in the free world to disengage itself from the "friendship" with Stalin that had prevailed in the war against Hitler. Not until Churchill's iron curtain speech did the pendulum of political friendship begin to swing from procommunism to anticommunism. And no one was more roundly abused as a false friend of freedom than Churchill. That "false friendship" however saved Western civilization.[40] I am consoled.

Mansfield did not retract by one inch his condemnation of the Declaration of Independence. In this he confirmed my thesis that rejection of the Declaration—and the acceptance of moral relativism—is the common core of present day conservatism no less than it is of present day liberalism. Genuine conservatism is then in greater danger from its putative friends than from its open enemies.

Mansfield abused me for pointing to the close resemblance of his disparagement of the proposition of human equality to that of John C. Calhoun. He said I was "obsessed" by Calhoun, and ordered me peremptorily to cease and desist from pronouncing his name.[41] Mansfield is so used to the deference accorded his neo-papal status in the college of cardinals of eastern Straussianism that it did not occur to him that, as I do not belong to his church, I am not subject to his authority. He cannot therefore use his authority to deflect attention from a fact that he cannot deny.

Mansfield believed he had refuted my objection to what he said about the alleged "self-evident half-truth" by hiding behind the authority of Tocqueville.[42] Tocqueville had warned against the danger of despotism arising from the passion for equality. Ergo: the doctrine of equality as propounded by Jefferson and Lincoln presents the danger of despotism. That the equality feared by Tocqueville was grounded in Rousseau, and that that propounded by Jefferson and Lincoln was grounded in Locke, is ignored by Mansfield. In what follows we will see the same difference—between Whigs and Jacksonian Democrats—that moved Tocqueville to make his warnings. Perhaps most revealing was Mansfield's pronouncement that the issue of slavery was over and done with, and that I should forget about it. According to Mansfield slavery belongs to the past and has nothing to do with present-day politics. I believe the fundamental issues underlying the Civil War are identical to the ones underlying present-day politics, and that the future of freedom is as much at risk now as then. Nothing illuminates this more than Mansfield's rejection of the doctrine of equality in Jefferson and Lincoln.

AN OPEN LETTER TO HARVEY MANSFIELD

> Polemarchus: it is still my opinion that justice is helping friends and injuring enemies.
> Socrates: Do you mean by friends those who seem to be good . . . or those who are, even if they don't seem to be . . . (Plato, *Republic*)

> Yet it would be thought be better, even necessary, to destroy what is closest to us, for the salvation of the truth, especially as we are philosophers: for both [our friends and the truth] are dear, but we must honor truth first. (Aristotle, *Nicomachean Ethics*)
> Amicus quidem Socrates, amicior veritas. (Thomas Aquinas, *Commentary on the Nicomachean Ethics*.)
> Solet Aristoteles quaerere pugnam. (Leo Strauss, Source Anon.)

Dear Harvey:

Your response to my analysis of your attack upon the Declaration of Independence, although beyond the bounds of civility, was not for that reason unwelcome. Like the lancing of a boil, it relieved the pressure of an infection, and may perhaps even have initiated a process of healing. It is in that interest that I now write.

For years now, my motives have been attacked by those who have assumed to themselves the authority of keepers of the tablets of Straussian orthodoxy. I have been denounced as a heretic for transgressing the permissible limits of opinion, without regard to whether those opinions were true or false. You too condemn me, not for being wrong, but for being faithless. You say that I am cowardly for not standing beside you in the struggle against the heathen, and treacherous for firing upon those I should treat as brothers. To attack someone's motives has been recognized for millennia as a means by which to make the weaker into the stronger argument. And it is unfailingly successful—when the audience is sufficiently gullible. But those who gain victory by these means do not gain honor with it.

Your accusations against me can have no other intention than to divert attention from the merits of the issues in dispute. But you are now going to have to defend yourself on the basis of the merits, or have your accusations turn against yourself.

You have portrayed yourself—as opposed to myself—as a front line fighter against our common enemies. Your stand against feminism, affirmative action, homosexuality, multiculturalism, and the other insanities of political correctness is something I have witnessed from afar, and have invariably praised. But Harvard is not the world. I have been doing exactly the same thing here, albeit without the visibility that Harvard affords.

In the spring of 1969 I attained an exceptional notoriety in opposing the Black Studies Center. I had written a letter to our trustees, urging them to make no decision until the violence and threats of violence ceased. By that time there had been two pipe bombings—one of which nearly killed and badly injured a 19 year old secretary—and 25 fires, one of which gutted one of the older buildings on campus. My letter was leaked to the press, and a storm of denunciation descended upon my head. The leader of the Black Student Union publicly urged that someone take a gun and shoot me. With a unit of the Black Panthers stationed nearby this was not an altogether idle threat. For some time I made it a habit of looking under my hood to make sure that there was nothing wired to my ignition. The situation at Claremont was far more dangerous than the much better publicized one at Cornell. We had no *New York Times* reporter here to advertise our plight. On the contrary, there was a conspiracy of the college administrations, the city government, and the local press, which shut off any avenue of support from the outside world. I might mention that unlike some of our famous friends I did not run away to Canada!

In recent years I have flooded the campus paper with essays, articles, and letters on diversity, multiculturalism, racism, homosexuality, etc. Two titles that exhibit my pusillanimity are "Why Sodomites Are Not Gay," and "How Homophobia Can Save Your Life." My pamphlet on "Homosexuality and the Natural Law" has been published by the Claremont Institute, and more than 10,000 copies distributed around the country. It has become something of a text book in furnishing a coherent, systematic set of arguments for the good people who recognize the immorality of homosexuality, but do not have the dialectical resources to fight against it. I have received letters of thanks from all over the country. I must also say that your own stand against homosexuality, although commendable for itself, has not had the depth of philosophical resource that only the natural law argument can provide.

Meanwhile, the "Gay-Lesbian Hotline" in Los Angeles has listed me as among their dangerous enemies. Where in the world you got the idea that I have been standing passively in the rear, letting others do the fighting, I cannot imagine.

While the foregoing relates to me personally, much more important has been the role of my students, or former students, in carrying the torch of the convictions they have drawn from my teaching, each according to his own lights, into the academy and into the affairs of our nation. It would be ungrateful to attempt any catalogue or list of their achievements. Instead, I place on record the tribute from Clarence Thomas—now Mr. Justice Thomas—in 1989, on the occasion of my "unretirement."

> I have had the good fortune of having two of Dr. Jaffa's students work with me here at the Equal Employment Opportunity Commission. They have increased my knowledge of political subjects immensely by articulating a reflective, principled, understanding of current and past political struggles. Having become acquainted with other students of Dr. Jaffa's in the academy and in government, I have renewed strength in my own mission, knowing I have thoughtful allies elsewhere. Dr. Jaffa's students have affirmed the beliefs and practices instilled in me from childhood and have given my innate conservatism further, deeper justification. I think it no exaggeration to say that the future of freedom and self-government in America depends upon the extent to which conservatism, the Republican party, and our nation take account of the wisdom of Harry Jaffa.

Professor Jaffa is not just another academic, neither in his learning and its great benefits nor in the uncompromising manner in which he displays it. Having seen multitudes of cowards and opportunists here in Washington, it is always refreshing to see someone who is utterly unafraid to speak his mind on the vital issues of the day, and for all time.

I count myself blessed for having become acquainted with Professor Harry V. Jaffa, his work, and his students.

In the course of your remarks, you claimed authority from Tocqueville for denouncing the "self-evident half-truth that all men are created equal." It is true the Tocqueville warned that the passion for equality could lead either to liberty or to despotism. And it is also true, as I said in our spoken exchange, that Tocqueville used "equality" without distinguishing clearly equality of rights from equality of ability or of virtue. However I do not recall Tocqueville ever speaking, as you do, in direct disparagement of the Declaration of Independence. Although Tocqueville lived until 1859, the views expressed in the *Democracy in America* were formed entirely from his visit to America during the Jacksonian period.

When Tocqueville came to America the Jacksonian revolution was in mid-course, and the struggle of parties deep seated. Jackson's attack upon—and destruction of—the Second Bank of the United States was conducted in the idiom of class warfare not altogether unlike that of the Marxists of a later generation. Jackson was presented as the tribune of the people, risen to defend them against sinister conspiracies. The anti-Jackson party, which became the Whigs, was actually the surviving remnant of the party of Hamilton and, like Hamilton, was committed to the national bank, and to tariffs and internal improvements promoted by the national government. It inherited the *Federalist*'s belief in the equal protection of unequal faculties of acquiring property, and both the propriety and utility for society as a whole of class distinctions arising therefrom. I cannot think of a better expression of the Whig attitude toward the creation of wealth than the following from a speech of President Calvin Coolidge in 1926.

After all, the chief business of the American people is business. They are profoundly concerned with producing, buying, selling, investing and prospering in the world. I am strongly of the opinion that the great majority of people will always find these are moving impulses of our life. . . . Wealth is the product of industry, ambition, character and untiring effort. In all experience, the accumulation of wealth means the multiplication of schools, the increase of knowledge, the dissemination of intelligence, the encouragement of science, the broadening of outlook, the expansion of liberty, the widening of culture. Of course, the accumulation of wealth cannot be justified as the chief end of existence. But we are compelled to recognize it as a means to well-nigh ever desirable achievement. So long as wealth is made the means and not the end, we need not greatly fear it.

A replay of the Jacksonian animus can be found in the slander of Coolidge by that tribune of the New Deal, Arthur Schlesinger, Jr.[43]

Abraham Lincoln was a Whig. He called Henry Clay his "beau ideal of a statesman." Among the banners carried by Lincoln supporters in the great campaign of 1858 was one that said "The Gals Link on To Lincoln, as their Mothers did to Clay." At one time Lincoln was denounced by the Democrats as a "bluestocking," a defender of wealth and privilege. Lincoln humorously repelled this charge by asking if anyone who saw his awkward and ill dressed figure could possibly believe it! The idea that the success of some must be at the expense of others has been a durable feature of party conflict in popular governments from ancient times. That it usually results from the envy of the successful[44] by the unsuccessful does not mean that it is not sometimes true. Popular governments breed both demagogues and malefactors of great wealth. Whether justified or unjustified, the levelling tendency within any popular government is always present. That is all the more reason why the principle of equality must be rightly understood.

The heart of the conflict during Tocqueville's visit to America is revealed more concisely in the Lincoln-Douglas debates of 1858 than in any other place. 1858 may seem like a late date for such a revelation. But Lincoln and Douglas had been debating, since the 1830s as representatives of the Jacksonian and Whig political creeds. Lincoln's Lyceum speech of 1838 had warned against the great destroyers of republics, Alexander, Caesar, and Napoleon, with the Whig suggestion that Jackson might have been their heir. (It had been Whig doctrine that Jackson's veto of the bill to re-charter the second Bank of the United States had been an unconstitutional exercise of executive power.) Douglas had built his career as a fire-eating advocate of the cause of the

Old Hero. He had vaulted into political prominence in 1844 as a member of Congress in a powerful speech in support of a bill restoring to Andrew Jackson a fine Jackson had paid for being in contempt of court, when he had imposed martial law in New Orleans in 1812. The case Douglas made for Jackson was—ironically—not very different from the one Lincoln would make out for himself when he suspended the writ of *habeas corpus* during the Civil War. But the justification of a claim of super-constitutional authority exercised "in the name of the people" fit the pattern of the Whigs warnings.

The issue in the Lincoln-Douglas debates came down to the simple question of whether there were, or were not, any objective moral boundaries within which alone the sovereignty of the people might operate. "Whenever," Douglas said, "you put a limitation upon the right of a people to decide what laws they want, you have destroyed the fundamental principle of self-government." Because of this Douglas, as a good Jacksonian, believed the people had a right to have slavery if they wanted it. He did not care, he said, whether slavery in the territories was voted up or voted down. He cared only for the sacred right of the people to decide. Lincoln, on the other hand, believed that the principle of self-government was itself authorized by a more profound principle: that all men are created equal, and endowed by their Creator with certain unalienable rights. The equal rights of man authorized majority rule: but only "to secure these rights," not to deny or disparage or destroy them. Slavery was an utter negation of the very rights which authorized the majority to rule. When Lincoln declared that a black woman had the same right as any other human being on earth to put into her own mouth the bread her own hand had earned, he was defending *all* property rights. As a Whig he had defended the property rights of those at the top of the social-economic pyramid. As a Republican he defended the property rights of those at the bottom of the same pyramid. But whether in defense of the rich or of the poor, the argument was the same.

Any argument in favor of majority rule must begin by defining the universe within which the majority is to be found. We saw in Madison's essay on sovereignty, echoing John Locke, that the unanimous consent of every individual, *freely given*, is the foundation of majority rule. But the will of the majority may rule only as the "plenary substitute" for the will of the whole. It may not do anything which might not be comprehended by the unanimous consent which made the political community a voluntary association. Even beyond that, it might not do anything that might not be done *rightfully* by unanimous consent. A gang of robbers is not authorized to embark upon of a career of plunder, because they are unanimously agreed to do so! The unanimous consent by which all lawful government is authorized arises from the equal rights with which all men are endowed by their Creator. It is the rights human beings possess *before* entering into the primordial social contract, their rights under the laws of nature, which determine the boundaries of majority rule. Any single exception to the proposition of equal human rights destroys the entire argument for majority rule, for minority rights, and for constitutional government altogether.

In the course of our oral argument, you said that you had placed the origin of American constitutionalism in the state of nature doctrine of both Hobbes and Locke. Here however is what you wrote:

> The great confidence of the constitutional generation—Our Fathers, Lincoln called them—arose from the modern idea of constructing politics from the pre-political beginning I mentioned, the state of nature. The foremost advantage to be had from beginning this way was to banish partisan opinion from constitution-making, for partisan opinion not only keeps us from discerning but also from applying truth in politics. Partisan opinion is confusing because it is diverse; partisan opinions differ over the nature of happiness, over the *ends* of action. By following Hobbes and turning to the passions that allegedly precede opinions, above all the passion of *fear*, we can discover a universal, non-partisan foundation for politics. We may not know what happiness is, but each of us can know or imagine the fear of death we would feel without government to keep the peace (since each fears dependably for his own death) expresses the individualism of modern politics and also gives rise to its emphasis on liberty together—uneasily—with peace.

In this passage you rely solely on Hobbes for your conception of American constitutionalism. In Locke, the state of nature—upon which lawful governments are founded, and by which they are regulated and interpreted—is governed by the law of reason. It is reason, not passion, and certainly not the passion of fear, to which Our Fathers looked for their non-partisan foundation. And, I repeat, you have not a single line of documentary evidence to the contrary.

You also express the view—a commonplace in your sect—that the American Founders, again following Hobbes, turned away from happiness as the end or purpose of government, because opinions as to what constituted happiness were always partisan and controversial. You say they followed Hobbes in believing that men might agree on what was evil when they could not agree on what was good. Once again you say something for which you have no shred of evidence. The Declaration of Independence speaks of the pursuit of happiness in the state of nature, but it speaks of "safety and happiness" as the ends pursued by a people bound by the social contract when they "institute new government." And Madison in the 43rd *Federalist* says that it is the "transcendent law of nature . . . that the safety and happiness of society are 'the objects at which all political institutions aim. . . .'" Nor is there any reason to think that the Founding Fathers regarded opinions concerning happiness to be merely subjective and idiosyncratic. If the happiness of society is the end of government then it is *social* happiness which is the foundation of *individual happiness*. This is exactly the thought expressed by Washington in his first inaugural, and it is in itself perfectly Aristotelian.

Let me finally reiterate that the ultimate non-partisan foundation of American constitutionalism is not anything found in Hobbes, but in the inferences drawn from the doctrine that "God hath made of one blood all the nations that dwell upon the earth." That at least is how the Founding generation understood itself, and how Lincoln understood the Founding generation.

Harry V. Jaffa
Claremont, California
April 28, 1996

IN DEFENSE OF THE PROPOSITION THAT ALL MEN ARE CREATED EQUAL: A SECOND OPEN LETTER TO HARVEY MANSFIELD

Dear Harvey:

Some days ago I received the transcript of the oral exchange between us that took place on April 19. When I addressed my open letter to you on April 28 I was unaware of the existence of the tape. I do not find that my memory served me ill when I wrote the first time, but the transcript enables me to quote you directly and has prompted some further thoughts.

You said:

There is a battle going on in this country between those, as you say, who want to continue America on the basis of its fundamental and original principles and those who do not. There is a front line to that battle. You're not in the front line.

There is indeed a battle going on. It is not a new one. The Civil War was fought between two sides, each of which insisted that it was committed to the fundamental and original principles upon which the nation was founded, and that the other side had betrayed those principles. Your facile assumption that you are on the side of the "fundamental and original principles" can hardly be warranted, especially when you characterize the most fundamental of all the original principles as a "self-evident half-truth." This is the proposition that Abraham Lincoln called the "central idea" of the Founding, and which he enshrined in the Gettysburg Address. There is indeed a battle going on, which is much more fundamental than that with the silly scions of political correctness.

The "Storm over the Constitution"[45] is far more profoundly a struggle between those who identify the principles of the Founding with a moral relativism completely alien to the thought of the Founding, and those who would reassert the moral realism inherent in the laws of nature and of nature's God. The genuine Founders believed in an objective moral order, knowable by reason, and confirmed by revelation,[46] that is the foundation of the constitutional regime. This is the side I am on, and I am in the thick of the fight, with no sympathy or help from you or your friends.

The insanities of "political correctness" are all grounded in a relativism which asserts that all moral choices are value judgments, and that all value judgments are equally non-rational. Dinesh D'Souza demonstrated that brilliantly in *The End of Racism* (as he had done earlier in *Illiberal Education*). Bill Bennett has said the same thing in a 1995 article in *Commentary*, and in many other places. However, neither D'Souza nor Bennett has been willing to acknowledge that the same moral relativism that is the heart of ideological liberalism is equally embedded in conservatism, although I have rubbed their noses in the evidence. Here is a classic case of seeing the mote in another man's eye, but not the beam in one's own!

The lunacy of "political correctness" cannot however be defeated by another team of moral relativists. If the choice comes down to which "value judgments" public policy is to serve, the ones that promise more unrestrained indulgences (like medieval pardoners) will always win. A good example of politically correct liberalism is the homosexual movement. The homosexuals demand that the government find a cure for AIDS. Every sodomite who kicks the bucket from AIDS is regarded as a martyr. To even suggest that his own behavior may have been the cause of his death is to generate the wildest of hysterical denunciations. To be a sodomite is now thought to be "gay," but to call sodomy by its right name is now considered worse than an ethnic, racial, or religious slur, even in conservative circles. And this notwithstanding the fact that sodomy has been a common law felony for centuries, and is still a felony on the statutes of nearly half the states. That the pleasures of buggery,[47] or any pleasures, are morally wrong—is abhorrent to the politically correct. A self-destructive hedonism is "in", and the idea that there are bad pleasures has become incomprehensible. General Washington drummed a continental soldier out of the ranks for the "abominable vice" of sodomy. Today Washington would himself be drummed out for using such "insensitive" language.

It is an unquestioned dogma today that a cure for AIDS is just another government entitlement to be paid for by all of us, whether we approve or disapprove. What is the "conservative" response? It is influenced, in large part, by the fact that the conservative ranks are shot through with homosexuals. They may be less militant than the left wing homosexuals (although some of them are not), but they are still highly visible. Rank and file conservatives, who have no sympathy for the sodomites, are nonetheless frightened into silence. You will look hard and long for conservatives—except fundamentalist religious conservatives—who will condemn sodomy as immoral. So a conservative position is one that votes less money for AIDS research than the liberals. A conservatism that cannot call the moral phenomena by their right names, that can only say "We promise you everything the liberals promise, only less," can never win.

❋ ❋ ❋

You say that if I have

criticisms to make of those on your side who are shooting at the enemy, tell it to them! Mention that they are shooting at the wrong target or they have the wrong aim or something like that.

If by "my side" you mean present day political conservatives, then I have been doing what you say I should be doing, without any thanks or even notice on your part. Your present reaction closely resembles that of Robert Bork, Lino Graglia, and Charles Cooper. They have noticed all right but not exactly with gratitude! William Rehnquist has not replied to me, since a sitting Chief Justice does not reply to "academic scribblers." In my essay for the Salvatori conference, as in the book and articles that preceded it, I have featured the astonishing oracle of the Chief Justice, that safeguards for individual liberty do not have any intrinsic worth, that they are not based upon any ideas of natural justice, and that they only represent political value judgments. And, according to Rehnquist, political value judgments, like all value judgments can be proved neither right nor wrong. One cannot imagine a more stark example of that "contemporary rejection of natural right [that] leads to nihilism—nay, [that] is identical with nihilism." (*Natural Right and History*, p. 3.) Here is the "self-destruction of reason" in all its nakedness. Here in sharpest focus is what Leo Strauss called the "crisis of the West." Can one imagine any assertion of moral relativism by a politically correct liberal more destructive than this? I have constantly presented the moral realism of classical rationalism, not merely as an alternative, but as a refutation of this conventional wisdom. In this I have followed the model of Leo Strauss with no help from you or your friends.

> The crisis of the West consists in the West's having become uncertain of its purpose. The West was once certain of its purpose—of a purpose in which all men could be united, and hence it had a clear vision of its future as the future of all mankind.

Thus Strauss in the Introduction to *The City and Man* (p. 3). The single most authoritative expression of the West's universal purpose, in which all can be united, with a vision of the future of all mankind, is the American Declaration of Independence.[48] July 4, 1776, was the first time in all of human history that any nation, or any people, justified its separate and equal station in the world, not because of any unique qualities or virtues of its own, but because of rights that it shared with all men everywhere. American exceptionalism and American universalism are indissolubly united. In the letter Jefferson wrote for the celebration of the 50ᵗʰ anniversary of the Declaration—the day, as it happened, that he and John Adams underwent their apotheosis—he wrote:

> May it be to the world, what I believe it will be (to some parts sooner, to others later, but finally to all) the signal of arousing men to burst the chains under which monkish superstition had persuaded them to bind themselves, and to assume the blessings of self-government. . . . All eyes are opened, or opening to the rights of man.

Contrast this with the belief that constitutional safeguards for individual liberty do not have any intrinsic worth, and that whatever moral rightness or goodness is attributed to them is derived solely from the fact that they have been adopted by a people. Here is Leo Strauss's direct response to Rehnquist.

> If principles are sufficiently justified by the fact that they are accepted by society, the principles of cannibalism are as defensible or sound as those of civilized life. From this point of view, the former principles can certainly not be rejected as simply bad. And, since the ideal of our society is admittedly changing, nothing except dull and stale habit could prevent us from placidly accepting a change in the direction of cannibalism. (*NR&H*, p. 3)

One need only substitute "political correctness" for "cannibalism" (not that there is that much difference!) and "dull and stale conservatism" for "dull and stale habit" in the foregoing. It follows necessarily from Rehnquist's premises that the safeguards for slavery in the original Constitution, "take on" the identical moral rightness or goodness as the safeguards for liberty. After all, they were adopted, not only by the same people, but at the same time. This conclusion cannot be evaded by noisily denouncing me for having a "fixation" on Calhoun.

The real "battle going on in this country" is between those who think safeguards for individual liberty are grounded in a right with which all men are endowed by their Creator, and those who regard safeguards, whether for liberty or for slavery, as intrinsically indifferent.

In his essay on "The Notion of a Living Constitution"[49] Rehnquist describes the political process as a contest between competing value judgments, with the majority having the "right"—insofar as anything can be called right—to enact their value judgments into law. Thus in Weimar Germany in 1933 the kind of political process endorsed by Rehnquist culminated in the victory of Hitler, who lost no time in enacting his value judgments into law. It follows from Rehnquist's premises that the Nuremberg laws—having taken on moral rightness and goodness—were fully entitled to judicial enforcement. And this follows no matter how violently Rehnquist himself would have disagreed with Hitler's value judgments. It also follows that as long as the slave power in the antebellum South had the votes it had the right to enact laws protecting slavery. What the slave power once had the right to do, the sodomites and the advocates of the total welfare state also will have the right to do, whenever they have the power. Rehnquist may be a man of the "right" in present day political terms, but his theory presents no objective or intrinsic ground for saying that anything his political enemies wish to do is "wrong." Thomas Jefferson, in the Virginia Statute of Religious Liberty of 1786, took note of the fact that the existing Virginia legislature could not bind future legislatures, whose authority would be no less than their own. Yet, he said,

> we are free to declare, and do declare, that the rights hereby asserted are of the natural rights of mankind, and that if any act shall hereafter be passed to repeal the present, or to narrow its operation, such act will be an infringement of natural right.

Abraham Lincoln, in the debates with Douglas, asserted categorically that the people of a territory had no right to vote for slavery because slavery was wrong. According to Lincoln, there was no such thing, whether for an individual or a people, as a right to a wrong. Jefferson wrote that the ultimate repository of the principles of the Constitution was the people *en masse*. They, he said, are independent of every authority except moral law. It was only within the primordial sovereignty of the laws of nature and of nature's God that the people itself may be sovereign. Rehnquist's idea of original intent has nothing in common with this.

* * *

In the transcript, you say

> As you know very well, it's true that Strauss is identified with a view that Locke is much closer to Hobbes than has been thought to be the

case by the great majority of commentators, at least those before Leo Strauss—except for the Canadian Maple Leaf Marxist, C. B. Macpherson. So that it makes a difficulty for your position which seem to depend on a real, deep division between Hobbes and Locke.

I replied that

I had referred to the view of the Founding Fathers, and to impute to the Founding Fathers the interpretation of Leo Strauss is, it seems to me somewhat anachronistic.

Let me say that "anachronistic" is much too mild a characterization. Leo Strauss taught us, as a fundamental hermeneutic principles, to understand the writers of the past as they understood themselves, before attempting to understand them differently or better. In dealing with the "Straussians" of your persuasion, I have come up against a blank wall of incomprehension when I say that we should understand the Lockeianism of the Founding as the Founders themselves (not Leo Strauss) understood Locke. These "Straussians" simply cannot get it into their heads, that there is no reading of Locke, not even Strauss's, which is a sufficient guide to what Washington or Jefferson or Hamilton or Madison or Adams believed to be the doctrine of the *Second Treatise*. This is all the more remarkable in that, according to Strauss, Locke did have an exoteric teaching which was traditional. Why would Strauss—or anyone—think that the Founding Fathers looked beyond the traditional Locke? They were not fooled by the exoteric doctrine. What they accepted is what they believed to be true and just. And I have argued that the doctrine in which they believed is in fact, true and just. That theirs was an Aristotelianized Locke is supported by innumerable texts, which I repeatedly cite, but which are simply dismissed by "Straussians." I am reminded of the story of the burning of the library at Alexandria, and of the Khalif who said of the books in the library, that if they agreed with the Koran they were superfluous, and if they contradicted it they were evil. A similar story is told of a 17th century scholastic, who refused to look through Galileo's telescope, because if it confirmed Aristotle's astronomy it was superfluous, and if it contradicted it, it was wrong! Leo Strauss was not a man who refused to look at evidence.

✻ ✻ ✻

Transcript:

HM: You say that Aristotle's argument about the political nature of man is essentially the same as Locke's argument about the state of nature, or that at least that if Aristotle did come back today (HJ: Yes.) he would have endorsed what Locke had to say about that.

HJ: Because of the difference between monotheism and politics. ["Politics" is an obvious error for "polytheism."]

HM: Well, I'm not sure I agree with that suggestion of yours. . . . That's because I think that when Aristotle said the nature of man is a political animal; he meant the nature of man, he didn't mean man in certain circumstances, such as circumstances of polytheism instead of monotheism.

You seem to approve of Aristotle's idea of human nature and, therewith, of the idea of nature itself as an unchanging ground of changing experience. "That all men are created equal" means precisely that all human beings share in a common nature. To call that proposition a half truth is either to divide the human race into different "natures"—some being superior and some inferior—or to deny altogether that there is a human nature. Surely you must see the potential for unlimited evil in either of those alternatives.

In the Introduction to *The City and Man* Leo Strauss wrote:

> The return to classical political philosophy is both necessary and tentative or experimental . . . the relative success of modern political philosophy has brought into being a kind of society wholly unknown to the classics, a kind of society to which the classical principles . . . are not immediately applicable. Only we living today can possibly find a solution to the problems of today. (p. 11)

To the foregoing I would immediately add Aristotle's pronouncement, in the *Nicomachean Ethics*, that all natural right is changeable. Of course, human nature does not change. The nature of the virtues, moral and intellectual, and their corresponding vices, remain exactly what Aristotle said of them in the *Nicomachean Ethics*. When George Washington spoke of the indissoluble union of virtue and happiness, he meant exactly what Aristotle meant. The trans-historical character of the moral phenomena is wonderfully illuminated in Strauss's letter to

Löwith, when he wrote that it was the example of Churchill that enabled him to understand what Aristotle meant by magnanimity. What
constitutes virtue, and what vice, is no different now than at any time in
the past. Pleasure and pain, and the passions attached either to the one
or the other, are no different. Human nature is always and everywhere
the same. It is the same notwithstanding the fact that human beings
may be either civilized or barbarous or savage (according to the Declaration of Independence no less than Aristotle). It has been said that
there is nothing new in the world, only new ways of committing old sins.
But there must also be new ways of committing old virtues. The Polish
cavalry charging the tanks of the Wehrmacht in 1939—like the Charge
of the Light Brigade in the Crimean War—represented courage of a
sort. But it looked more like foolhardiness.

Our changed political circumstances are revealed in Aristotle's remark that what the law does not command, it forbids. This is the same
conception of law that informed the laws of Moses, and of all ancient
cities. Yet today it would be as foolish as the Polish cavalry charging
tanks. To apply Aristotle's text as a practical directive would be utterly
destructive of Aristotle's intention.[50] It would be a formula for tyranny,
not for justice. As we learn from Fustel de Coulanges, the ancient city
grew out of an aggregation of families, clans, and tribes. It was rendered
cohesive by allegiance to gods that were originally gods of separate
families, and that (by a syncretistic process) grew to embrace all the
clans and tribes of the city. The Pan-Hellenic gods grew out of an
extension of the same process. In deference to that development, the
Greek cities suspended their wars during the Olympic games. The
growth of Israel from Abraham, Isaac, and Jacob, to the 12 (and later 2)
tribes is prototypical. Periclean Athens was divided along tribal lines.
The first chapter of the Gospel of Matthew, authenticates Jesus's credentials (he is called the son of David, the son of Abraham) by his direct
descent—through 42 generations—from Abraham and David. Jesus
will, by the Christian dispensation, transform a community of blood into
a community of faith. But Jesus's qualifications for doing this depended,
a priori, upon his bloodlines, upon the fact that he himself was the
direct heir of Abraham and David. In ancient Israel as in any ancient
city, family, city, law, and God (or gods) formed a seamless web. In it,
how to worship (or whether) was no more a matter of individual right

than how (or whether) to obey the law. In it, separation of church and state, or of state and society, would have been unintelligible.

Of all the natural rights celebrated in the American Founding, none takes precedence of the free exercise of religion. Yet neither Plato nor Aristotle nor any ancient thinker, even alludes to such a right. Imagine Moses, descending Sinai, and finding the cult of the golden calf, and being told by Aaron that the people had just discovered their natural right to religious freedom! That would be a little like a Connecticut Yankee in King Arthur's court. Although Socrates was condemned to death for impiety, he never even suggested that the court of Athens had no proper jurisdiction over this question. He simply denied the impiety. In the ancient city a man was bound to his family and his city by the ancestral gods of his family and city. Yet in *Pilgrim's Progress*, Christian runs away from his wife and children, crying "What shall I do to be saved?" Christianity established a direct personal relationship between the individual human being and the one and only God, a relationship which was unknown to the ancient world. The salvation sought by Christian was dependent upon the state of his own soul and was independent of the goodness of his political community, or even of his family. This is the origin of modern individualism. In its secularized version it has become the basis of free government in the post-classical world. However, it was more than a millennium before that free government took form. It did so, only in and by the American Revolution. Its presence is recorded in the proposition that all men are created equal.

As Jesus distinguished—and separated—obedience to God from obedience to Caesar, Christianity separated obedience to law and obedience to God. In Shakespeare's *King John*, when the King refuses to obey the Pope's legate, he is told that he will be excommunicated, and his subjects enjoined to kill him as a tyrant. (It is however difficult to see who is the more tyrannical: the Pope or the King.) In the end, the King is forced to bow to the authority of the Pope to retain his crown. No classical philosopher had encountered such a struggle between secular and religious authority, each striving for supremacy. To overcome such a disjunction of authority called for a solution that Aristotle himself would not have found in the *Politics*. That does not mean however that an Aristotelian solution was not possible or necessary.

By the principles of the Declaration of Independence, civil society will be formed by a voluntary agreement, by individual human beings acting to secure the rights with which they have been endowed by their Creator. Political sovereignty is inherent in these rights, and the authority of any people will be the result of a contract, in which each pledges to all, and all to each, their mutual protection. The authority of any government will be the result of a delegation of powers from the people to that government. It will be limited by the nature of that delegation, which in turn will be limited by the nature of the original rights. For example, there can be no governmental power over the rights of conscience, because the nature of such rights is that the government can only protect them, it cannot interfere with them. The equal protection of the natural rights of every contracting member, is the end of the government. No one can reserve greater protection for himself or his rights, than for anyone else's. No one would enter into a contract with someone who stipulated a superior claim to the protection of his rights to those of others. Distinctions may and must arise within civil society, making one life more entitled to protection than another: for example, the general's rather than the private's. But such distinctions are necessities arising in the service of the equal protection of all. They do not arise from any original claim of inherent or natural superiority. A free society is possible only upon the acknowledgement of equal rights as the only foundation upon which legitimate governmental power arises.

The aforesaid government will moreover derive not any powers, but only *just powers* from the consent of the governed. Those powers are accordingly limited to what may rightfully be inferred from the original contract. Aristotle today would certainly say, as a general rule, that "Whatever the law does not forbid, it permits." Yet the authority of government itself is not less of divine origin than in ancient Israel. God channels His authority from the bottom up, from the people as a whole, rather than from the top down. Nor is the source of authority that of individuals merely. *It is individuals insofar as they have been endowed with certain unalienable rights by their Creator.* Neither individually nor by a people, can those rights be exercised merely at pleasure. They must be exercised in accordance with the morality of the laws of nature from which they are derived. This implies a duty to respect the equal rights of others. The distinction between civilization, on the one hand, and barbarism and savagery, on the other, consists precisely in the mutual recognition of the rights with which all possess as members of the human race. Within the system arising from the aforesaid mutual recognition there can then be no such conflict between piety and law as we saw in *King John*.

To repeat, no government governs in its own right, or by delegation from above. God does not hand down municipal laws from Sinai. They are enacted by a people, pursuant to the exercise of their God-given natural rights. There is no license from the rights mentioned in the Declaration of Independence to wage aggressive war, or to enslave other human beings who have the identical rights from the same God. Here is the heart of that decent constitutionalism that Leo Strauss said should command our unhesitating loyalty.

For the just powers of government to be derived from the consent of the governed, it is necessary that there be government by majority rule. Until the American Revolution, the Christian West had been torn, first by the conflict between Popes and Emperors, and later between Catholics and Protestants. Sectarian conflict and sectarian persecution were anathema to the Founding Fathers. They hated them in themselves, and they hated them because government by the consent of the governed was impossible as long as the governed were divided by sectarian passions, passions which turned them into barbarians and savages. No ancient city was divided, as was Christendom, between those who believed, and those who did not believe, in such dogmas as transubstantiation. (Or, we might add, between the Big-enders and the Little-enders in Lilliput.) No Catholic could accept a decision on transubstantiation by a majority of Protestants, and no Protestant could accept a decision by a majority of Catholics. Majority rule was possible only if such differences were excluded from the political process. For popular government to become possible, sectarian religious differences had to be removed from politics. In Jefferson's words, a man's civil rights should no more depend upon his opinions in religion, than in physics or geometry.

Locke's *Letters on Toleration* (themselves instructed largely by Spinoza's *Theological-Political Treatise*) were adapted and adopted in Jefferson's Statute of Virginia for Religious Freedom. The principles of that statute—beginning with "Whereas Almighty God hath created the mind free"—have become doctrinal for the Founding as a whole and are now incorporated not only in the federal Constitution, but in the constitutions of all 50 states. And they are perfectly consistent with an enlightened piety that sees sectarian differences as a manifestation of human freedom, and not as the snares of Satan.

Tocqueville called religion the first of political institutions in America, meaning thereby that there was a common morality taught by all the churches, irrespective of their doctrinal differences. Because doctrinal differences were not political differences, the majority shared a common moral framework with the minority. What Tocqueville failed to see, however, was that this common morality was not merely an empirical consensus within the framework of biblical religion, but was according to the laws of nature and of reason. Cooper's sermon of 1780, which I often quote, makes clear something that is not clear in Tocqueville: that the dictates of right reason are the voice of God no less than sacred scripture, and that these dictates are in accordance with the same laws of nature to which the Congress appealed in the Declaration of Independence. It was because religion in America acknowledged the authority of reason—of the laws of nature—no less than of revelation, that religion became the first of political institutions. In short, religion adapted itself to the principles of the Founding, and thereby became a buttress and support of the Founding. This is what made republican government—government of, by, and for the people—a practical possibility. It assumes no change whatever in human nature. It is a dispensation of practical wisdom that can certainly be called Aristotelian, although what it is called is less important than what it is.

❖ ❖ ❖

Transcript:

HM: It has been, you say, it has been well said that "it was easier for Moses to get the Jews out of Egypt than to get Egypt out of the Jews." I think that's a beautiful example of the point that I was going to make. That, for Aristotle, there isn't anything behind the political. That if the Jews weren't Jews, they were Egyptians. They were one thing or the other. And on page 57, you say, "Typically, there must be a founding lawgiver, a powerful political leader who forges a political community." It's a political leader; that again is my point, that politics is already present in the leadership of the man who puts a political community together.

To say that, "for Aristotle, there isn't anything behind the political" is to misunderstand the nature of the political as Aristotle understood it. In the example of Moses and the Jews, what was behind the political was God! Moses only did what he did because, after a good deal of reluctance, he accepted God's instructions, and carried them out. George Washington said repeatedly, that Divine Providence had led the way to American freedom, a thesis asserted prospectively in the Declaration of Independence itself. This thesis is asserted in the Declaration on the basis of an understanding of the laws of nature and of nature's God. It was supported by the conviction of the Congress that its intentions were approved by God. Their conviction that they were acting in accordance with the will of the Creator was not essentially different from that of Moses!

In Aristotle, the best regime is the guiding light for legislators. It is a regime which may not be actual anywhere, or at any time, yet it is the basis of all law-giving. Law-giving in practice is the prudent adaptation of the best regime—what is inherently right or just—to what is possible here and now. You can't make a silk purse from a sow's ear, nor can you make a free republic out of barbarians and savages. With the latter, the question is, How do you make them less barbarian and less savage? But the difference between barbarism or savagery and civilization is fixed in the nature of things, and is not dependent upon any political process. On the contrary, understanding and directing the political process is dependent upon the nature of things.

Political things, as we see them, are always in a state of change. When we speak of the political process, we mean a process of change. The question of our time, of all time, is whether there is or is not a timeless standard, an unchanging reality by which political reality can be judged and directed. For Moses, it was God. For Aristotle, it was the best regime, the regime in accordance with human nature, a nature which itself is rooted in an eternal order. For the Continental Congress, it was the laws of nature and of nature's God. Whether these transcendental standards are the same or different, whether or how they may be reconciled or justified, are important questions. But they are agreed that there can be no political process, properly so called, without an unchanging trans-political standard informing the political mind. Today, however, the universities—the places where elites should be formed that the people can recognize and accept—deny the possibility of any knowledge of these trans-political standards. When those who should form the elites deny any rational ground for the claims of elites, what kind of elite claims can you expect?

* * *

HM: The third point is about equality in the sense of my statement that the Declaration is a selfevident half-truth. Now, you say on page 97, "Mansfield knows perfectly well that any exception to the 'all' in 'all men created equal' has been and can be a justification of slavery. He knows that equality refers only to rights, and not to brains, beauty, or virtue." There are other things one might mention: talents, athletic ability, sexual prowess, things like that. All those are inequalities. You go on to say, on page 68, you, Jaffa: "I can see no basis whatever for any emendation of that doctrine into a half-truth." I didn't say that the doctrine was a half-truth, I said the statement was a half-truth. You're the one who said the equal protection of unequal faculties was inherent from the outset in the doctrine of human equality in the American Founding. (HJ: Yes.) So there is a basis for saying that the equality of man is—that "all men are created equal" is—a half-truth, if all men are also created unequal.

There has been a good deal of discussion since the conference, as to whether you had actually said that the proposition in the Declaration of Independence—and in the Gettysburg Address—that all men are created equal is a self-evident half-truth. The transcript seems to leave no doubt upon that point. You make some sort of a point however that you didn't say the *doctrine* was a half-truth but rather that the *statement* was a half-truth. I don't know what benefit you expect from this distinction. The proposition, as it occurs within the Declaration and the Gettysburg Address, is certainly the statement of a doctrine. You have called that statement of that doctrine a self-evident half-truth, notwithstanding the fact that it refers *only* to rights and in no way to *abilities*. At no point, moreover, do you concede that, in their right to life, liberty, and the pursuit of happiness, all men are created equal. It seems to me that you only confirm my earlier identification of you with Jefferson Davis, in his debate with Henry Wilson, in the Senate, in 1860.

You do however attempt to defend yourself by saying that "there is a basis for saying that 'all men are created equal' is a half-truth, if all men are also created unequal." You had quoted me, saying that you (Mansfield) knew that the equality proclaimed in the Declaration referred "only to rights and not to brains, beauty, or virtue." To these you added "talents, athletic ability, sexual prowess,[51] things like that." But your silence was deafening on whether all men are created equal in any respect at all. You quoted me as saying that "the equal protection of unequal faculties was inherent from the outset in the doctrine of human equality in the American Founding." Without the slightest justification you had assumed that I had conceded that "all men are also created unequal."

It does not seem to occur to you that it is impossible to recognize those respects in which human beings are unequal until one has recognized the respect in which all men are created equal. Let us turn to the passage in Locke's *Second Treatise* which is clearly the principal source of the statement in the Declaration of Independence. Here is the beginning of the second chapter, "Of the State of Nature."

> To understand political power aright, and derive it from its original, we must consider what state all men are naturally in, and that is a state of perfect freedom to order their actions and dispose of their possessions and persons as they think fit, within the bounds of the law of nature, without asking leave, or depending upon the will of any other man.
>
> A state also of equality, wherein all the power and jurisdiction is reciprocal, no one having more than another; there being nothing more evident than that creatures of the same species and rank, promiscuously born to all the same advantages of nature, and the use of the same faculties should also be equal amongst another, without subordination or subjection, unless the Lord and Master of them all should by any manifest declaration of His will set one above another, and confer on him by an evident and clear appointment an undoubted right to domination and sovereignty.

Elsewhere Locke refers to this state of equality as an equality of "dominion." That is to say, no one has by nature a right to rule another, more than another has the right to rule him. I have often rendered this thought by saying that there is no such difference between man and man, as there is between man and dog, that makes one by nature the ruler of another. When man meets dog, ruler meets ruled, in virtue of the difference of species. There is no such difference within the human species that marks the ruler from the ruled. It is this primordial natural equality of dominion that determines that the just powers of government must be derived from the consent of the governed. This is the original foundation of the constitutionalism that emerged from the American Revolution. This is the reason why the American Revolution was consummated only by the abolition of slavery, and by the adoption of the Civil War amendments.

How profoundly Locke's doctrine (or statement!) influenced the Americans in the Revolution, may be seen from the opening of the "Declaration of the Causes and Necessity of Taking up Arms." This bears the date of July 6, 1775, two days short of a year before the Declaration of Independence.

> If it was possible for men, who exercise their reason to believe, that the divine Author of our existence intended a part of the human race to hold an absolute property in, and an unbounded power over others, marked out by his infinite goodness and wisdom, as the objects of a legal domination never rightfully resistible, however severe and oppressive, the inhabitants of these colonies might at least require from the parliament of Great Britain some evidence, that this dreadful authority over them has been granted to that body.

The foregoing is clearly an elaborate paraphrase, heavy with sarcasm, of the second paragraph of second chapter of the *Second Treatise*, quoted above. The Congress is saying that is not possible for anyone who exercises his reason, to believe that any one part of the human race is invested with a right of property in or dominion over any other part. This refers to human persons, whether considered individually or as members of societies. There is "nothing more evident," which is to say that it is self-evident, that members of the same human species are not marked out, some to rule and others to be ruled. Here is the doctrine of human equality asserted without equivocation or ambiguity a year before Declaration of Independence. Inequality of ability or talent or virtue (or sexual prowess), has nothing to do with the equality of right asserted by the Congress. It is notable moreover that in asserting a right to liberty that belonged to mankind as mankind, the Congress condemned human slavery everywhere. To attempt to emend the Declaration, as you do, to say that "all men are also created unequal," is to call into question, if not actually to destroy its force as an antislavery document. I repeat therefore that I cannot see any difference between the position you take and that of Jefferson Davis, in the exchange with Henry Wilson in the Senate in 1860.

The assertion of the doctrine that all men are created equal was intended, as Locke says, and as our Revolutionary forebears believed, to enable us to understand political power aright. To have taken their bearing from human inequality would have been to understand political power wrongly. It would have led to a justification of hereditary aristocracy and hereditary monarchy, in short, to the *ancien regime*. It was then necessary, first of all, to establish the proposition that there were no differences within the human species that established a right of dominion within the species. But they did not assert or imply the obvious untruth that there were no differences at all within that species, or that none of those differences were irrelevant in deciding who should rule, or for what ends. Here is Jefferson on natural aristocracy (letter to John Adams, October 28, 1813).

> For I agree with you that there is a natural aristocracy among men. The grounds of this are virtue and talents. . . . There is also an artificial aristocracy, founded on wealth and birth, without either virtue or talents; for with these it would belong to the first class. The natural aristocracy I consider as the most precious gift of nature, for the instruction, the trusts, and government society. And, indeed, it would have been inconsistent in creation to have formed man for the social state, and not to have provided virtue and wisdom enough to manage the concerns of the society. May we not even say, that that form of government is the best, which provides the most effectually for a pure selection of these natural aristoi into the offices of government? The artificial aristocracy is a mischievous ingredient in government, and provision should be made to prevent its ascendency.

That man is by nature political is asserted by Jefferson no less unequivocally than by Aristotle.[52] That to be political means to be neither beast nor God is also intended no less by Jefferson than by Aristotle. You mentioned athletic ability as among the things in which human beings were unequal. But animals other than man run faster and jump higher than human animals. Before we have an athletic competition, we are assured that the competitors are equally human, before discovering

among them inequality in the ability to run or to jump.[53] In the 1936
Olympics Hitler dismissed the triumphs of Jesse Owens by denying that
he was a human competitor. The equality of man, in the sense of the
Declaration of Independence, is the necessary condition for athletic
competition no less than for defining the universe within which there
can be majority rule.

Jefferson says that there is a natural aristocracy. It never seems to
occur to him that this contradicts in any way the proposition that all
men are created equal. Nor would it have seemed so to John Adams.
Adams was the author of the Massachusetts Bill of Rights of 1780,
which began "all men are born free and equal, and have certain natural,
essential, and unalienable rights. . . ." Although the just powers of
government are derived from the equal rights of all, the question arises,
Who is to exercise those powers to the greatest advantage of the political community? Here we see Jefferson warning against the "artificial
aristocracy." Just as there were false claims to superiority in the *ancien
regime*,[54] so there have been false claims in respect to equality in democracies. Jefferson understood this as well as Tocqueville. Notwithstanding his well known diatribe against Plato, Jefferson's attempt to
provide for a pure selection of the natural *aristoi* into the offices of
government came as near to the theory of Plato's Republic as has ever
been suggested by anyone. Jefferson wished to have universal public
primary education. Free secondary education would be offered to the
top 10 percent of the primary pool. Free higher education would be
offered to the top 10 percent of the secondary pool. We thus see Plato's
three classes emerging from a perfectly open competitive academic
process, with the guardian class constituting no more than 1% of the
original community. The offices of government would however be filled
by an open political process. The guardian class would have no prescrip-
tive rights to office. Merit from any source might be recognized. But
Jefferson thought that there would be a natural disposition by the people to choose from that 1 percent that had proved itself in open educational competition. Of course, everything would depend upon the quality of the educational system by which these guardians were selected.
Jefferson certainly expected that they would be "studiers" of the laws of
nature. He never imagined that the universities would be dominated by
those who denied that there were such laws, much less any who studied
them. Jefferson never could have imagined that a Chief Justice of the

United States—or any justice—or any civilized person—could say that
constitutional safeguards for individual liberty were without any intrinsic worth. He would have been dumbfounded at the news that such was
the conventional wisdom of the universities that were to train the minds
of the future guardians of those safeguards.

In "What Is Liberal Education?" Leo Strauss wrote:

> Liberal education is the ladder by which we try to ascend from mass
> democracy to democracy as originally meant. Liberal education is
> the necessary endeavor to found an aristocracy within democratic
> mass society.

When Strauss speaks of "democracy as originally meant" he is clearly
referring to the American Founding, not democracy in the ancient city.
It is altogether probable here that Strauss had in mind Jefferson. This
probability is based in part upon the fact that in his essay "On Classical
Political Philosophy" Strauss found "the natural answer of all good men
to the natural question of the best political order" by quoting what
Jefferson said about the pure selection of the natural *aristoi* in the letter
to Adams.[55]

What Strauss says "we" must attempt is what Jefferson had in mind,
but never could put directly into practice.[56] That is to have a system of
education to discover and train the natural aristocracy. However, it
cannot be repeated too often, that identification of such an aristocracy
is possible only within a universe in which the only advantage of birth *a
priori* is of being "promiscuously born to all the same advantages of
nature, and the use of the same faculties" as other members of the
human species. It is also possible only in virtue of an education that
takes its bearings by the moral distinctions grounded in nature.

The pure selection of the natural *aristoi* into the offices of government would be made by the people as a whole. The tacit premise is that
civilized and intelligent human beings recognize their own lack of competence in many of the offices of life. In those disciplines in which they
recognize wisdom superior to their own, they wish to be ruled, not by
themselves, but by the wise. Accordingly, in matters of health we do not
wish to be ruled by ourselves, but by the physician, as in other circumstances by the architect, the attorney, the economist, the general, the
engineer. But in every case, we also wish to choose, or to share in
choosing, the one who is to rule us. It is the part of wisdom that,

although the skill of the physician may benefit us as we cannot benefit ourselves, there is nothing in his medical training alone to make him wholeheartedly devoted to benefiting us. Physicians have been known to conspire against their patients.[57] The Hippocratic oath is itself recognition that the moral dimension of the medical profession is not something intrinsic to medical skill, or that it results from medical training. We do not moreover rely on the Hippocratic oath. We expect the doctor to be dependent upon our good opinion for the economic success of his practice. There are also laws, both civil and criminal, by which the doctor may be punished for negligence or malice. We see then that the consent of the governed is not meant to be a way in which the unwise rule, but rather a way of assuring that rule of the wise may be beneficial to the unwise. Of course, we presuppose a people sufficiently enlightened and intelligent to show competence in choosing their doctors. The system we endorse would have no relevance in a pre-scientific society in which medical practice was conducted by witch-doctors. And even in the most enlightened society there will be an abundance of fools and charlatans. Yet, to a remarkable degree, the claims of wisdom and consent are brought into a harmony with each other.

It is thought however that political government differs from medical government. What constitutes the health pursued by medical government, it is said, is not essentially controversial. But there is no similar agreement as to what constitutes the health of the body politic. It is assumed that because there is no such agreement, there is no objective or rational knowledge of political health. But disagreement as to what is the truth does not mean there is no truth, or that it is not within our power to know it.[58] It means, at most, that both sides (or all sides) may be wrong. It does not mean that one side may not be right. The most profound disagreement as to what constitutes health in the body politic is between those who condemn tyranny and despotism, and those who praise it. The argument condemning tyranny is a long one, but it is summarized in the proposition that all men are created equal, and that the just powers of government are derived from the consent of the governed. That, said Lincoln, is the sheet anchor of American republicanism. Here however is an adversarial view of the causes and consequences of Lincoln's speeches and deeds.

Since the Civil War, in which the Southern States were conquered, against all historical logic and sound sense, the American people have been in a condition of political and popular decay. . . . The beginnings of a great new social order based on the principle of slavery and inequality were destroyed by that war, and with them also the embryo of a future truly great America.

Can there be no rational dissent to the judgment rendered above? Are all opinions on the relative merits of slavery and freedom equal? Lincoln compared slavery to a cancer in the body politic. Calhoun compared, not slavery, but abolitionism, to a cancer. The moral relativist would say that both are value judgments, and that neither is "right" and neither is "wrong". Is contented slavery the best condition for all human beings, as the Grand Inquisitor said, or is it good only for "inferior races," as the defenders of slavery in the antebellum South maintained? Did God and nature intend the principles of civil and religious liberty for some human beings but not for others? Are we, with Rehnquist, Bork, and their positivist cohorts seriously to believe, that there is no more ground in reason for civil and religious liberty than for the slavery or the despotism espoused by the Grand Inquisitor, Calhoun, and Adolf Hitler?

The medical doctor is not expected to reach a consensus with witch doctors, voodoo, or shamans. Statesmanship requires that we reject the rejection of the principles of civil and religious liberty, whether by defenders of the Confederacy or of the Third Reich. The consent of the governed can however serve the ends of wisdom, whether medical or political, only if there is sufficient rationality or enlightenment both in the claims of those supposed to be wise, and of those who are to consent to their rule. Thus Jefferson:

If a nation expects to be ignorant and free . . . it expects what never was and never will be.

That human beings ought not to be ruled as if they were beasts, or as if their rulers are gods, rests upon premises as accessible to reason as do those of medical science. Human beings are not born with saddles on their backs, to be ridden by priests or kings or demagogues. This is the truth embodied in the proposition that all men are created equal. Understood as Lincoln and Jefferson understood it, this is the basis upon which wisdom and consent, aristocracy and democracy, can be harmonized.

Transcript:

> **HM**: What happens, what tends to happen, in the American regime is that the state of nature which . . . was a pre-political basis or foundation of politics, has become a principle of politics in the Aristotelian sense, the ruling principle, the *arche*. So that the state of nature is not understood simply as a basis from which we would prepare to rule, but a basis upon which we would continue to rule.

The state of nature was never intended solely as a pre-political foundation for politics. It was always intended to furnish a ruling principle in the Aristotelian sense. Consider the following from the second chapter of the *Second Treatise*:

> The state of nature has a law of nature to govern it, which obliges every one; and reason, which is that law, teaches all mankind who will but consult it, that, being all equal and independent, no one ought to harm another in his life, health, liberty, or possessions. For men being . . . all the servants of one sovereign Master . . . furnished with like faculties, sharing all one community of nature, there cannot be supposed any such subordination among us, that may authorize us to destroy one another, as if we were made for one another's use, as the inferior ranks of creatures are for ours.

A little later Locke says that

> the municipal laws of countries . . . are only so far right as they are founded on the law of nature, by which they are to be regulated and interpreted.

Is it not self-evident that we ought not to harm others who do not harm us, or threaten to harm us, whether within civil society or in the state of nature? Locke is clear that "municipal laws" are not only founded on the law of nature, but "regulated and interpreted" by it. Does not the law of nature condemn slavery within civil society? Does it not condemn as barbarous or savage all violations of what today we call human rights? As I have often said, the defect of our human rights policy is that we no longer proclaim it as a dictate of the law of nature and of reason but as just another set of value judgments. We at once scold others for not living up to our standards, while telling them that there is no reason why they should live up to them! It is true that we attempt to secure recognition of human rights by means of the United Nations and other instruments of international positive law. But such agreements may reflect no more than American power. They are not in themselves arguments for any wisdom except that of superior force.

The law of nature tells us not to treat other humans as if they were made for our use, like the inferior creatures. Notwithstanding the exigencies of self-preservation and the dispensations of prudence, this is a moral injunction that in itself admits of no exception, whether within civil society or outside of it. Aristotle himself finds the origin of friendship among birds and other animals, but most of all in man, in belonging to the same race or species. For this reason, he says, we praise those who are known as lovers of their fellow men. (*N.E.* 1155 20) The injunction not to harm others of our species is not the same as "Love thy neighbor as thyself . . ." but is not less a dictate of right reason.

Aristotle divides justice into two: justice in exchanges, and justice in distributions. The former, is reducible to numerical equality, as follows. The relationship of any two individual human beings may be understood, *a priori*, as zero equals zero. If I slip on a banana peel that you have negligently left on your sidewalk, you will have injured me. My injury is then understood to constitute your gain. If my loss by the injury is judged (reasonably) to equal $1,000, then you are held to have gained the same amount as I have lost. You must then pay me $1,000, to eliminate my loss and your gain, restoring our *a priori* relationship of zero zero. What constitutes justice here—and in all other exchanges—has nothing whatever to do with the wisdom, virtue, or sexual prowess[59] of the parties. It does not matter whether they are equal or unequal in any respect but one.

All buying and selling, all torts, all contracts, constitute a zero sum game, in which justice requires that there be a numerical equality at the beginning and the end of every transaction. This equality applies only to mature human beings of sound mind. Contracts cannot be made with dogs or horses, or with children, or with the mentally retarded. In the antebellum South, enforceable contracts could not be made by slaves or with slaves, since legally they had the same status as horses or dogs.[60] Nor can contracts be made with barbarians or savages who do not or cannot understand the terms of the contract. But the justice in an exchange is intrinsic to the transaction itself. It does not depend upon the personal qualities of the parties to the transaction. A good man has the same obligation to pay a debt to a bad man as to another good man. Nor can he plead in extenuation that he needs the money more than the one to whom it is owed. The parties to an exchange are equal in a precise numerical sense. How one honors one's obligations in exchanges with others does however determine one's own character for justice. A just man will pay his debts to a poor man who could not enforce the payment of the debt, as well as to a rich man who could. When Lincoln said that a black woman had the same right to put into her mouth the bread that her own hand had earned, he was saying that, in a precise Aristotelian sense, she had the same—or equal—right to justice as every other human being in the world. The labor that produced the bread at the same time produced her right to that bread, and its appropriation by anyone else constituted theft. This equality of right admits of no exceptions, on Aristotelian grounds no less than upon Jeffersonian or Lincolnian.

Justice according to Aristotle is also present in distributions. The first finisher in a race is entitled to the first place prize, and the second finisher, the second place prize, and so on. In each case, the prize must equal the place. If dividends from corporate profits are distributed, someone who has twice as many shares as someone else should receive twice as much in dividends. For the one with double the shares to receive the same amount would not be equal but unequal. Equality rightly understood means recognition of proportional equality in distributions no less than numerical equality in transactions. Once again, this is Aristotle's understanding no less than Lincoln's.

Transcript:

HM: And this is the argument of Tocqueville's *Democracy in America*, a book which you do not sufficiently appreciate. That book says that we live in the midst of a democratic revolution, that is, we live in a certain kind of democracy, a democracy that democratizes. It has a continuing tendency to make itself more and more democratic as it proceeds. So, it's, I think, not enough, then, to stick simply to the principle that "All men are created equal" if one wants to combat this democratizing tendency which is, I believe, a fundamental dan-

ger, perhaps the fundamental danger of our democracy as so identified by Tocqueville.

We live, you say, in a certain kind of democracy, one that democratizes.
What is the other kind? One that monarchizes? When Tocqueville visited here in the mid-1830s, the United States was on the eve of the
debate that culminated in the Civil War. The idea of rights enshrined in
the laws of nature was being replaced by rights having their origin in
history, in which the "ought" is identified with the "is". According to the
historical school, the course of events from pre-history onwards, which
resulted in the freedom of the free, also resulted in the slavery of the
slave. The free deserved their freedom because they had it. And the
slaves deserved their slavery for the same reason! That in a nutshell is
the argument that persuaded Calhoun. Slavery, from being considered
evil, even if sometimes a necessary evil, was now said to be a positive
good. In a century which culminated in Darwinian evolution, "science"
was discovering new "laws of nature," entirely different from those
known to Jefferson. What Jefferson believed to have been disproved by
science, was now held to be proved by science. Science now declared
that some human beings were in fact born "with saddles on their backs,"
to be ridden by a master race. The "equality" of mankind only applied
to a superior race. It applied only to whites of British descent, or whites
of European descent, or whites of European descent who were not
Catholics. Moreover, the equality of those who deserved to be "equal"
was enhanced and promoted by slavery. Consider the following:

> With us [of the South] the two great divisions of society are not the
> rich and poor, but white and black; and all of the former, the poor as
> well as the rich, belong to the upper class, and are respected and
> treated as equals, if honest and industrious, and hence have a posi-
> tion and pride of character of which neither poverty nor misfortune
> can deprive them. [Calhoun, Speech on the Oregon Bill, 1848]

And again:

> I am a Southern man and a slaveholder—a kind and merciful one, I
> trust—and none the worse for being a slaveholder. I say, for one, I
> would rather meet any extremity on earth than give up one inch of
> our equality—one inch of what belongs to us as members of this
> great republic! What! acknowledged inferiority! The surrender of life

is nothing to sinking down into acknowledged inferiority! [Calhoun, Speech on Resolutions on the Slave Question, 1847]

Here we see that differences of wealth, or of talent, or of virtue, are reduced to insignificance because they pale in comparison with the all-consuming difference of race and color. We are told that death is better than the slightest loss of equality. That the slaves might feel anything demeaning from the far greater indignity of slavery seems never to have cast the slightest shadow on Calhoun's consciousness. I don't think Calhoun thought servitude any more demeaning to his slaves than to his dogs. The equality Calhoun defends is identified with state rights, but state rights divorced completely from natural rights. Compare Calhoun's praise of slavery as promoting social equality with Jefferson's denunciation of slavery in the *Notes on Virginia*, in which he says slavery not only injured the slaves but corrupted the morals of the master class.

The doctrine of state rights today still has the odor it acquired in the defense of slavery and Jim Crow. No matter how much we praise Rehnquist—as I myself often do—for attempting to revive the constitutional status of the states, that odor still adheres. And the reason is that Rehnquist denies natural rights as much as Calhoun. It cannot be repeated too often that natural rights are the foundation of individual rights, and individual rights are the ground of the recognition of individual achievement and individual merit. The erosion of the natural rights of the Founding—the erosion of the idea of the equality of man as man—was the necessary if not the sufficient cause of Tocqueville's strictures on that subject. It was impossible, whether in Jacksonian America or today, to degrade equality rightly understood without at the same time degrading that recognition of merit which is inequality rightly understood. This is what you fail to understand.

> One must begin to take account of and to justify the inequalities which are in our country: that diversity . . . only exists when people are thought to be unequal and not just equal; and I've, in my writings, tried to emphasize that point time and again, that you cannot have diversity without inequality. So the problem today is not so much to put down slavery, but it's to hold down this democratic revolution. To do that, one has to promote, one has to show that

> America is full of the promotion and encouragement of inequality as well as equality. So, I think that the two principles must be understood together. It's perfectly true that you can understand equality as equal treatment before the law, but it has to be emphasized, and emphasized time and again, that equality before the law means toleration, or even promotion, of inequality. And so, I really differ with you on the tactics or the strategy for defending our original principles today.

In saying that "the two principles must be understood together" you seem to have conceded, at long last, that there is a principle of equality that deserves recognition. But "equality before the law" is a feature of the positive law of the Constitution. Unless the equality of positive law is grounded in some conception of equality antecedent to the positive law, "equal treatment before the law" can mean almost anything. "Separate but equal" was once used to represent equal treatment before the law. In fact, it still represents equal treatment, only it is now called by a different name. The demand for preferential treatment by race or gender is now known under the general rubric of affirmative action. But it is not different in principle from the old separate but equal. All that has changed is the intended beneficiaries and the intended victims. The changes in question represent only a change in power, not a change in right or wrong. The first Justice Harlan, in his dissenting opinion in *Plessy*, declared that the Constitution did not recognize any classes or subclasses of citizens. Segregation by race was wrong, he said, not because of any supposed injury to one or another class of citizen. It was wrong because there were no classes of citizens. His tacit premise was "that all men are created equal," and that this equality ought to be reflected in the law of the Constitution. The recognition of separate or disparate classes of citizens meant the substitution of group rights, or collective rights, for individual rights. This is exactly what happened when Calhoun divorced state rights from natural rights. "Equal treatment before the law" except as a translation into the Constitution of the principle that all men are *without exception* created equal, is worthless.

Taney in *Dred Scott* said that Negroes were not included in the proposition that all men are created equal. He said that the rights affirmed in the Declaration did not apply to every human individual. They applied only to those who enjoyed a preferred status because of the color of their skin. That is to say, they enjoyed their preferred status because of their membership in one of the groups into which humans were divided. Their rights were group or collective rights, not individual rights. To be white, as Calhoun said, was to be a member of an upper class. To be white was to be part of an hereditary aristocracy. Something like this happens whenever the unqualified truth of the proposition of human equality is denied.

Taney said that as a justice of the Supreme Court, he was bound by the meaning of the Constitution that prevailed in the minds of those who had framed and ratified it. In their minds, he said, blacks were so far inferior that they had no rights which white men were bound to respect. That this was so, he offered in evidence the alleged fact that the proposition in the Declaration of Independence that all men are created equal did not include blacks. According to Taney, if the Founding Fathers, as moral men, had believed what they said, they would have abolished slavery. Taney seems to have assumed that moral men were those who acted in accordance with Kant's categorical imperative. As good Kantians they would have acted solely on the basis of their judgment that slavery was wrong, paying no attention whatever to considerations of prudence. Taney failed to notice that the Declaration itself rejected Kant when it appealed to the dictates of prudence. Now Taney knew perfectly well that in 1776 or 1787 no American government had the power to abolish slavery throughout the United States. Between 1776 and 1787 all the states north of the Mason Dixon line had adopted plans for the gradual elimination of slavery. The Congress of the Confederation had in 1787 adopted the Northwest Ordinance, which excluded slavery from all the territory north of the Ohio River, the only territory directly controlled by the central government. The first Congress under the Constitution re-adopted the Northwest Ordinance. I do not believe there is a single piece of documentary evidence to support what Taney said was the prevailing view of the Founding generation, and there are innumerable expressions that directly contradict it—for example the 1775 Declaration of the Causes and Necessity of Taking Up Arms. What is astonishing is not that Taney's anachronistic Kantianism should have been taken up by the defenders of slavery in 1857, but that it has been taken up today by the so called civil rights establishment. John Hope Franklin, Leon Higginbotham, Thurgood Marshall, have been among the leading spokesmen for the view that the Declaration did not include Negroes, that the Founding was indeed racist, and therefore that the original intentions of those who framed and ratified the Constitution ought not to have any authority. But it is not only the radicals of the Left who say this. Virtually all the paleocon scholars, like Willmoore Kendall and M. E. Bradford say the same thing. The legal positivists—like Rehnquist and Bork—do not assert it directly, but their identification of the "ought" with the "is" amounts to the same thing. Irving Kristol thinks that anything written by the anti-slavery author of the Declaration of Independence is not worth reading! The Right and the Left do not differ on whether the Founding was racist. They only differ as to whether this was or was not a good thing. And they draw different practical conclusions. Those on the Left say— inconsistently, to be sure—that since the Constitution has always been racist, race based remedies ought to be adopted. Those on the Right oppose them, not because they oppose race based benefits, but because the wrong race is being benefited. Both Right and Left however are wrong for the same reason that Taney was wrong. The proposition that all men are created equal means and always has meant that all human beings, everywhere and always, have the rights to life, liberty, and the pursuit of happiness.

You say that you have tried "time and again" to emphasize "that you cannot have diversity without inequality." But what diversity, and what inequality? Slavery and Jim Crow were outstanding examples of diversity and inequality.[61] Their counterparts today are found grouped under the rubric of affirmative action: for blacks, women, Latinos, Eskimos, Native Americans, homosexuals, the otherwise enabled, or anyone else who can find his or her way into the "rainbow coalition." You say the problem is not "to put down slavery" but to "hold down the democratic revolution."[62] But it is precisely because the justification of slavery, as embodied in Taney's opinion in *Dred Scott*, has never been put down, that racism is alive and well today. What you call the democratic revolution is in fact the revolution against democracy. It is against that aristocracy of merit in a regime of equal rights that Jefferson envisaged as democracy, and which Leo Strauss called democracy as originally meant.

You say that you and I really do "differ". . . on the tactics or the strategy for defending our original principles. . . . I say that where we really differ is not on tactics or strategy, but on the original principles themselves. The equality in the Declaration of Independence—which you attack—is the equality in nature which distinguishes what is lower than man—the bestial—from what is higher—the divine. Aristotle says that reason is the most divine thing in us, and should be cultivated above everything else. But moral relativism tells us that reason is impotent to know anything about the just and the unjust, right and wrong, good and bad. The laws of nature and of nature's God represent that objective order from which we, like Aristotle and the Founding Fathers, may take our moral and political bearings. The enemy of "our original principles" is that relativism that denies either the existence, or the accessibility to reason, of such an order. It is impossible to defend "our original principles" except by defending them against this moral relativism. When are you going to begin?

Harry V. Jaffa
Claremont, California
July 8, 1996

Third Open Letter from Jaffa to Mansfield

November 30, 1999
Professor Harvey C. Mansfield, Jr.
Department of Government, Harvard University
Cambridge, Massachusetts 02138
Dear Harvey:

I understand that, in conversation with some Claremont students at Santa Monica, you said that I had attacked everyone I had ever loved. I don't know if these were you precise words, but I believe they convey your meaning.

I don't know why you would say such a thing. I don't know why you would think it. However, it is consistent with your diatribe against me at the April 1996 25th anniversary conference of the Salvatori Center. What is notable is not the disparagement, then and now, but the absence of any reasoned argument addressed to the issues that divide us. You impute bad motives to me without showing that they are in the service of bad reasoning.

After last year's meeting, I addressed two open letters to you, amounting between them to something like 100 pages. Eighteen months later, not a word of reply. At least, not a word of reply to me. I assume however that what you said at Santa Monica about me you have been saying elsewhere. To attack someone's character when you cannot deal with his reasons is Standard Operating Procedure for someone "tied by interests he cannot admit to an argument he cannot defend." To discredit your opponent when you cannot refute him is also known—apart from Machiavelli—as "poisoning the well." It is consistent with this that you now seem to relish "victim" status, so popular (and successful) among present day Liberals. It is however, strange for someone who lectures on manliness!

❋ ❋ ❋

The highest kind of friendship according to Aristotle (and the final cause of all lesser forms of friendship) is philosophic. The ultimate end of such friendship is to test each other's arguments. What greater betrayal of such a friendship can there be, than to confirm another in a falsehood, lest one fall out of his favor? It is always easier, and more socially acceptable, to flatter by agreeing. If we are true to our vocation we must be prepared, at one time or another, to play the role of the physician being tried by a jury of children, on charges brought by the pastry chef.

What follows is an account by Leo Strauss of the classics' understanding of friendship.

> Since the philosopher is the man who devotes his whole life to the quest for wisdom, he has no time for political activity of any kind: the philosopher cannot possibly desire to rule. His only demand on the political men is that they leave him alone. He justifies his demand by honestly declaring that his pursuit is purely theoretical and does not interfere in any way with the business of the political men. This simple solution presents itself at first glance as the strict consequence from the definition of the philosopher. Yet a short reflection shows that it suffers from fatal weakness. The philosopher cannot lead an absolutely solitary life because legitimate "subjective certainty" and the "subjective certainty" of the lunatic are indistinguishable. Genuine certainty must be "intersubjective." The classics were fully aware of the essential weakness of the mind of the individual. Hence their teaching about the philosophic life is a teaching about friendship: the philosopher is as philosopher in need of friends. To be of service to the philosopher in his philosophizing, the friends must be competent men: they must themselves be actual or potential philosophers, i.e., members of the natural "elite." Friendship presupposes a measure of conscious agreement. The things regarding which the philosophic friends must agree cannot be known or evident truths. For philosophy is not wisdom but quest for wisdom. The things

regarding which the philosophic friends agree will then be opinions or prejudices. Hence there will be a variety of groups of philosophic friends: philosophy, as distinct from wisdom, necessarily appears in the form of philosophic schools or sects. Friendship as the classics understood it offers then no solution to the problem of "subjective certainty." Friendship is bound to lead to, or to consist in, the cultivation and perpetuation of common prejudices by a closely knit group of kindred spirits. It is therefore incompatible with the idea of philosophy. The philosopher must leave the closed and charmed circle of the "initiated" if he intends to remain a philosopher. He must go out to the market place; the conflict with the political men cannot be avoided. And this conflict by itself, to say nothing of its cause or its effect, is a political action. [Leo Strauss, *On Tyranny,* revised and expanded edition, eds. Victor Gourevitch and Michael S. Roth, New York: Free Press, 1991; originally published 1963) 194–195]

A full commentary on this extraordinary passage would take a book by itself. It seems clear to me however that some "Straussians" have become a sect, more concerned to cultivate and perpetuate their sectarianism, than to pursue the truth. That the American Founding is wholly modern, that the equality celebrated in it can only be understood as Hobbesian, that its purposes can be consummated only by the extinction of all influence of biblical religion—and religious morality—are some of the common opinions which have become unquestioned and unquestionable. Any Straussian who ventures beyond their precincts will find himself in the position of a Communist Party member of the 1930s who dared to question democratic centralism.

* * *

You and I differ as to whether the proposition that all men are created equal is a whole or a half-truth. I maintain that it is a whole truth, if understood as it was intended to be understood by Jefferson and Lincoln, in the Declaration and in the Gettysburg Address. You identify the proposition with the democrats, as represented in the third book of the *Politics,* who say that justice is equality. So it is, says Aristotle, for equals. But not for unequals. So the identification of justice with equality is a half-truth, and for like reason the proposition that all men are created equal is a half-truth. That I take it, briefly stated, is your position.

What is wrong with it is the identification of the democratic argument in the *Politics* with the proposition celebrated in the American mind of the founding and in the Gettysburg Address. The latter is not a partisan assertion within a regime. It is a species specific proposition about man, God, and the universe. It is an example of what Thomas Aquinas called the natural law, the rational creature's participation in the eternal law. Its true parallel is in the first book of the *Politics,* when Aristotle says that man is by nature a political animal, and that whoever is not part of a *polis* by nature is either a beast or a god. The perception of the "great chain of being" as one that distinguishes man, beast, and God (or god), is common to Aristotle and the Declaration of Independence. It is the ground *a priori* not of democracy as such, but of the rule of law. No such disparity exists between man and man, as exists between man and God, or man and beast, as would justify arbitrary rule. Hence ruling and being ruled, the essence of political life, properly so called, is natural to man. Disparities in human excellence may of course exist, so of which may even justify government without consent—barbarism and savagery, or criminal conduct. But these apparent exceptions do not constitute exceptions to the great chain of being itself. They are not beasts or gods arising from human parents.

The distinctions that arise among the human types that constitute a polity will always justify some being preferred to others, in the constitution of a government. The "pure selection of the natural *aristoi* into the offices of government" is as much to be desired in a democracy as in any other form of government. Jefferson's point is that it is more likely to take place in a democracy, where the privileges of the artificial aristocracy have been abolished. This is what Strauss meant by "democracy as originally meant."

That there are men (and women) of such superlative ability—and ambition—as to challenge the equality in nature proclaimed in the Declaration is observed both by Aristotle and the Founders. Lincoln's Lyceum speech is addressed to this problem. But Lincoln's solution, as Aristotle's and Strauss's, is that the very greatness of such natures can be manifested only in their ultimate devotion to the rule of law. Anyone who advanced his claim to rule on the basis of such superiority—as for example Napoleon or Hitler—would, *ipso facto,* be revealed as a charlatan.

Crisis of the House Divided was acclaimed almost universally—that is by those who read it. As it turned out, however, very few of its admirers understood or accepted the thesis that, in Lincoln, classical virtue had proved its possibility, and even its success, in a regime otherwise modern. Many who liked the book did so because of an emotional commitment to Lincoln, and because I seemed to elevate the ground of their admiration. But that higher ground was usually an ersatz Aristotelianism, either Nietzschean or Hegelian.

As I interpret you, classical philosophy and biblical religion, and even more, the morality common to them, have been dealt a death blow by Machiavelli, and whatever of either deserved to survive does so in one or another of the form of Machiavelli's teaching. From your point of view, if I can penetrate the layers of your onion, neither moral rationalism, grounded in nature, nor biblical morality, are either defensible or desirable. Machiavelli's version of "natural right" was domesticated by Hobbes and Locke, and constitutional formalism becomes the simulacrum of morality. The "effectual truth" of executive power leaves the private citizen free for the unhindered pursuit of property and pleasure. Your lecture on the *Mandragola* many years ago—one of the most brilliant I ever heard—made it clear, I thought, that the effectual truth of Machiavellian politics was ultimately in the service of something like the bourgeois menage that emerges at the end. Respectable immorality. Machiavelli's bourgeois menage is very much like the one about which Karl Marx waxed sarcastic. But Marx saw clearly that bourgeois immorality was only a half-way house to a utopian state in which there would be no forbidden pleasures, nor any reason for pleasures to be forbidden. It seems to me that, judged by this standard, present day America is closer to the ultimate Communist ideal than was ever even imagined by Lenin or Stalin.

The foregoing, as it seems to me, is the direction in which you, and Machiavelli, would take us. In saying so much, let me hasten to add that many elements of Machiavelli are classical, and deserve to be included in an enlightened present day classicism. Machiavelli's critique of Christianity is I believe incorporated by Shakespeare (the greatest scholar of Machiavelli before Leo Strauss!) In Shakespeare however it is in the service of a more enlightened and tolerant Christianity, such as that presided at the American Founding. Consider the restoration of the family at the end of *Measure for Measure*—*the* play presided over by Shakespeare's version of the Prince—with the family at the end of the *Mandragola.*

I welcome your opposition to homosexuality. I do not find in it however the moral realism based upon the intrinsic connection between morality and nature that I find in my own. I enclose a copy of my recent "Why Sodomy Is Not Gay," and a letter to Ward Connerly, who wants the laws of nature to condemn racial preferences, but not sodomy!

These make clear my approach, for whatever it is worth. Do you still say that I skulk in the rear, while others carry on the fight?

With best wishes,
Sincerely,
Harry V. Jaffa

P.S. If I do not have any response in, let us say, a month's time, I will consider this an open letter.

NOTES

1. The word "gay" as referring to homosexuality is for the first time in the 1989 edition of the Oxford English Dictionary. It is said to be of American origin and slang. The word "homophobia" is not to be found even in this, the latest O.E.D.

2. In 1987 Professor Michael Zuckert published an article in the *Review of Politics* (Summer 1987, 319–339) in which he argued that "We hold these truths to be self-evident" did not mean "We believe in the truth of what we hold to be true." The Declaration, he argued, held forth certain propositions because they were convenient for the justification of the purposes of the Congress. This of course would make the Congress disingenuous in its appeal to God. Although Zuckert pursued an ingenious course to prove that this is what the Declaration might have meant, he did not produce a scrap of evidence to show that this is what it did mean to Jefferson or any of his contemporaries of '76, Zuckert's interpretation also has about the same validity as having Aristotle crib his works from the library at Alexandria.

3. This is not the place to repeat any of my differences with Judge Bork. They are spelled out in *Original Intent and the Framers of the Constitution: A Disputed Question*, and in *Storm Over the Constitution*. The present example

is taken from a letter of his in *Commentary*, which had no reference whatsoever to our differences.

    4. The author of this apt phrase is Richard Hofstadter. The *Communist Manifesto* was presented to the world in 1848. The *Disquisition on Government* was published in 1851, after Calhoun's death in 1850.

    5. The date of this essay is January 29, 1989.

    6. Of the foregoing five, only Hart is still alive. To his credit and honor, he has been as forward as could be wished in his defense of Israel.

    7. It should be noted, however, that opposition to Davis within the Confederacy was often focused on the fact that Benjamin was a Jew.

    8. A possible exception is Lew Lehrman's article appealing to the right to life in the Declaration of Independence to condemn abortion. Lehrman's *NR* article—and a similar one in *The American Spectator*—had been referred to approvingly by Clarence Thomas in speeches and articles when he was the head of EEOC. For this he was roundly abused during the hearings on his nomination to the Supreme Court. Thomas made no attempt to defend his approval of Lehrman's articles, or of the Declaration of Independence, in this venue. Although it is not generally known, Lehrman's article was condemned by many paleoconservative anti-abortionists because of its appeal to the detested Declaration of Independence. °Editor's note: William F. Buckley, Jr. and Charles R. Kesler, eds. *Keeping the Tablets: Modern American Conservative Thought in the Twentieth Century* (New York: Harper&Row, 1988); this is a revised edition of William F. Buckley, Jr., ed., *American Conservative Thought in the Twentieth Century* (New York: Bobbs-Merrill, 1970).

    9. The Lincolnian understanding was given prominence throughout the book in Kesler's editorial comments.

    10. Kendall's widely quoted phrase was that the Gettysburg Address had "derailed" the American political tradition, by giving to the idea of equality an importance that it had hitherto lacked.

    11. A much more accurately descriptive expression than "anti-Semite."

    12. The reasons for this are too complex to elaborate here. For the moment, we only point to the fact that if there had been a Jewish government in the councils of the allies the rail lines to Auschwitz would almost certainly have been bombed. That alone could have saved—at the least hundreds of thousands of Jewish lives. Allied planes flew over Auschwitz many times to bomb military targets, but no military resources could be "diverted" to save Jews.

    13. Under the Nuremberg laws, one Jewish grandparent was all that was necessary to qualify for extermination. Hence untold numbers of non-Jewish Americans were Jews by Hitler's definition. This is a seldom expressed reason—perhaps more often felt than actually understood—why there is such widespread support of Israel among Americans.

14. See my article "The Right Rights," attacking an *NR* editorial, and defending the Israeli position on the West Bank, in *NR*, November 10, 1989.

15. In 1946 Dean Acheson said he "would not turn his back" on Alger Hiss!

16. I am an enthusiastic subscriber to the *Standard*—as I have been for many years to *Commentary*, *The Public Interest*, and *The National Interest*.

17. My 1980 essay, "The Moral Majority and the American Founding" may have anticipated similar pronouncements by Kristol. I have lectured at CBN University, and appeared on Pat Robertson's 700 Club TV program. An essay of mine on the Declaration of Independence was featured in the inaugural issue of Robertson's *Journal of Christian Jurisprudence*.

18. This lecture is included in Kristol's recent book *Neoconservatism: The Autobiography of an Idea* (New York: Free Press, 1995).

19. John R. Alden, *The American Revolution* (New York: Harper & Row, 1954), 76–77.

20. Irving Kristol has also found me "unanswerable" but "worth ignoring." It is good to be in the company of Tom Paine and George Washington!

21. See previous reference to Amos and Andy.

22. Robert Goldwin and Robert S. Licht, eds., *The Spirit of the Constitution* (Washington, D.C.: The AEI Press, 1990), 81.

23. President of the Ethics and Public Policy Center, Washington, D.C. In the *Los Angeles Times*, November 19, 1995 (the anniversary of the Gettysburg Address).

24. And a great friend and major inspiration in the life and career of Winston Churchill.

25. "The Character of American Political Order" in Robert L. Utley, Jr., ed., *The Promise of American Politics: Principles and Practice after Two Hundred Years* (Washington, D.C.: University Press of America, 1989), 13–14.

26. I learned this bit of folk wisdom from my late brother-in-law, Percy (Whitey) Butler.

27. *Liberalism Ancient and Modern* (New York: Basic Books, 1968), 256.

28. *Political Sermons of the American Founding Era, 1730-1805*, Ellis Sandoz, ed. (Indianapolis: Liberty Press, 1990), 637.

29. Like T. S. Eliot's "Bleistein."

30. A foreign observer who was not without astuteness, and who had no doubt that the civil war was a historical turning point, said that

> Since the Civil War, in which the Southern States were conquered, against all historical logic and sound sense, the American people have been in a condition of political and popular decay. . . . The beginnings of a new social order based upon the principle of slavery

and inequality were destroyed by that war, and with them also the
embryo of a future truly great America.

That observer was Adolf Hitler in 1933. Hermann Rauschning, *The Voice of
Destruction* (New York, Putnam, 1940), 68, 69.

31. It is sometimes forgotten that both the Douglas Democratic platform
and the Breckenridge Democratic platform of 1860 called for the acquisition
of Cuba. The Ostend Manifesto of 1854 had called for the acquisition of Cuba,
either by purchase or conquest.

32. "Eastern" Straussians have almost without exception assumed that the
Founding Fathers read Locke as Leo Strauss read him in *Natural Right and
History*. This is about as anachronistic as thinking that Aristotle stole from
African authors in the library at Alexandria.

33. *The Works of Alexander Hamilton*, ed. Henry Cabot Lodge (New York:
GP Putnam's Sons, 1904), Vol. I, 61, 62.

34. Judaism and later Islam continued the tradition of the ancient city, by
understanding themselves primarily as law. But the world in which they have
attempted this continuation has made the attempt utopian, or fatuous, or
merely tyrannical. The tyrannical is clearly visible in the attempts to create
Islamic republics, as in Iran. Jews, trained by centuries in the Diaspora, have
learned to obey their own law while not calling into question the non-Jewish
law of the countries in which they reside. Modern Israel, for all the uniqueness
of its historic role, remains just another country of the Diaspora. It is a modern
democracy, deriving the authority of its non-Jewish laws from the rights of man
in the state of nature.

35. The quotation from "the judicious Hooker" in chapter 2—"Of the State
of Nature"—of Locke's *Second Treatise* is an extended paraphrase and commentary on the Golden Rule. For Jefferson it formed an unbreakable bond
between the ethics of the Gospels and the principles of the Declaration of
Independence.

36. The session was moderated by Professor Charles Kesler of the Government Department, Claremont-McKenna College, and was transcribed by Tim-
othy W. Caspar.

37. At the 25th anniversary symposium of the Henry Salvatori Center,
Claremont McKenna College, April 19, 1996. (Patriots' Day, commemorating
the shot heard round the world.)

38. F. E. Smith (later Lord Birkenhead) once remarked that "Winston
[Churchill] has devoted some of the best years of his life to the preparation of
his impromptu speeches."

39. This is called "fragging" in the military.

40. That Stalin was a greater danger than Hitler was Churchill's own assessment in 1946, and was followed to the end of his life by Leo Strauss. The reason why Stalin was a greater danger was precisely because so many in the West believed him to be at bottom a liberal, differing perhaps in means, but not in ends.

41. The resemblance to Thrasymachus, declaring certain definitions of justice as off-limits to Socrates, is striking.

42. Every one of his "arguments" was an argument from authority.

43. *Coolidge and the Historians* (Durham, NC: Carolina Academic Press, 1983), by Tom Silver, is a brilliant exposure of the misrepresentation to which a supposedly accredited historian will resort to gain credit with his political favorites. Schlesinger had himself vaulted into prominence with a book about Jackson, hailing him as a precursor of Franklin D. Roosevelt.

44. Before World War I, Asquith was once asked why the dislike of Churchill was so general. "It is," he said, "the envy with which mediocrity always views genius."

45. See *Storm Over the Constitution: Jaffa Answers Bork* (Center for the Study of the Natural Law, The Claremont Institute, 1994).

46. The excerpt from the sermon of Rev. Samuel Cooper, quoted in "The Decline and Fall . . .", should go a very long way to dispel any doubt on this.

47. Buggery and sodomy are both common law terms, the former being genus and the latter species.

48. It is no accident that Strauss began *Natural Right and History* with the Declaration of Independence, as an example of that natural right that had been replaced by history and nihilism.

49. Editor's note: See Harry V. Jaffa, *Original Intent and the Framers of the Constitution* (Washington, D.C.: Regnery Gateway, 1994).

50. Aristotle himself says that it is the intention of the lawgiver, not the letter of the law, that is the law.

51. We all know how to recognize and reward inequalities of athletic ability or of talent. But who is the Babe Ruth or the Yascha Heifetz of sexual prowess? Who do you have in mind? King Solomon? Don Giovanni? Errol Flynn? Wilt Chamberlain? Is prowess in chastity counted? For example, as in the case of Joseph resisting Potiphar's wife. Or Joseph Andrews, who is pursued by Lady Booby through 300 pages, saving his virtue for his beloved Fanny to the end? And what about female prowess? Are we to disregard Cleopatra? Nell Gwynn? Lady Hamilton? Fanny Hill? Elizabeth Taylor? Are male and female prowess—whether for doing or for don'ting—measured on the same scale? Which Lucretia showed the greater prowess, the one celebrated by Shakespeare, or the one celebrated by Machiavelli?

52. Aristotle would not of course have spoken of "creation." But for the Founding generation, the created world and the natural world meant substantially the same thing.

53. In women's competitions, questions have arisen as to whether certain persons were female.

54. The Duke of Gloucester is reported to have said that what he liked about the Garter is that it had no damned nonsense about merit.

55. It is also a remarkable fact—pointed out to me by Professor Colleen Sheehan—that the sentence embodying Jefferson's formula for the best regime appears to be at the very precise center of Strauss's essay on classical political philosophy. I can think of no more powerful symbol of the presence of classical political philosophy within the compass of the Founding presided over by the author of the Declaration of Independence.

56. Of course, Jefferson hoped to accomplish something of what he intended for the nation as a whole by his founding of the University of Virginia. The establishment of the land grant colleges of the Midwest during Lincoln's presidency had something of the same intention.

57. We leave aside the fact that in war medical science may be used to injure the health of the enemy.

58. See *Natural Right and History*, pp. 9, 10.

59. Unless, of course, it is a contract for sexual services!

60. If I injure your horse—or if your horse injures me—the claims cannot be made by the horse or against the horse. The claims can be made by the owner of the horse, or against him. The same held true with respect to damages to or caused by slaves. However, the criminal law of the slave states— quite inconsistently—held the slaves themselves responsible *as persons*, not chattels, for certain offenses.

61. I might add that the current tax code is an outstanding example of diversity and inequality. That is why I am in favor of a flat tax.

62. "Holding down the democratic revolution" is a great campaign slogan. It seems already to have inspired many of our conservative luminaries.

8

THOMAS AQUINAS MEETS THOMAS JEFFERSON

INTRODUCTION

Harry Jaffa finds a unity where most contemporaries would see a radical difference: That Thomas Aquinas and Thomas Jefferson share fundamental premises about morality and politics. While separated on any number of key points, their agreement on moral-political life, Jaffa maintains, transcends differences as fundamental as natural law versus natural rights and of course ancients versus moderns. Jaffa argues that: "What Washington says about the 'indissoluble union between virtue and happiness' is as succinct a précis of the *Nicomachean Ethics* as can be imagined. Clearly, the 'pursuit of happiness' and the pursuit of virtue—'the pure and immutable principles of private morality'—are one and the same." The Declaration of Independence is the crucial text for reconciling the seemingly divergent paths of Aquinas and Jefferson.

But how does this reconcile the faithful Thomas with the doubting one who abridged the Gospels? In the modern world, equality and government by consent replace the ancient city of Plato, Aristotle, and Moses. But after Christianity, "The task of connecting the universal God with a particular regime would have to await the realization that mankind had been endowed by their Creator with certain unalienable rights." Jaffa asks in conclusion, "Wherein does this differ from Thomas Aquinas's concept of the natural law, as the rational creature's participation in the eternal law? This, freed from the obscurantism of historicism, relativism, and nihilism, is our true inheritance."

The editors thank *Interpretation* for permission to reprint from *Interpretation* Vol. 33, No. 2 (Spring 2006).

THOMAS AQUINAS MEETS THOMAS JEFFERSON BY *HARRY V. JAFFA*

The conventional, the more or less received view, of the relationship of Aquinas's thought to Jefferson's, is that the former represents the gloomy ages of monkish superstition, and the latter the skeptical and scientific Age of Enlightenment. In due time, it is said, the progress of History replaced the former with the latter. Of course, the same progress has in our time replaced the Age of Enlightenment with the Age of Nihilism, also known as Post-Modernism. A meeting of the two Thomases today—assuming such a thing were possible—would then be a meeting of two minds, each locked within the confines of its own age, unable to understand each other, and both made obsolete by Progress. Thomas, as a quasi-official philosopher of the church, may still be of interest to some pious Roman Catholics, and to some marginal non-Catholics, who have not yet discovered that they are also prisoners within their own time and place.

Leo Strauss, in blissful defiance of what everyone else knew (or thought they knew) used to say that Socrates had more in common with any intelligent American than with any stupid Athenian. For Strauss, the difference between intelligence and stupidity was more important than any difference between an ancient Athenian and a modern American. According to Strauss, there was something called the "human condition" which was common to all human beings, apart from their time and place. What was common to all human beings made possible a common understanding which, however difficult to achieve, was nonetheless in principle accessible to all human beings. That principle was once called "philosophy." (This was before a doctorate in philosophy—PhD—might be in any subject other than philosophy.) The understanding of what was important to all human beings as human beings was once regarded as a measure of one's distance from barbarism. Notwithstanding their great differences within this common understanding, the Great Books of the Western tradition constituted the basis of what we call Western Civilization. Today, something called "cultural relativism," a feature of what is called "political correctness" holds that what is unique to particular times and places has within itself a greater truth than what is common. At the same time, they deny the possibility of intelligent communication between different times and places. Strangely, the proposition that all vital human communication is sealed within its own time and place, is a generalization about all times and places which exempts itself from its own edict. The essence of post-modernism was captured in the ancient world by the Cretan who declared that all Cretans were liars.

"Deconstructionism" is the literary wing of post-modernism fashionable on our campuses today. It abandons any quest for objective meaning in literature but studies instead the subjective reaction of the reader. Among the historians, documents are studied for what they mean *to us,* not what intrinsic meaning they might have, or what meaning they once had to those whose lives were directly affected by them. Ken Burns, at the end of his long Civil War documentary, observed that the promise of equality in the Gettysburg Address had not been fulfilled, since there was still discrimination against sodomites (Burns however used the false neologism "gay"). It is difficult to imagine anything in 1863 further from the mind of Abraham Lincoln or the defenders of the Union than the association of the cause of freedom with that of sodomy. Lincoln did say however that Jefferson in the Declaration of Independence had embodied an "abstract truth, applicable to all men and all times." The idea of such a truth, trans-historical and trans-cultural, would have been as familiar to Thomas Aquinas, Thomas Jefferson, and Abraham Lincoln, as it would have been strange to Ken Burns, and to most present-day academic historians.

The most famous sentence in the political literature of the world, embodying the abstract truth that commended itself to Lincoln, and the one most pregnant with consequences for all mankind, is as follows.

> We hold these truths to be self-evident, that all men are created equal, that they are endowed by their Creator with certain unalienable rights, that among these are life, liberty, and the pursuit of happiness.

Lincoln at Gettysburg said that the nation, at its birth, had been "dedicated to the proposition that all men are created equal." We see however that in its original form, that proposition was the first in a series of propositions, all of which are regarded as self-evident. The evidence for the latter is however contained within the former. That is to say, the sense in which all men are said to be equal implies *a priori* the rights which they are said unalienably to possess.

There is only one respect however in which "all men" (meaning all human beings) are held to be equal. That is in what John Locke calls "dominion." By nature, no man is the ruler of another. There is no natural difference between one human being and another, such as there is between the queen bee and the workers or drones. Nor is there any such difference between one human being and another, as there is between any man, and any dog or horse or chimpanzee, by reason of which the one is the ruler and the other is the ruled. Jonathan Swift to the contrary notwithstanding, men ride horses by self-evident natural right. The "enslavement" of the horse by his rider is not against nature, and is therefore not unjust. But the enslavement of one human being by another violates that same order of nature which justifies the rider of the horse. There is here no intention to say that human beings are equal, among themselves, with respect to intelligence, strength, size, beauty, or virtue. Nor are they thought to be equal in any of those qualities which are generally regarded as desirable in those who fill the offices of government. George Washington was the first president of the United States. It is doubtful that there was then another human being in the world with the experience, the wisdom, the self-control, the justice, and the confidence of his countrymen, who could fill that office, and launch the new Constitution upon its path of glory. But Washington did not choose himself, nor did his virtues, of themselves, entitle him to office. He was indeed chosen because of his virtues, but he was chosen in a constitutional process, decided upon by the American people, embodying the consent of the governed. Let us follow the logical process whereby the proposition that all men are created equal might result in the superior virtues of George Washington being placed at the service of the American people.

It was an oft-repeated saying of James Madison, that "compact is the essence of free government." What Madison meant is neither more nor less than what is meant by "all men are created equal." That human beings are by nature equal in "dominion" means that human beings are not by nature under government. While human beings remain equal in dominion, with none having authority over another, they are in what is called the state of nature. The transition, by which human beings become citizens or subjects of government, is accomplished by something called the social contract (or "compact"). This is an agreement of each with all, and of all with each, that they form a government whose object shall be the better security of the equal and unalienable rights with which each has been endowed by his Creator. For someone to be a party to such a contract, he must, first of all, recognize that each one of his partners to the contract possesses the same unalienable rights, and that each therefore has the same claim to the security of those rights. No one can, *a priori,* lay claim to greater protection of his rights, than can be afforded anyone else. Not George Washington, or anyone with George Washington's virtues, can lay claim to such protection. Nor can anyone claim any exemption from an equal share of the burdens which must be borne if the government is to be able to furnish the protection for which it is founded.

No one can claim as a right exemption from taxation or military service. The most urgent reason for the formation of the political community is protection from all violence, both foreign and domestic. Prior to government—in the state of nature—each individual had to furnish his own protection. In such a state he would remain extremely vulnerable. Now his fellow citizens will join together to help protect him. But it would be irrational to demand protection for himself, and be unwilling to join in protecting the others. No one can claim advantages not equally shared with others, or exemptions from the burdens equally shared by others. Anyone who tries to exempt himself from the common burdens, which are the price to be paid for the common benefits, cannot be accepted as a fellow citizen. He will remain in a state of nature. What, you may ask, about the Quakers, who set the pattern of conscientious exemption from military service that has remained part of the American political tradition? That exemption has not been a right, but rather a privilege granted, out of consideration for those whose mode of worshiping God requires that they abstain from violence, even in self-defense. It is an act of prudent generosity towards otherwise good citizens, a privilege that can only be granted to a few, for otherwise the political community would be disabled from performing its most urgent reason for existence.

The formation of the community, by the social contract, is by unanimous consent. This consent is based upon the mutual recognition of the common humanity of the contracting members. In the ancient city—the city of Plato and Aristotle and Moses and of Fustel de Coulanges—human beings commonly recognized each other as members of the same family, or clan, or tribe, or city, or nation. To ask them to recognize each other first and foremost as members of the human race is to reverse the order of priority of what hitherto had been the ordinary experience of mankind. Hitherto that experience had been linked to the self-understanding of the ancient city as the creation of the gods (or God) of that city. The Old Testament in this respect—in the self-understanding of the Mosaic polity as the creation of the God of Israel—is typical of all ancient cities. The God of Israel gave Israel its laws, but did not give laws to Athens or Rome or Sparta. In the post-classical world of the Christian West however the God of Israel became the God of all mankind. In so becoming, He ceased being the lawgiver that was the God of Moses. Municipal law, the law of particular regimes, is no longer the law of a particular god, since the particular gods are all dead! The task of connecting the universal God with a particular regime would have to await the realization that mankind had been endowed by their Creator with certain unalienable rights. From the perspective of the American Founding, the governments of the West had, from the fall of the Roman Empire (in the words of the *Federalist*) depended for their political constitutions "on accident and force" rather than on "reflection and choice." Lincoln grouped all of the former together as based upon "the divine right of kings," which he considered in principle the same as slavery. Slavery represented the quintessence of force without right, but any form of government without a foundation in the consent of the governed was a form of slavery. The precise point in the long human story at which accident and force was replaced by reflection and choice was the point at which human equality determined the form of the unanimous consent by which the state of nature was transformed into civil society.

For more than a millennium and a half the Christian West had been afflicted by the hiatus between the authority of God and the authority of the law. By unanimous consent the authority of God became once more the authority for law, but this authority now emanated from the people, not from autocratic kings or aristocracies of wealth or birth. This was by reason of the fact that each human individual participating in the creation of a free civil society had been equally endowed by his Creator with the rights which entitled him to enter into the social contract. It was understood moreover that the exercise of these rights (among them "life, liberty, and the pursuit of happiness") was confined to the purposes for the sake of which they had been endowed by their Creator. When the Signers of the Declaration appealed to the "supreme judge of the world" for the "rectitude of [their] intentions" they acknowledged the divine government of the world as the framework within which their rights might be exercised. The Declaration was moreover issued in the name of "the good people of these colonies." In a letter to Spenser Roane, many years later, Jefferson said that the ultimate repository of the principles of the Constitution was "the people *en masse.*" They, he said, are independent of everything "but moral law." The people however does not make the moral law, the moral law makes the people. Without the moral law, a human assemblage, even one formed by consent, may be nothing more than a gang of robbers. Consent is then more than an act of will, it is an act of will informed by understanding of the moral law, which is also God's will. We see here how closely Jefferson is attuned to the natural law doctrine of Thomas Aquinas.

The community formed by unanimous consent will act by the will of the majority. The will of the majority is however restrained *a priori* by the limits intrinsic to unanimous consent. According to James Madison, in his great essay on Sovereignty, the majority may do anything that can be done *rightfully* by unanimous consent. But free governments cannot govern by unanimous consent. Majority rule is a substitute for unanimity, authorized by the social contract. The purpose of majority rule is to find the means to serve the ends of government already embodied in the unanimous consent. The ends served by majority rule are not themselves decided by majority rule.

It is amazing how little of this most basic of the elements of political right is understood today even in the highest places. Mr. Justice Scalia, in his famous Rome interview (*Origins,* vol. 26, no. 6 [June 27, 1996]), declared that "The whole theory of democracy . . . is that the majority rules; that is the whole theory of it. You protect minorities only because the majority determines that there are certain minority positions that deserve protection." And again: "You either agree with democratic theory or you do not. But you cannot have democratic theory and then say, but what about the minority? The minority loses, except to the extent that the majority, in its document of government, has agreed to accord the minority rights."

Justice Scalia, like all legal positivists, denies to the Declaration of Independence any constitutional status whatever. But one would think the most elementary reasoning—the natural law in its pristine form—would instruct him that there can be no legitimacy to majority rule without minority rights. What rightful authority can be attributed to an election in which there is no freedom of speech, or of the press, or of the right of the people peaceably to assemble? The plebiscite has been a favorite instrument of tyrants since Napoleon. In the last election conducted by Saddam Hussein he received 99% of the vote, doing better even than Hitler and Stalin. One of the main concerns of the authors of the *Federalist* was to prevent the tyranny of the majority.

The idea that the majority "accords" rights to the minority is the ultimate absurdity. The purpose of majority rule is to secure the rights possessed equally by every citizen. Strictly speaking, there are no minority rights, there are only individual rights. The Bill of Rights of the Constitution is not an act of condescension by the majority; it is a recognition of rights with which we have been "endowed by [our] Creator." Only because majority and minority have the same rights, and therefore a common interest, is majority rule a legitimate means of governing.

We said earlier that George Washington had been elected first president because of his great virtues. Once a political community has been formed, the people rightly seek those they think best qualified to find the means to secure their rights. Democracy, understood from the principles of the Declaration of Independence, is not only consistent with aristocracy, it is aristocracy. Consider the following passage from one of Jefferson's letters to John Adams.

> For I agree with you that there is a natural aristocracy among men. The grounds of this are virtue and talents. . . . The natural aristocracy I consider as the most precious gift of nature for the instruction, the trusts, and government of society. And indeed it would have been inconsistent in creation to have formed man for the social state, and

not to have provided virtue and wisdom enough to manage the concerns of the society. May we not even say that that form of government is the best which provides the most effectually for a pure selection of these natural *aristoi* into the offices of government.

The last sentence in the above was quoted by Leo Strauss, in his essay "On Classical Political Philosophy," to express the very essence of the idea of the best regime in Plato and Aristotle, the very heart of classical political philosophy. The theme of nature's fitting man for the social state, and providing virtue and talents for government, could hardly be more Aristotelian had it been written by Thomas Aquinas. We might call the American Founding as a whole, taking into account both the Declaration and the Constitution, as prudently classical, recalling Aristotle's dictum, that of natural right, all is changeable. The equal rights of the Creator were necessary to replace the law-giving gods of the ancient city. This replacement required a democratization of the ancient idea of aristocracy. But the change in form was less a change in substance than it might at first seem to be. Consider the following from Washington's inaugural address as president.

> [T] he foundations of our national policy will be laid in the pure and immutable principles of private morality. . . . I dwell on this prospect with every satisfaction . . . since there is no truth more thoroughly established than that there exists in the economy and course of nature an indissoluble union between virtue and happiness . . . since we ought to be no less persuaded that the propitious smiles of Heaven can never be expected on a nation that disregards the eternal rules of order and right which Heaven itself has ordained.

What Washington says about the "indissoluble union between virtue and happiness" is as succinct a précis of the *Nicomachean Ethics* as can be imagined. Clearly, the "pursuit of happiness" and the pursuit of virtue—"the pure and immutable principles of private morality"—are one and the same. There is no patronage here of the notion, popular today, that the pursuit of happiness means "doing your own thing," no matter what that "thing" is. Finally, we see Washington asserting that the boundaries of national policy, the actions of citizens and statesmen, whether private or public, must conform to "the eternal rules of order and right."

Wherein does this differ from Thomas Aquinas's concept of the natural law, as the rational creature's participation in the eternal law? This, freed from the obscurantism of historicism, relativism, and nihilism, is our true inheritance.

9

DRED SCOTT REVISITED

INTRODUCTION

Harry Jaffa frequently berated conservative legal luminaries such as Judge Robert Bork and Chief Justice William Rehnquist for completely missing the core of the *Dred Scott* case—and thereby misunderstanding its role in causing the Civil War. Thus, *Dred Scott*'s significance lies not in "judicial activism," "substantive due process," or other concepts of contemporary jurisprudence but in its perversion of the Declaration of Independence's role in constitutional interpretation, that is, in American self-understanding. In his own life, Taney completely betrayed the anti-slavery meaning of the Declaration, and replaced it with his infamous assertions in *Dred Scott*; his biography paralleled that of the nation in its rejection of the meaning of the Declaration.

If students of the law cannot understand the most consequential Supreme Court case of American history, can they get anything else right about the Constitution and our laws? In his last essay devoted to this subject Jaffa reiterated the themes he has emphasized since 1987 but with an even greater emphasis on the meaning of the founding principles for Western civilization.

Jaffa understands *Dred Scott* in light of the entire American political tradition and the political roles all three branches sought to play in order to extend the "Slave Power." The Compromise of 1850 had repealed the Missouri Compromise, and the Kansas-Nebraska Act of 1854 invited judicial review of the spread of slavery to that vast territory. Through these laws Congress and Presidents had invited the Court to act in further defense of slavery. In his "House Divided" speech Lincoln responded that a conspiracy of "Roger [Taney], Franklin [Pierce], Stephen [Douglas], and James [Buchanan]" sought to nationalize and thereby make perpetual "the Slave Power." This was not a renegade Court, and Lincoln's conspiracy charge was not overblown political rhetoric. "*Dred Scott* was not primarily in the interest of judicial power. It was in the interest of the Slave Power."

This was the challenge Lincoln and his often unreliable allies faced. This is the America and the world one sees when one takes the Declaration of Independence with the seriousness it deserves.

Harry V. Jaffa, "Dred Scott Revisited," *Harvard Journal of Law & Public Policy* 31:1 (Winter 2008), 197–327. Reprinted with permission.

DRED SCOTT REVISITED

I

It has been many years since I first wrote that the American Revolution was, at once, an event in time and an idea out of time.[1] Lincoln meant no less when he wrote that Jefferson enshrined in the Declaration of Independence "an abstract truth, applicable to all men and all times."[2] It was a commonplace among the Founders (and Lincoln) that the American experiment in self-government was not for Americans alone, but for all mankind.[3] This was not merely an expression of national pride. It was a sober judgment. It was almost as impossible then, as it is now, to imagine circumstances more favorable to the success of this experiment than those that existed at the Founding. It was, and is, hard to imagine this experiment succeeding elsewhere if it failed here. The Civil War clearly was a test, as Lincoln said at Gettysburg, of whether any nation "conceived in Liberty, and dedicated to the proposition that all men are created equal" could long endure.[4] The test came when eleven states "seceded" following the election of Abraham Lincoln in 1860. The Republican platform in that year contained a pledge to end any further extension of slavery into the new territories from which new states might be formed.[5] The seceding states found it intolerable that all new states would be free states, so that eventually three-fourths of the states might be able to abolish slavery by constitutional amendment, without the consent of the slave states. As Lincoln put it in his first inaugural, "One section of our country believes slavery is *right,* and ought to be extended, while the other believes it is *wrong,* and ought not to be extended. This is the only substantial dispute."[6]

Lincoln believed that the Constitution established a regime within which such disputes might be resolved peacefully. The states, in ratifying the Constitution, bound themselves to accept the results of elections held according to the rules of the Constitution. To set aside the results of an election because of dissatisfaction with those results, as the secessionists proposed, would make a mockery of the very idea of government by elections. It would leave tyranny or anarchy as the only alternatives. Lincoln set out this argument—ballots or bullets—with mathematical simplicity and clarity. He conceded, however, that if any constitutional rights or privileges had been denied to the discontented states in the elections, or if there was any future threat by the Republicans to such rights or privileges, the states' withdrawal from the Union might be justified.[7] Lincoln took the greatest pains to deny that any such rights or privileges had been denied or threatened. He could not, however, deny their differences concerning slavery. Nor did he deny that a difference on this subject could turn friends into enemies and make a common citizenship impossible.[8]

In all his speeches, from Peoria in 1854,[9] to Cooper Union in 1860,[10] and finally to Gettysburg in 1863,[11] Lincoln insisted that the central idea of the Founding, from which all its minor thoughts radiated, was the proposition that all men are created equal. The slavery that existed in the Founding generation was an inherited evil that could not be eradicated instantly, but it was, in accordance with the principles of the Declaration, to be "put in course of ultimate extinction."[12] All the legal rights of white men depended finally upon the recognition of a common human nature. The Declaration itself was addressed to a "candid world,"[13] which included all races and nations. There could be no such thing as equal rights of slavery and freedom. Property in human beings could not be compared indifferently to property in non-human chattels. To make chattels of other human beings was a violation of the laws of nature, and this nation was founded upon "the Laws of Nature and of Nature's God."[14]

To justify their claim to the same rights in the territories as in the free states, leading Southerners transformed the assertion of equality of the rights of individual human beings into a claim of equality of rights of the states. They contended that the federal government could not discriminate between the property of settlers from free states and settlers from slave states, since the territories were the joint property of all the states. This argument was elaborated by John C. Calhoun.[15] To make it, he had to deny any authority to the Declaration's proposition of equality. This "hypothetical truism," he said, was "the most false and dangerous of all political errors."[16] For the Slave South, Calhoun became a prophet of unrivalled authority. His argument suffered, however, because it was based upon a candid rejection of the Founders, who were still revered in the antebellum South. Jefferson he regarded as a fanatic.[17]

To turn the Founders against the Founding, to expunge the authority of the idea of the equality of the rights of individual human persons, was the task to which Chief Justice Roger Taney set himself in *Dred Scott* 150 years ago. To accomplish this task, Taney did not merely have to ignore the generally accepted historical view of the Founding, accepted even by Calhoun; he actually had to reverse the facts in the case. Here is how he did it:

> It is difficult at this day to realize the state of public opinion in relation to that unfortunate race, which prevailed in the civilized and enlightened portions of the world at the time of the Declaration of Independence, and when the Constitution of the United States was framed and adopted.
>
> They had for more than a century before been regarded as beings of an inferior order, and altogether unfit to associate with the white race, either in social or political relations; and so far inferior, that they had no rights which the white man was bound to respect; and that the negro might justly and lawfully be reduced to slavery for his benefit. . . . This opinion was at that time fixed and universal in the civilized portion of the white race.[18]

Taney was a firm advocate of what is known now as a jurisprudence of original intent. According to this view, the words of the Constitution are always to be interpreted as they were understood by those who framed and ratified them. No change in how those words might come to be understood at any later period authorizes a departure from that original meaning. Only an amendment to the Constitution by the authority that made the Constitution can authorize an emendation in that original understanding.[19] Taney's approach in *Dred Scott,* however, was counterfeit originalism. He placed this perfectly sound jurisprudential doctrine in the service of an incredible misrepresentation of the Founding ideals shared by those who framed and adopted the Declaration of Independence and the Constitution.

It is true that blacks at the time of the Founding were regarded in some generalized sense as inferior. This remained true throughout the nineteenth century and beyond. But such alleged inequality of blacks and whites was not necessarily regarded as greater than that ordinarily seen among whites. Jefferson, for example, once observed that although Sir Isaac Newton may have been the most intelligent man in the world, this gave him no dominion over Jefferson's person or his property.[20] The inequality *within* species must be distinguished from the inequality *of* species. There is no inequality within the human species such as that between man and beast, or between man and God. Unequal abilities among human persons, regardless of color, nationality, or gender, do not determine what the rights or privileges of said persons ought to be.[21]

When Taney says that blacks during the Founding era were regarded as inferior, he is not exaggerating. But when he says that they were regarded as having "no rights which the white man was bound to respect"—as if they were animals of a different species—he is simply wrong. Historian Don Fehrenbacher has pointed out that a free black man in late eighteenth century America had, in some respects, more legal rights than a married white woman.[22] Free blacks could marry, inherit and bequeath property, buy and sell, sue and be sued.[23] Nor is it true that they could "justly and lawfully be reduced to slavery."[24] In fact, there was never a time or place at which a free black in America could be lawfully reduced to slavery. A free black man, like a free white man, could be deprived of his liberty only when he had been duly convicted of a crime.[25]

Taney invented a proslavery Founding and a proslavery jurisprudence of original intent. After quoting in full the passage in the Declaration beginning, "We hold these truths to be self-evident," he comments:

The general words above quoted would seem to embrace the whole human family, and if they were used in a similar instrument at this day would be so understood. But it is too clear for dispute, that the enslaved African race were not intended to be included, and formed no part of the people who framed and adopted this declaration; for if the language, as understood in that day, would embrace them, the conduct of the distinguished men who framed the Declaration of Independence would have been utterly and flagrantly inconsistent with the principles they asserted; and instead of the sympathy of mankind, to which they so confidently appealed, they would have deserved and received universal rebuke and reprobation.[26]

Taney's assertion that the words of the Declaration "seem to embrace the whole human family" is remarkable, and it becomes even more remarkable when joined with the further assertion that these same words would be so understood "today," that is, in 1857. Taney assumes without question that he knows that the so-called African race belongs to the "human family." But he implies that those who wrote the Declaration in 1776, and those who subsequently framed and adopted the Constitution, did not know this. We know the meaning of their words, but they did not! Taney does not explain, or apparently think there is any need to explain, why we should be governed by the Founders' allegedly defective understanding, rather than by our own superior understanding. Yet, the doctrine of original understanding presupposes a Constitution based upon the laws of nature and of nature's God— human nature as it really is. Without this legitimacy, the Constitution would have no intrinsic moral authority or claim on our fidelity to original meaning.[27]

Taney implies that if the Framers had understood the meaning of their own words, they would have abolished slavery. But he does not explain why, if we today (in 1857) know that the words of the Declaration "embrace the whole human family," do we not act to end slavery? Why should we who know better not make that better understanding the basis for interpreting the Constitution? Why does Taney pile Pelion on Ossa to prove that because the Founders did not abolish slavery (something they had no power to do!), they did not think blacks belonged to the human family? Taney's contention was that public opinion in 1857 was more favorable to the recognition of a black man's humanity than it was at the Founding. But this is clearly the reverse of the truth. It is the reverse, not only of what dissenting Justice Curtis and Abraham Lincoln thought, but also of what virtually everyone—including the most vocal partisans of the Slave South—thought.

Taney wrote that the opinion that blacks did not belong to the human family was "fixed and universal" in the civilized world in 1776 and 1787.[28] In fact, the "fixed and universal" opinion was almost the exact opposite. Consider, for example, the following passage from Alexander Stephens's "Cornerstone" Speech of March 22, 1861. Stephens was Vice President of the Confederate States of America, which had become a completely organized and functioning government at least two weeks before Abraham Lincoln was sworn in as President of the United States. Stephens explained:

> The prevailing ideas entertained by [Jefferson] and most of the leading statesmen at the time of the formation of the old Constitution were, that the enslavement of the African was in violation of the laws of nature; that it was wrong in principle, socially, morally, and politically. It was an evil they knew not well how to deal with, but the general opinion of the men of that day was that, somehow or other, in the order of Providence, the institution would be evanescent and pass away. This idea, though not incorporated in the Constitution, was the prevailing idea at the time.[29]

Stephens recognized in the Founding principles the exact opposite of the assertion Taney called "fixed and universal." He recognized, too, that the principles of the Declaration of Independence, although not explicitly incorporated in the Constitution, are the necessary ground for distinguishing the Constitution's principles from its compromises, something hotly denied and disputed today no less than before the Civil War. While acknowledging the racial egalitarianism of the Founding, Stephens goes on to say that it has now been superseded:

> Our new government is founded upon exactly the opposite idea [to that of the equality of the races]; its foundations are laid, its cornerstone rests upon the great truth that the negro is not equal to the white man. That slavery—subordination to the superior race—is his natural and moral condition.
>
> This, our new government, is the first in the history of the world based upon this great physical, philosophical, and moral truth.[30]

Stephens goes on to compare the reluctance to accept this "truth" to the tardy acceptance of all new scientific discoveries, such as those of Galileo and Harvey.[31] He is confident that this scientific discovery, like others that have preceded it, will eventually triumph, and with it will come the vindication of "our new government." It is sufficient for present purposes to repeat once again that Stephens's account of the opinion of the civilized world on the subject of race in the latter part of the eighteenth century is the exact opposite of Taney's. Yet, Taney does not subscribe to the "scientific" racism of Stephens. The aforesaid "science," along with a host of other variants on the theory of evolution, was sweeping over the western world in the later nineteenth century, virtually obliterating consciousness of the natural rights doctrine of the Declaration of Independence. Darwin's *Origin of Species* was published in 1859, but the seminal ideas therein had been germinating since Rousseau's 1754 *Discourse on the Origin of Inequality.*

There is yet another witness against Taney, one more unlikely and potent than even Alexander Stephens. The following is a speech to a jury in 1819 by a young lawyer in Frederick, Maryland. His client was Jacob Gruber, a Methodist minister who had delivered an abolitionist sermon to an audience of some 2,600, including some 400 blacks, many of whom were slaves. Gruber was indicted for inciting the slaves to rebellion. The young lawyer delivered this remarkable (and successful) speech to the jury:

> Any man has a right to publish his opinions on that subject [slavery] whenever he pleases. . . . It is a subject of national concern, and may at all times be freely discussed. Mr. Gruber did quote the language of our great act of national independence, and insisted on the principles contained in that venerated instrument. He did rebuke those masters, who, in the exercise of power, are deaf to the calls of humanity; and he warned them of the evils they might bring upon themselves. He did speak with abhorrence of those reptiles, who live by trading in human flesh, and enrich themselves by tearing the husband from the wife—the infant from the bosom of the mother: and this I am instructed was the head and front of his offending. Shall I content myself with saying he had a right to say this? That there is no law to punish him? So far is he from being the object of punishment in any form of proceeding, that we are prepared to maintain the same principles, and to use, if necessary, the same

language here in the temple of justice, and in the presence of those who are the ministers of the law. A hard necessity, indeed, compels us to endure the evil of slavery for a time. It was imposed upon us by another nation, while we were yet in a state of colonial vassalage. It cannot be easily, or suddenly removed. Yet while it continues it is a blot on our national character, and every real lover of freedom confidently hopes that it will be effectually, though it must be gradually, wiped away; and earnestly looks for the means, by which this necessary object may be best attained. And until it shall be accomplished: until the time shall come when we can point without a blush, to the language held in the Declaration of Independence, every friend of humanity will seek to lighten the galling chain of slavery, and better, to the utmost of his power, the wretched condition of the slave.[32]

A modern scholar, nay, Lincoln himself, could not have composed a better epitome of Lincoln's speeches and writings on slavery. It is all there: the recognition of the slaves' humanity, the recognition of "colonial vassalage" as the cause of the presence of slavery at the Founding, the reliance on the authentic antislavery meaning of the Declaration of Independence, and the avowal that the honor and future of the United States depended upon the "ultimate extinction" of slavery.[33] The young lawyer who in 1819 authored this speech was, of course, Roger B. Taney. He was, therefore, the greatest among all witnesses against the Chief Justice who espoused the opposite point of view in 1857. There is no question that the public opinion from which the Declaration was fashioned was favorable to the rights of black human beings, and that in 1857, the Constitution ought to have been interpreted in that light. Yet, against this condemnation of the Taney of 1857, we must nonetheless recognize the faint echo of 1819, which reveals that Taney's mind (unlike Alexander Stephens's) had not been completely submerged in the rising tide of a false "scientific" racism.

II

There is no more erroneous opinion about *Dred Scott* today than that it represented an attempt by the Supreme Court to usurp power belonging to the elected branches of government. A prominent critic of the Taney Court has written:

The Court in *Dred Scott* decided that all of the agitation and debate in Congress over the Missouri Compromise in 1820, over the Wilmot Proviso a generation later, and over the Kansas-Nebraska Act in 1854 had amounted to absolutely nothing. It was, in the words of Macbeth, "A tale told by an idiot, full of sound and fury, signifying nothing." According to the Court, the decision had never been one that Congress was entitled to make; it was one that the Court alone, in construing the Constitution, was empowered to make.[34]

This analysis skips from the Wilmot Proviso of 1846–1847 to the Kansas-Nebraska Act of 1854, omitting any mention of the territorial laws passed as part of the great Compromise of 1850. The laws adopted in 1850 for the Territories of Utah and New Mexico, from which five states were eventually formed, provided that the people of those territories could apply for admission to the Union with constitutions that permitted or prohibited slavery, as the people might at that time decide.[35] This was, as far as it went, "popular sovereignty" for the territories. Senator Stephen A. Douglas adopted these laws as the authority for his version of popular sovereignty that he incorporated into the Kansas-Nebraska Act of 1854.[36] But there was a difference, which Douglas (but not Lincoln) conveniently overlooked: according to the territorial laws of 1850, the decision for or against slavery was to be made by the people of the territories at the time they framed their state constitutions.[37] Nothing, however, was said in 1850 of the legal status of slavery *during* the territorial period, before the people of the territories framed their state constitutions.[38] The facts on the ground during this interim period would determine what the people of the territories would decide when they framed their constitutions, but on the all-important question of the status of slavery during the territorial period, Congress could not and did not make up its mind. Congress was divided into so many different factions that none commanded a majority. Its solution was to provide in the territorial laws that any dispute over slavery arising during the territorial period could be appealed directly from the supreme court of the territory to the Supreme Court of the United States.[39] Hence, jurisdiction on the question of the status of slavery in a territory during the territorial period was given to the Court by Congress. It was not seized by the Court from Congress.

Dred Scott was not a judicial power grab but rather part of a Slave Power conspiracy involving two Presidents, a Chief Justice, and a Unit-

ed States Senator (with many unnamed co-conspirators). An indispensable guide to understanding the politics surrounding *Dred Scott* is Lincoln's "House Divided" speech, which set in motion his 1858 campaign
for the Senate seat held by Stephen A. Douglas. The speech places
Dred Scott in the context of a national conspiracy. But the speech must
also be seen from the perspective of the struggle within the Republican
Party between Illinois Republicans and the East Coast Republicans
who wanted Illinois Republicans to support Douglas for reelection. The
House Divided speech was delivered to a state convention that had
assembled for the express purpose of declaring that Abraham Lincoln
was the first, last, and only candidate of the Republican Party of Illinois.[40] Until the firing on Fort Sumter, Lincoln regarded Douglas (rather than the followers of John C. Calhoun) as the greatest threat to the
nation. This was because Douglas offered, in popular sovereignty, a
temptingly easy way out of the sectional crisis. Douglas's claim was that
if the people of each territory were allowed to determine the status of
slavery in that territory, then the slavery question could be confined
within territorial boundaries and need not roil Congress or the nation.
What made Douglas all the more attractive was his leadership of the
Congressional Republicans in the recent struggle over the Lecompton
Constitution—the draft state constitution proposed by proslavery forces
in Kansas. According to Lincoln, however, Douglas's easy way out
would delay but not end the crisis over slavery. Furthermore, such
appeasement of slavery would only make the crisis, when it came, more
difficult. For Lincoln, only a principled rejection of slavery could end
the crisis.

In the House Divided speech, Lincoln accused Douglas, along with
Taney and two Presidents of the United States, of participating in a
conspiracy to spread slavery, not only to all the new territories, but to
the free states as well:

> A house divided against itself cannot stand.

> I believe this government cannot endure, permanently half *slave* and
> half *free*.

> I do not expect the Union to be *dissolved*—I do not expect the house
> to *fall* —but I *do* expect it will cease to be divided.

It will become *all* one thing, or *all* the other.

Either the *opponents* of slavery, will arrest the further spread of it, and place it where the public mind shall rest in the belief that it is in course of ultimate extinction; or its *advocates* will push it forward, till it shall become lawful in *all* the States, *old* as well as *new—North* as well as *South*. [41]

No more fateful words have ever been spoken here, or perhaps anywhere, or at any time in human history. Lincoln's account of events, from the Kansas-Nebraska Act of 1854 to *Dred Scott* in 1857 and beyond, cannot be stated more concisely, more profoundly, or more brilliantly than Lincoln himself did in the House Divided speech. It cannot be doubted that there existed a common understanding and common goal among the four "workmen—Stephen, Franklin, Roger, and James," as Lincoln described them. [42] "Roger" was certainly not acting alone. *Dred Scott* was not primarily in the interest of judicial power. It was in the interest of the Slave Power.

The results of the Presidential Election of 1856 signaled the looming threat to the Slave Power and were surely on Taney's mind when he began writing the opinion in *Dred Scott*. Democrat James Buchanan had been elected with 174 electoral votes to Republican John C. Fremont's 114; Millard Fillmore received only 8 electoral votes but garnered 873,053 popular votes to Buchanan's 1,836,072 and Fremont's 1,342,345. [43] Fillmore's American Party was largely the residue of the old Whig party. Thus, the further alienation of old Whigs (like Lincoln), together with Know Nothings and Free Soil Democrats, would soon engulf the presidential electoral process. That would mean the end of slavery's expansion and, eventually, of slavery itself.

How to preserve slavery within the Union and prevent the impending Republican victory were the problems facing Taney when he sat down to write the opinion of the Court in *Dred Scott*. To this end he devoted all his energy and considerable talent.

This was not a task in which he was acting alone. Pierce and Buchanan were the preeminent "Doughface" Presidents (Northern men with Southern principles). [44] Pierce in his final State of the Union Address[45] and Buchanan in his Inaugural Address,[46] endorsed, in advance, the forthcoming *Dred Scott* decision. The two Presidents joined in calling on all good Americans to accept *Dred Scott* as a final settlement of all outstanding constitutional questions in regard to slavery. Both of these Presidents knew that *Dred Scott* would "settle" these questions in a way most satisfactory to the Slave Power. Stephen A. Douglas also endorsed *Dred Scott* in advance,[47] although it is doubtful that he knew how the decision would undercut "popular sovereignty."

At the time of Buchanan's inauguration on March 4, 1857, the forces of slavery had tenuous control of the presidency, the Senate, and the Supreme Court. This gave slavery a moment of political power not likely to occur again in the foreseeable future. The election of a Republican President would mean no more proslavery appointments to the Court. It would mean a veto of any legislation likely to add a slave territory or a slave state to the Union. The Court in *Dred Scott* attempted to provide a permanent constitutional status for slavery within the Union. But should that status be denied to it by the forthcoming elections, *Dred Scott* also would provide a constitutional justification for secession. Secession could be made to appear not as an attack on the Union, but as a defense of the Constitution as interpreted by the Supreme Court.

Exactly how, then, did Taney in *Dred Scott* propose to resolve the existing constitutional impasse? First, he declared that the right to property in slaves was "expressly affirmed" in the Constitution.[48] This was another example of a straightforward lie—like the one about the subhuman status of the Negro at the time of the Founding—which he knew to be false, but which he also knew would be believed by those who had an interest in believing it. Taney then observed that if the right of property in slaves was an expressly affirmed constitutional right, any law or state constitution that denies it is itself unconstitutional.[49] Hence, the Missouri Compromise's exclusion of slavery from the Louisiana Territory, or any law limiting a slaveowner's access to any United States territory, was unconstitutional.[50] Although Taney's opinion directly addresses only slavery in the territories, its logic applied to the states as well, by virtue of the Supremacy Clause.[51] The "tenons and mortices" of the four workmen, when fitted together, made a structure of legal reasoning in which slavery would be lawful not only in every territory, but in every state, old as well as new, North as well as South.[52]

Lincoln foresaw this threat. When I was writing *Crisis of the House Divided,* some fifty years ago, the most influential historians refused to take seriously Lincoln's assertion of an imminent threat of slavery be-

coming lawful in the free states.[53] They saw Lincoln's argument as a
scare tactic in the service of his personal ambitions.[54] They believed
that the great historical trends were against slavery.[55] They supposed
that with or without Lincoln, and without a civil war, slavery was destined for the dust bin of history.[56] But in the second of their seven joint
debates, at Freeport, Lincoln read at length from a speech in which
Douglas denounced the Washington *Union*—*the* mouthpiece of the
Buchanan administration. Here are Douglas's words, as quoted by Lincoln:

> When I saw that article in the Union of the 17th of November,
> followed by the glorification of the Lecompton Constitution on the
> 18th of November, and this clause in the [Lecompton] Constitution
> asserting the doctrine that a State has no right to prohibit slavery
> within its limits, I saw that there was a fatal blow being struck at the
> sovereignty of the States of this Union.[57]

Here is direct confirmation, from Douglas himself, of Lincoln's
charge in the House Divided Speech that slavery could become lawful
in all the states, as well as in all the territories. Lincoln's quoting of
Douglas on the threat of slavery becoming lawful in the states, no less
than in the territories, was a lightning bolt, an illumination of the entire
political landscape.

The third of the questions (or "interrogatories") put by Lincoln to
Douglas at Freeport was as follows:

> If the Supreme Court of the United States shall decide that States
> can not exclude slavery from their limits, are you in favor of acquiesc-
> ing in, adopting and following such decision as a rule of political
> action?[58]

Here is Douglas's reply:

> I am amazed that Lincoln should ask such a question. ("A school boy
> knows better.") Yes, a school boy does know better. Mr. Lincoln's
> object is to cast an imputation upon the Supreme Court. He knows
> that there never was but one man in America, claiming any degree of
> intelligence or decency, who ever for a moment pretended such a
> thing. It is true that the Washington *Union,* in an article published on
> the 17th of last December, did put forth that doctrine, and I de-

nounced the article on the floor of the Senate, in a speech which Mr.
Lincoln now pretends was against the President. . . . He casts an
imputation upon the Supreme Court of the United States by supposing that they would violate the Constitution of the United States. I
tell him that such a thing is not possible. (Cheers). It would be an act
of moral treason. . . .[59]

Douglas is simply blustering; he never answers the question. The
Washington *Union* was Buchanan's mouthpiece, and the article in question was a sighting shot in the war that was beginning between Douglas
and the Buchanan Administration on the proslavery Lecompton Constitution. In that war, Douglas led the Republicans to victory over the
leadership of his own party. This gave Douglas at least a temporary
standing in the Free Soil movement. Lincoln, however, would destroy
that standing by pointing to the inconsistency between Douglas's support of *Dred Scott* and his attempt to annul the consequences of *Dred
Scott* by popular sovereignty. The imputation of moral treason that
Douglas says Lincoln cast upon the Supreme Court was not speculative.
The moral treason had already been committed. To call property in
slaves an *expressly affirmed* constitutional right would make it the supreme law of the land, overriding any state constitution or law to the
contrary.

The second question put to Douglas by Lincoln at Freeport has
been wrongly celebrated in the popular lore about the debates, for its
significance is not equal to that of the third question. The "Freeport
question" and the reply to it are nonetheless worth examining in their
original forms:

> Can the people of a United States Territory, in any lawful way,
> against the wish of any citizen of the United States, exclude slavery
> from its limits prior to the formation of a State Constitution?[60]

Douglas replied:

> I answer emphatically, as Mr. Lincoln has heard me answer a hun-
> dred times from every stump in Illinois, that in my opinion the peo-
> ple of a Territory can, by lawful means, exclude slavery from their
> limits prior to the formation of a State Constitution. . . . It matters
> not what way the Supreme Court may hereafter decide as to the
> abstract question whether slavery may or may not go into a territory

under the constitution, the people have the lawful means to intro-
duce it or exclude it as they please, for the reason that slavery cannot
exist a day or an hour anywhere, unless it is supported by local police
regulations. . . . Those police regulations can only be established by
the local legislature, and if the people are opposed to slavery they
will elect representatives to that body who will by unfriendly legislation effectually prevent the introduction of it into their midst. If, on
the contrary, they are for it, their legislation will favor its extension.
Hence, no matter what the decision of the Supreme Court may be
on that abstract question, still the right of the people to make a slave
territory or a free territory is perfect and complete under the Nebraska bill.[61]

Douglas, as one of the four "workmen," had committed himself in
advance to accepting the decision of the Supreme Court in *Dred Scott*
as the solution to all outstanding questions on slavery. Yet he now tries
to escape the Court's conclusion that there is no power under the Constitution to prevent a slave-owner from lawfully carrying his slave property into a territory. Douglas was quite wrong in asserting that slavery
cannot exist without local police regulations. As Lincoln explained, slavery had often been protected by the informal collaboration of slave
owners.[62] Readers of *Huckleberry Finn* will recall the slave patrol on
the Mississippi that forced Jim to hide under the raft.[63] Such patrols
were commonplace in the antebellum South, as was the *posse comitatus*, a system of police enforcement that did not require legislation.[64]

Douglas's distinction between an "abstract" constitutional right and
an effectual one was utterly fallacious, and Lincoln took pains to see
that it did not gain acceptance. He did so by comparing the right to hold
slave property in a territory, as set forth in *Dred Scott,* to the constitutional right to reclaim runaway slaves. The Fugitive Slave Clause provides that,

> No Person held to Service or Labour in one State, under the Laws
> thereof, escaping into another, shall, in Consequence of any Law or
> Regulation therein, be discharged from such Service or Labour, but
> shall be delivered up on Claim of the Party to whom such Service or
> Labour may be due.[65]

The Constitution does not say how or by whom a runaway slave is to be
pursued, captured, or incarcerated, or how the owner's claim is to be

adjudicated. The words "shall be delivered up," however, leave no room for doubt that appropriate legislation, whether by the states or by Congress, must be forthcoming to implement this constitutional right. Lincoln supported the Fugitive Slave Act of 1850, much as he hated to see runaway slaves hunted down and forcibly returned to their unrequited labor. He did so because the commanding word "shall" in the Constitution bound whoever took an oath to support the Constitution to support such legislation as well.[66] The obligation to do so could not be evaded by calling the right in question "abstract."

In the course of the debates, Lincoln pointed out the abolitionists' claim of a right to deny enforcement of the Fugitive Slave Law of 1850. He then pointed to Douglas's analogous claim of a right to deny enforcement of a slaveholder's right to be secure in his slave property when emigrating to a territory. Lincoln would show that, just as the Fugitive Slave Clause could not be evaded, neither could Douglas use his doctrine of popular sovereignty to evade the "abstract" constitutional right of slave ownership, if *Dred Scott* were correct.[67] Lincoln concluded the last of the joint debates, at Alton, as follows:

> I defy any man to make an argument that will justify unfriendly legislation to deprive a slaveholder of his right to hold his slave in a Territory, that will not equally, in all its length, breadth and thickness furnish an argument for nullifying the fugitive slave law. Why there is not such an Abolitionist in the nation as Douglas, after all.[68]

This ironic comparison of Douglas's Freeport Doctrine to abolitionism, pursued relentlessly by Lincoln, effectively destroyed Douglas as a national leader. Its culminating effect came at the Democratic Convention in Charleston in April of 1860. A majority of the delegates wanted Douglas as the Democratic candidate for President, but they could not attain the two-thirds majority that the party's rules required. The seven states of the Deep South would not support Douglas unless he supported federal enforcement of slaveholders' rights in any United States territory. They took their stand upon these concluding words in Taney's opinion in *Dred Scott:*

> Now, as we have already said . . . the right of property in a slave is distinctly and expressly affirmed in the Constitution. . . . And no word can be found in the Constitution which gives Congress a great-

er power over slave property . . . than property of any other description. The only power conferred is the power *coupled with the duty* of guarding and protecting the owner in his rights.[69]

The italicized words may be the most portentous in American history. No one who accepted them could have been elected dog catcher in any free state. Yet they convinced the Deep South that it was an absolute constitutional necessity that Congress provide federal police protection for slave property in any territory that did not itself provide that protection. The South believed that a denial of this alleged constitutional right was a breach of the compact from which the Union under the Constitution derived its being. It became the foundation of their soon to be claimed right of secession.

These words—the words of Roger Taney—denied the nomination of a united Democratic party to Douglas and, in effect, assured the Election of 1860 to Lincoln and the Republicans.

NOTES

1. See *Harry V. Jaffa*, Equality and Liberty 120 (1965).
2. Letter from Abraham Lincoln to Henry L. Pierce and Others (April 6, 1859), in *The Collected Works of Abraham Lincoln*, pp. 374, 376 (Roy P. Basler ed., 1953).
3. See, e.g., *The Federalist* No. 1, at 27 (Alexander Hamilton) (Clinton Rossiter ed., 1999). ("It has been frequently remarked that it seems to have been reserved to the people of this country, by their conduct and example, to decide the important question, whether societies of men are really capable or not of establishing good government from reflection and choice, or whether they are forever destined to depend for their political constitutions on accident and force.")
4. Abraham Lincoln, Gettysburg Address (November 19, 1863), in *This Fiery Trial: The Speeches and Writings of Abraham Lincoln*, pp. 183, 184 (William E. Gienapp ed., 2002).
5. Republican Convention 1860: Platform of 1860, in *Text-Book for 1860*, pp. 26, 26–27 (Horace Greeley & John F. Cleveland eds., 1860).
6. Abraham Lincoln, First Inaugural Address (March 4, 1861), in *This Fiery Trial: The Speeches and Writings of Abraham Lincoln*, *supra* note 4, pp. 88, 94.
7. *Id.*, p. 93.

8. *Id.*, pp. 93–97.

9. Abraham Lincoln, *The Legitimate Object of Government* (July 1, 1854?), in *This Fiery Trial: The Speeches and Writings of Abraham Lincoln*, *supra* note 4, pp. 27–28.

10. Abraham Lincoln, Speech at the Cooper Union (February 27, 1860), in *This Fiery Trial: The Speeches and Writings of Abraham Lincoln*, *supra* note 4, pp. 71, 78–80.

11. Abraham Lincoln, *supra* note 4, p. 183.

12. Abraham Lincoln, Speech at Chicago, Illinois (July 10, 1858), in *Abraham Lincoln: Speeches and Writings, 1832–1858*, pp. 445, 446 (Don E. Fehrenbacher ed., 1989).

13. The Declaration of Independence, para. 2 (U.S. 1776).

14. *Id.*, para. 1.

15. See, e.g., John C. Calhoun, Senate Speech on the Oregon Bill (June 27, 1848), in *Union and Liberty: The Political Philosophy of John C. Calhoun*, pp. 563, 565–70 (Ross M. Lence ed., 1992).

16. *Id.*, p. 565.

17. See *id.*, 569–70 ("[The belief in equality] had strong hold on the mind of Mr. Jefferson, the author of [the Declaration of Independence], which caused him to take an utterly false view of the subordinate relation of the black to the white race in the South; and to hold, in consequence, that the former, though utterly unqualified to possess liberty, were as fully entitled to both liberty and equality as the latter; and that to deprive them of it was unjust and immoral.")

18. *Dred Scott v. Sandford*, 60 U.S. 393, 407 (1857).

19. See *id.*, pp. 409–11. Taney might also be said to be a disciple of Aristotle's maxim that the intention of the legislator is the law.

20. Letter from Thomas Jefferson to Henri Gregoire (February 25, 1809), in The Works of Thomas Jefferson, pp. 99, 100 (Paul Leicester Ford ed., 1905).

21. Lincoln expressed this Aristotelian idea, which makes a lie of natural slavery, with exquisite logic:

> If A can prove, however conclusively, that he may, of right, enslave B, why may not B snatch the same argument and prove equally, that he may enslave A?
>
> You say A is white and B is black. It is *color*, then; the lighter, having the right to enslave the darker? Take care. By this rule you are to be slave to the first man you meet, with a fairer skin than your own.
>
> You do not mean *color* exactly? You mean the whites are *intellectually* the superiors of the blacks, and therefore have the right to enslave them? Take care again. By this rule, you are to be slave to the first man you meet, with an intellect superior to your own.
>
> But, say you, it is a question of *interest;* and, if you make it your *interest*, you have the right to enslave another. Very well. And if he can make it his interest, he has the right to enslave you.

Abraham Lincoln, Fragment on Slavery (1854), in *Abraham Lincoln: Speeches and Writings*, 1832–1858, *supra* note 12, p. 303.

22. Don E. Fehrenbacher, *The Dred Scott Case: Its Significance in American Law and Politics*, 349 (1978).

23. *Id.*

24. *Dred Scott,* 60 U.S. at 407.

25. Fehrenbacher, *supra* note 22, pp. 348–49.

26. *Dred Scott,* 60 U.S. at 410.

27. Some qualifications concerning the jurisprudence of original intent are here in order. As a general doctrine governing the relationship of judges to law, originalism must meet the objection that it applies only to a morally defensible legal system. Could a judge in Nazi Germany conscientiously apply Nazi law—for example, the Nuremberg laws—governing Jews? He could if he were a Nazi with a Nazi conscience (if that is not an oxymoron). If he were instead a decent human being, he would do his best to frustrate the law, and to make it as unburdensome to the Jews as possible. He might go along with it to some extent, on the assumption that his replacement would be a true Nazi. But, as a non-Nazi he could not commit himself to a jurisprudence of Nazi intent. To paraphrase Aristotle, a good man is a good citizen (or a good judge) only in a good regime. He is a bad citizen in a bad regime. Only a bad man can be a good citizen in a bad regime. Justice Thurgood Marshall believed the regime of the Founding was bad because he believed it was based upon slavery and racism, not unlike the regime of Adolf Hitler. Clearly, the Founders thought the regime they were founding—based upon the principles of the Declaration of Independence—was a good one. They regarded slavery as an exception to the principles of the Declaration, not as consistent with those principles. A Nazi judge would have regarded the Nuremberg laws as perfectly consistent with the Nazi principles of Adolf Hitler. A Jefferson (or a Lincoln) could not regard the presence of slavery in the Constitution of 1787 as consistent with the principles of the Declaration or the Constitution.

28. *Dred Scott,* 60 U.S. at 407.

29. Alexander H. Stephens, "African Slavery: The Corner-stone of the Southern Confederacy (March 22, 1861)," in *Pulpit and Rostrum*, pp. 65, 69 (1862). The date of this speech was at almost an exact midpoint between Lincoln's inauguration on March 4 and the firing on Fort Sumter on April 13, at a time before there was any certainty of a coming civil war. Hence there was no clear reason for Stephens at that time to have doubted the permanence of the Confederate government.

30. *Id.*, p. 70.

31. *Id.*, p. 71.

32. Clement Eaton, *The Freedom-of-Thought Struggle in the Old South*, p. 132 (Harper & Row 1964) (1940).

33. Abraham Lincoln, "House Divided" Speech at Springfield, Illinois (June 16, 1858), in *Abraham Lincoln: Speeches and Writings, 1832-1858, supra* note 12, pp. 426, 428.

34. William H. Rehnquist, The Notion of a Living Constitution, *Texas Law Review* 54, pp. 693, 701–702 (1976), reprinted in *Harvard Journal of Law and Public Policy* 29, pp. 401, 410 (2006) (footnote omitted).

35. Act of September 9, 1850, ch. 51, § 1, 9 Stat. 453, 453 (establishing a territorial government for Utah); Act of September 9, 1850, ch. 49, § 2, 9 Stat. 446, 446–47 (establishing a territorial government for New Mexico).

36. See Abraham Lincoln, Speech on the Kansas-Nebraska Act at Peoria, Illinois (October 16, 1854), in Abraham Lincoln: Speeches and Writings, 1832–1838, *supra* note 12, pp. 307, 344.

37. § 1, 9 Stat. at 453; § 2, 9 Stat. at 447. In his Peoria Speech, Lincoln definitively refutes the idea that the territorial laws of 1850 supplied a precedent for the concept of popular sovereignty embodied in the Kansas-Nebraska Act. Lincoln, *supra* note 36, pp. 344–46.

38. See generally § 1, 9 Stat. 453; § 2, 9 Stat. 446.

39. See § 1, 9 Stat. at 455–56; § 2, 9 Stat. at 450.

40. See Lincoln, *supra* note 33, p. 426.

41. *Id.*

42. *Id*, p. 431. Lincoln was referring of course to Stephen A. Douglas, Franklin Pierce, Roger Taney, and James Buchanan.

43. *Congressional Quarterly, Guide to U.S. Elections* 1, pp. 682, 767 (5th ed. 2005).

44. Northern Democrats were said to have faces of dough that Southerners could shape as they wanted.

45. Franklin Pierce, Fourth Annual Address (December 2, 1856), in *The State of the Union Messages of the Presidents, 1790-1966*, vol. 1, pp. 918, 922 (Fred L. Israel, ed., 1966).

46. James Buchanan, Inaugural Address (March 4, 1857), in *Inaugural Addresses of the Presidents of the United States from George Washington 1789 to Harry. S. Truman 1949*, pp 103, 104 (1952).

47. See Robert W. Johannsen, *Stephen A. Douglas*, p. 546 (1973).

48. *Dred Scott*, 60 U.S. at 451.

49. *Id.*, pp. 451–52.

50. *Id.*, p. 452.

51. U.S. Constitution, Article VI, § 2 ("This Constitution, and the Laws of the United States which shall be made in Pursuance thereof, . . . shall be the

supreme Law of the Land . . . any Thing in the Constitution or Laws of any State to the Contrary notwithstanding").

52. Lincoln, *supra* note 33, pp. 431–32.

53. See Harry V. Jaffa, *Crisis of the House Divided*, pp. 19–27 (1959) (identifying historians making these arguments).

54. *Id.*, pp. 23, 27.

55. See *id.*, p. 22.

56. See *id*

57. Abraham Lincoln, Second Debate, Freeport, Illinois: Lincoln's Rejoinder (August 27, 1858), in *Abraham Lincoln: Speeches and Writings, 1832-1858, supra* note 12, pp. 573, 579.

58. Abraham Lincoln, Second Debate, Freeport, Illinois: Lincoln's Speech (August 27, 1858), in *Abraham Lincoln: Speeches and Writings, 1832-1858, supra* note 12, pp. 537, 542.

59. Stephen A. Douglas, Second Debate, Freeport, Illinois: Douglas' Reply (August 27, 1858), in *Abraham Lincoln: Speeches and Writings, 1832-1858, supra* note 12, pp. 549, 553–54.

60. Lincoln, *supra* note 58, pp 541–42.

61. Douglas, *supra* note 59, pp. 551–52.

62. Abraham Lincoln, Third Debate, Jonesboro, Illinois: Lincoln's Reply (September 15, 1858), in *Abraham Lincoln: Speeches and Writings, 1832-1858, supra* note 12, pp. 602, 618.

63. Mark Twain, *Adventures of Huckleberry Finn*, pp. 155–57 (Susan K. Harris ed., Houghton Mifflin Co. 2000) (1884).

64. *See* Lincoln, *supra* note 62, p. 618; see also Fugitive Slave Act of 1850, ch. 60, § 5, 9 Stat. 462, 462–63 (authorizing enlistment of *posse comitatus* and commanding "all good citizens" to aid enforcement of fugitive slave law).

65. U.S. Constitution, Article IV, § 2, cl. 3.

66. Abraham Lincoln, Seventh Debate, Alton, Illinois: Lincoln's Reply (October 15, 1858), in *Abraham Lincoln: Speeches and Writings, 1832-1858, supra* note 12, pp. 790, 813 ("Why then do I yield support to a fugitive slave law? Because I do not understand that the Constitution, which guarantees that right, can be supported without it.")

67. *Id.*, pp. 813–14.

68. *Id.*, p. 814.

69. *Dred Scott,* 60 U.S. at 451–52 (emphasis added).

10

THE LEGEND OF SLEEPY HOLLOW

INTRODUCTION

Harry Jaffa's April 2010 remarks on the passing of Irving Kristol on September 18, 2009, present an autobiographical memoir. After expressing his gratitude to Irving Kristol for "his encouragement and support" for his pathbreaking study of Lincoln, Jaffa intensifies his earlier critique of Kristol from his 1978 book, *How to Think About the American Revolution: A Bicentennial Cerebration*. Noting his refusal to address his criticisms of thirty years, Jaffa mocks Kristol's dismissal of "the American political tradition [as] an inarticulate tradition" and his subsequent dismissal of the Civil War from the course of American politics. In this, the influential Kristol ignored the theory and practice of Jefferson, among other founders, to say nothing of Lincoln. Jaffa confronts this "mindless conclusion that the American Revolution ushered in an era of mindless peace, prosperity, and fellowship." And in this same vein Jaffa continues his criticism of Martin Diamond as well, reiterating his earlier critique of his former colleague's failure to acknowledge the guidance the Declaration gives to republican governance.

But, more notably, Jaffa raises issues that he did not dwell on in 1978. Now he focuses on "the theological-political framework of the Declaration of Independence." He quotes at length from George Washington's Circular Letter of 1783, observing: "No prophet of Israel ever prophesied more wisely than Washington does here." But that

theological-political teaching needs Jefferson's Virginia Statute of Religious Liberty as well as the political wisdom of his First Inaugural. This
account of Washington and Jefferson contrasts with Kristol's assertion
that "the authors of the Constitution . . . were for the most part not
particularly interested in religion." Jaffa's deepened understanding of
the founding leads him to intensify his critique of Kristol and restate the
need to approach the study of America with both the most obvious and
the highest questions in mind. "It was only by breaking the deadlock
over slavery that the United States could open its gates to immigrants
from eastern Europe, whence came my forebears and Kristol's." To
sleep through the American Revolution is to open up America to the
tyranny of headless horsemen and other fantasies.

The editors thank Hillsdale College for permission to print this previously unpublished essay.

IRVING KRISTOL AND THE LEGEND OF SLEEPY HOLLOW

I

Irving Kristol was one of the leading public intellectuals of our time. In
that category, in the last generation, he may have had no peer. As an
influence peddler—apart from his role as public intellectual—he may
have had no peer since Felix Frankfurter peopled the New Deal with
his happy hot dogs. I can testify to Irving's virtuosity as a promoter of
young scholars since he once promoted me—some sixty years ago when
I was a young scholar. And for that I remain grateful.

I met Irving some time in the middle 1950s. I had discovered the
Lincoln-Douglas debates in 1946, when browsing in a Fourth Avenue
bookstore, not far from the New School for Social Research, where I
was a graduate student. I had already begun my doctoral dissertation,
which would be published in 1952 by the University of Chicago Press as
*Thomism and Aristotelianism: A Study of the Commentary by Thomas
Aquinas on the Nicomachean Ethics.* I had been completely infatuated,
sitting in Leo Strauss's classes, listening to him cite medieval commentaries on Aristotelian texts. At the same time I was overwhelmed by
Lincoln's speeches and writings, outraged at the mindlessness of the
academic writing about him, and convinced that he deserved the same

kind of thoughtful care that Strauss gave to philosophic texts. I met Kristol some time during this phase of my career when I was lecturing wildly to anyone who would listen (and there was no one who listened more devoutly than Leo Strauss) to my tale of Lincoln's greatness, and the complete failure of Lincoln scholarship to recognize that greatness.

Strauss himself had devoted his great gifts to Great Books in the philosophic tradition. But his hermeneutic principle applied more widely. All scholarship of the past implied a primary responsibility to understand the documents of the past as their authors had understood them, before attempting to understand them differently or better. This principle was certainly more fruitful, the more intelligent the author one was studying. But it was no less necessary as an axiom of all historical scholarship if there was to be objectivity in our understanding of the past. Before one could judge an opinion to be vicious or stupid (or wise), one had to characterize it accurately.

Clearly, Straussian hermeneutics applied to political speech or writing no less than to philosophic books. Strauss's thesis in *Persecution and the Art of Writing* seemed particularly applicable to American history in an age dominated by the problem of slavery. No American historian had however applied a Straussian hermeneutic to the debates over slavery, or showed the least awareness of its applicability. The opinion dominating Civil War historiography when I began my study was that the agitation over slavery leading to the Civil War was perfectly mindless, because modern philosophy had assured us that reason could not resolve moral differences. Unscrupulous politicians both North and South had, it was said, exploited these differences for political advantage. And none had done so to greater advantage than Abraham Lincoln. The historians who condemned Lincoln *a priori* on the basis of their own presuppositions did not however examine what he actually said on the subject of slavery. They dismissed him on the basis of their (assumed) superior knowledge of the supposed truth that there was no possible rational resolution to the differences concerning slavery. It had however become clear to me that Lincoln's intentions in his speeches in the 1850s were perfectly opaque in the absence of an awareness of his reserve, especially with regard to the subject of racial equality. This meant carrying Strauss's enterprise forward from political philosophy to political history. This became the dominating theme of my career. It was inspired in part by Strauss's essay "On Classical Political Philosophy,"

published in 1946, which maintained a continuity between pre-philo-
sophic political opinion and philosophic political opinion, the latter
bringing rationality into the former. From its outset I had Strauss's
enthusiastic encouragement and support. At its outset I also had encouragement and support from Irving Kristol.

   The first fruit of my Lincolnian passion was an essay entitled "Expe-
diency and Morality in the Lincoln-Douglas Debates." It was originally
a lecture at St. Johns College, Annapolis, in the Fall of 1951. As a break
with mainstream Lincoln scholarship, it was not surprising that I could
find no one to publish it. Irving Kristol generously volunteered to find a
publisher, and succeeded in placing it in the first (1957) issue of the
Anchor Review, edited by his friend Melvin Lasky. I like to say that I
made Vladimir Nabokov famous, since the same issue of the *Anchor
Review* published the first excerpts from *Lolita.* When an eager public
rushed out to read what I had to say about Lincoln and Douglas they
stumbled over the work of Nabokov! (I still think however, that *Lolita*
was nothing but pornography pretending to be literature.)

   Irving Kristol's benevolence did not stop here. Although two years
my junior—at a time when I had my foot unsteadily on (or below) the
very bottom rung of the academic ladder—he had become an international eminence in the *avant garde* literary and publishing worlds, both
in London and in New York. On his initiative he negotiated a contract
for me with Doubleday, then the largest publisher in the free world, for
the publication in 1959 of *Crisis of the House Divided.*

   I had come to know Kristol because of his long-standing friendship
with Martin Diamond. They had been fellow students and Trotskyites,
at the City College of New York in the 1930s. Both met their wives in
the same revolutionary circles, and both families followed the same
trajectory across the political spectrum. I had come to know Diamond
as one of the elite corps of graduate students that formed around
Strauss after he began teaching in Chicago in the spring quarter of
1949. I had joined Strauss in Chicago in July of 1949, after he had
secured a teaching position for me in the Great Books program in the
downtown College. I was given an office on campus which was the
anteroom to Strauss's office, where I served *de facto* as his research
assistant. All his visitors, including all his graduate students, with whom
I soon became acquainted, had to pass through my office to reach him.
At that time, I believe, I had a certain prestige among those students—

many of whom have since become quite famous—since I had studied with Strauss for five years before he came to Chicago, and I was publishing a very Straussian book on Aristotle and Aquinas. Also on some few occasions, when Strauss was indisposed, I took his classes. I also gave a course on the Lincoln-Douglas debates in the Department of Political Science in the spring quarter of 1950, thereby introducing Chicago Straussians to the study of American political thought.

I left Chicago for Columbus, Ohio, and Ohio State University, in the fall of 1951. The chairman of the Political Science Department at Ohio State was Harvey Mansfield, who had been a professor in my first political science course at Yale, and had been my freshman faculty advisor. In that capacity he had advised me, or rather warned me (in the spring of 1936) that my "ethnicity" made an academic career impossible. And indeed he had said nothing less than the truth. Before World War II, the faculty of the American liberal arts college was at least 98% off limits to Jews, blacks, and women. The roster of the past and present members of the Ohio State Political Science Department in 1951 did not show one Jewish name before 1947, the year Mansfield became chairman. And now, fifteen years and a world war later, Mansfield recommended my appointment to my first tenure track position. In time he also sponsored my tenure, my promotion to associate, and, in 1959, to a full professorship at Ohio State.

In 1952–1953 I had a Ford Foundation fellowship, and devoted the entire year to a single-minded study of classical Greek. In 1956–1957 I had a Rockefeller Foundation fellowship to pursue my study of the Lincoln-Douglas debates. For this year I moved my family to Chicago, to profit from the intense vitality—and the intense interest in my Lincoln project—of the community Strauss had created around himself. Many illuminating conversations during the year with Allan Bloom, Martin Diamond, Robert Goldwin, and Joseph Cropsey, in addition to Strauss, fired my messianic zeal to understand Lincoln as he understood himself.

During my fellowship year in Chicago there developed a special sense of community and mutual assistance of the Jaffa and Diamond families, in part because of the birth of the Jaffa daughter in December of 1956, and of the Diamond son some five months later. The Diamonds moved to Claremont in 1959, and soon thereafter set in motion the happy events leading to the Jaffas joining them there in 1964. Unfortunately, the story of the two families does not have a happy ending. In the mid '60s, *Time* magazine in a cover story listed Diamond as one of the ten greatest college teachers in America. Shortly thereafter the Diamond marriage ended in a blaze of ferocious hostility and violent recrimination that left no room for their bewildered friends who tried to remain loyal. This personal note would not enter here but for the fact that Diamond left Claremont in 1970, and pursued a "second sailing" of his career, now in the penumbras of an eastern conservatism, both paleocon and neocon, which was profoundly hostile to Lincoln and the Declaration of Independence. It was also hostile to the original form of Diamond's pathbreaking scholarship on the *Federalist,* as it had been to my work on Lincoln. Everything in Lincoln's thought and action turned on his conception of the relationship of the principle of equality in the Declaration of Independence to the form of the Constitution and of popular government. Diamond's brilliant early work on the *Federalist* was a denial of the Progressive era's belief that the Constitution represented an oligarchic reaction against the egalitarian democratic impulse of the Declaration of Independence. According to Diamond's account, and according to Diamond's account of the *Federalist*'s account, the Constitution was a wise and prudent incorporation of the principles of the Declaration. It was in no sense a rejection, or a distancing from those principles. In this new phase of his career, however, Diamond took care to fit himself within the boundaries of the reactionary conservatism which now enveloped him; Diamond turned against his own thesis, by declaring that the Declaration of Independence gave "no guidance" either to the framing or interpretation ("construction") of the Constitution. This was in direct denial of the Republican party platform of 1860, on which Lincoln had been elected, and which had quoted the text of the Declaration and affirmed that its principles had been incorporated into the Constitution. This is what Diamond and Kristol now denied, and what informs the debate between us, a debate which, I believe, contains within itself the future of the Republic.

II

Diamond's "no guidance" theme is taken from his lecture entitled "The Revolution of Sober Expectations," the second in the American Enterprise Institute's Distinguished Lecture Series on the Bicentennial of the United States. This series may rank as the most ambitious of its kind, celebrating with appropriate fanfare one of the greatest events in the history of the world. AEI pulled out all the public relation stops in ceremonies surrounding the lectures. They were published separately in pamphlets of the finest rag paper. They were broadcast nationally on public radio and television. The first two lectures were published together by the Seagram Corporation in a fantastically expensive edition, although they were later combined with the others in a single volume.[1]

The Inaugural Lecture in this elaborate setting, entitled "The American Revolution as a Successful Revolution," was by Irving Kristol. His selection was meant both to confirm and enhance his eminence as the spokesman of American Conservatism, as it was meant to confirm and enhance the leadership of the American Enterprise Institute in the Conservative movement.

They could not have made a worse choice. Kristol's lecture resonates hardly a single fact about the American Revolution, and what it does resonate are the author's ideological preconceptions of what the Revolution ought to have been rather than anything that it actually was. These preconceptions seem to be shaped more by the idea of revolution he once held as a youthful follower of Trotsky than by anything associated with Jefferson or Tom Paine, both of whom he loathed.

In the Marxist idea of proletarian revolution, the elimination of private property is believed to eliminate the sole remaining source of political conflict among human beings. According to the Hegelian-Marxist dialectic, each revolution brings about a synthesis of the antecedent thesis and antithesis. That synthesis, representing a new form of property, generates its own antithesis. The last revolution, however, eliminating all private property, generates no antithesis, hence no further politics.

This is the conception of a revolution to end all revolutions, and hence all politics, and indeed to end History. History began with the institution of private property and ends with its elimination. Kristol seems to have retained the conclusion of this analysis, although no trace of the analysis itself remains. But there is no other explanation of his mindless conclusion that the American Revolution ushered in an era of mindless peace, prosperity, and fellowship.

Kristol's preconceptions also have much in common with the doctrines of John C. Calhoun and his latter day heirs. Calhoun may best be remembered for calling the idea of equality, as expressed in both the Massachusetts Bill of Rights of 1780 and in the Declaration of Independence, as "the most false and dangerous of all political errors." Kristol never repeats this precisely, but his contempt for anything Jeffersonian was profound. It is worth noting that Karl Marx and Calhoun were contemporaries, the Communist Manifesto being dated 1848 and Calhoun's Oregon speech, with its centrality in the Calhoun canon, given in the same year. Calhoun's *Disquisition on Government* was published in 1851, although its composition must have been in the late 1940s.

In *A New Birth of Freedom* I argued that Calhoun and Marx were, respectively, right-wing and left-wing Hegelians. And I believed they had more in common as Hegelians than what separated the right from the left. Hofstadter's title for his chapter on Calhoun, "The Marx of the Master Class," in *The American Political Tradition,* was a brilliant inspiration. (Marx might with equal justice have been called the "The Calhoun of the Proletariat.") What united Marx and Calhoun was a belief in a determinism that subordinated reason to passion and nature to history. Wisdom resulted not from Socratic speculation but from discerning the path of necessity laid out in history and by history, rightly understood. In his writing on the American Revolution, Kristol's idea of what history ought to have been overrides every fact that stands in its way. Here in his own words is the theme of his Distinguished Lecture.

> To begin at the beginning, the American Revolution was successful in that those who led it were able, in later years, to look back in tranquility at what they had wrought and to say that it was good. This was a revolution which, unlike all subsequent revolutions, did not devour its children: the men who made the revolution were the men who went on to create the new political order, who then held the highest elected positions in this order, and who all died in bed. Not very romantic perhaps. Indeed, positively prosaic. But it is this very prosaic quality of the American Revolution that testified to its success. It is the pathos and poignancy of unsuccessful revolutions which excite the poetic temperament; statesmanship which successfully accomplishes its business is a subject more fit for prose. Alone among the revolutions of modernity, the American Revolution did not give rise to the pathetic myth of 'the revolution betrayed.' It spawned no literature of disillusionment; it left behind no grand hopes frustrated, no grand expectations unsatisfied, no grand illu-

sions shattered. Indeed, in one important respect the American Revolution was so successful as to be almost self-defeating: it turned the attention of thinking men away from politics, which now seemed utterly unproblematic, so that political theory lost its vigor, and even the political thought of the Founding Fathers was not seriously studied. This intellectual sloth, engendered by success, rendered us incompetent to explain this successful revolution to the world, and even to ourselves. The American political tradition became an inarticulate tradition.

One knows not whether to laugh or weep at the imagined spectacle of Madison, Jefferson, Adams, Franklin, and Washington, sitting around a table, at a loss to know what to say to each other! I am reminded of the beginning of Plato's *Apology of Socrates,* in which Socrates says of his accusers, that they spoke so powerfully that he scarcely recognized himself, yet nothing they said was true. No generation of political men since the world began, was less at a loss for words or more articulate than the men who made our Revolution and wrought the constitutional order we have inherited.

No authority on our Revolution and Founding ranks higher than—or even equals—that of George Washington. In a Circular Letter to the States, June 14, 1783, from which we now excerpt, he carries us back to that period when, according to Kristol, nothing politically important was happening and nobody was talking about it.

The citizens of America, placed in the most enviable condition, as the sole Lords and Proprietors of a vast tract of continent . . . abounding with all the necessities and conveniences of life are now by the late pacification acknowledged to be possessed of absolute freedom and independence. They are from this period to be considered as the actors on a most conspicuous theater which seems to be peculiarly designated by Providence for the display of human greatness and felicity. . . . The foundation of our empire [i.e. forms of government] was not laid in the gloomy age of ignorance and superstition but at an epoch when the rights of mankind were better understood and more clearly defined than at any former period; the researches of the human mind, after social happiness, have been carried to great extent; the treasures of knowledge, acquired through a long succession of years by the labors of philosophers, sages, and legislatures, are laid open for our use, and their collective wisdom may be happily applied in the establishment of our forms of government. . . . At this auspicious period the United States came into existence as a nation, and if their citizens should not be completely free and happy, the fault will be entirely their own.

Such is our situation, and such are our prospects; but notwithstanding the cup of blessing is thus reached out to us, notwithstanding happiness is ours if we have a disposition to seize the occasion and make it our own; yet, it appears to me there is an option still left to the United States of America, that it is in their choice, and depends upon their conduct, whether they will be respectable and prosperous or contemptible and miserable as a nation. This is the time of their political probation; this is the moment when the eyes of the whole world are turned upon them; this is the moment to establish or ruin their national character forever; this is the favorable moment to give such a tone to our federal government as will enable it to answer the ends of institution; or this may be the ill fated moment for relaxing the powers of the union, annihilating the cement of the Confederation, and exposing it to become the sport of European politics, which may play one state against another to prevent their growing importance, and to serve their own interested purposes. For according to the system of policy the states shall adopt at this moment, they will stand or fall; and by their confirmation or lapse, it is yet to be decided whether the Revolution must ultimately be considered as a blessing or a curse; a blessing or a curse not to the present age alone, for with our fate will the destiny of unborn millions be involved.

No prophet of Israel ever prophesied more wisely than Washington does here. According to Washington, these were years when the American people were not only rejoicing in the freedom earned by their victory (under Washington's leadership), but were also wallowing in the imbecilities of the Articles of Confederation. These imbecilities are described with unsurpassed precision and eloquence in the first nine numbers of the *Federalist,* which seem not to have been on Kristol's reading list. As Washington makes clear, the mid-1780s were years of decision not only for the American people, but for mankind. History, as Washington characterizes it, is a theater and the American people the actors in a drama produced by Providence. But the outcome will not be scripted by Providence, it will be the result of the character of the American people. Washington rejects historical determinism. God in his wisdom has left man free to act wisely or unwisely. Without the possibility of failure there would be no meaning to success. When Washington wrote, the success of the Revolution was entirely open. Kristol seems however to have slept as soundly through this history as Rip van Winkle slept through the Revolution itself.

Here we may insert a footnote to the remark that the Founding Fathers all died in bed. One of those who did so was Alexander Hamilton. The former Secretary of the Treasury died in bed after being shot by the Vice President of the United States. It is true that the shooting took place in a duel, but the duel itself took place because of the intensity of the conflict which engaged these rival leaders in New York politics. We are reminded that in the presidential election of 1800, Burr and Jefferson ended with the same vote in the Electoral College. That was because under the Constitution of 1787 each elector cast two votes for president. There was no separate vote for vice president. The runner up became vice president. The Republican electors clearly intended Jefferson to be president, and Burr vice president, but the ballots made no such distinction, and the election went therefore to the House. It was moreover the Federalist House, elected before 1800, and in it Hamilton could exert his considerable influence, which he did, so that his great rival Jefferson became president. The end result was however certainly in accord with the will of the people, exerted through the ballot box. But Burr never forgot that it was Hamilton who prevented him from becoming president.

Kristol says that a successful revolution is one that sets out to be as little revolutionary as possible. But Washington seems to contemplate the freedom with which Providence had endowed the American people as an occasion for bringing the free exercise of reason, or the quest for excellence, not mere tradition, to bear upon the new political order. He seems almost to call for a re-convening of the Court of Athens, supplemented by recent researches of the Enlightenment. The American mind, he thought, ought to be open to the best that had been thought, or said, or tried, in the long course of civilization. Washington accordingly set the agenda for the coming Constitutional Convention, over which he would preside.

A constitutional government is one whose just powers are derived by reason in agreement with revelation from the consent of the governed. When men who are created equal—equal, as Locke said, in "dominion" or authority—come together to form a government, the compact or agreement which is to govern them must be unanimous. The government to be formed will offer equal protection to the God-given rights of each citizen, and each citizen will be under an equal obligation to support the government, whether by bodily service or by taxes. The government thus formed operates on the basis of majority rule. The majority however may rightfully do only those things that are implicit in that unanimous agreement. By reason of that unanimous agreement, the majority represents and acts in the name of those in the minority no less than those in the majority.

Our bill of rights for example includes many things with respect to which there are no just powers of government. Foremost among them is the free exercise of religion. No majority has the right to tell a Catholic to be a Protestant, a Protestant to be a Catholic, a Jew to be a Christian, or anyone to be of any faith other than his own. Only if sectarian religious preferences are kept out of the political process can the majority represent the minority, only then can there be government by majority rule. The civil wars of the Reformation, beginning in the 16th century, with the merciless slaughter of millions of Christians by other Christians were a vivid memory of the Founding Fathers. That memory (of which Irving Kristol seems to have no memory) constituted the principal motivating force behind nearly all the institutional arrangements that we call the Founding.

In 1783, when Washington wrote the circular letter quoted above, constitutional government as we know it, with sectarian religious differences excluded from the political process, was impossible elsewhere in the world. Here is the key to the inner meaning of the idea of American exceptionalism. This also explains why American history can be understood as messianic in a sense altogether rational. But Americans did not think that separating church and state, and making the free exercise of religion an entirely private right, meant to sacrifice in any way the strictures of morality or the blessings and the consolations of revealed religion. Most Americans were, or were descended from, men and women who had come to these shores to escape religious persecution. They did not at first renounce religious persecution, they sought only to escape it. In time however the idea gained strength that, in accordance with the social contract, they could be friends and fellow citizens, each reinforcing the rights of the other, while each worshiping God in his own personal way.

The foregoing process, which culminated in the words "Congress shall make no law . . ." was the result of the great battle over establishment led by Madison and Jefferson. What may be called the fighting in the political trenches in Virginia, in the mid 1780's, was conducted largely by Madison, whose *Memorial and Remonstrance* was a very mine of the arguments for religious freedom upon which Jefferson drew in the Statute. But the headwater of this great river of freedom was undoubtedly John Locke's *Letters on Toleration*. The *Letters* bore a relationship to the Virginia Statute similar to the relationship of the *Second Treatise* to the Declaration of Independence. Encompassing both however—less obviously but more profoundly—was the *Reasonableness of Christianity*. The sermons of the Revolution are notable for the harmonization of the laws of reason, nature, and God. Here is Jefferson, in his inaugural, congratulating the American people on their possession of

> a benign religion, professed, indeed , and practiced in various forms, yet all of them inculcating honesty, truth, temperance, gratitude, and the love of man; acknowledging and adoring an overruling Providence, which by all its dispensations proves that it delights in the happiness of man here and his greater happiness hereafter.[2]

Burke's attack on the French Revolution was notable for its denunciation of the atheism of the revolutionaries. But the Christianity he defended was an abstraction from the differences of Protestantism and Catholicism. (One of his parents was Protestant and the other Catholic.) We can see that Jefferson (even before Burke) takes Burke's argument a step farther, in abstracting from the differences of all biblical religions and their sectarian divisions. We hear a great deal these days, particularly in conservative circles, that the American form of government is based upon "Judeo-Christian morality." Neither Jefferson nor Lincoln had ever heard of "Judeo-Christian morality," a phrase of recent coinage, yet both were instrumental in bringing it into existence. When we have made the necessary abstractions from the different biblical religions, what remains is the theological-political framework of the Declaration of Independence. There is only one Creator God for all. There is but one God of the laws of nature. There is but one supreme Judge of the world, and but one Divine Providence whose protection the Signers claimed. The Judeo-Christian morality corresponds with that "benign religion" which is wisely not give a name, but which unites Americans nonetheless, in perhaps the profoundest meaning of *e pluribus unum.*

George Washington's greatest fear in 1783, as it would be in the later Farewell Address, was for the survival of the union of the states. As he said in 1783, any weakening of the bonds of union would be the occasion for foreign intervention, against the interest of all Americans. Twice in our history has an alleged malign foreign influence taken front stage in American politics. Most recently it was in the 1950s in the so called McCarthy era, with one side defending Communists as citizens exercising their civil rights under the Constitution, the other declaring the nation's right of self-defense against those conspiring with a foreign power to overthrow the government. What is important here is to recognize that nearly all the positions on both sides in the 1950s were also taken in the 1790s, with the division over the French Revolution approximating that over the Communist-Bolshevik Revolution in Russia. It happened that the Republican party, headed by Jefferson and Madison, was from the outset friendly to the French, believing their revolution to represent the spread abroad of the influence of the American Revolution. They saw events in Europe as a league of crowned heads and their anointing priests to defeat republicanism and restore the fraudulent inequalities of the *ancient regime.* The intensity of the party conflict at a time when, according to Kristol, there was no conflict, was almost beyond imagination. The XYZ affair, in which French agents attempted to address the American people over the heads of the Federalist government, resulted in the Alien and Sedition Acts of 1798. These in turn elicited the protests of the ever-famous Virginia and Kentucky resolutions.

It should be remarked that Jefferson represented the American government in Paris at the outset of the French Revolution when it still showed a more moderate face. But Jefferson's will to believe that the French Revolution was inspired by the American Revolution led him to ignore the dynamics that pointed to tyranny, dynamics evident to Edmund Burke from the outset. Yet Jefferson experienced daily in pre-Revolutionary France, as Burke did not, a thousand examples of intolerable repression and corruption. He saw the revolution as a necessary means for correcting such great evils. Here are some examples, from

Paris, of Jefferson's reactions to the unreformed Europe that preceded the French Revolution.

> Experience declares that man is the only animal which devours its own kind; for I can apply no milder term to the governments of Europe, and to the general prey of the rich on the poor.[3]

> I hold it, that a little rebellion now and then is a good thing, and as necessary in the political world as storms in the physical.[4]

> What country before ever existed a century and a half without a rebellion. . . . The tree of liberty must be refreshed from time to time with the blood of patriots and tyrants. It is its natural manure[5]

Of the foregoing, the remark about the tree of liberty is the best known. It was, however, inspired not only by the revolution going on before his eyes but by Jefferson's intimate knowledge of English constitutional history, particularly that culminating in the Glorious Revolution of 1689. The last, ending in the victory of parliamentary supremacy over hereditary divine right monarchy, represented in many ways the archetype of constitutional change for the American Founding Fathers. What is of immediate interest here is that historically all popular liberty, as Jefferson understood it, had been advanced by rebellion and revolution, none by free elections. This puts in context Jefferson's remarkable rhetoric in the Kentucky Resolutions of 1798, and the still more remarkable rhetoric of his inaugural address in 1801, in which he in effect repudiates, at least in part, what he had said three years earlier.

For a further understanding of 1800 we note that both the Alien and Sedition acts were written to expire in 1801. We note then that these acts, on the one hand, and the Virginia and Kentucky resolutions, on the other, represent what we might call the bookends of partisan controversy in the election of 1800. That election is of world historical importance as the first time in human history (so far as we know) in which a government was turned over to its bitterest rivals on the basis of a free election without the losers being executed, imprisoned, or exiled.

The precedent thus established in 1800—of elections replacing rebellions or revolutions—was followed here until 1860, when it was repudiated in the secession of 11 southern slave states that refused to accept the election of Abraham Lincoln as president. We are so accustomed to elections as a means of resolving partisan differences that it is difficult to realize how comparatively recent a phenomenon it was in 1861. We have learned recently from a number of foreign examples (e.g., the election of Hamas in Gaza) that a free election is not of itself a sufficient title to legitimacy. Why Lincoln's election should have been regarded as beyond the boundaries of the Constitution, or why the extension of slavery should have been regarded as an indefeasible personal and constitutional right, are questions that, in one form or another, have roiled American politics from the beginning. Free elections may result in unfree governments, as happened in Weimar Germany in the coming to power of Hitler, as well as when they are carried by religious fanatics. As we have seen, the exclusion of sectarian religion from the political process was understood at our Founding to be a necessity of free constitutional government. But Jefferson sees the division in American politics over the French revolution as a threat to republican freedom not unlike that of religious fanaticism. He does not say anything openly here about slavery, but he admits that there are threats other than religion that can fatally disrupt the republican form of government.

Here is Jefferson in his inaugural of 1801, reviewing the events of 1800.

> During the contest of opinion through which we have passed the animation of discussions and of exertions has sometimes worn an aspect which might impose on strangers unused to think freely and to speak and write what they think; but this being now decided by the voice of the nation, announced according to the rules of the Constitution, all will, of course, arrange themselves under the will of the law, and unite in common efforts for the common good.

> All too will bear in mind this sacred principle, that though the will of the majority is in all cases to prevail, that will to be rightful must be reasonable, that the minority possess their equal rights, which equal law must protect, and to violate would be oppression.

> Let us then fellow citizens unite with one heart and one mind. Let us restore to social intercourse that harmony and affection without which liberty and even life itself are but dreary things. And let us reflect that, having banished from our land that religious intolerance

under which mankind so long bled and suffered, we have yet gained little if we countenance a political intolerance as despotic, as wicked, and capable of as bitter and bloody persecutions. During the throes and convulsions of the ancient world, during the agonizing spasms of infuriated man seeking through blood and slaughter his long lost liberty, it was not wonderful that the agitation...should reach even this distant shore; that this should be more felt and feared by some and less by others and should divide opinion as to measures of safety. But every difference of opinion is not a difference of principle. We have called by different names brethren of the same principle. We are all Republicans, we are all Federalists. If there be any among us who would wish to dissolve this Union or to change its republican form, let them stand undisturbed as monuments of the safety with which error of opinion may be tolerated where reason is left free to combat it.[6]

I have quoted so much—and shall quote more—from this magnificent document of human freedom, which is also a document of that history through which our Rip van Winkle has so soundly slept. I have done so, because selective quotation often obscures the sweep and brilliance of great literature, and Jefferson's inaugural, even apart from its historical and political importance, is a classic of the literature of the English speaking peoples.

Perhaps the most quoted line from this speech is that saying we are all Republicans, all Federalists. No one had offended against this hypothetical friendship in the campaign of the 1790's more than Jefferson himself. He can take satisfaction in the outcome, in part, of course, because of his own victory. But it was in Jefferson's interest now that he had to govern to gain the good will of his erstwhile adversaries, and to imply that a victory of the other party would also have been legitimate. Jefferson's olive branch is an invitation to the Federalists to become a loyal opposition and thereby become part of a system of party governance by cooperation as well as by opposition, of majority and minority. We know—from no less a source than John Quincy Adams (see *Documents Relating to New England Federalism*, edited by Henry Adams[7])—that there were already treasonable movements among some Federalists to take New England out of the Union and rejoin the British empire. They were sufficient to lead John Quincy Adams to leave his father's party and join Jefferson's. The seeds of the secessionism that came to fruition in 1861 were sowed here.

Jefferson's acute dissertation on the limits of majority rule within a constitutional system implied a promise by the leader of a victorious majority to respect the rights of the defeated minority. But Jefferson distinguishes "brethren of the same principle" from those of a different principle. The apparent "other" principle was that of the *ancien regime,* that of those who believed there were "angels in the form of kings" to govern us. Jefferson wrote that not every difference of opinion is a difference of principle. By this he conceded that some differences of opinion *are* differences of principle. Jefferson does not imply that those of a different principle are entitled to the equal protection to which legitimate minorities are entitled.

In a magnificent passage he writes

> If there be any among us who would dissolve this Union or change its republican form, let them stand undisturbed as monuments of the safety with which error of opinion may be tolerated where reason is left free to combat it.

This is not an ACLU-type defense of free speech, as if the right of free speech can stand alone apart from other rights which the government is also bound to protect. It is a prudential judgment that the rational defense of republicanism will by its evident and intrinsic superiority overcome its adversaries in the open political process of free government. As an example of triumphant reason Jefferson writes:

> Sometimes it is said that man can not be trusted with the government of himself. Can he then be trusted with the government of others? Or have we found angels in the form of kings to govern him? Let history answer this question.

We recall that Jefferson had compared the existing governments of Europe, relics of feudalism and divine right monarchy, to cannibals. The sarcastic reference to angels in the form of kings reminds us of what Lincoln would call the abstract truth, applicable to all men and all times, that Jefferson had wisely and gloriously incorporated in the Declaration of Independence. Lincoln would himself incorporate into the Gettysburg Address the truth that all men are created equal. That truth condemned American slavery no less than European aristocracy and monarchy. That truth required that we recognize the equal humanity of those below us in the social or economic classes into which the political community may at any time be divided, whatever their wealth or poverty, whatever their color or ethnicity. We may in turn rightly demand the same recognition of the rights of our humanity from those above us. Those who do not recognize our humanity, who would use political power to strip us of our rights as human beings, are not entitled to share in the power stemming from the protection of those rights. In our time that has certainly referred to both Nazis and Communists and white supremacists. We note that Jefferson advocated leaving divine right monarchists "undisturbed." As we have seen, that is because he thought that they were essentially harmless, as their fallacies could so easily be refuted, and there was no Third Reich or USSR rising up behind them. If they were ever to actually disturb or threaten to disturb our safety, we would be under no obligation—on Jefferson's premises—to leave them undisturbed. It is notable that in the 1950's Irving Kristol led a movement of liberal anti McCarthyite anti-Communists. A group of ACLU-type liberals were demanding that the State Department issue a visa to a Soviet school teacher who would tour the United States explaining Soviet communism to American children and their teachers. This was of course in the interest of promoting the indefeasible good of international understanding. Irving held that such international understanding might indeed be achieved if an American school teacher toured the Soviet Union at the same time, explaining American democracy and capitalism to Soviet children and their teachers. Of course, the Stalinists and Stalinoids of that day, whether here or in the USSR, wanted no part of such a deal. Their kind is still present, however, in the form of politically correctoids who deny that our form of government, or any form of government, is better than any other. Governments and ways of life differ, they say, but none is better than another. However, anyone who says his way of life is better than any others, e.g. those who assert American exceptionalism, is by that fact to be condemned! For his stand against Stalinism sixty years ago, on campuses dominated by hysterical anti- McCarthyism, I honored Irving Kristol, and still do. Upon what grounds, however, could Kristol reject (as he did) both Soviet communism and Nazi racism? We turn to the underlying conflict identified by Jefferson as that between "error of opinion" and the reason that must be left free to combat it. We turn again to our statement of first principles. According to the Declaration of Independence, the rider rides the horse by the natural right of the human species (*homo sapiens*) to rule the lesser species, who are without reason in the order of creation. This right comes to us directly from God and nature. We do not have to ask the horse or the ox to consent to be governed. Within the human species, apart from the contract by which civil society is brought into being, there is no natural order of rule. The only rule that is legitimate arises from the exercise of the freedom of the rational will by the logic of consent. Human beings can agree, and ought to agree, to form governments to secure their natural rights. In the interest of this security there can be (and must be) laws and government which command our obedience. But laws and governments have no other purpose but to secure those equal, God-given natural rights. To fill the offices of such governments, however, differences among human beings do matter. To protect our equal rights we want not anyone but the best. We want the best men and women to be our generals, judges, and public policymakers. It is not sufficient to be human. A true democracy strives to become a true aristocracy.

Marxism replaces the distinction of species with the distinction of class: the proletariat can rightfully use, enslave, or destroy, as if they were subhuman species, its class enemies. Similarly, the Nazis regarded all non-Aryans as inferior species, subject to rightful enslavement or destruction. In April of 1861, before the firing on Fort Sumter, Alexander Stephens, Vice President of the Confederate States of America, in his Cornerstone speech, hailed the advent of the Confederacy as the first government in the world founded upon what Stephens asserted was a recent scientific discovery: that of the inferiority of the Negro race, and of the alleged scientific fact that in chattel slavery lay the optimum possible relationship for both races. (Darwin's *Origin of Species* was published in 1859, but Stephens does not tell us where he found the science he says proved black inferiority.) Inferior races might be governed or used without their consent as much as horses or oxen. We can see here the beginning of that "scientific" racism, that popular synthesis of Hegel and Darwin that would dominate the mind of western civilization by the end of the nineteenth century. Such triumph of error over reason would virtually consign to oblivion that order of nature and of nature's God that Jefferson and Lincoln believed was the ground of reason's triumph over error. It was no longer believed that there were angels in the form of kings, but that there were races or classes genetically or historically authorized to rule or destroy those asserted to be inferior. This was and is a return of the dark ages, but now with the vilest superstition masquerading as science. This has proved to be the most insidious superstition the world has ever seen: an appeal to what is called science to deny the authority of reason. Irving Kristol could consistently have taken the stand he did take against both communism and Nazism—not to mention its offshoots in American liberal progressivism—by recognizing that equality of right within the human species central to the doctrine of the Declaration of Independence. Turning against this principle of the Founding and of Abraham Lincoln meant turning against his own better self.

III

We return to Kristol's contention that those who led the Revolution were able in their later years to look back in tranquility upon what they had wrought. It is too bad that Kristol has not identified for us any of the expressions of tranquility upon which he seems to have relied. We begin our survey with a line from Jefferson's *Summary View of the Rights of British America*, August 1774.

> The abolition of domestic slavery is the great object of desire in the colonies where it was unhappily introduced in their infant state. But previous to the enfranchisement of the slaves we have, it is necessary to exclude all further importations from Africa.

In Jefferson's draft of the Declaration of Independence there was a ringing denunciation of the foreign slave trade, a denunciation most unfortunately deleted by the Congress. It is notable that in 1774 Jefferson speaks of the *abolition* of domestic slavery. The foreign slave trade must be ended previous to *enfranchisement*. If anyone had used such language in Illinois in 1838 he might have been lynched, as the abolitionist Elijah Lovejoy was lynched. But in 1774 we have the purer air of the Revolution. It was in the *Summary View* that Jefferson ended with the electrifying peroration that once was known to every American school child.

> The God who gave us life, gave us liberty at the same time; the hand
> of force may destroy, but cannot disjoin them.

That the principles of the Revolution are color-blind is shown by the
first sentence of the *Declaration of the Causes and Necessity of Taking
Up Arms,* sent forth by the Congress July 5, 1775, one day less than a
year before the Declaration of Independence. Its magnificent irony and
contempt of Parliament seems to imply an independence already
achieved.

> If it was possible for men who exercise their reason to believe, that
> the Author of our existence intended a part of the human race to
> hold an absolute property in, and unbounded power over others,
> marked out by his infinite goodness and wisdom, as the objects of a
> legal domination never rightfully resistible, however severe and op-
> pressive, the inhabitants of these colonies might at least require from
> the Parliament of Great Britain some evidence that this dreadful
> authority over them has been granted to that body.

Clearly, it is not possible for men who exercise their reason to believe that any part of the human race—whether the King and Parliament of Great Britain or slave owners in America—can hold an absolute right of property in other human beings, with a domination never
rightfully resistible. The only argument to the contrary, the only sus-
pension of the rule of reason, would be a certified miracle. The
American Congress is in effect demanding of the British Parliament:
"You got miracle? Prove it!"

Jefferson and John Dickinson were co-authors of the aforesaid Declaration, but Jefferson alone in the *Notes on Virginia,* (1781 and 1782)
wrote of American slavery as follows:

> And can the liberties of a nation be thought secure when we have
> removed their only firm basis, a conviction in the minds of the peo-
> ple that these liberties are of the gift of God? That they are not to be
> violated but with his wrath? Indeed I tremble for my country when I
> reflect that God is just; that his justice cannot sleep forever.[8]

Jefferson added: "I think a change already perceptible, since the
origin of the present revolution. The spirit of the master is abating, that
of the slave rising from the dust, his condition mollifying, the way I

hope preparing under the auspices of heaven, for a total emancipation, and that this is disposed, in the order of events, to be with the consent of the masters, rather than by their extirpation." Jefferson seems cautiously optimistic in 1783 as to the possibility of "total emancipation." And indeed in the 12 years from independence until the ratification of the Constitution all the states north of the Mason and Dixon line had either abolished slavery or set in motion a process that would end slavery within their jurisdiction. When however the Congress in 1785 failed to exclude slavery from the draft of the Northwest Ordinance (although they would repair this omission the following year, after Jefferson had left for Paris) Jefferson had this to say:

> What a stupendous, what an incomprehensible machine is man! Who can endure toil, famine, stripes, imprisonment, and death itself in vindication of his own liberty, and, the next moment, be deaf to all those motives whose power supported him through his trial and inflict on his fellow man a bondage one hour of which is fraught with more misery than ages of that which he rose in rebellion to oppose.[9]

The characterization here of American slavery is scarcely less harsh than that of the European governments Jefferson would accuse of cannibalism. In the 1780s he could still believe that the spirit of the Revolution was working towards universal emancipation. By 1820 however that had changed. The invention of the cotton gin here and of the power loom in England touched off an industrial revolution that made slavery vastly more profitable. At the same time, the positive good theory, which no one had even heard of in the age of the Revolution, soon came forward to justify the huge profits now to be made from the slave's labor.

In the Missouri crisis of 1820 Jefferson's tone is very different from what it had been in 1783. Concerning whether Missouri should be admitted as a slave state he wrote,

> this momentous question . . . like a fire-bell in the night, awakened and filled me with terror. I considered it at once as the knell of the Union. It is hushed indeed for the moment. But this is a reprieve only. . . . I regret that I am now to die in the belief that the useless sacrifices of themselves by the generation of 1776 to acquire self-

government and happiness to their country, is to be thrown away . . .
and my only consolation . . . that I shall not live to weep over it.[10]

Where is the tranquility that Kristol thought would comfort the last
years of the Founding generation? Even in the *Notes on Virginia* Jefferson was not exactly tranquil when he remembered that God is just and
threatened a merciless race war. In 1820, Jefferson predicts an even
more merciless war over slavery, but with the whites divided against
themselves, a war that closely resembles what actually came to pass in
1861.

Irving Kristol compares the "successful" American Revolution with
the bloodier and disastrous French and Bolshevik revolutions. According to Kristol the American Revolution alone did not give rise to the
"pathetic and poignant myth of 'the Revolution betrayed.'"

We have already noted the "poetic" miseries that—according to
Kristol—attended the French and Bolshevik revolutions, but which we
prosaic Americans avoided by being successful. But the American Revolution did not end at Yorktown. If it could properly be said to have
ended at all (which it cannot) it would not be at Yorktown but at Appomattox. The European revolutions were severe (and unsuccessful) not
because they tore down and replaced a political superstructure, but
because they tore up a social substructure of more than a thousand
years, a substructure of blood-sucking privileged classes rooted in feudalism and divine right. What Kristol calls the American Revolution
replaced only the political superstructure of the former British colonies.
As we have seen, however, the announced goals of the American Revolution called for the abolition of slavery no less than of divine right
monarchy. The genuine American Revolution could only be completed
with the total abolition of slavery. And the war—our Civil War—that
tore up the foundations of the social order rooted in slavery had all the
ferocity of the European revolutions. If we add the death toll of the
Civil War to that of the War of Independence, as we should, we have a
better basis for comparison with the European revolutions.

As we have shown again and again, Kristol's imaginary American
Revolution has no existence in historical reality. It belongs among the
Legends of Sleepy Hollow. There is the South of "Gone With the
Wind," the South celebrated by the "Confederates in the Attic," the
unregenerate mystical legions of the South that shall rise again, this

time to victory over the hated Yankees and their infamous leader, Abraham Lincoln.

The immunity to reality of Kristol's imaginary American Revolution is attested by what he wrote in a 1989 essay on "The Character of the American Political Order."[11]

> The American people seem never to have been torn by conflicting interpretations of the American political tradition, though scholars may be. Even our very bloody Civil War had surprisingly little effect on the course of American history. If one were to write an American history textbook with the chapter on the Civil War dropped out, to be replaced by a single sentence to the effect that slavery was abolished by constitutional amendment in 1865, very little in subsequent chapters, as now written, would need revision.

Once again, one knows not whether to laugh or to weep. Might not anyone reading Kristol's revised American history textbook ask *why* slavery was abolished in 1865? Why does Kristol mention the 13th but not the 14th and 15th amendments? The 13th amendment ended slavery but it did not make the freed slaves citizens. Before the Civil War it was generally assumed that state citizenship was primary and federal citizenship derivative. By the 14th amendment one was first of all a citizen of the United States and incidentally a citizen of the state wherein one resided. This made anyone, born and residing in the United States, and subject to the jurisdiction thereof, a citizen of the United States as well as of the state wherein he was residing. This entitled him, as a United States citizen, without regard to his race, color, or previous condition of servitude, to federal protection of his constitutional rights. It is only the addition of the 14th and 15th amendments that made possible the political career of Martin Luther King, Jr. There could have been no civil rights revolution had there not been a victorious Union army, an army victorious with the addition of 200,000 black troops who by their blood and courage earned the right to all the benefits of citizenship under the Constitution.

Kristol also writes that

> The Civil War had even less effect on the American political tradition, since there never really was a distinctively Southern political tradition, nor did the war give rise to one. A textbook in American

intellectual history could safely ignore the Civil War, were it not for the fact that one feels it to be almost sacrilegious that so much suffering should be so barren of consequence. The Civil War was and is a most memorable event—but not any kind of turning point in American history. [12]

No Southern political tradition? John C. Calhoun put to bed with Rip van Winkle? No debates between Webster, Hayne, and Calhoun? No Proclamation against Nullification by Andrew Jackson, no Repeal of the Missouri Compromise, no Dred Scott decision, no Lincoln Douglas Debates, no John Brown?

The Civil War not a turning point and barren of consequences? Turning 4,000,000 black slaves and their descendants into United States citizens inconsequential? It was only by breaking the deadlock over slavery that the United States could open its gates to immigrants from eastern Europe, whence came my forebears and Kristol's. When Lincoln gave the House Divided speech, June 16, 1858, he said that the nation was at a point of decision: it would become either all free or all slave. At that very moment, by the logic of the Dred Scott decision, as Lincoln proved in the debates, the nation was already in principle all slave. The Chief Justice had asserted that the right to own slaves was "expressly affirmed" in the Constitution. By the supremacy clause, this would make it a constitutional right, and as such belonging to the supreme law of the land, anything in any free state constitution to the contrary notwithstanding. To prevent this outcome was Lincoln's historic mission. The complex series of arguments and actions between 1854 and 1861 by which Lincoln, first of all, prevented the Union from becoming all slave, and then prevented it from being divided, is a tale of statesmanship unsurpassed, and perhaps never equaled, in mankind's long story. This story is moreover encapsulated in the Gettysburg Address, by which it is now (at least until we are advised by Kristol) enshrined in historic memory.

IV

As a final emanation from the penumbras of Sleepy Hollow, we turn to a 1990 publication entitled *The Spirit of the Constitution,* in which Kristol is quoted as saying that "the authors of the Constitution ... were for the most part not particularly interested in religion, especially Jefferson who wrote nothing worth reading on religion or almost anything else."[13] When I read in 1974 that it would be wise to ignore Tom Paine, I suspected that Kristol's real animus was directed not at Paine but at Jefferson. That suspicion is confirmed here. Consider that Kristol wants to abolish from our history the central event of that history. Abraham Lincoln disappears from the scene. And we have here dismissed from all consideration the author of two documents, the Declaration of Independence and the Statute of Virginia for Religious Liberty, two immortal works central to the cause of human freedom, now and forever. What can be the fate of a conservatism nurtured on such a doctrine?

Harry V. Jaffa
Claremont, California
April 2010

NOTES

1. *America's Continuing Revolution: An Act of Conservation* (Washington, D.C.: American Enterprise Institute, 1975). Iterations of the lecture and subsequent article, as well as other works by Kristol, can be found at http://contemporarythinkers.org/irving-kristol/. This and all other footnotes are from the editors.

2. First Inaugural, March 4, 1801.

3. Letter to Edward Carrington, January 16, 1787.

4. Letter to James Madison, January 30, 1787.

5. Letter to William S. Smith, November 13, 1787.

6. First Inaugural, March 4, 1801.

7. Henry Adams, ed., Documents Relating to New-England Federalism: 1800-1815 (Boston: Little, Brown, 1877).

8. *Notes on the State of Virginia*, Query XVIII.

9. Letter to Jean Nicolas Démeunier, June 26, 1786.

10. Letter to John Holmes, April 22, 1820.

11. "On the Character of American Political Order," in *The Promise of American Politics: Principles and Practice after Two Hundred Years*, ed. Robert Utley (Lanham, MD: University Press of America, 1989), 363.

12. Ibid., 363–364.

13. Robert Goldwin and Robert Licht, eds., *The Spirit of the Constitution Five Conversations* (Washington, D.C.: American Enterprise Institute, 1990), 81.

INDEX

Abraham, 199–200
Adams, John, 242, 243
Adams, John Quincy, 177, 313–314
Afrocentrism, 152–154
Alien and Sedition Acts, 159, 177, 311
American Conservatism and the American Founding (Jaffa), 121
American Conservative Thought (Buckley), 173
American Founding, 13–15, 177, 264n52; Bloom and, 59–60, 63–67, 76; Calhoun against, 278; democracy in, 243; *Dred Scott v. Sanford* and, 251–252; in "Eliot", 165–168; in "Equality", 12; equality and, 205–206, 212; Hobbes and, 223–224; human equality in, 163; individual rights in, 207; intentions and, 157–158; Kristol on, 176–177, 261n18, 317, 320; Lincoln on, 6, 161; Locke and, 63–64, 197, 210, 230, 262n32; Mansfield on, 204–205; natural right in, 113; principles of, 225, 229, 235–236, 302; as racism, 253; reason in, 223–224; religion and, 183–184, 297–298; *Republic* and, 75; self-preservation and, 63–64; sex and, 63; slavery in, 66–67, 158, 163, 178, 251–253, 318; state of nature in, 223; Strauss on, 75–76, 229, 230; Taney against, 278–281, 281; in "Thomas Aquinas Meets Thomas Jefferson",

273; time and, 276, 292n3; virtues in, 65–66; Washington on, 305–306. *See also* Aristotle and Locke in American Founding; Jefferson, Thomas; Madison, James
"The American Founding as the Best Regime: The Bonding of Civil and Religious Liberty" ("American Founding") (Jaffa), 121, 122; autonomy in, 142–143; consent of the governed in, 131–132, 137; divine right of kings and, 141; election of 1800 in, 128–129; equality in, 126; faith in, 143; God in, 137–139; individualism in, 141–142; liberty in, 122–124, 124; limiting in, 122, 136; natural justice in, 125–126; radical modernity in, 134; reason and revelation in, 134, 136; religion in, 127–128, 131, 133, 137–139; sovereignty in, 126–127, 137; U.S. Constitution in, 122–124, 124, 125, 127–128, 129, 132; Virginia Statute of Religious Liberty in, 136–137; Western civilization in, 133–134. *See also* Jefferson, Thomas
American Revolution, 13–15, 128, 240, 276; Civil War related to, 320; France and, 29; Kristol and, 176–177, 179–180, 303–304, 307, 320–321; Locke and, 61, 240; Paine and, 179; rights of man and, 132; secession

related to, 65, 69; Washington and, 29, 307, 308

"The American Revolution as a Successful Revolution" (Kristol), 303, 305–307, 320

anarchy, secession as, 194, 277

anti-Semitism, 174, 180, 182, 260n11; of Eliot, 169–172, 173–174

Aquinas, Thomas, 140–141, 165, 217, 257, 265–266

aristocracy, 242, 264n54, 272–273, 273, 316. *See also* natural aristocracy

Aristotle, 5, 6, 31, 124, 217, 298; Afrocentrism and, 152; Churchill and, 232; on friendships, 247, 255; Hobbes and, 108; on intention, 232, 263n50; Jefferson and, 241–242, 264n52; on justice, 207, 247, 248; on law, 7–8, 232, 263n50; Locke and, 231; *Metaphysics* by, 141; Moses related to, 236; on nature of man, 231; Nazism and, 294n27; political community of, 197–198, 203; regimes and, 205, 237; scientific rationality and, 108; state of nature and, 44, 196, 196–197, 197–198, 211; Strauss and, 198, 273; *See also Nicomachean Ethics*; *Politics*

"Aristotle and Locke in American Founding", 5, 6; authority and, 8–9; church and state separation and, 9; cities in, 7–8; Galileo and, 9–10; God in, 8; law and, 7, 7–8, 260n10; Lincoln and, 6; religion in, 5–6; Shakespeare and, 8, 10; social contract and, 7, 9; Strauss and, 9–10; Washington and, 7

"artificial aristocracy", 242, 264n54

authority, 8–9; on ancient Rome, 200–201; Aristotle on, 44; in Christianity, 233; in consent of the governed, 234–235, 244–245, 307–308; in "Equality", 18, 18–20, 22, 23; from God, 188; of Tocqueville, 216–217, 220, 263n42; unanimous consent for, 270–271; in U.S. Constitution, 124, 280, 287; of U.S. Declaration of Independence, 60, 227–228, 263n48

Becker, Carl, 166–167

Bellow, Saul, 58–59

Benjamin, Judah, 173, 260n7

Bennett, Bill, 225–226

Benson, George C. S., 98–99

Berns, Walter, 40–41

Bible, 133; ancient Israel in, 138–139; Bloom and, 54–55, 55–56; equality in, 104–105; Israel in, 138–139; law and, 198–199; Lincoln on, 55, 202; Locke and, 61; Psalms, 192; "Reichstag" related to, 104–105; U.S. Declaration of Independence and, 56, 137

Bill of Rights, U.S., 22, 155–156, 159, 272, 308; Massachusetts, 33, 242; Virginia, 37–38, 122–124

Black Power movement, 98; Black Panthers and, 88–89, 218; Black Students Union in, 90–91, 218; Bloom and, 74–75, 85, 86, 87; bombings in, 87–90, 218; demands in, 87, 90, 91–92; Nazism related to, 97; proposal in, 92–93, 96; publicity and, 218–219; racially exclusive "centers" in, 92–93, 98; relativism in, 93–95, 97; Strauss and, 86, 95, 97; threats in, 90, 91, 218; trustees and, 96, 218; voting related to, 96, 97, 98; white education and, 93, 97

Bloom, Allan, 48, 49, 54, 62; American Founding and, 59–60, 63–67, 76; Bible and, 54–55, 55–56; Black Power movement and, 74–75, 85, 86, 87; on Civil War, 67–68; grandparents of, 54–56; on great books, 47–48, 56–59, 81; on Heidegger, 52–53, 77–78, 79, 80, 82; Lincoln and, 76–77; on Locke, 61, 63; morality and, 48–52; on Nietzsche, 52–53, 77–78, 79, 80, 82; Plato and, 79–80, 81; relativism of, 52–54; *Republic* and, 74–75; on sex, 49–51, 63; on "The Sixties", 74–75; on slavery, 70–71, 72; Strauss and, 62, 78–79, 80, 81, 81–82

Bolshevik revolution, 310, 320

Bonaparte, Napoleon, 114; Jews and, 173–174; Kirk and, 162–163

Bork, Robert, 160, 161, 259n3

Buchanan, James, 286, 286–287, 295n44

Buchanan, Pat, 174, 175

CONTRIBUTOR BIOGRAPHIES

ABOUT THE EDITORS

Edward J. Erler is professor of political science emeritus at California State University, San Bernardino, and is a senior fellow of The Claremont Institute. He is the author of *The American Polity: Essays on the Theory and Practice of Constitutional Government*, co-author of *The Founders on Citizenship and Immigration*, and has published numerous articles in law reviews and professional journals. Among his most recent articles are "The Decline and Fall of the Right to Property: Government as Universal Landlord"; and "The Second Amendment as a Reflection of First Principles"; he has also published several articles in the *Encyclopedia of the American Constitution*. Dr. Erler was a member of the California Advisory Commission on Civil Rights from 1988 to 2006 and served on the California Constitutional Revision Commission in 1996. He has testified before the House and Senate Judiciary Committee on birthright citizenship, voting rights, and other civil rights issues.

Ken Masugi is a nonresident senior fellow at the Claremont Institute. He teaches graduate courses for Johns Hopkins University's Center for Advanced Studies in American Government in Washington, D.C., and has held positions at a variety of universities and college programs, including a federal prison and Princeton University. He taught for three years at the U.S. Air Force Academy, where he was John M. Olin Distinguished Visiting Professor. Masugi has also served in the federal government for ten years, as a special assistant and speechwriter to the heads of the Departments of Labor and Justice and the U.S. Equal Employment Opportunity Commission. He is the co-author, co-editor, or editor of ten books on American politics and author of over 100 articles and reviews on American politics, political philosophy, constitutional development, and films.

ABOUT THE AUTHOR

Harry V. Jaffa (1918–2015) was a distinguished fellow of the Claremont Institute, and the author of numerous articles and books, including his widely acclaimed study of the Lincoln-Douglas debates, *Crisis of the House Divided: An Interpretation of the Lincoln-Douglas Debates* (University of Chicago Press, 1959).

Dr. Jaffa was a professor of government at Claremont McKenna College and the Claremont Graduate School. He received his BA from Yale in 1939, where he majored in English, and holds a PhD from the New School for Social Research.

His other books include *Thomism and Aristotelianism* (1979), *The Conditions of Freedom* (1975), *How to Think About the American Revolution* (1978), *American Conservatism and the American Founding* (1982), *Original Intent and the Framers of the Constitution: A Disputed Question* (1994), and *A New Birth of Freedom: Abraham Lincoln and the Coming of the Civil War* (2000).

Professor Jaffa's last published work was *Crisis of the Strauss Divided: Essays on Leo Strauss and Straussianism, East and West* (2012).